Microsoft

Word 2003 TOP 100 Simplified®

Tips & Tricks

by Jinjer Simon

Wiley Publishing, Inc.

Word 2003: Top 100 Simplified® Tips & Tricks

Published by
Wiley Publishing, Inc.
111 River Street
Hoboken, NJ 07030

Published simultaneously in Canada

maranGraphics, Inc.
5755 Coopers Avenue
Mississauga, Ontario, Canada
L4Z 1R9

Library of Congress Control Number: 2003112056

ISBN: 0-7645-4131-5

Manufactured in the United States of America

10 9 8 7 6 5 4 3 2 1

1K/RY/QZ/QT/IN

Trademark Acknowledgments

Important Numbers

For U.S. corporate orders, please call maranGraphics at 800-469-6616 or fax 905-890-9434.
For general information on our other products and services or to obtain technical support please contact our Customer Care Department within the U.S. at 800-762-2974, outside the U.S. at 317-572-3993 or fax 317-572-4002.

Permissions

U.S. Corporate Sales

Contact maranGraphics at (800) 469-6616 or fax (905) 890-9434.

U.S. Trade Sales

Contact Wiley at (800) 762-2974 or fax (317) 572-4002.

CREDITS

Editorial Manager/ Project Editor:
Rev Mengle

Development Editor:
Dana Rhodes Lesh

Acquisitions Editor:
Jody Lefevere

Product Development Manager:
Lindsay Sandman

Copy Editor:
Jill Mazurczyk

Screen Artist:
Jill A. Proll

Illustrators:
Ronda David-Burroughs,
David E. Gregory

Technical Editor:
Allen Wyatt

Editorial Assistant:
Adrienne Porter

Manufacturing:
Allan Conley,
Linda Cook,
Paul Gilchrist,
Jennifer Guynn

Book Design:
maranGraphics, Inc.

Production Coordinator:
Nancee Reeves

Layout:
LeAndra Hosier,
Kristin McMullan,
Kathie Schnorr

Cover Design:
Anthony Bunyan

Proofreader:
Linda Quigley

Quality Control:
Laura Albert
Andy Hollandbeck
Brian H. Walls

Indexer:
Johnna VanHoose

Vice President and Executive Group Publisher:
Richard Swadley

Vice President and Publisher:
Barry Pruett

Composition Director:
Debbie Stailey

AUTHOR'S ACKNOWLEDGMENTS

Although the author typically gets the credit, the efforts of many individuals behind the scenes are necessary to complete a project of this type. I would like to acknowledge the efforts of some key individuals, particularly: Rev Mengle, the project editor, who did a fantastic job on this book while still maintaining his other responsibilities as an editorial manager; Jill Mazurczyk, copy editor, who has worked on my other books in the past and did a great job again on this one; and Dana Lesh, who helped edit the chapters and did an excellent job. I also would like to thank my technical editor, Alan Wyatt, who provided some very good input on the book. This series requires a lot of extra work from the graphics and production staffs at Wiley. Although I do not know all the names of the individuals involved, I appreciate all their efforts in making sure the book came together. Finally, I would like to thank my acquisitions editor, Jody Lefevere, for getting this book started and coordinating all the scheduling and contract issues.

maranGraphics is a family-run business
located near Toronto, Canada.

At **maranGraphics**, we believe in producing great computer books–one book at a time.

Each maranGraphics book uses the award-winning communication process that we have been developing over the last 28 years. Using this process, we organize screen shots and text in a way that makes it easy for you to learn new concepts and tasks.

We spend hours deciding the best way to perform each task, so you don't have to! Our clear, easy-to-follow screen shots and instructions walk you through each task from beginning to end.

We want to thank you for purchasing what we feel are the best computer books money can buy. We hope you enjoy using this book as much as we enjoyed creating it!

Sincerely,

The Maran Family

Please visit us on the Web at:

www.maran.com

HOW TO USE THIS BOOK

Word 2003: Top 100 Simplified® Tips & Tricks includes the 100 most interesting and useful tasks you can perform using Word 2003. This book reveals cool secrets and timesaving tricks guaranteed to make you more productive.

Who is this book for?

Are you a visual learner who already knows the basics of Word 2003, but wants to take your Word 2003 experience to the next level? Then this is the book for you.

Conventions In This Book

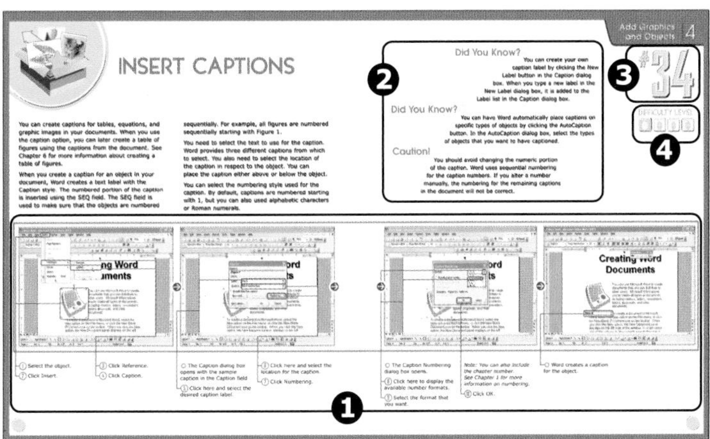

❶ Steps

This book walks you through each task using a step-by-step approach. Lines and "lassos" connect the screen shots to the step-by-step instructions to show you exactly how to perform each task.

❷ Tips

Fun and practical tips answer questions you have always wondered about. Plus, learn to do things in Word that you never through were possible!

❸ Task Numbers

The task numbers, ranging from 1 to 100, indicate which self-contained lesson you are currently working on.

❹ Difficulty Levels

For quick reference, symbols mark the difficulty level of each task.

 Demonstrates a new spin on a common task

 Introduces a new skill or a new task

 Combines multiple skills requiring in-depth knowledge

 Requires extensive skill and may involve other technologies

TABLE OF CONTENTS

1 Create and Lay Out a Word Document

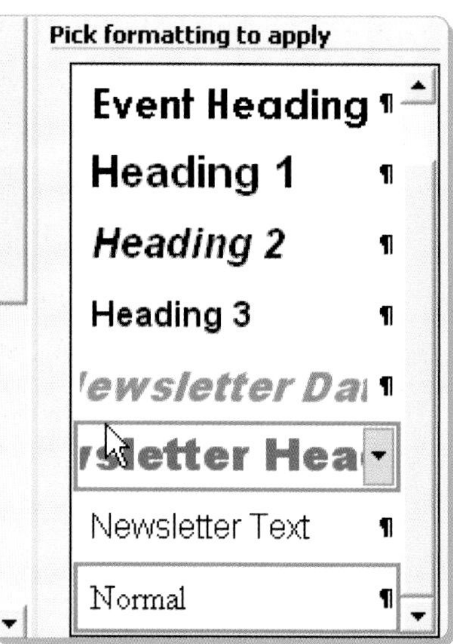

2 Change the Text Formatting

3 Work with Tables and Columns

Sales

2002 Sales Results

Sales during 2002 were at record n figures are in for each office, and t each office have been selected.

Office	Name
Dallas	Jones
Houston	Wilson
New York	Anderson
Los Angeles	Hansen

4 Add Graphics and Objects

TABLE OF CONTENTS

5 Using Macros and Fields

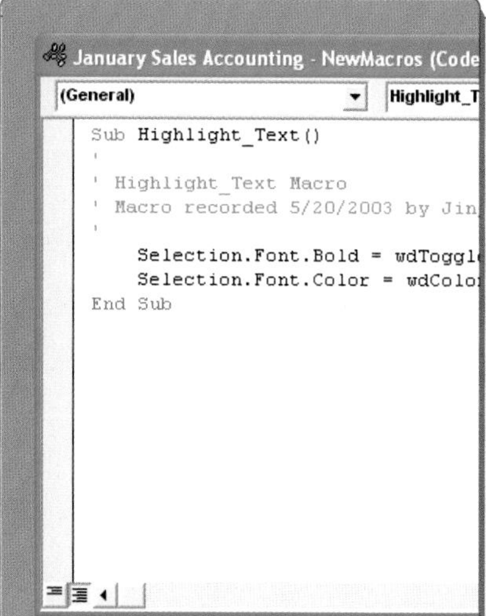

6 Work with Large Documents

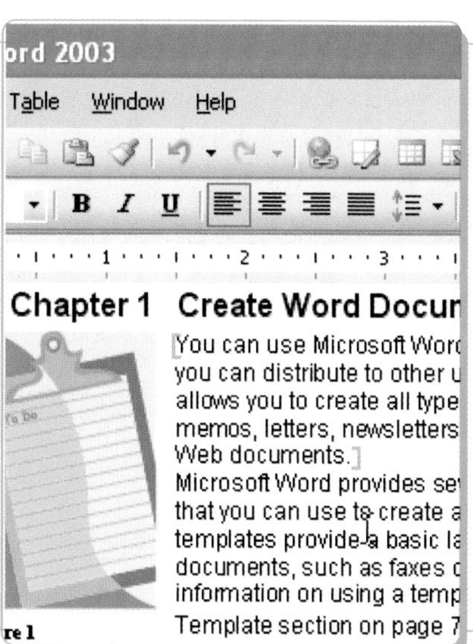

7 Printing Documents

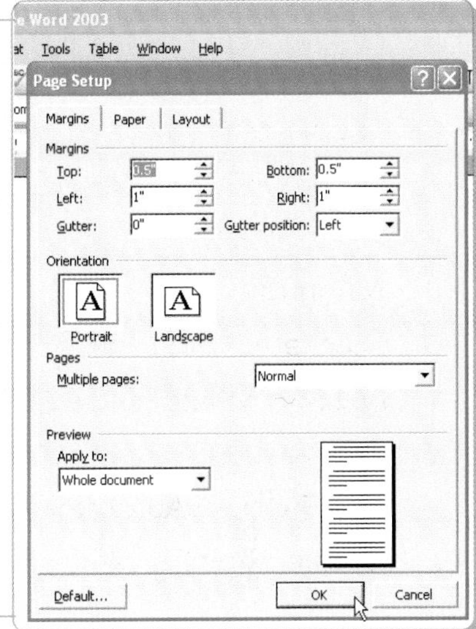

8 Using Automation and Proofing Tools

9 Create Web Pages

10 Using Mail Merge

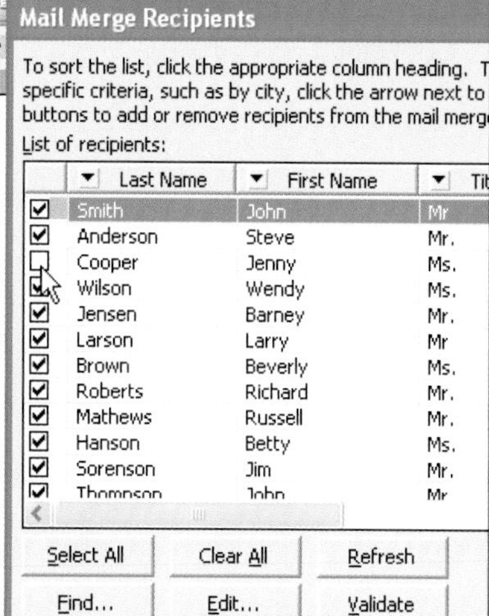

Create and Lay Out a Word Document

Microsoft Word allows you to create several different types of files. Although the default file type is to create a .DOC Word document, you can also create .DOT template files, HTML files, XML files, and even text files. Word can also open files from many different file formats. As you open different file formats, Microsoft Word converts those files to a .DOC format.

If you have several files that you want to convert to Word documents, you can use the Batch Conversion Wizard to automate the task. You also can use the Wizard to convert multiple Word documents to a different format.

You can create new Word documents using a template file that provides styles and formatting for the document. You can use any of the built-in templates, or you can create your own template by saving any document as a template. By using templates and styles, you can keep the layout of your Word documents consistent.

You can customize the layout of your documents by specifying the look and placement of the page numbering. Page numbering is always associated with a header or footer on the page. Because Word allows you to create different headers and footers for odd and even pages, you can also have two different page number schemes in a document. You can also create a different page number scheme for the first page in the document. You can restart or change the page numbering in the middle of a document by inserting section breaks.

TOP 100

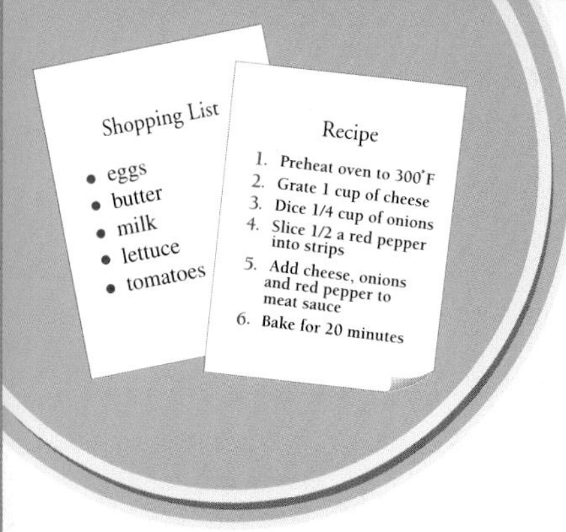

Apply styles from ANOTHER TEMPLATE

Word gives you the flexibility to copy certain styles from another template into your current document. For example, you can copy a style you created to highlight a person's name in a document. You copy styles using the Organizer dialog box.

While you can also apply the entire template to your document by copying styles instead you can get only the specific styles you want and avoid the confusion of unneeded styles. Also, when you apply a template to a document, Microsoft Word automatically updates styles with the same name to reflect the styles of the template; so if you have a style in the document that you want to keep, Word changes it, whether or not you want it changed. For example, if both the template and document contain a Normal style, the document style updates to reflect the settings of the Normal style in the template. By copying only the desired styles from the template, all other styles in the document remain unchanged.

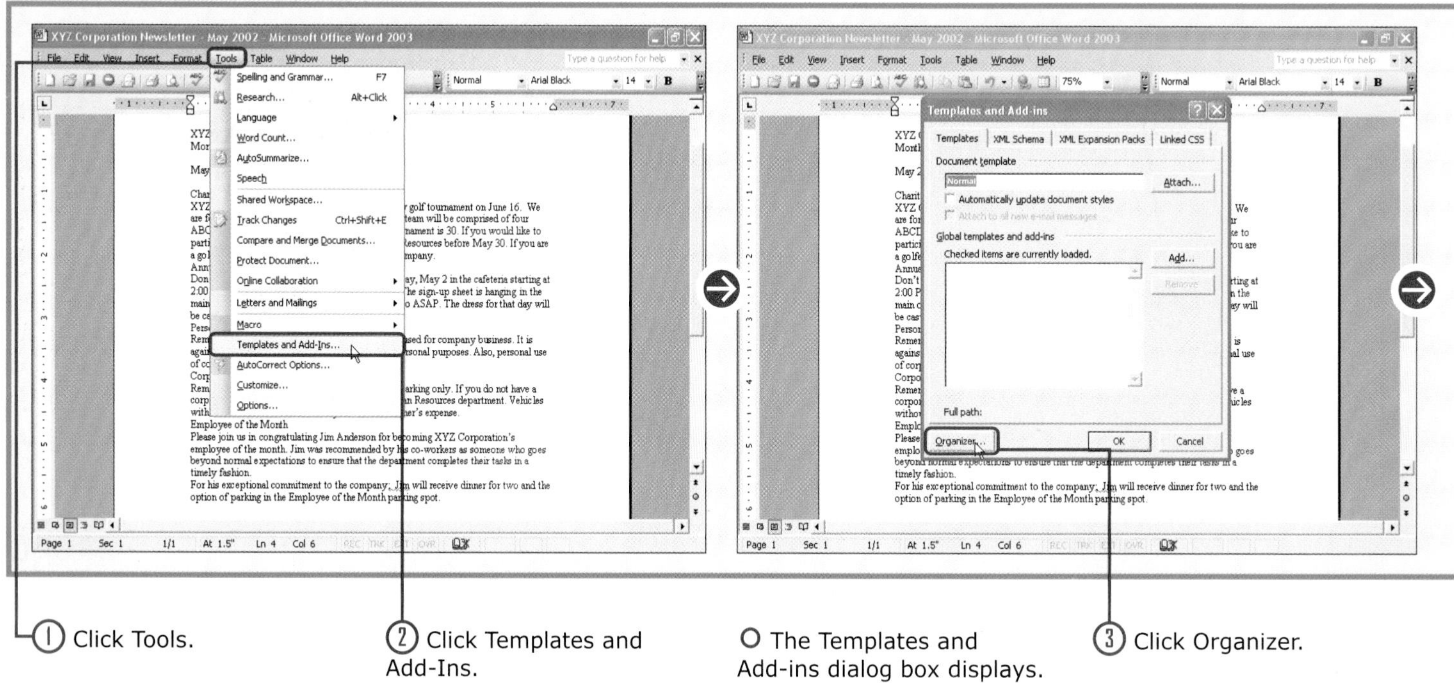

① Click Tools.

② Click Templates and Add-Ins.

○ The Templates and Add-ins dialog box displays.

③ Click Organizer.

#1

DIFFICULTY LEVEL

Did You Know?

If you want to use all of the styles in a template, you can just attach the template to the document in the Templates and Add-ins dialog box. To replace the current template, click Attach and select the desired template. Keep in mind, any styles in the document that match the template will be updated to use the settings in the template. For example, the Normal style in the document updates to use the font settings of the Normal style in the template.

Did You Know?

Microsoft Word applies a style to everything that you create. By default, Word applies the Normal style to all text, so if you do not apply any additional styles, all text within your document will have the Normal style.

When you create a style, Word bases the new style on the currently selected style. If you change the font settings for the original style, Word automatically adjusts the settings of all styles that are based upon that style.

CONTINUED

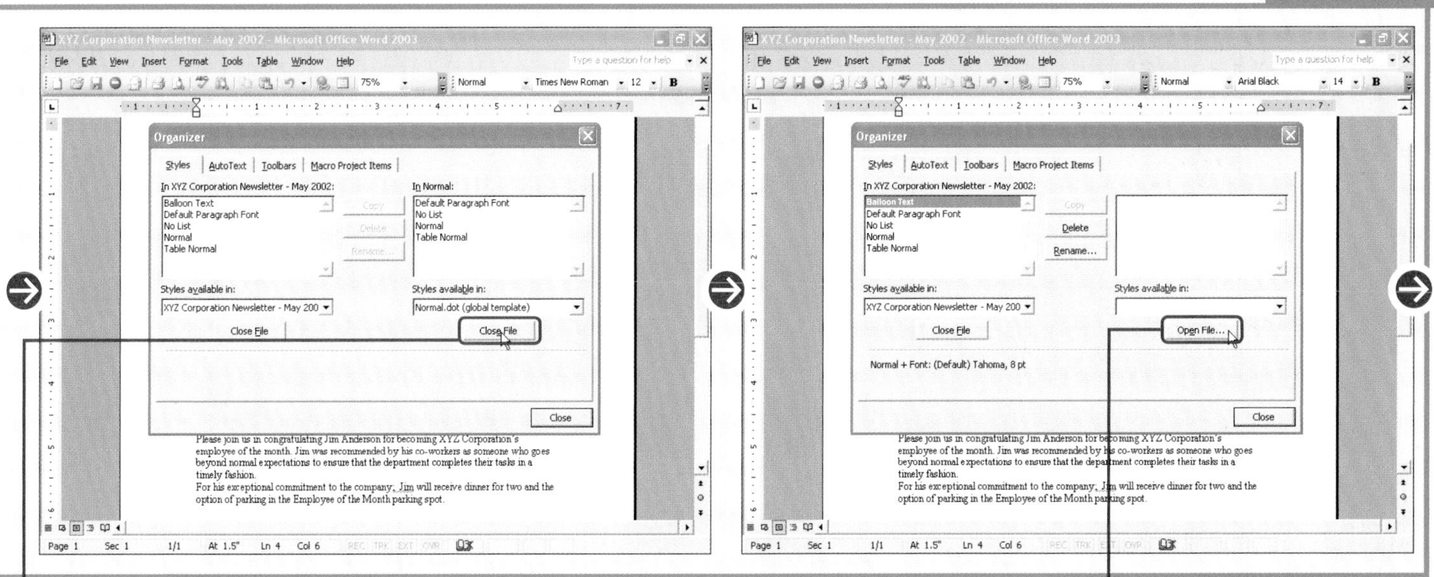

- The Organizer dialog box displays the current document and attached template styles.

4. Click Close File to close the current template.

Note: You can also click the Close File button under the document to open styles for another document or template.

Note: Closing a template or document on the Organizer dialog box does not affect the open documents in Word.

- Word clears the styles from the list box and the Close File button becomes Open File.

5. Click Open File.

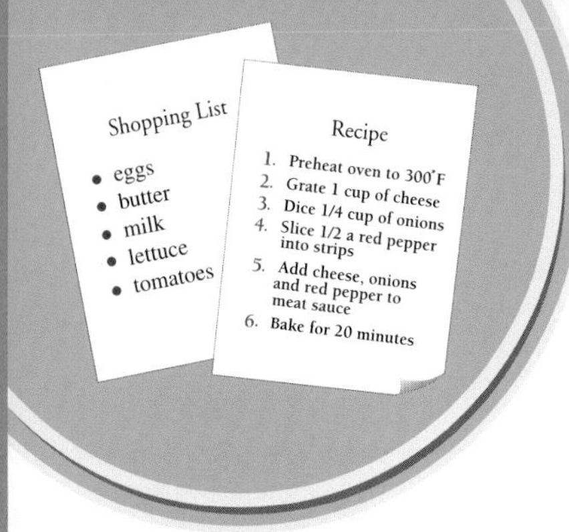

Apply styles from ANOTHER TEMPLATE

The Organizer dialog box allows you to copy styles between any documents and templates by opening that associated file in the Organizer dialog box. Word displays the styles in the current document in the left list box and the styles in the attached template in the right list box. Word displays the corresponding document or template name above the list box. By default, Microsoft Word looks for templates in the default Templates folder when you select Open File from the Organizer dialog box.

When you select a style in either one of the list boxes, the formatting settings for the style are listed in the bottom of the Organizer dialog box. Be aware that you cannot change the settings of a style from the Organizer dialog box.

You can open any Word document or template from which to copy styles by opening the corresponding documents. You can use this option to copy styles between any available documents and templates without having to use the Organizer dialog box. After styles are copied to a document or template, the new styles appear in the Style list.

CONTINUED ▶

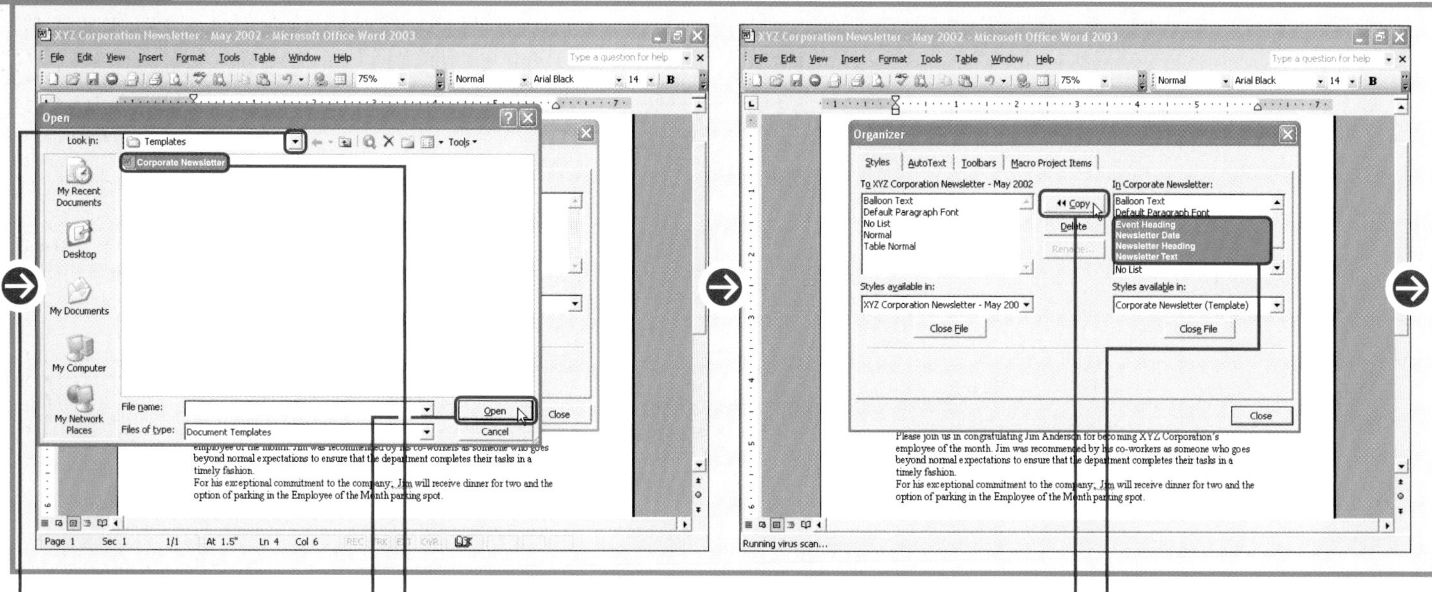

○ The Open dialog box displays the default Templates folder.

6 Click the Look in down arrow to select the folder containing the document or template.

7 Click the name of the document or template.

8 Click Open to view the styles in the specified document or template.

○ The styles from the selected document or template display in the list box.

9 Highlight the styles you want to copy.

10 Click Copy.

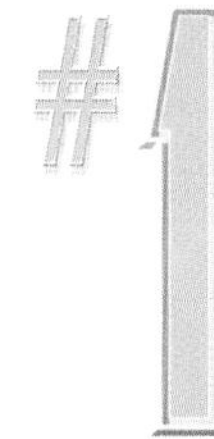

Apply It!

If you intend to distribute your document to other users, consider copying the styles from the attached template directly into the document. Doing so eliminates the need to distribute your template with the document.

CONTINUED

Did You Know?

You can also copy custom toolbars and macros among different documents and templates using the Organizer dialog box. You copy these items by selecting the appropriate tab and then following the same process outlined in the task. You can also copy AutoText entries using the Organizer dialog box, although you can only copy AutoText entries between different templates.

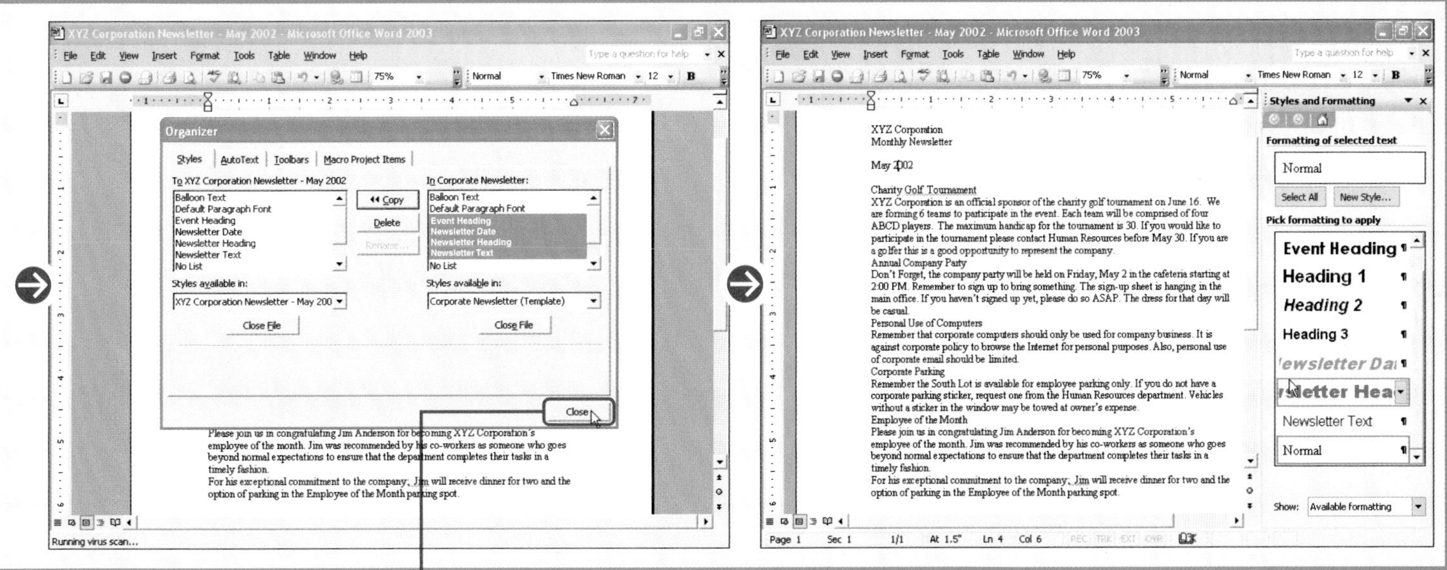

- Microsoft Word copies the selected styles to the document.
- Repeat steps **9** and **10** to copy additional styles from the same template.

11. Click Close to close the Organizer dialog box.

- The newly copied styles appear in the Style list.

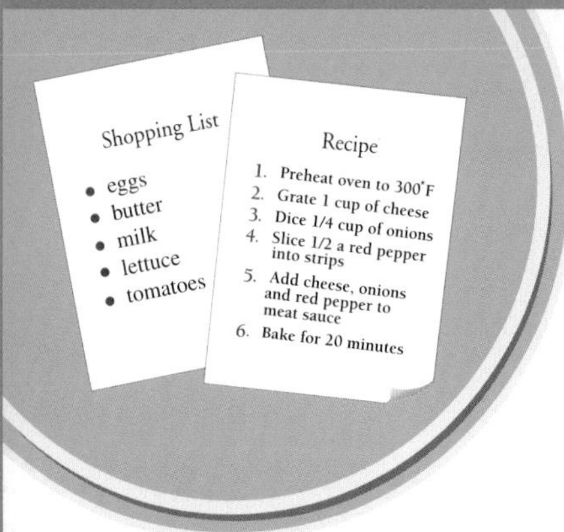

Open an ENCODED TEXT FILE

You can open encoded text files in Microsoft Word. *Encoded* files are text files that are saved using a specific encoding standard that assigns a numeric value to each character in the file. You typically use encoded text files when you are working with files from different languages that use special characters, such as Chinese or Japanese.

When you open an encoded text file, you need to tell Word how to interpret the numeric values in the file. You do so by selecting an encoding standard from the list. To make the process easier, the File Conversion dialog box provides a Preview window to show you the results of the selected encoding standard. By default, Word attempts to find a default encoding standard for you to use. If the selected encoding is not correct, you can select another one from the list.

Be aware that if you open a text file that uses the same encoding standard you are using for Windows, Word automatically detects the encoding and opens the text file without displaying the File Conversion dialog box.

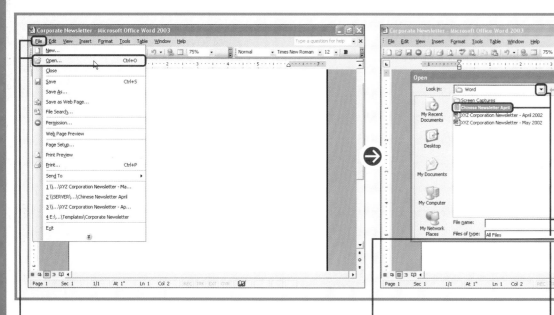

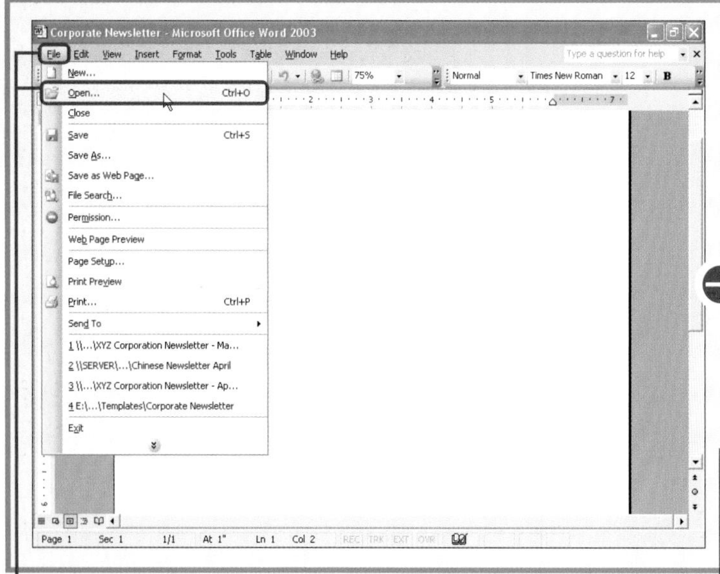

1. Click File.
2. Click Open.

- The Open dialog box displays.

3. Click the Files of type down arrow and select All Files to make all files in a folder visible.
4. Click the Look in down arrow and locate the folder containing the encoded text file.
5. Click the desired text file.
6. Click Open.

DIFFICULTY LEVEL

Apply It!

To create an encoded text file, click File and then click Save As. In the Save As dialog box, select Plain Text in the Save as type field. When you click Save, the File Conversion dialog box displays. Select the encoding standard to use. If you select Windows (Default), Word encodes the document based upon the current language selection within Windows.

Word provides several different encoding standards you can use to open text files. You can load additional encoding standards by running the Office setup. In the Advanced Setup screen, click the Office Shared Features option, and then click International Support. Click the encoding standards you want to add and then click Run from My Computer.

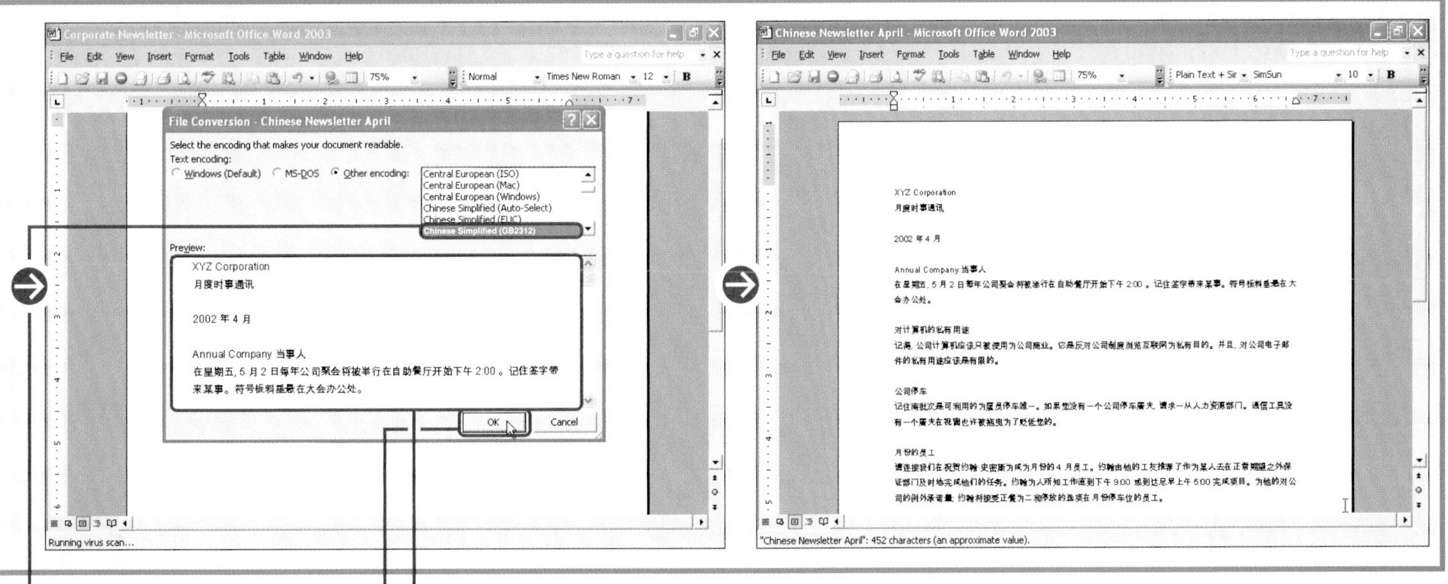

- The File Conversion dialog box displays.

⑦ Select the encoding that matches the text file you are opening.

- A preview displays for the encoding selection.

⑧ Click OK.

- The encoded text file opens in Word using the specified encoding.

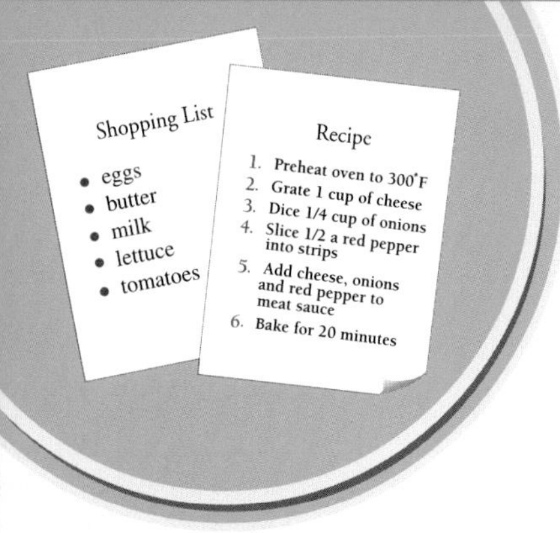

Using two different PAGE-NUMBERING SCHEMES

You can create different page-numbering schemes within the same document. For example, you may want to use alphabetic numbering for the first section and numeric numbers for the second section.

When you create a page-number format in a Word document, Word uses that same page-numbering format for all pages within the same document or section, so the only way to change the page numbering for the remaining pages is to create a new section.

By default, when you create a new section, Word links all headers and footers to the previous section. In order to create a new page-number scheme, you need to remove the link to the previous section. You can create section breaks at any location within a Word document. If you have a section break, you can change the layout of the page-numbering scheme for that section.

You use the Insert Page Number button to add the page number in the desired location. You can combine the page number with any other text.

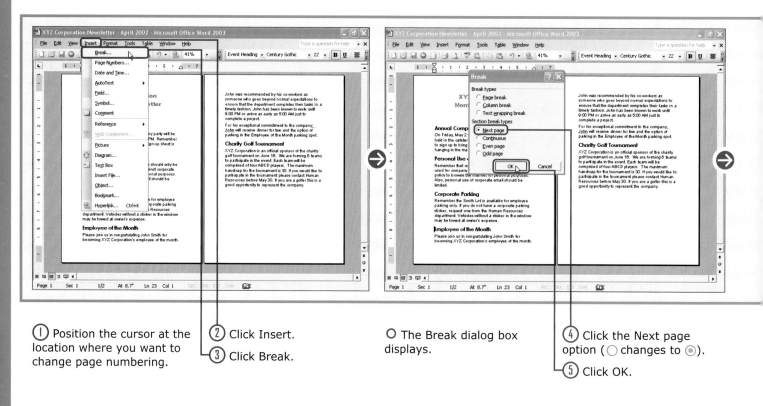

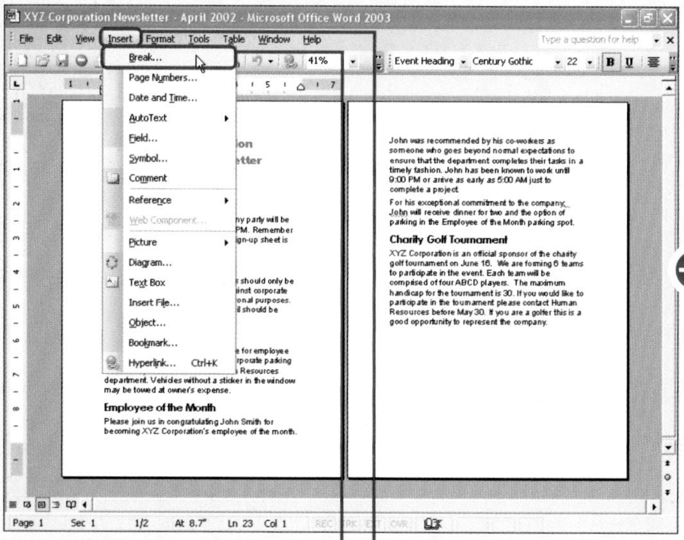

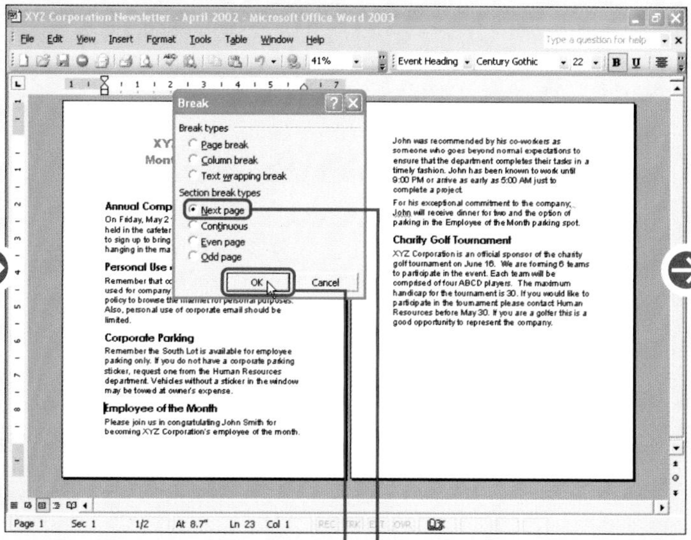

① Position the cursor at the location where you want to change page numbering.

② Click Insert.

③ Click Break.

○ The Break dialog box displays.

④ Click the Next page option (○ changes to ◉).

⑤ Click OK.

Apply It!

You can modify the headers and footers in a section even more by creating different headers for odd and even pages. You can also specify different headers and footers for the first page in the section.

In order to have these types of headers and footers, click File and then Page Setup to display the Page Setup dialog box. If you only want these header settings for the current section, select This section in the Apply to field.

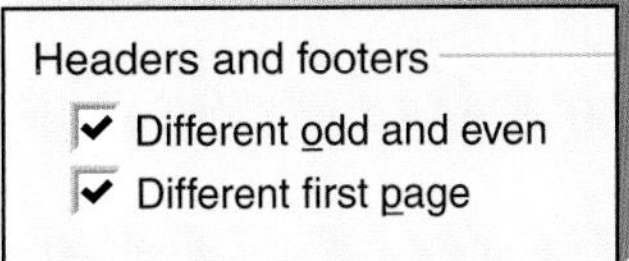

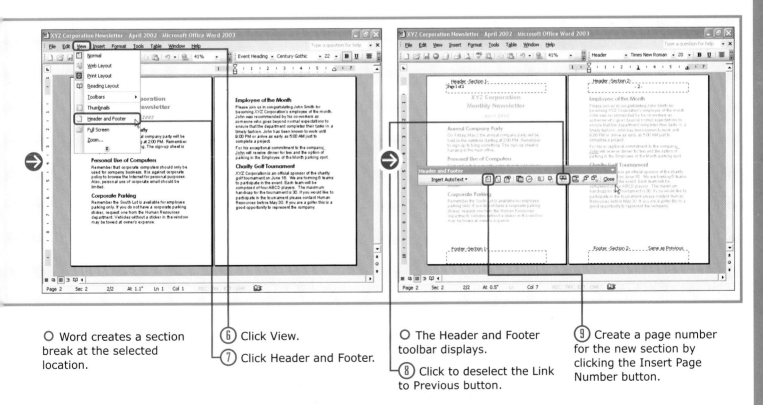

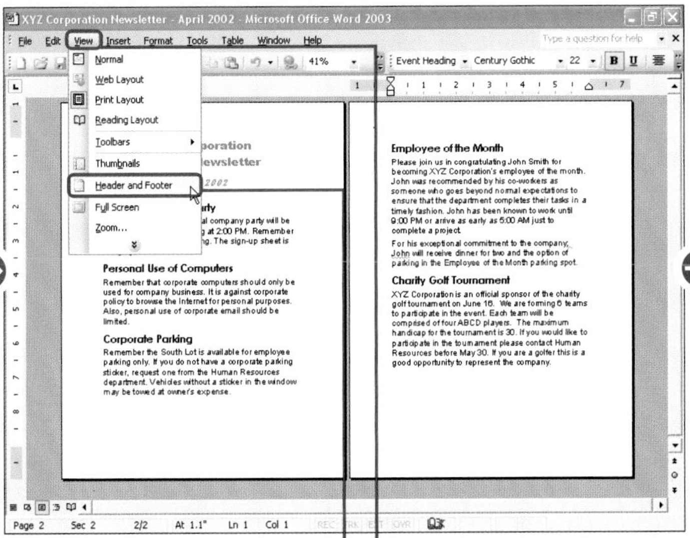

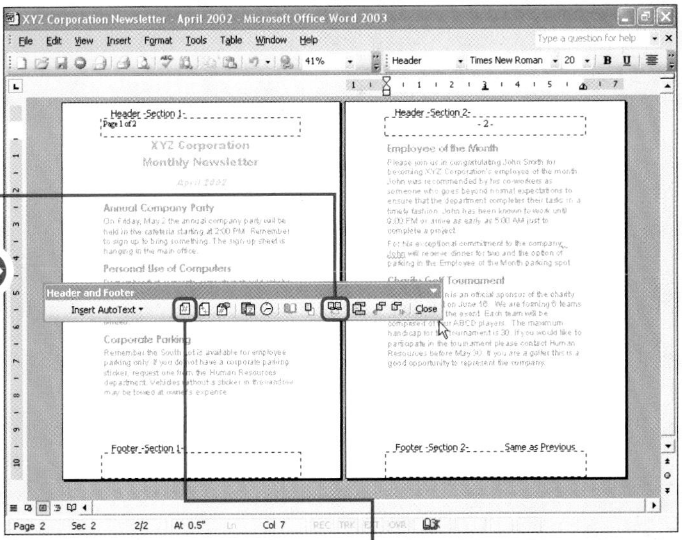

○ Word creates a section break at the selected location.

6 Click View.

7 Click Header and Footer.

○ The Header and Footer toolbar displays.

8 Click to deselect the Link to Previous button.

9 Create a page number for the new section by clicking the Insert Page Number button.

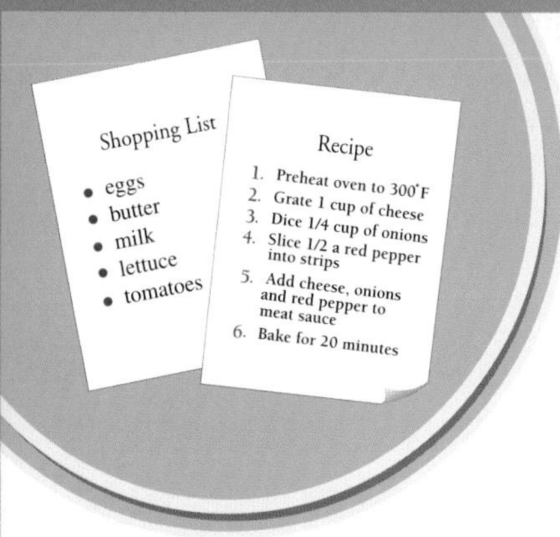

RESTART PAGE NUMBERS

for each chapter or section

You can restart the page numbering in each section of your Word document. This is especially useful when creating chapters in which you want each chapter to start numbering again at one.

In each section, you can specify the positioning and formatting for the page numbers. You can use numbers, letters, or Roman numerals by selecting the desired number format in the Page Numbers dialog box. For example, when creating a large document, such as a book, the introductory pages are typically numbered using either Roman numerals or alphabetic characters.

You can insert page numbers using either the Header and Footer toolbar — see task #3 — or the Page Numbers dialog box. This example uses the Page Numbers dialog box.

In the Start at field, type the number that represents the first page number for the section. This must be a numeric value even if you are using alphabetic or Roman numerals. For example, if you have Roman numerals selected, to start with page iv, you need to type 4.

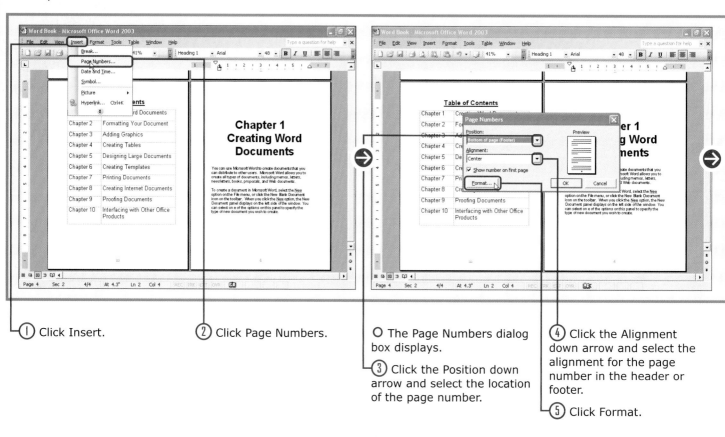

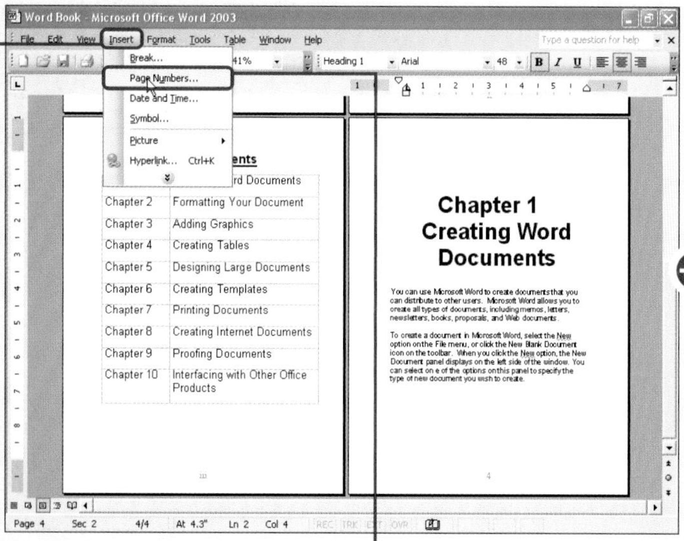

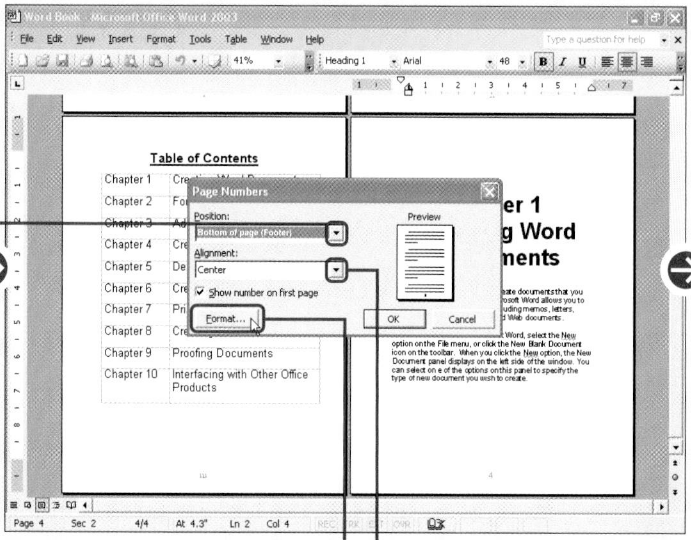

① Click Insert.

② Click Page Numbers.

○ The Page Numbers dialog box displays.

③ Click the Position down arrow and select the location of the page number.

④ Click the Alignment down arrow and select the alignment for the page number in the header or footer.

⑤ Click Format.

DIFFICULTY LEVEL

Put It Together!

You can have Word automatically insert the chapter or section number as part of the page number by checking the Include chapter number check box on the Page Number Format dialog box. With that option checked, for example, the second page of Chapter 1 would be 1-2.

Did You Know?

If you want to autonumber chapters or sections within your document, you need to create a style for the chapter or section heading that uses the automatic numbering format. For example, you can create a NumberSections style that use a numbering style. Then on the Page Number Format dialog box, select the Include chapter number option and select that style.

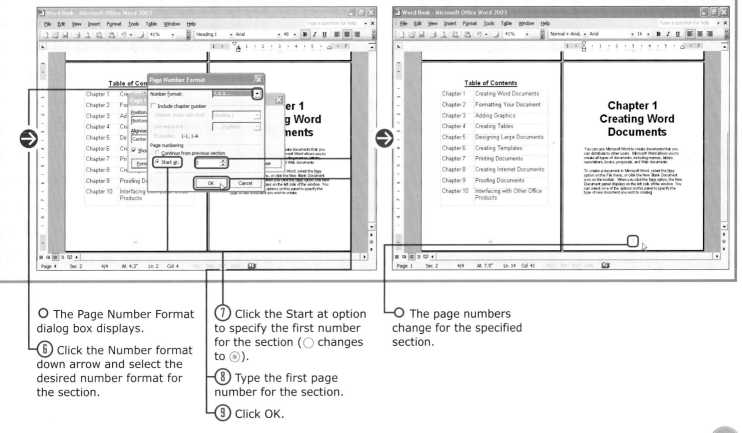

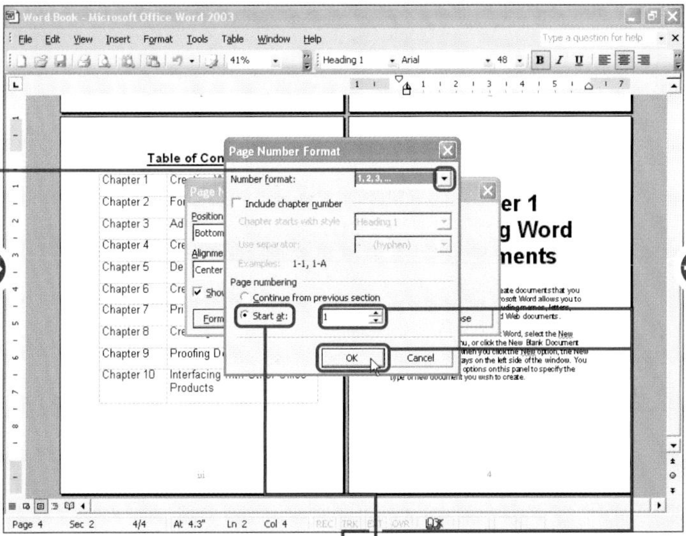

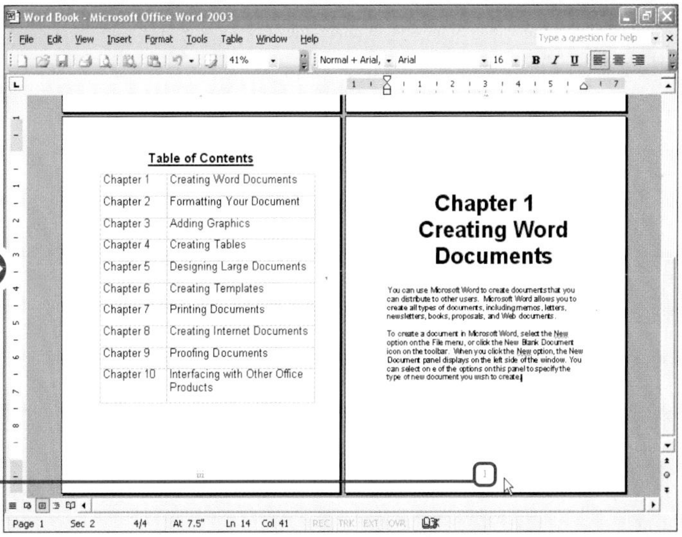

- The Page Number Format dialog box displays.

6 Click the Number format down arrow and select the desired number format for the section.

7 Click the Start at option to specify the first number for the section (○ changes to ◉).

8 Type the first page number for the section.

9 Click OK.

- The page numbers change for the specified section.

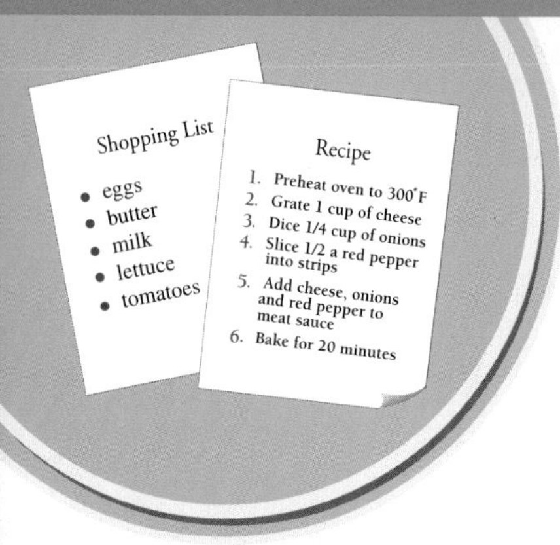

MOVE PAGE NUMBERS

outside of a header or footer

You can have page numbers appear anywhere on the page of your Word document. By default, Word places the page number in the header or footer of the document, but you can move the page number out of the header or footer and place it at another location in the document.

In order to move the page number, the page number must have been originally inserted using the Page Number dialog box. When you use this dialog box, Word places the page number on the page in a frame, whereas when you insert page numbers using the Header and Footer toolbar, Word places the page number directly in the text. See task #4 for more information on the Page Numbers dialog box.

If you are not sure how you added the page number, you can quickly check by clicking on it. If a frame appears around the page number, you can drag the page number on the page. If not, you need to re-create the page number using the Page Number dialog box.

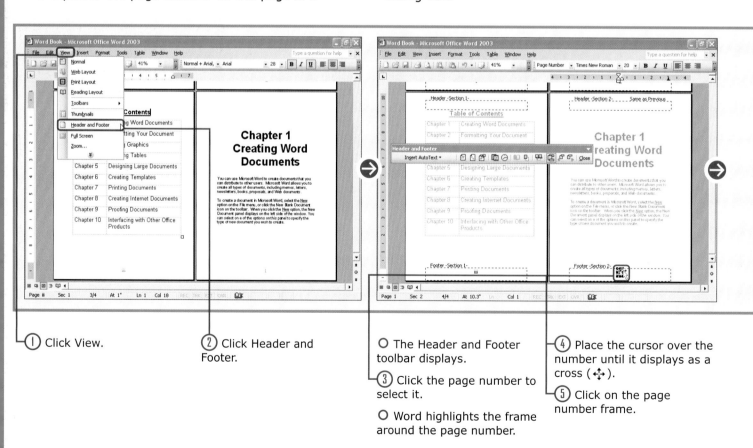

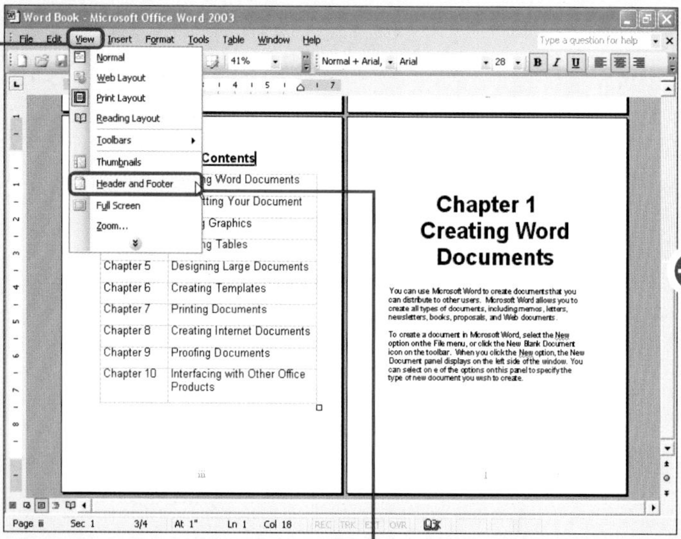

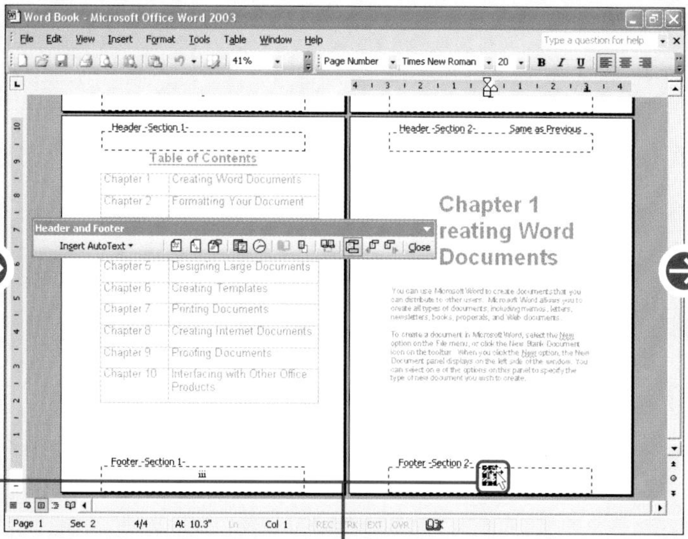

1 Click View.

2 Click Header and Footer.

○ The Header and Footer toolbar displays.

3 Click the page number to select it.

○ Word highlights the frame around the page number.

4 Place the cursor over the number until it displays as a cross (✥).

5 Click on the page number frame.

Did You Know?

When you move a page number outside of a header or footer, Word still associates the page number with the original location. In order to modify or move the page number, you must use the Header and Footer toolbar.

DIFFICULTY LEVEL

Did You Know?

If you drag and drop the page number frame on a location that contains text, Word moves the text to provide space for the page number.

Customize It!

If you want to add additional text to the page number, you must first size the frame to make it larger. To do so, select the frame and drag one of the sides. Type the desired text before or after the page number.

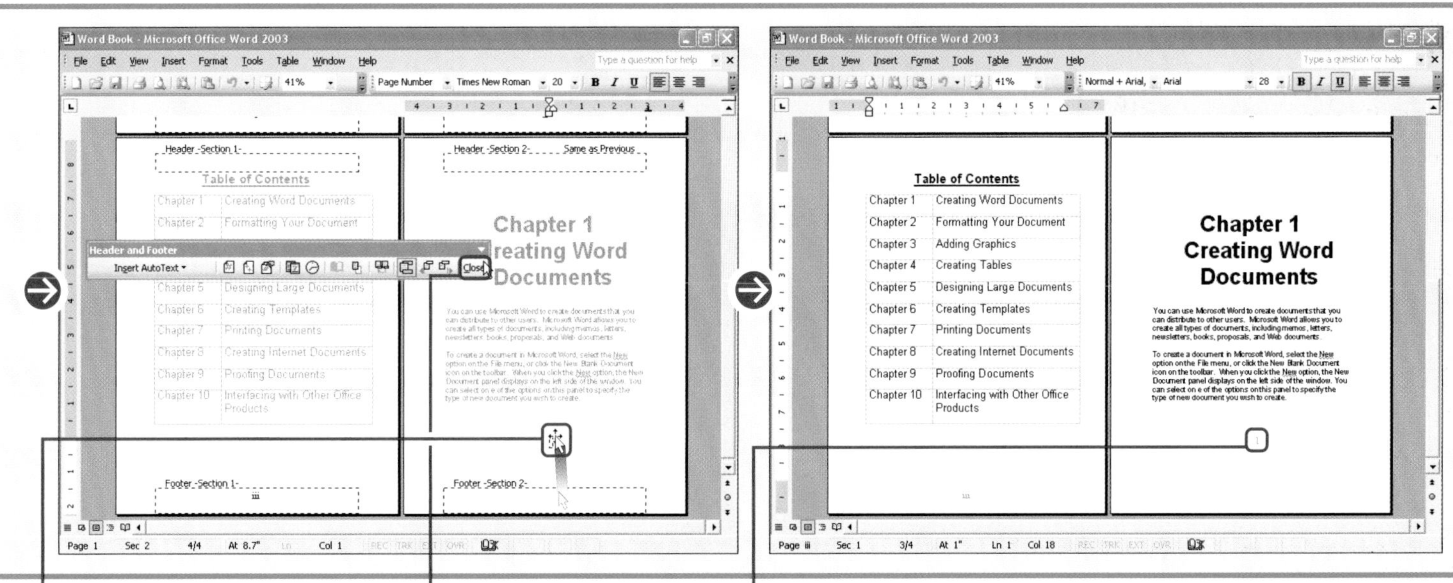

⑥ Drag the page number frame to the desired location.

⑦ Click Close to close the Header and Footer toolbar.

○ The page number displays in the new location.

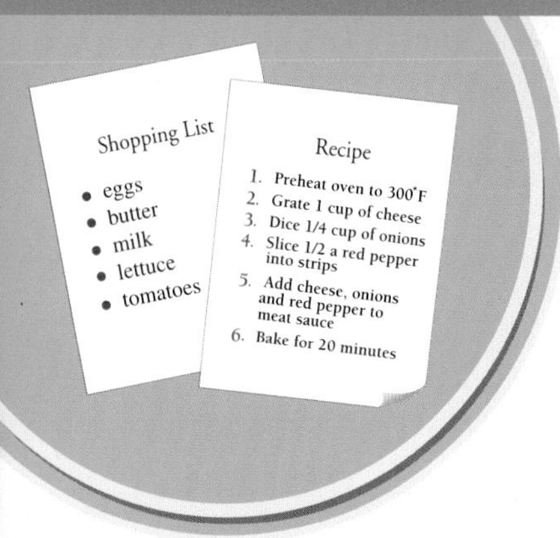

CREATE GUTTER MARGINS

for a bound document

You can set up your page layout to allow for the space necessary for binding. For example, if you are creating a report for a 3-ring binder, you can allow space for the 3-hole punch and still have a margin between the binding and the text.

Word refers to the space you allow for binding as a *gutter*. Because different binding styles have specific size requirements, you can set the gutter size in the Page Setup dialog box.

Word creates the gutter outside the corresponding margin. Therefore, if you have a 1-inch gutter on the left side and a 1-inch left margin, when the document prints you will actually see a 2-inch left margin.

If you intend to create pages printed on the front and back, you should set up your document to use Mirror margins. This option specifies that you want the margins on the odd pages to be a mirror or opposite of the even pages, so Word creates the gutter on the right side of the even pages and left side of the odd pages.

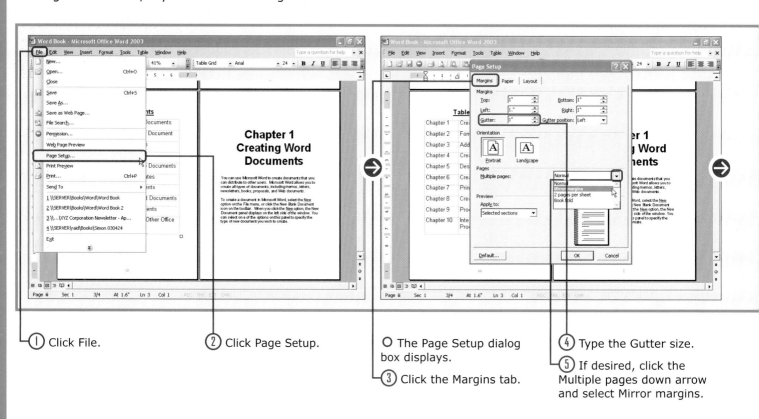

1. Click File.
2. Click Page Setup.

- The Page Setup dialog box displays.

3. Click the Margins tab.
4. Type the Gutter size.
5. If desired, click the Multiple pages down arrow and select Mirror margins.

DIFFICULTY LEVEL

Apply It!

You can place the gutter in different locations on the page. For example, place the gutter at the top of the page if you plan to staple or bind the pages from the top. Select Normal in the Multiple Pages field in the Page Setup dialog box, and then specify the gutter position in the Gutter Position field.

Margin settings should be visible when you view the document in Normal or Print Layout view. If the margins are not visible, click Tools ⇨ Options and select the View tab. To view margin settings in Normal view, select the Wrap to window check box. To view margin settings in Print Layout view, select the White space between pages check box.

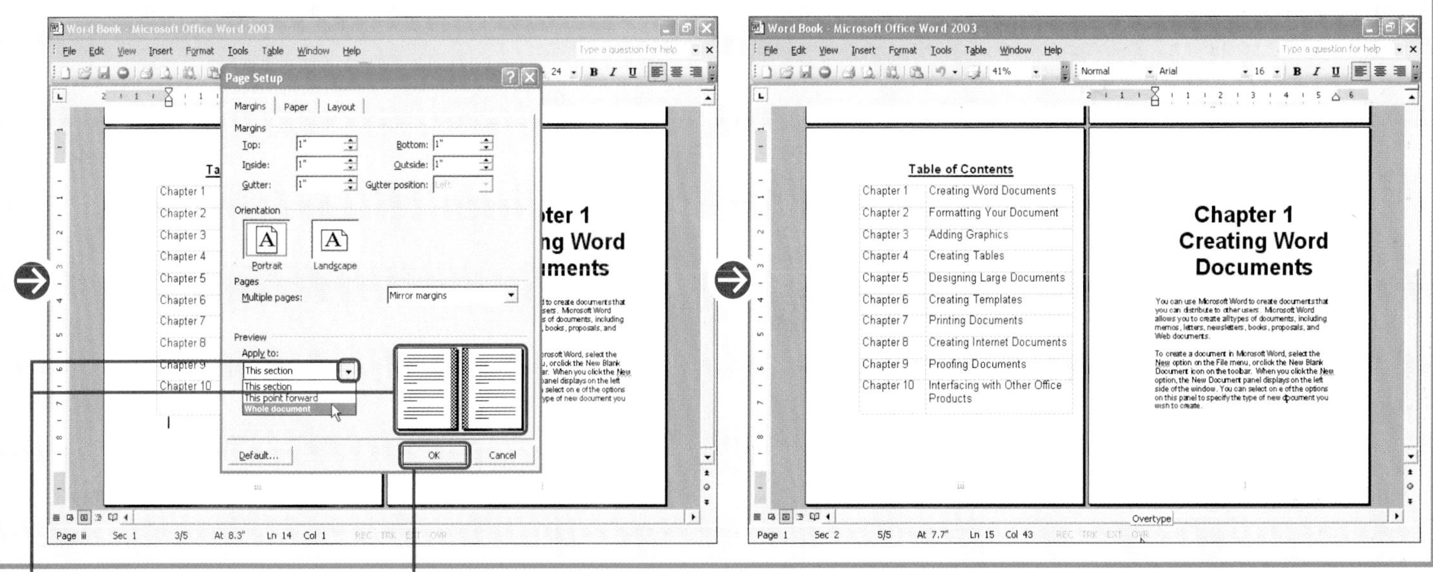

- The Preview changes to reflect the gutter margin settings.

6. Click the Apply to down arrow and highlight Whole document to apply the gutter settings to the entire document.

7. Click OK to apply the gutter margin settings.

- Word adjusts the margin sizes to reflect the changes.

Note: Resizing tables and other graphics to adjust for the new margin settings may be necessary.

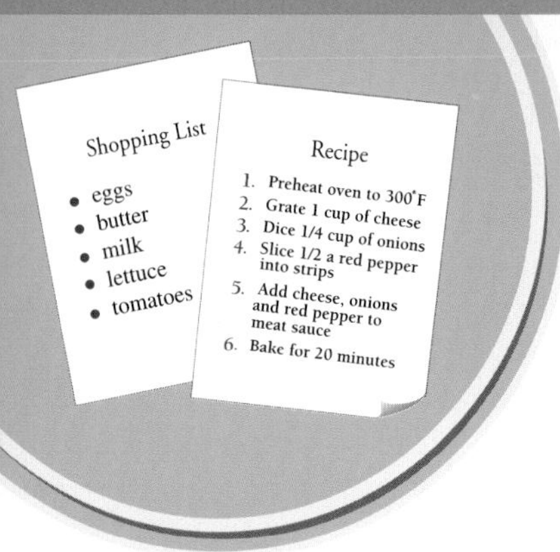

Number custom HEADING LEVELS

You can specify the heading levels for custom styles that you create in Word. By default, Word provides styles that you can apply to your document. These default styles, such as Heading 1 and Heading 2, have associated outline and table of contents levels. For example, if you view an outline of a document, all text with the Heading 1 style displays as level 1 in the outline. If you create a table of contents, the Heading 1 text displays as the first level.

By default, Word assigns a level of Body Text to all styles you create. This means that when you view a document outline or create a table of contents, your custom styles are treated like normal text. To alter this, you need to assign an outline level between 1 and 9 to each style. An outline level of 1 is considered the highest level. You typically want to apply this level to section or chapter headings.

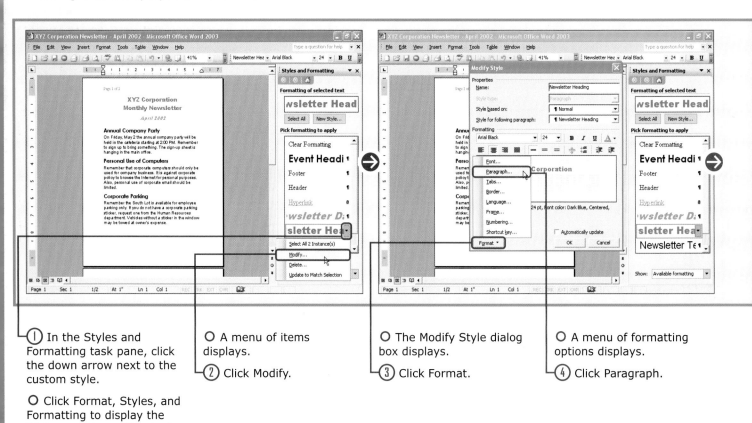

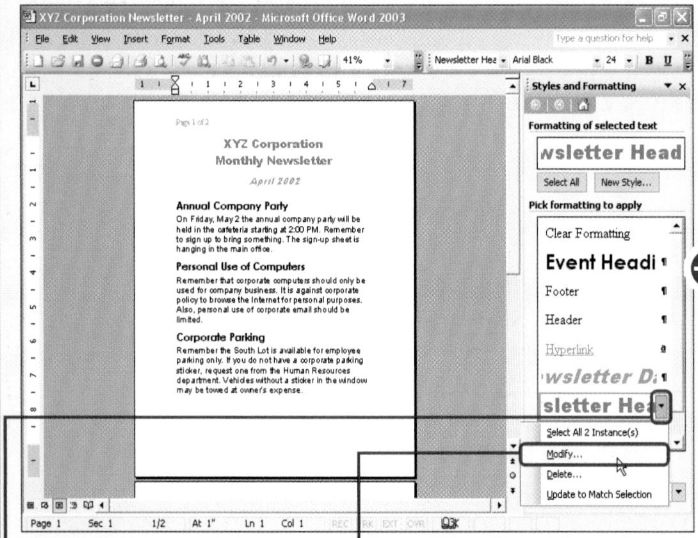

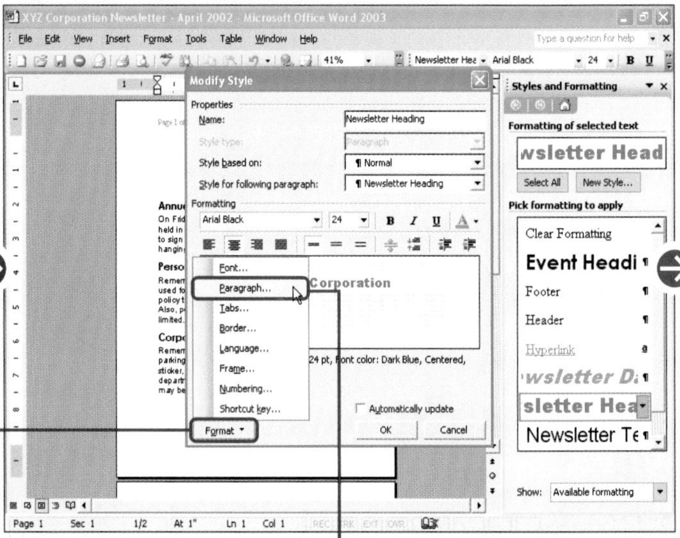

1. In the Styles and Formatting task pane, click the down arrow next to the custom style.

- Click Format, Styles, and Formatting to display the Styles and Formatting task pane.
- A menu of items displays.

2. Click Modify.

- The Modify Style dialog box displays.

3. Click Format.

- A menu of formatting options displays.

4. Click Paragraph.

DIFFICULTY LEVEL

Did You Know?

By default, the Styles and Formatting task pane lists all available custom and built-in styles. To display only selected styles, click the Show field down arrow and select Custom to display the Format Settings dialog box. Click the check boxes next to the styles you want displayed. In the Category field, select the name of the category you want to use for the selected styles.

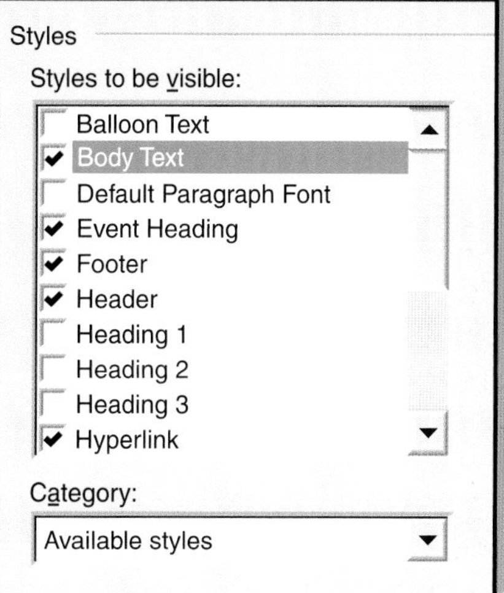

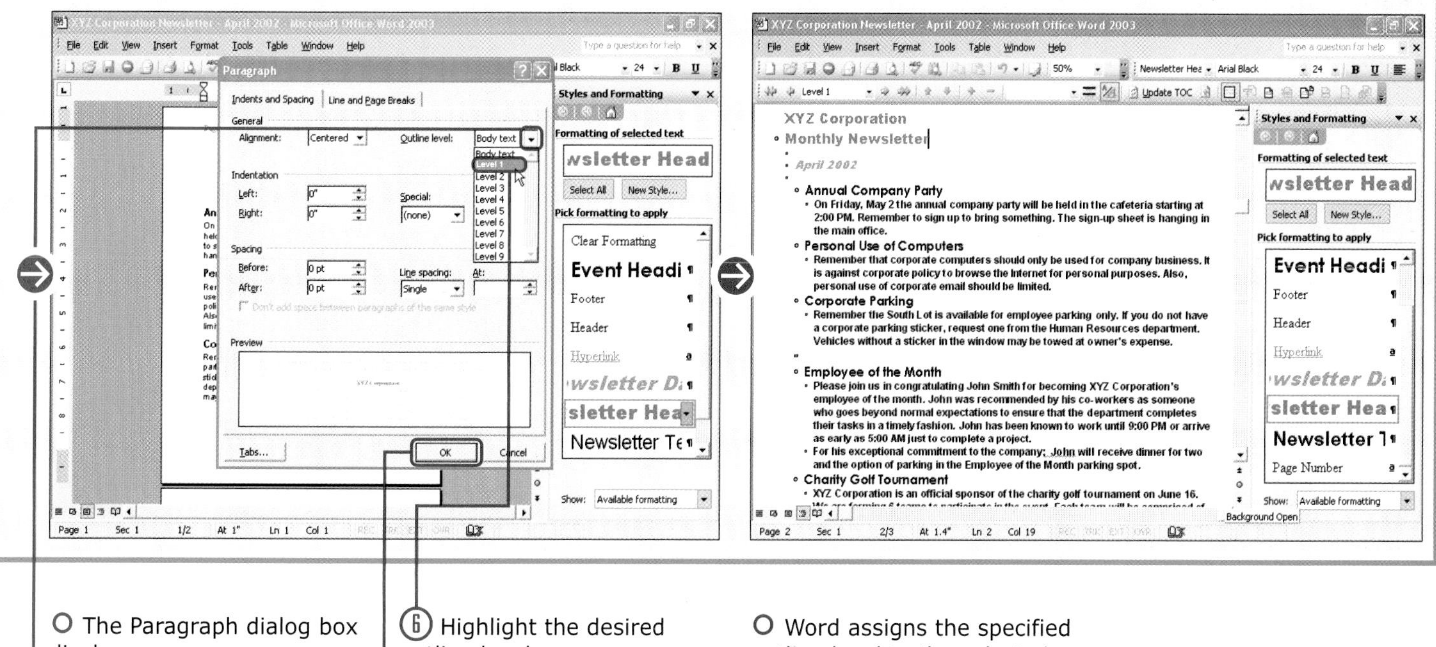

- The Paragraph dialog box displays.
- 5 Click the down arrow next to the Outline level field to view levels.
- 6 Highlight the desired outline level.
- 7 Click OK.
- Word assigns the specified outline level to the selected style when it creates an outline or a table of contents for the document.

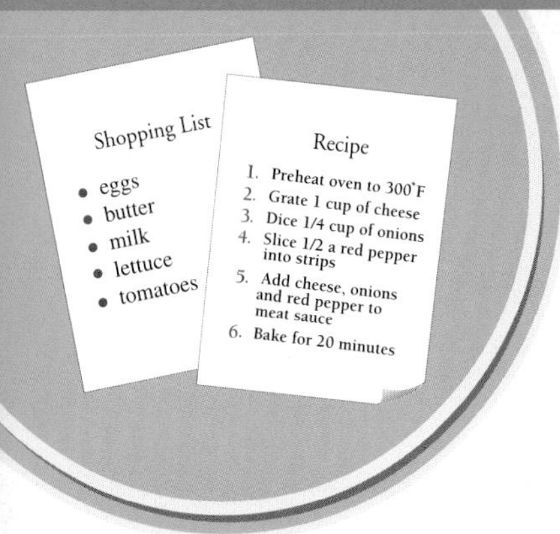

Create custom BULLET IMAGES

You can customize the image used for each bullet in a bulleted list. You can replace the bullet with another character or with any graphic image. You can also assign a different image to each bullet, or use the same image for the entire list.

Although you create bulleted lists using the Bullets button, to customize a bulleted list you need to use the Bullets and Numbering dialog box available on the Format menu. You specify the desired bullet image using the Customize Bulleted List dialog box.

If you want to use a character, you can select any character from any font installed on your machine. If you select a picture bullet, you can use one of the pre-installed bullet pictures.

If you are creating a new bullet list, you can apply the new bullet to each list item as you type. To do this, first select the desired bullet image for the bullet style and then create your list. Each time you press Enter, Word creates a new bulleted item with the selected bullet style.

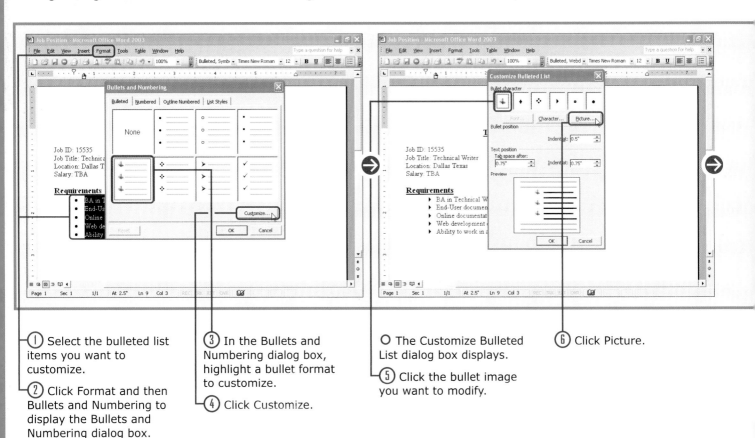

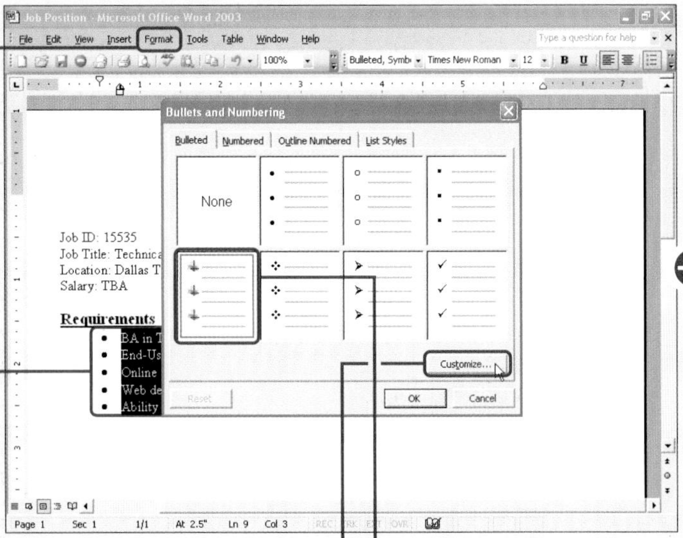

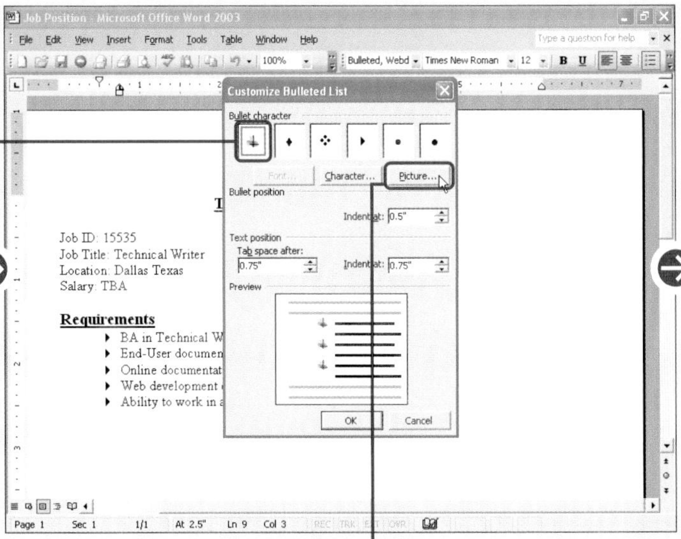

1. Select the bulleted list items you want to customize.
2. Click Format and then Bullets and Numbering to display the Bullets and Numbering dialog box.
3. In the Bullets and Numbering dialog box, highlight a bullet format to customize.
4. Click Customize.

- The Customize Bulleted List dialog box displays.

5. Click the bullet image you want to modify.
6. Click Picture.

DIFFICULTY LEVEL

Customize It!

You can create your own bullet images to import into Word by creating a GIF image of the desired bullet. Typically, bullet images are no larger than 20 by 20 pixels. You can import the image into Word by clicking the Import button in the Picture Bullet dialog box.

Apply It!

You can reset your bullet styles back to the default values. Because Word actually only maintains seven different bullet styles, any custom styles you create replace one of the default styles in the Bullets and Numbering dialog box. To reset the bullet styles back to the original defaults, click the Reset button in the Bullets and Numbering dialog box. Clicking Reset does not affect the bullets in your current documents.

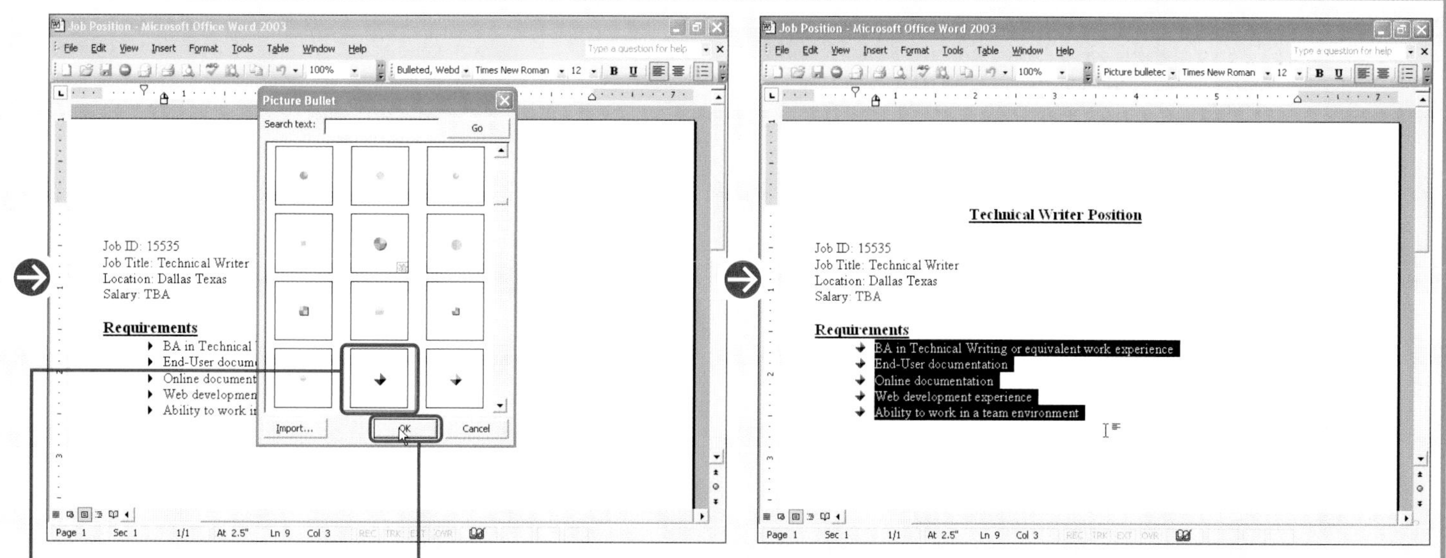

- The Picture Bullet dialog box displays.

7 Click the desired bullet image.

8 Click OK.

- The bulleted list image changes to reflect the selection.

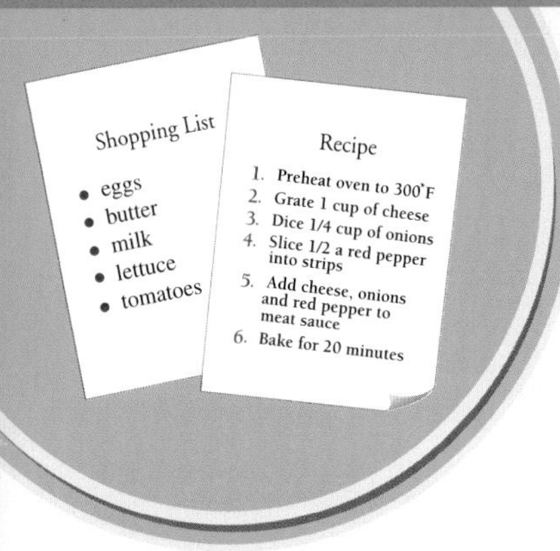

Change the file format for MULTIPLE DOCUMENTS

You can have Word convert multiple documents simultaneously from one format to another. This process is a great timesaver when you have several documents that you want to place on a Web site. By using a batch conversion, you can quickly convert the files to an HTML format. This eliminates the process of selecting the Save As option for each individual file.

To convert documents, you need to specify the folder location of the documents you want to convert and the location where you want to place the converted files. If the documents are in multiple locations, you need to either place them in the same folder or you will have to repeat the process for each folder location. When you convert files, the original files remain in the original format.

You can convert files using the Batch Conversion Wizard. You can either convert a series of Word documents to a different format or convert other files to Word documents. In either case, you have to select the other format.

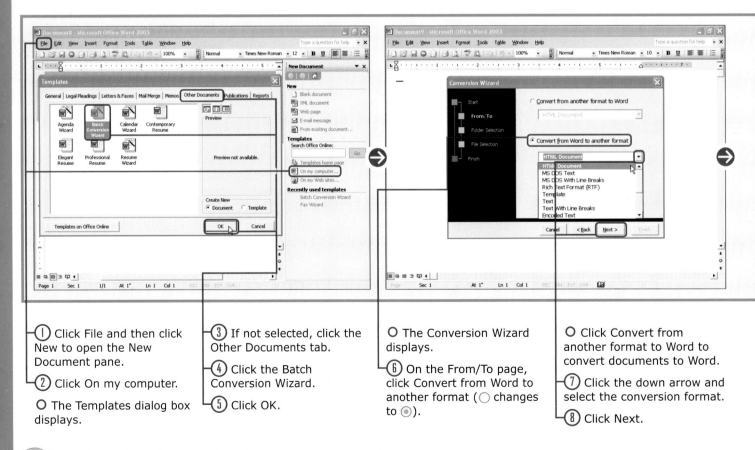

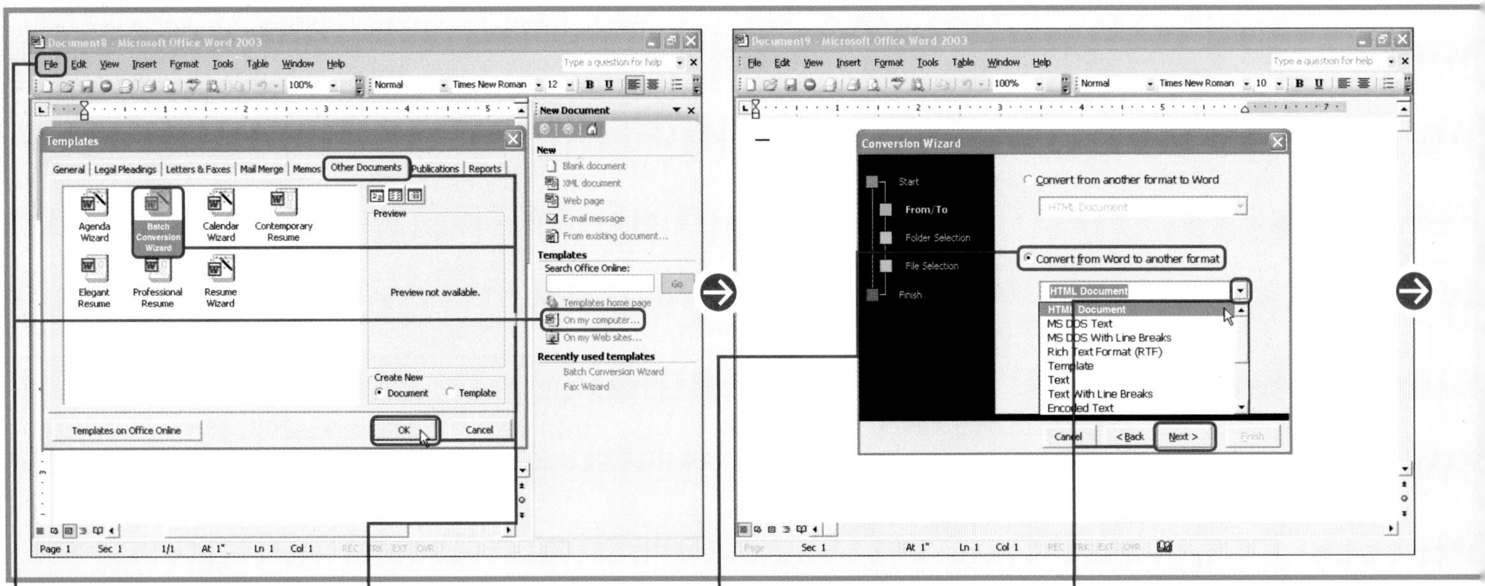

(1) Click File and then click New to open the New Document pane.

(2) Click On my computer.

○ The Templates dialog box displays.

(3) If not selected, click the Other Documents tab.

(4) Click the Batch Conversion Wizard.

(5) Click OK.

○ The Conversion Wizard displays.

(6) On the From/To page, click Convert from Word to another format (○ changes to ◉).

○ Click Convert from another format to Word to convert documents to Word.

(7) Click the down arrow and select the conversion format.

(8) Click Next.

#9

DIFFICULTY LEVEL

Did You Know?

When you select the Save option, Word always uses the default Word format to save the document. To change the default format, open the Options dialog box by clicking Tools and then Options. Click the Save tab and select the desired format for the Save Word files as field.

Did You Know?

When you open .HTML, .MHTML, .XML, .RTF, or .TXT files, Word automatically converts the files to Word documents. If you want to be aware of converted files, you can instruct Word to display the Convert File dialog box whenever you open a non-Word file. To do so, click Tools and then click Options to display the Options dialog box. On the General tab, click Confirm Conversion at Open.

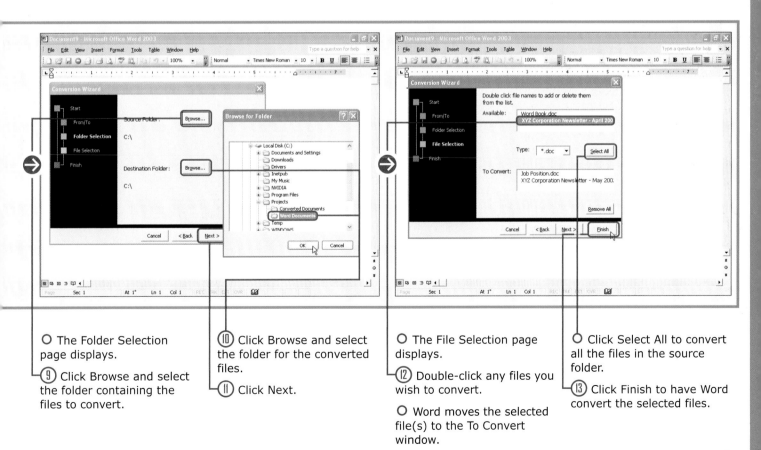

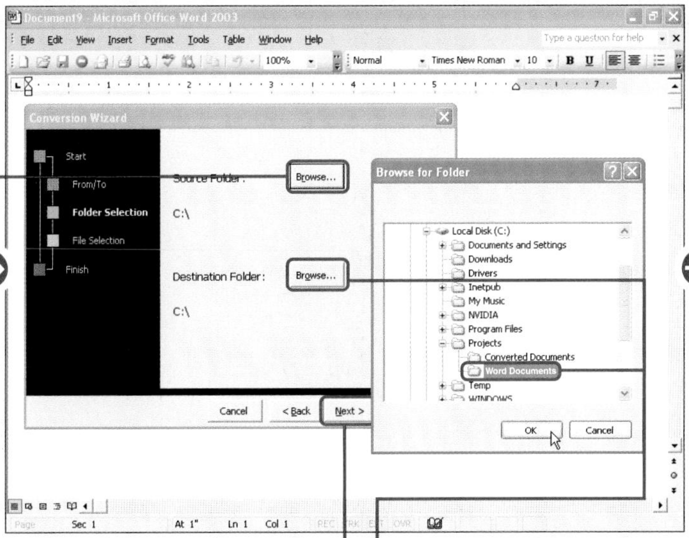

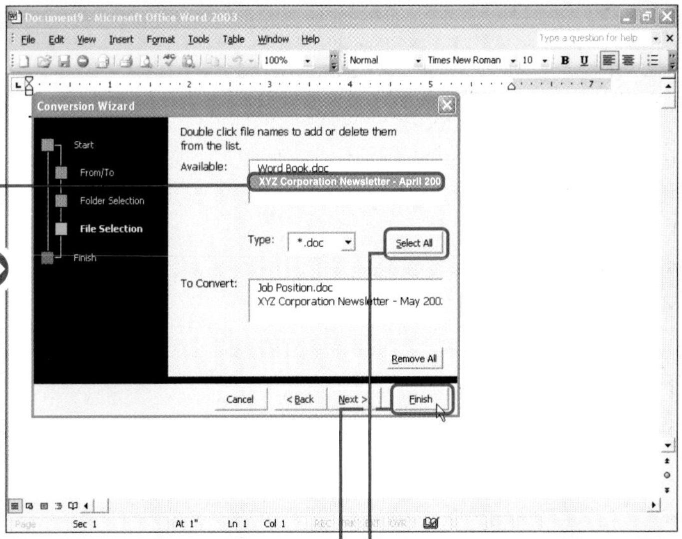

- The Folder Selection page displays.

9. Click Browse and select the folder containing the files to convert.

10. Click Browse and select the folder for the converted files.

11. Click Next.

- The File Selection page displays.

12. Double-click any files you wish to convert.

- Word moves the selected file(s) to the To Convert window.

- Click Select All to convert all the files in the source folder.

13. Click Finish to have Word convert the selected files.

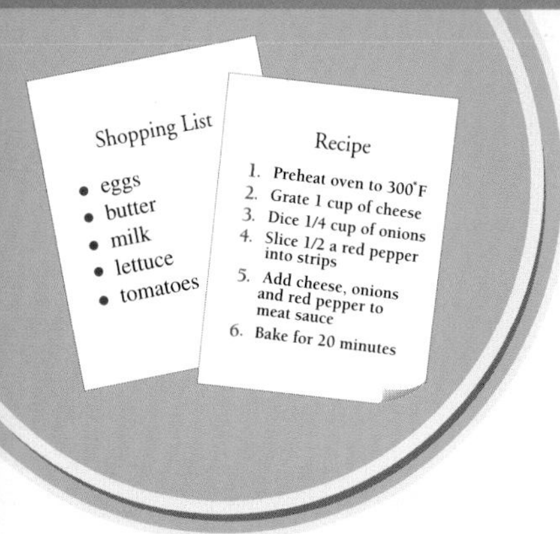

Specify SUBSTITUTION FONTS for converted documents

Word documents from other sources may use fonts that are not available on your machine. When this occurs, Word automatically selects substitution fonts from your available fonts. You can specify the substitution fonts that Word should use if the specified fonts do not exist on your machine so that the converted document looks as close as possible to the original.

You specify the font substitutions using the Font Substitution dialog box. The font substitutions that you specify are only used by Word when the fonts required by the document do not exist on your machine.

While you may be specifying font substitutions for just one document, keep in mind that Word remembers those selections the next time you open a document with the same missing fonts and automatically changes the missing font to the font you last specified. For example, if the document uses the Chicago font, and you specify a substitution of Arial, the next document you open with the Chicago font will be substituted with Arial.

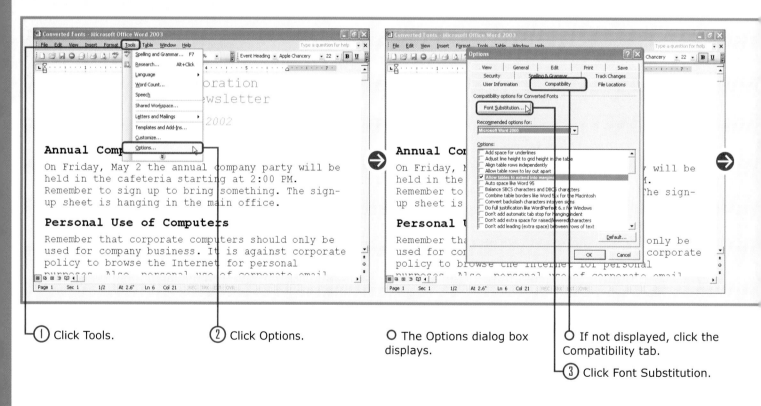

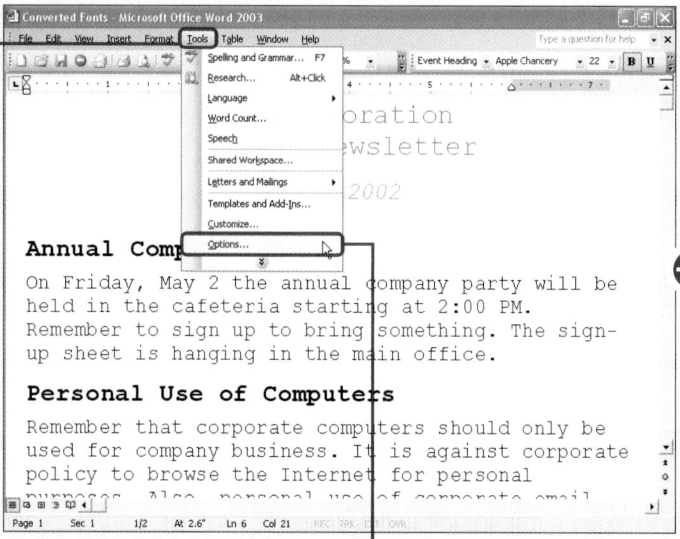

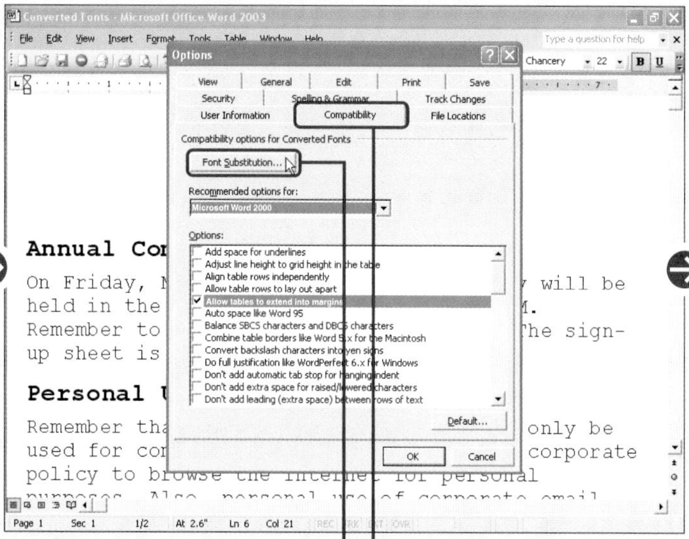

1. Click Tools.
2. Click Options.

- The Options dialog box displays.
- If not displayed, click the Compatibility tab.

3. Click Font Substitution.

DIFFICULTY LEVEL

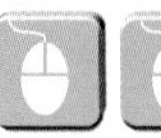   

Did You Know?

You can customize the appearance of documents that Word opens from different formats by using the Compatibility tab of the Options dialog box. Select the format you want to customize in the Recommended options for field and then select the appropriate check boxes. Remember that the options you select only control how the document displays in Word; they do not change the actual file.

Caution!

When you save Word documents in other non-.DOC or non-.DOT formats, such as text files, any formatting or other content not supported by that file format will be omitted, including graphics. Before this occurs, Word first displays a warning message informing you that some formatting may be lost.

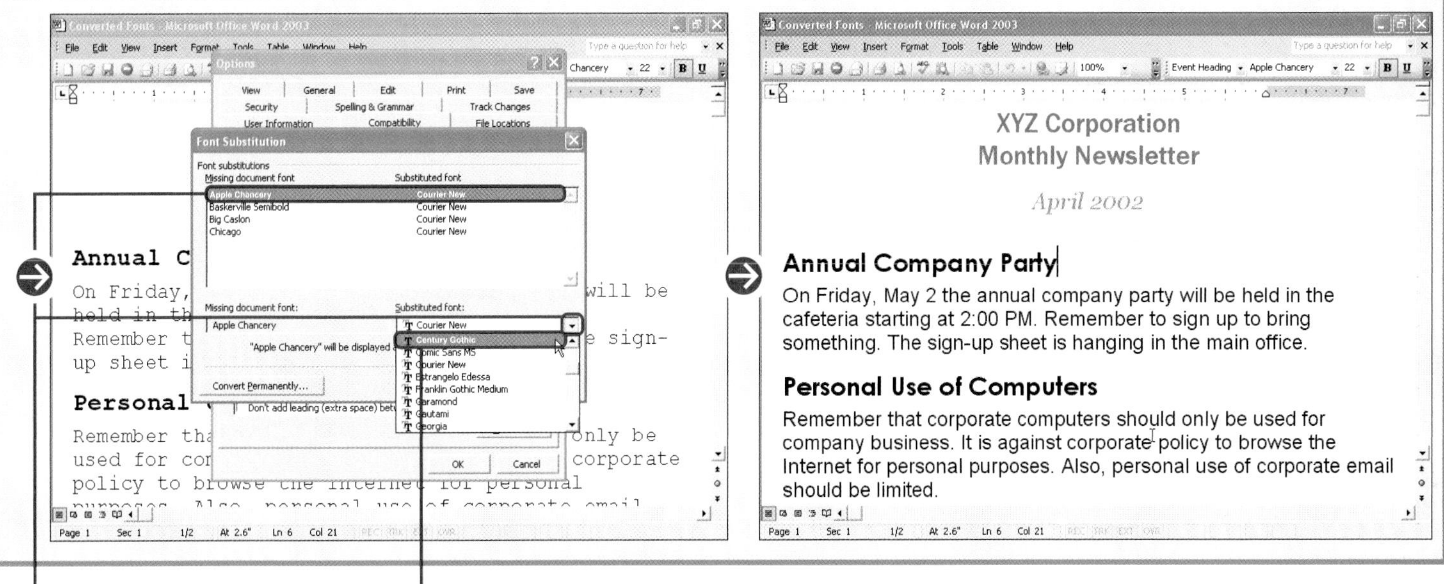

- The Font Substitution dialog box displays.

4. Click the font substitution you want to change.

5. Click the Substituted font down arrow.

6. Click the desired substitution font.

- Repeat steps **4** to **6** for each font substitution you wish to change.

7. Click OK in the Font Substitution dialog box.

- Word makes the specified font substitutions to the document.

Change the Text Formatting

Word provides several different features for changing the formatting of the text in your document. Text formatting ranges from changes to a font type or color to the placement of text within margins.

Word has several built-in formatting rules to help automate the creation of documents. For example, when you type text that resembles a hyperlink, Word automatically formats it and creates a link in the document. If you do not want that type of formatting, you can turn off the hyperlink feature.

Bulleted and numbered lists enable you to display a list of information. One way that you can customize the look of lists is by changing the spacing between list items. You can also control the numbering used by a numbered list by indicating what number the list should start with. If you want numbering to occur within a paragraph of text, you cannot use the Numbering option; instead, you can use the ListNum field, which enables you to insert a numbered item at any location in your document.

The document map can help you work through a large document. You can customize the appearance of the document map to make it easier to use. The Outline view also helps you to work with large documents. Using this view, you can quickly change the layout of a document by moving sections.

This chapter looks at some different ways of changing the format of text in your document to achieve the layout that you want.

TOP 100

Place NUMBERED ITEMS within a paragraph

You can create a numbered list of items within a paragraph using the ListNum field. Although Word does provide a numbered list option, this option does not enable you to place the numbered items on the same line.

You can insert the ListNum field code at any location within the special field brackets ({}). Although regular brackets are available on the keyboard, you must insert field brackets by pressing Ctrl+F9, or Word will not recognize them as field characters. The ListNum field uses the following syntax:

{LISTNUM "Name" [Switches]}

Use the Name instruction to link a list of related items. For example, if you have a list of grocery items, you can name the list "Grocery".

There are two switches you can use, /l and /s. Use the /l switch to indicate the level of the list. For example, /l 2 indicates that the list is a second level list. Use /s to specify the start value, if it is something other than 1. The start value should always be a number, even if the list is numbering in Roman numerals or alphabetic characters.

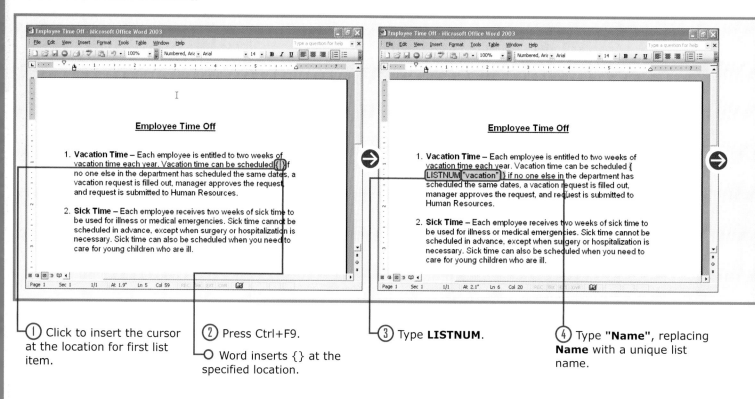

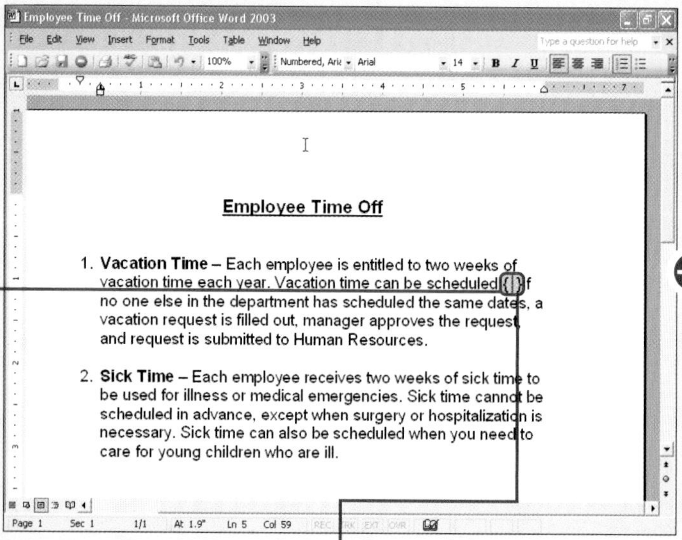

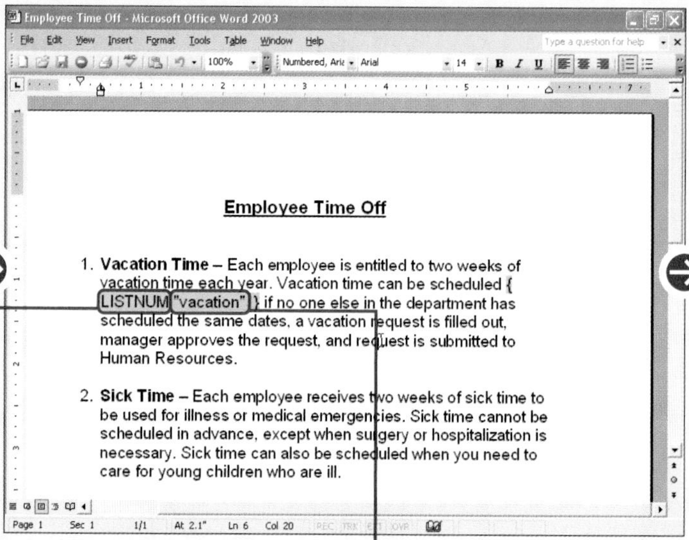

① Click to insert the cursor at the location for first list item.

② Press Ctrl+F9.

○ Word inserts {} at the specified location.

③ Type **LISTNUM**.

④ Type **"Name"**, replacing **Name** with a unique list name.

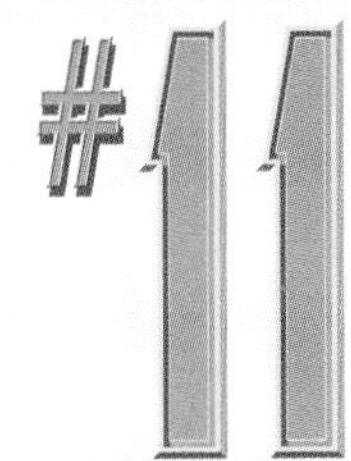

Did You Know?

You can change the level of a numbered list by pressing Ctrl and clicking the Increase Indent button to increase the level or pressing Ctrl and clicking the Decrease Indent button to demote the list.

Did You Know?

You can use the Name instruction to create specifically formatted lists. Word has three built-in formats for creating numbered lists; to use one of these formats, you type the corresponding name for the Name instruction.

Name	Description
NumberDefault	Inserts numbers followed by a close parenthesis, such as 1).
OutlineDefault	Inserts numbers using the outline style, such as II.
LegalDefault	Inserts numbers using the legal format typically used to number legal or technical publications, such as 1.2.

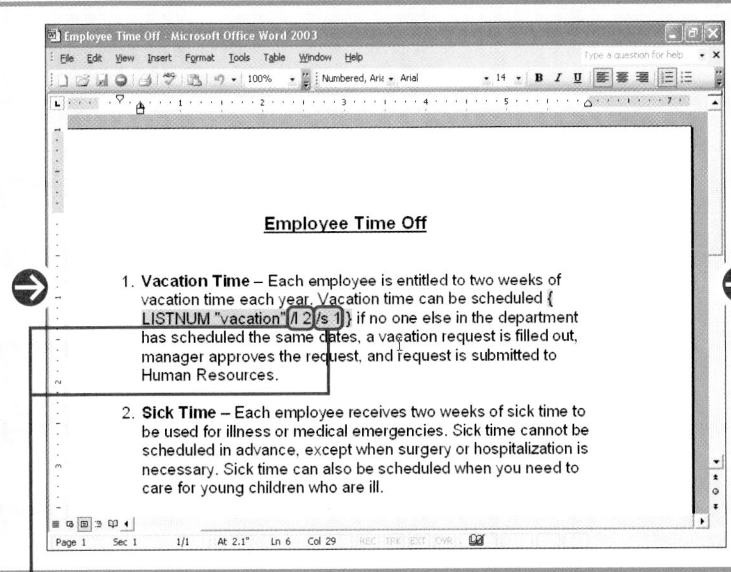

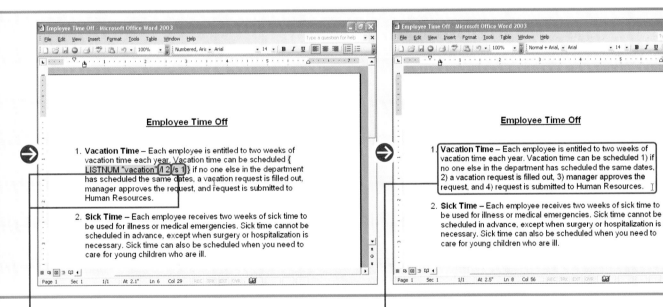

⑤ Type **/l 2**, replacing 2 with the level for the list.

○ You can also type **/s 1**, replacing 1 with the start value for the list.

⑥ Repeat steps **1** to **5** for each item in the list.

⑦ Press Shift+F9.

○ Word hides the field codes and displays the list numbers.

Add LINE NUMBERS to margins

You can have Word automatically add line numbers to the left margin. Line numbers are commonly used in legal documents to make it easier to refer to sections of the document.

Word automatically determines a position for the numbers. You can customize the location of the page number within the margin by specifying the distance of the page number from the text on the page. Make sure that you know what the size is for the left margin. If you specify a distance that is greater than the margin size, the line numbers will not be visible.

You can specify the first line number and the number to count by. For example, if you want to display only every other line number, you can specify to count by the value of 2. Keep in mind that Word coordinates the Start At and Count By values. If you specify a Count By value of 2 and a Start At value of 1, Word places even numbers in the document starting with 2 on the second line of text.

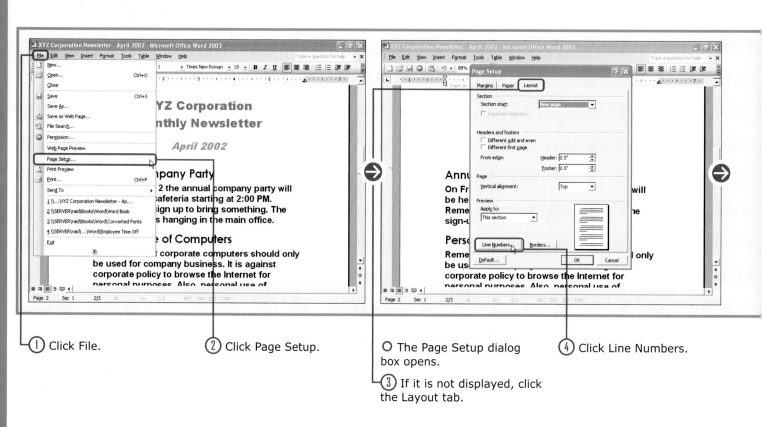

1. Click File.
2. Click Page Setup.

- The Page Setup dialog box opens.

3. If it is not displayed, click the Layout tab.
4. Click Line Numbers.

DIFFICULTY LEVEL

Did You Know?

You can have line numbers continue numerically throughout the entire document by clicking Continuous in the Line Numbers dialog box (○ changes to ◉). If you want the line numbers to restart for each section of the document, click Restart Each Section (○ changes to ◉).

Customize It!

You can have Word number only a section of text within the document. To do so, highlight the section of text that you want to number and then perform the steps to specify line numbers. When Word inserts the lines numbers, a page break will occur in your document before and after the text with line numbers.

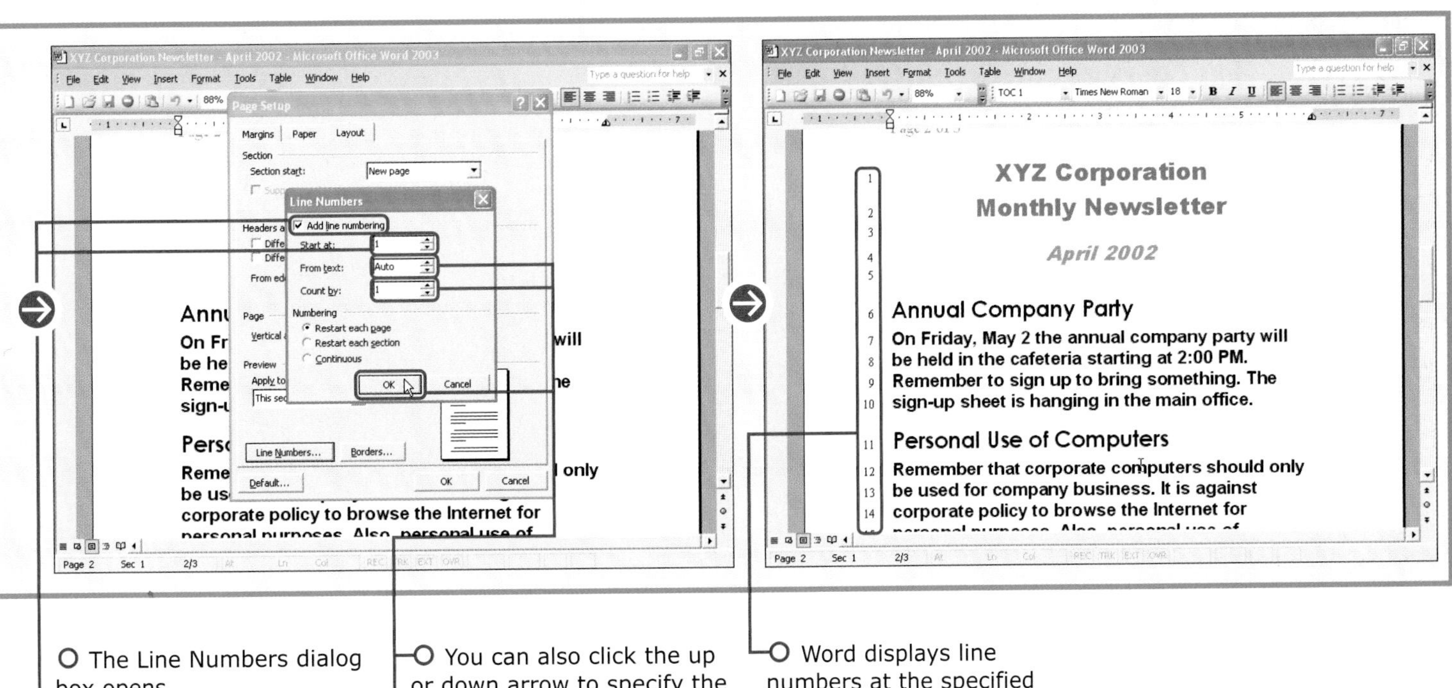

- The Line Numbers dialog box opens.

5. Click Add line numbering (☐ changes to ☑).

- You can also type a beginning line number.

- You can also click the up or down arrow to specify the distance for the numbers from the text.

- You can also type a number to indicate the frequency of line numbers.

6. Click OK.

- Word displays line numbers at the specified location in the left margin.

RESUME NUMBERING within the document

When you insert a new numbered list, you can have the numbering resume where the previous list left off. This is necessary when you have a numbered list that is separated by non-numbered text, such as a bulleted list.

Whenever you create a numbered list, Word automatically checks to see if a numbered list precedes it. If there is a numbered list directly above it, Word automatically continues numbering at that point. If the lists are separated by other word elements, such as plain text or a bulleted list, Word starts the numbering at 1 when you click the Numbering button.

In the Bullets and Numbering dialog box, you have the option of selecting not only which style of numbering you use but also whether the numbering restarts or continues from the previous list. Whichever option you select, the numbering option in the Bullets and Numbering dialog box changes to reflect the numbering that will be applied. For example, if the next number in the list is 6, Word shows the numbering starting at 6.

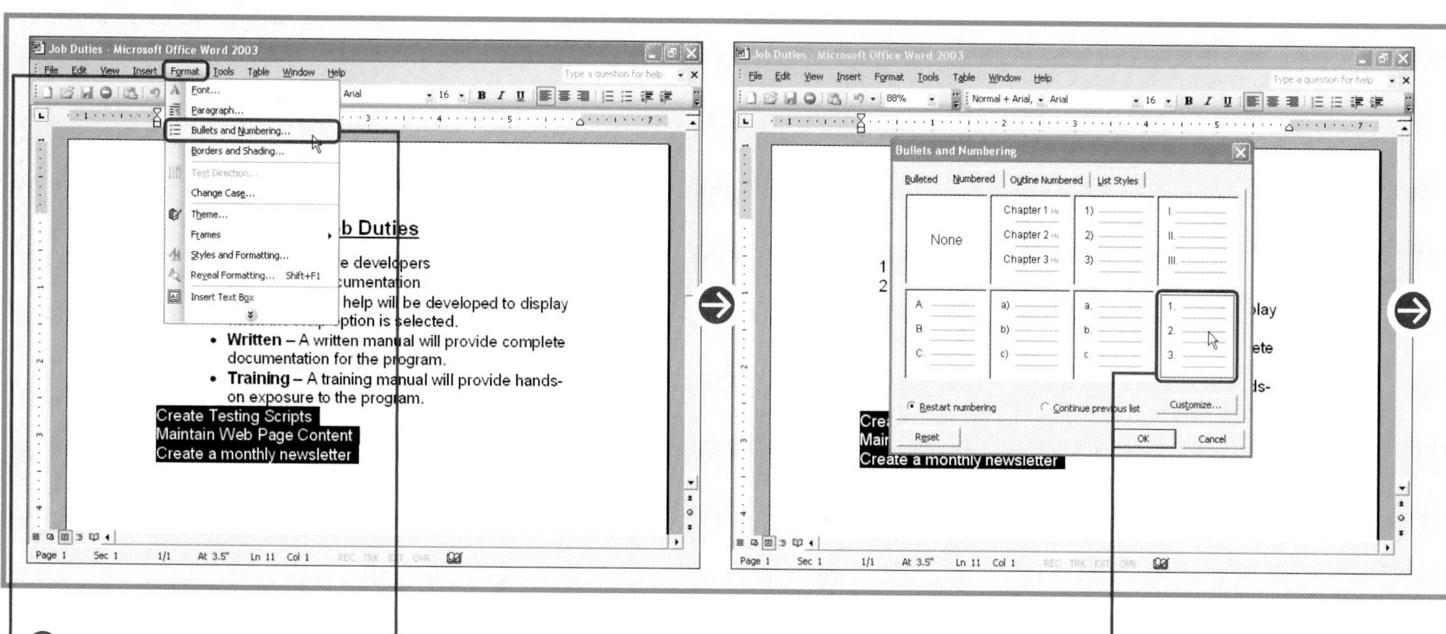

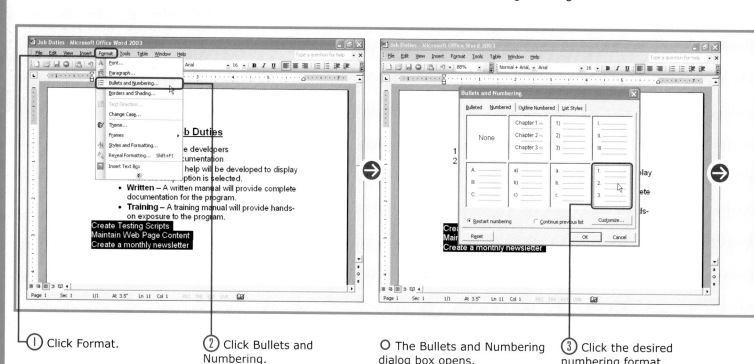

① Click Format.

② Click Bullets and Numbering.

○ The Bullets and Numbering dialog box opens.

③ Click the desired numbering format.

Did You Know?

You can use automatic numbering for table cells. To number table cells, first select the cells that you want to number and then select the Numbering button. If you move a numbered cell, Word renumbers the cells based on their locations. For example, if you move the cells in the third row to the beginning of the table, those cells become the first numbered cells, and all cells that remain are renumbered.

Did You Know?

You can make the formatting of the numbers different than the formatting of the text in the list. To do so, click a number and then select the formatting options that you want to apply. Any formatting that you select will apply to all numbers in the same numbered list.

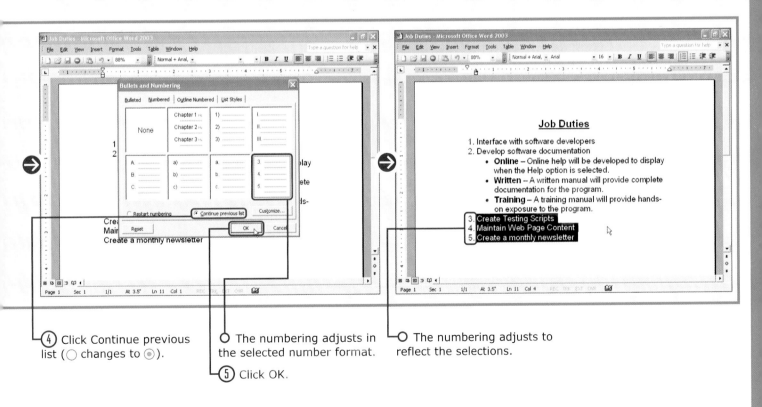

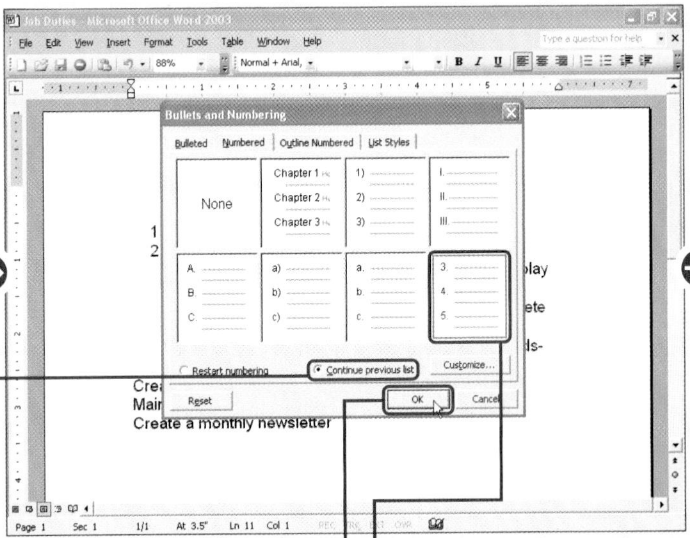

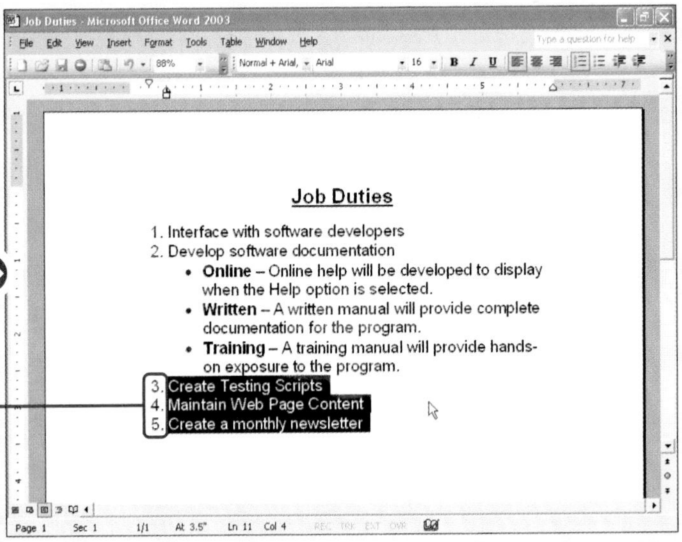

(4) Click Continue previous list (○ changes to ◉).

○ The numbering adjusts in the selected number format.

(5) Click OK.

○ The numbering adjusts to reflect the selections.

Eliminate automatic HYPERLINK FORMATTING

You can eliminate the automatic hyperlink formatting that Word applies to your documents. When you do so, all hyperlinks that you type are displayed using the same formatting as the surrounding text.

By default, when you type a hyperlink in a document, Word automatically formats the hyperlink so that if it is clicked, the corresponding Web address is displayed in a Web browser. Word also changes the formatting of the text for the hyperlink so that when the document is viewed, the hyperlink is obvious: Typically, the hyperlink appears in a bold blue font and is underlined, but you can also customize that formatting.

If you plan on printing your document, you probably do not want the hyperlinks to be formatted. When you turn off the automatic formatting, Word ignores all hyperlinks that you type. If you want special formatting applied, you can apply it manually. You may want to create a specific style that you can apply to each hyperlink to ensure that they all have the same formatting in your document.

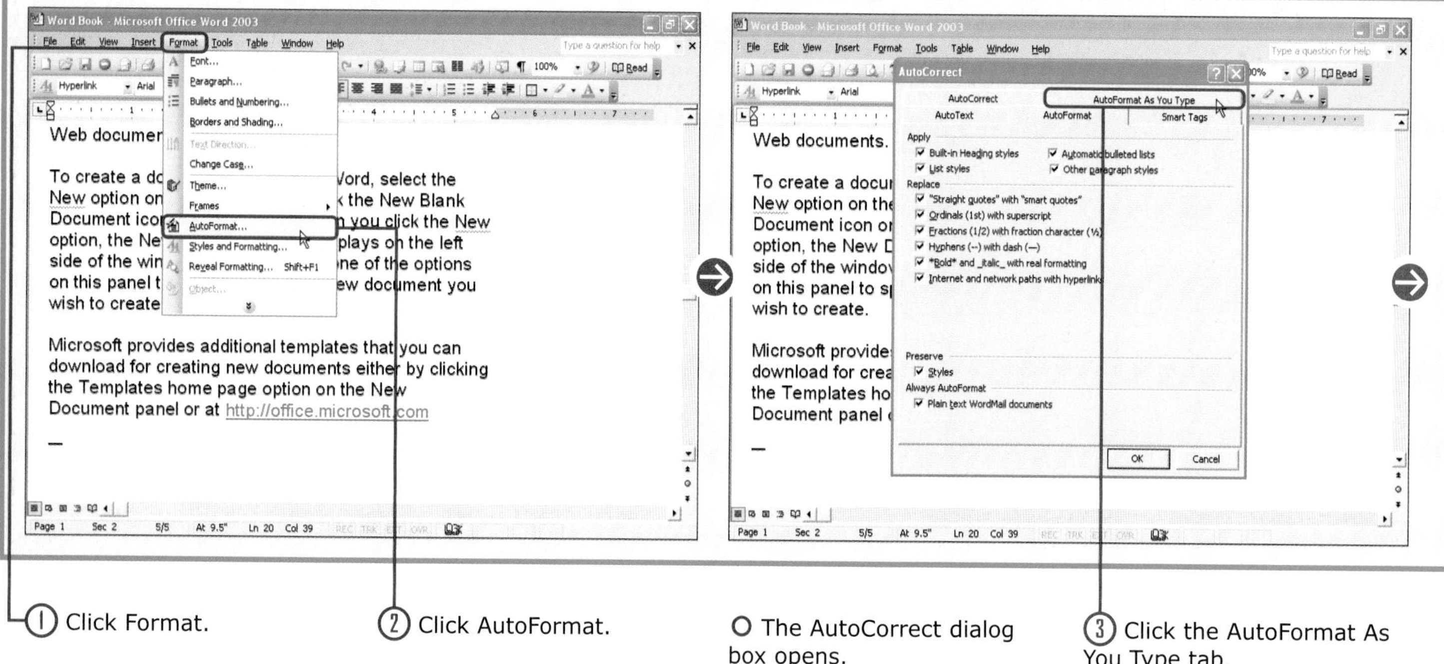

1. Click Format.
2. Click AutoFormat.

- The AutoCorrect dialog box opens.

3. Click the AutoFormat As You Type tab.

DIFFICULTY LEVEL

Did You Know?

If you do not want to turn off the formatting of all hyperlinks, you can also manually stop hyperlink formatting. To do so, right-click on a formatted hyperlink and click Remove Hyperlink. Word removes the hyperlink formatting, but the text remains.

Did You Know?

When you turn off the automatic formatting of hyperlinks, Word does not alter any hyperlinks that already exist in the document. If you want to eliminate the hyperlink formatting for existing hyperlinks, you need to do so manually by using the Remove Hyperlink option.

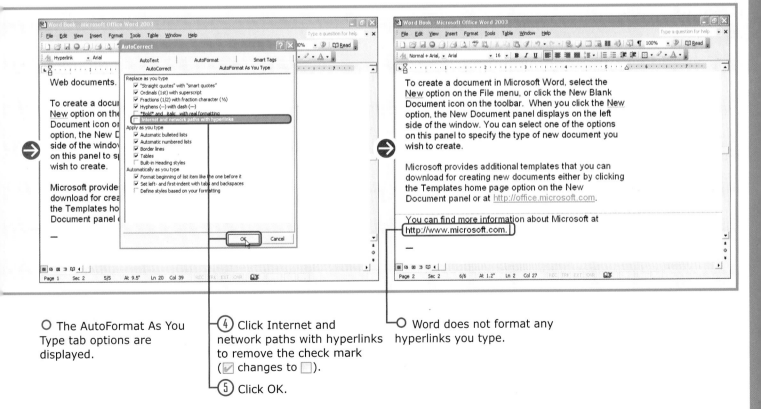

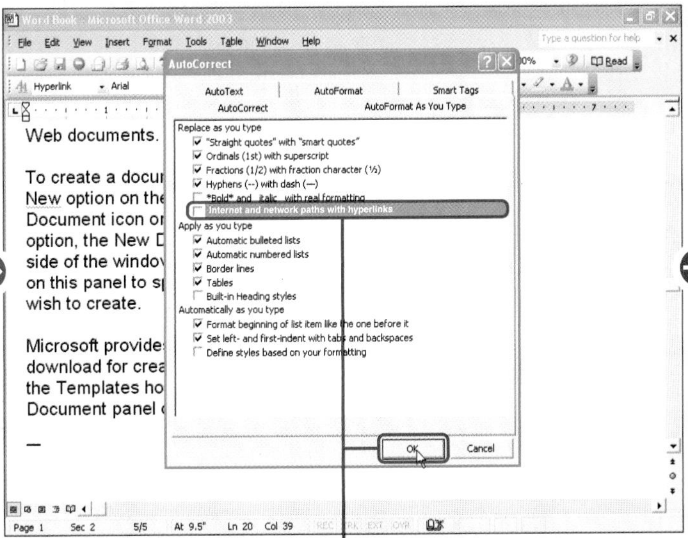

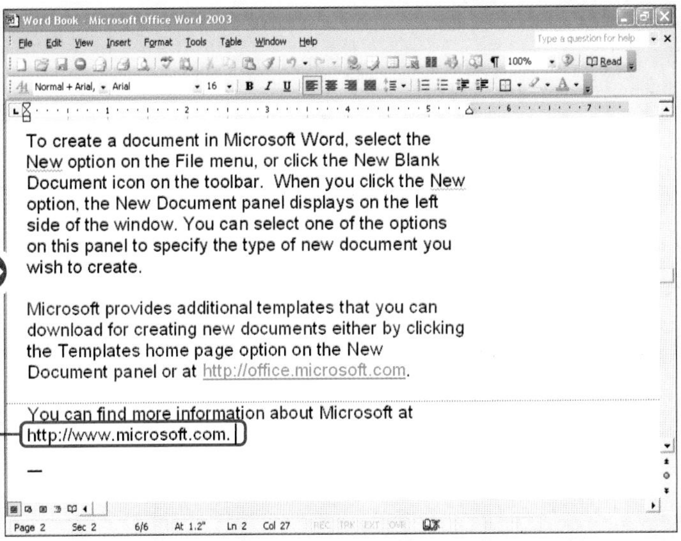

- The AutoFormat As You Type tab options are displayed.

4. Click Internet and network paths with hyperlinks to remove the check mark (☑ changes to ☐).
5. Click OK.

- Word does not format any hyperlinks you type.

DOUBLE-SPACE
bulleted and numbered lists

You can change the spacing between lines for both numbered and bulleted lists. By default, Word single-spaces between items in lists.

To change the spacing for a list, you have to use the paragraph formatting options in the Paragraph dialog box because Word sees each item in a list as a separate paragraph.

You need to specify the amount of spacing to insert before each item in the list. You specify the value in the Before field. To make the list double-spaced, you need to insert a value equal to the font size. For example, if you are using a 12-point font, you type 12 in the Before field. If you prefer, you can use the After field and insert the spacing after a list item.

If you want the same spacing to appear after the list, you need to repeat the process of changing the spacing by either selecting the last item in the list and setting the After field or setting the spacing before the first paragraph that follows the list.

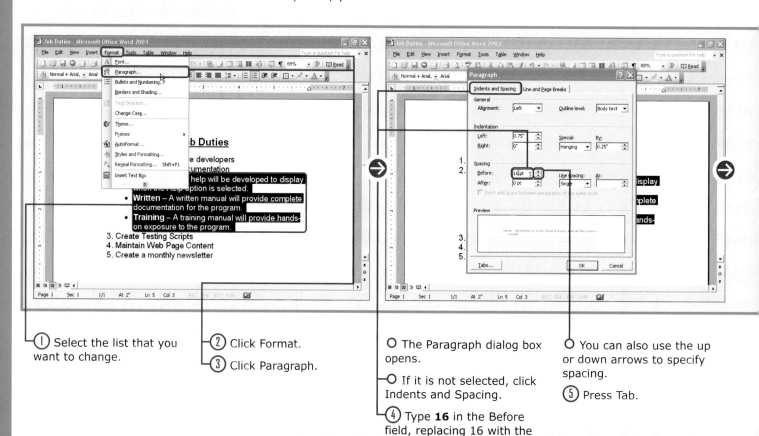

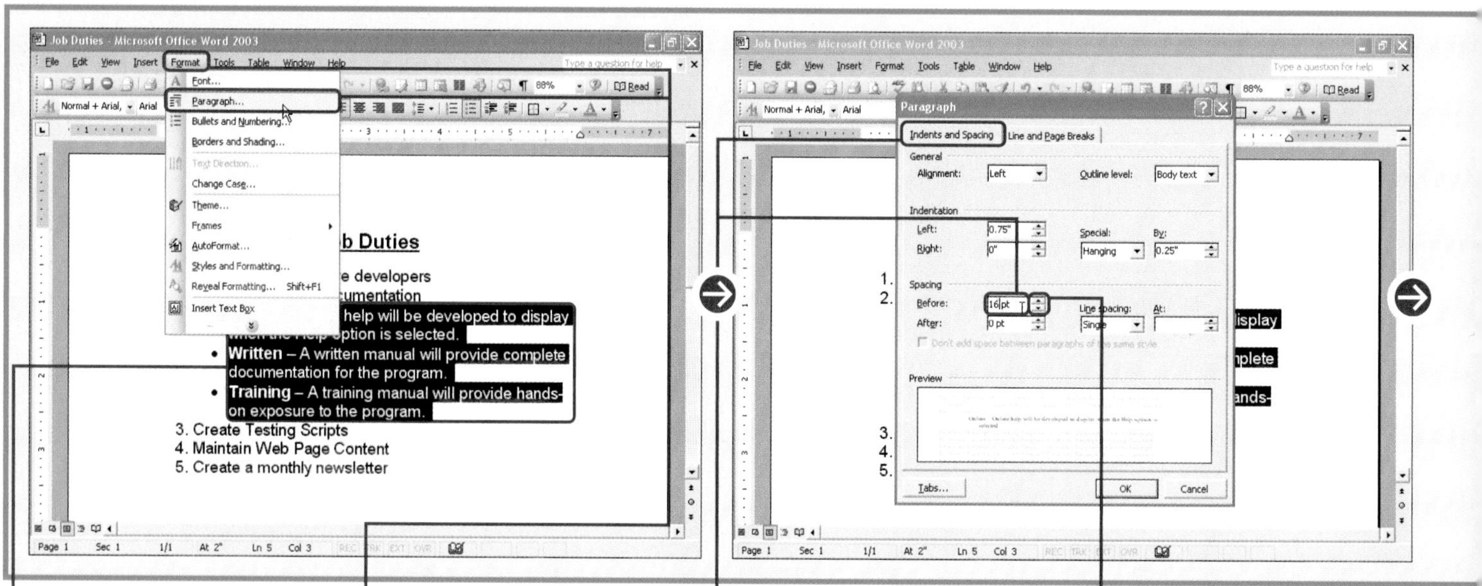

① Select the list that you want to change.

② Click Format.

③ Click Paragraph.

- The Paragraph dialog box opens.
- If it is not selected, click Indents and Spacing.

④ Type **16** in the Before field, replacing 16 with the current font size.

- You can also use the up or down arrows to specify spacing.

⑤ Press Tab.

DIFFICULTY LEVEL

Did You Know?

You can also change the spacing between the text and the bullet or number by selecting the list and clicking Format ➪ Bullets and Numbering. In the Bullets and Numbering dialog box, click Customize. In the Customize dialog box, type the amount of space you want between the text and bullet or number in the Tab Space After field. You should also change the Indent At field to the same value so that the lines under the bullet will be in line with the first line.

Did You Know?

If you want to double-space between every line within the selection, you can use the Line Spacing option in the Paragraph dialog box, or you can select the Line Spacing button.

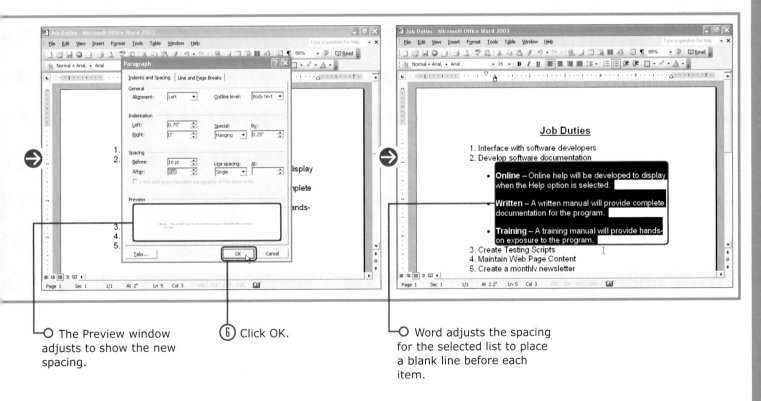

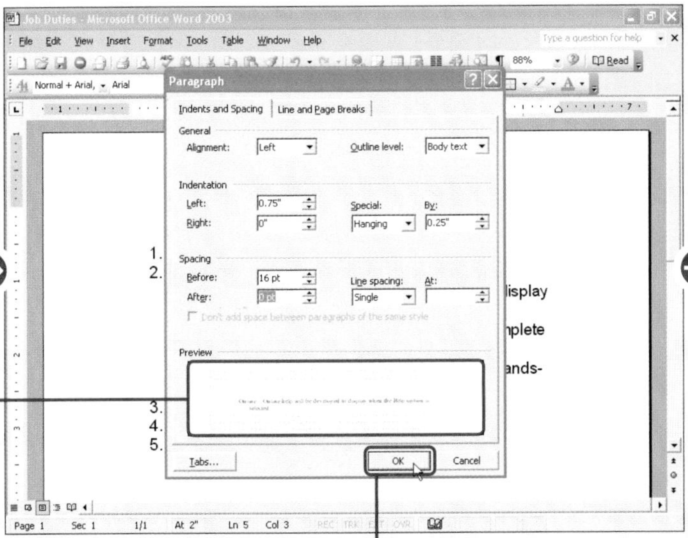

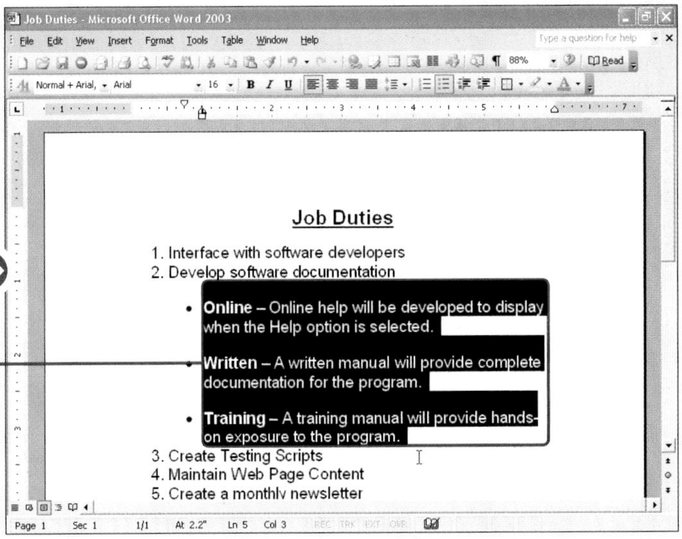

- The Preview window adjusts to show the new spacing.

6. Click OK.

- Word adjusts the spacing for the selected list to place a blank line before each item.

Change the formatting of the DOCUMENT MAP

You can change the formatting that Word uses to display the document map. A *document map* is a layout of the entire document that enables you to view different parts of the document by clicking on their corresponding links. The document map shows only the styles with a corresponding outline level. See Chapter 1 for information on creating custom headings.

If you do not like the appearance of the document map, you can change the style used to display the map text. Any formatting changes made to the document map do not affect the formatting of your document.

To change the formatting of the document map, select the Document Map style in the Styles and Formatting task pane. Because this style is not typically displayed, you need to use the Format Settings dialog box to make the Document Map style visible. After the style is visible in the Styles and Formatting task pane, you can change the font settings for all text that is displayed in the document map. The changes that you make to the style will be applied to the entire document map.

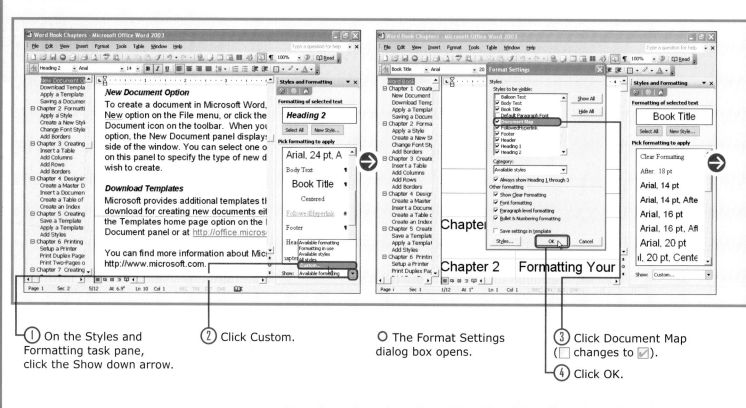

1. On the Styles and Formatting task pane, click the Show down arrow.
2. Click Custom.

- The Format Settings dialog box opens.

3. Click Document Map (☐ changes to ☑).
4. Click OK.

DIFFICULTY LEVEL

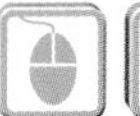

Did You Know?

To use the document map feature, you must have styles applied to your document that use the outline levels. The Heading styles automatically use outline levels. See Chapter 1 for information on setting levels for custom styles.

After you specify the desired formatting for the document map, you can remove it from the Styles and Formatting task pane by removing the check mark from the Document Map option in the Format Settings dialog box.

Customize It!

You can use the Format Settings dialog box to customize the list of styles that are listed in the Styles and Formatting task pane by setting a list of styles for each category. To do so, select the desired category in the Category field and then select the desired styles.

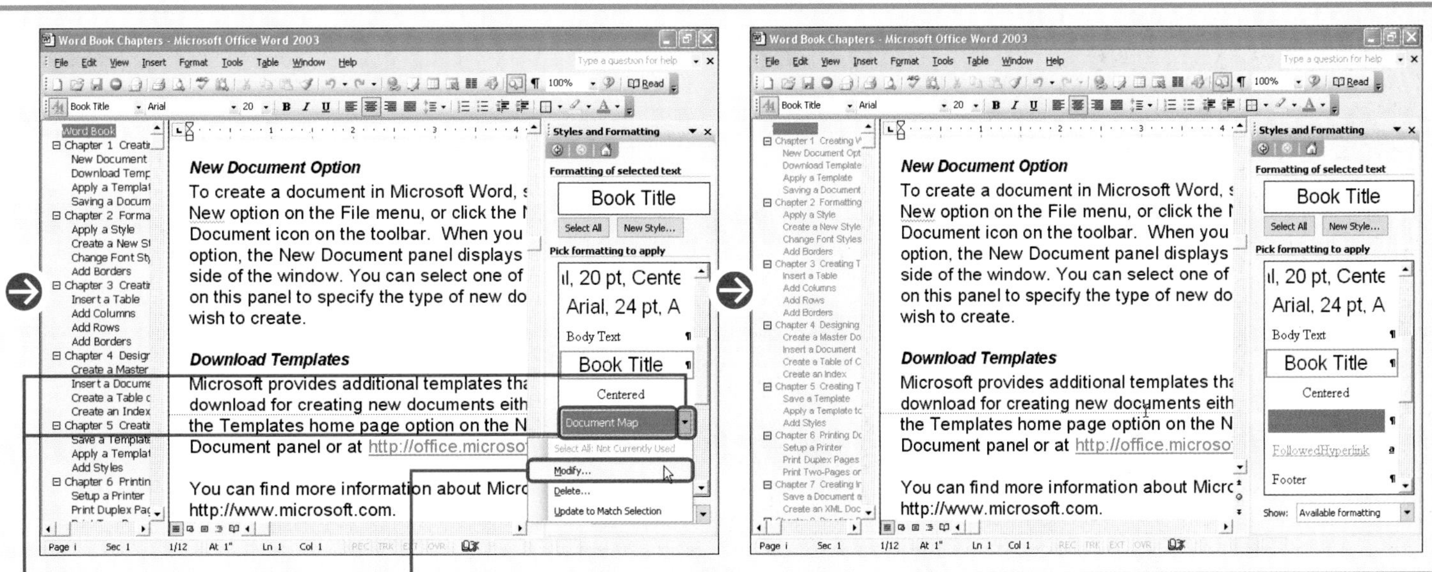

- The Document Map style is displayed in the Styles and Formatting task pane.

5. Click the down arrow to display a menu.

6. Click Modify.

- Make the formatting changes in the Modify Style dialog box.

Note: See Chapter 1 for more information on editing styles.

- The document map changes to reflect the formatting changes.

Edit a DOCUMENT OUTLINE

You can make modifications to the layout of a document using the Outline view. When you view a document outline, you can look at the layout of the document.

To use the Outline view, you need to set up your original document to use styles with assigned outline levels. If you use the built-in heading levels, they already have assigned outline levels. Typically, you use Heading 1 for the chapter title, Heading 2 for the next level, and so on. Based on the assigned heading levels, Word lays out your document by indenting each level. An icon resembling a plus sign appears next to each heading. You can click this icon to expand and collapse the document.

In Outline view, you can rearrange your document by moving the headings associated with sections. If you move a section heading, all text and subheadings within that section move. Make sure that the section is collapsed under the heading.

You can also change the heading level by using the Promote and Demote buttons. If you change a Heading 3 to a Heading 2, all subheadings within that section are promoted.

MOVE A SECTION

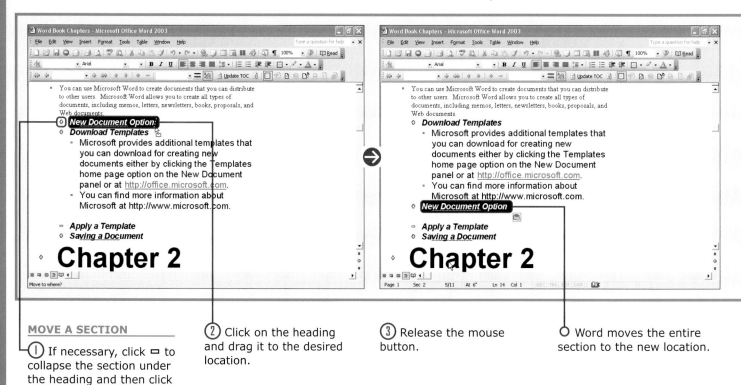

① If necessary, click ▭ to collapse the section under the heading and then click ✥ to select the heading.

② Click on the heading and drag it to the desired location.

③ Release the mouse button.

○ Word moves the entire section to the new location.

  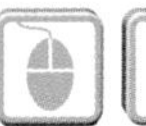 

Did You Know?

You can also use the keyboard to change the level of a heading in any view. Press Alt+Shift+left arrow to promote a heading or Alt+Shift+right arrow to demote a heading.

Apply It!

You can use the Outline view to quickly lay out the document headings before adding the body text in Normal view.

Did You Know?

When you view the document outline, Word automatically expands the document to show all levels. If you want to see only level 2 and level 1 headings, you can select the option Show Level 2 in the Show Level field on the Outline toolbar. This works well when you want to change the layout of the document.

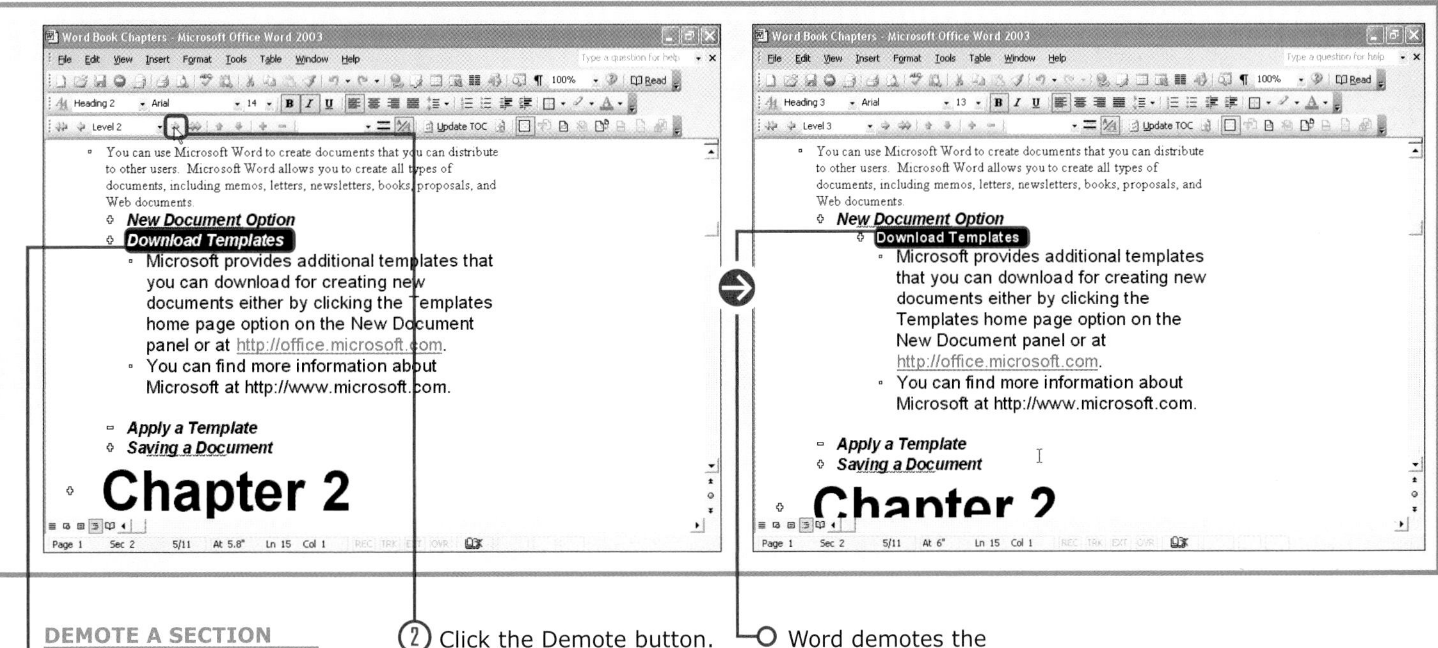

DEMOTE A SECTION

1. Click the heading you want to change.
2. Click the Demote button.

- Word demotes the heading by changing it to the next lower level.

COMPARE FORMATTING

of two sections of text

You can compare two sections of text within the same document to determine if there are any formatting differences. This enables you to verify that the formatting throughout your document is consistent.

To accomplish this, you use the Reveal Formatting pane. The Reveal Formatting pane summarizes all the formatting settings applied to the currently selected text. The Reveal Formatting pane provides links to each of the dialog boxes for changing the formatting of the text selection. For example, if you click Font, the Font dialog box opens.

When you compare two sections of text, Word specifies the differences between the formatting of the two sections. The format setting of the first section is displayed first, followed by the setting for the second section. For example, if the font of the first section is Arial and the second is Times New Roman, Word displays the font settings as Arial ➪ Times New Roman.

If the formatting for the two selected sections is the same, Word displays the text No formatting differences in the Formatting Differences window.

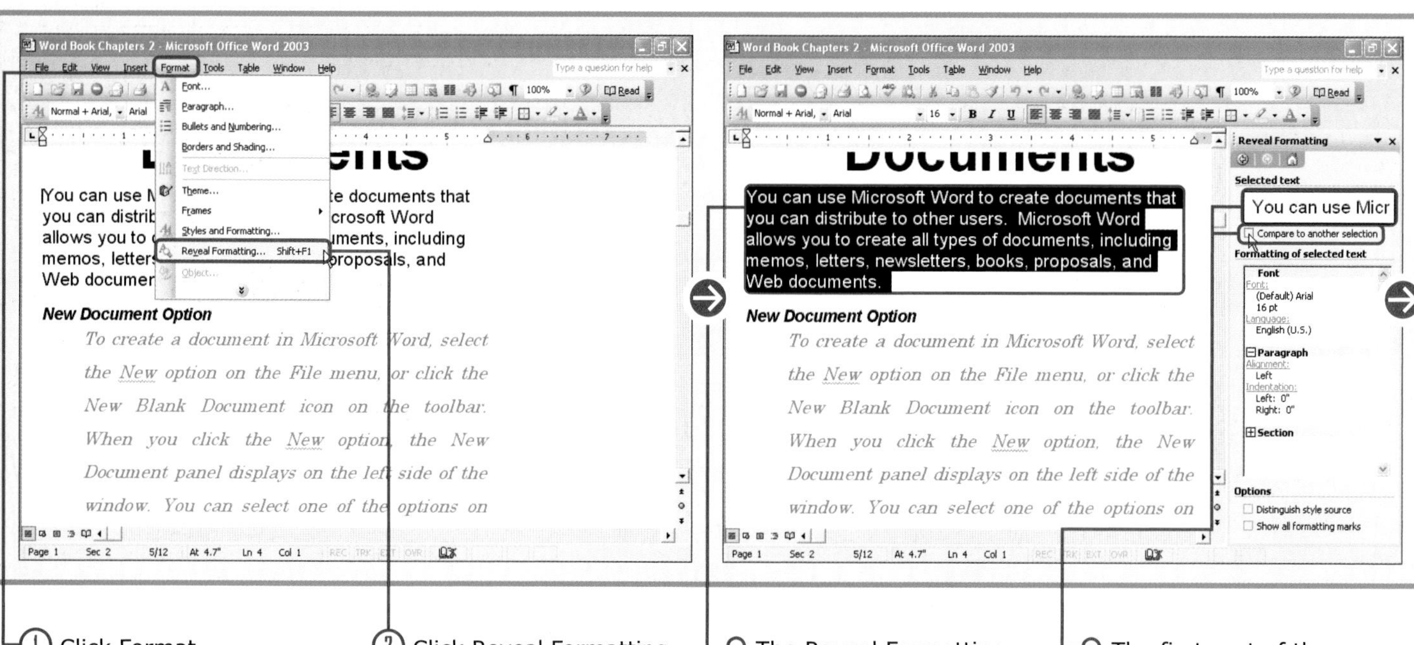

1. Click Format.
2. Click Reveal Formatting.

- The Reveal Formatting pane appears.

3. Select the first text section.

- The first part of the selected text is displayed in the Preview window.

4. Click Compare to another selection (☐ changes to ☑).

DIFFICULTY LEVEL

Did You Know?

You can apply the formatting from the first section to the second section. To do so, click the second Preview window. Click the down arrow next to that window to display a menu. Click Apply Formatting of Original Selection. When you select the option, all the formatting from the section is applied to the second section.

Did You Know?

You can have Word determine if all the text in the document is formatted the same as the selection by having it select the text with the same formatting. To do so, click the down arrow next to the second Preview window and then click Select All Text with Similar Formatting. Word will examine the entire document and highlight all text that matches the formatting of the selected text.

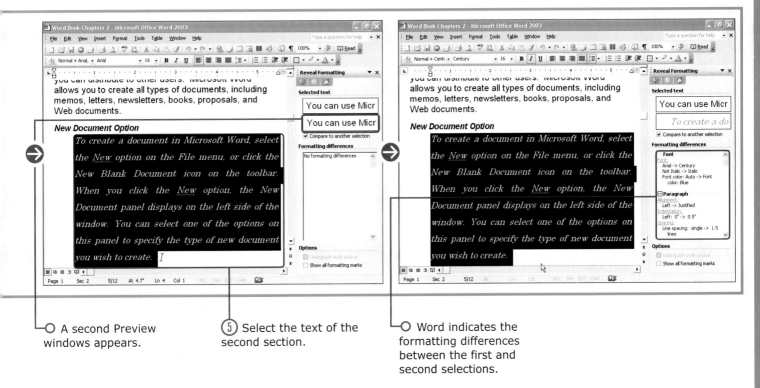

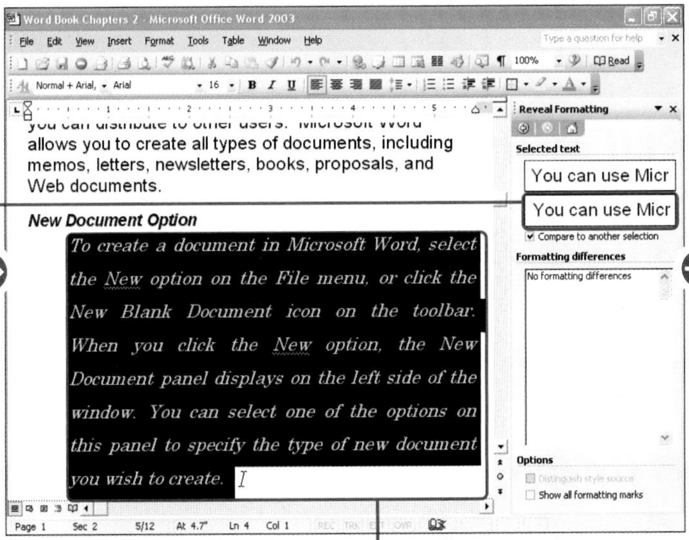

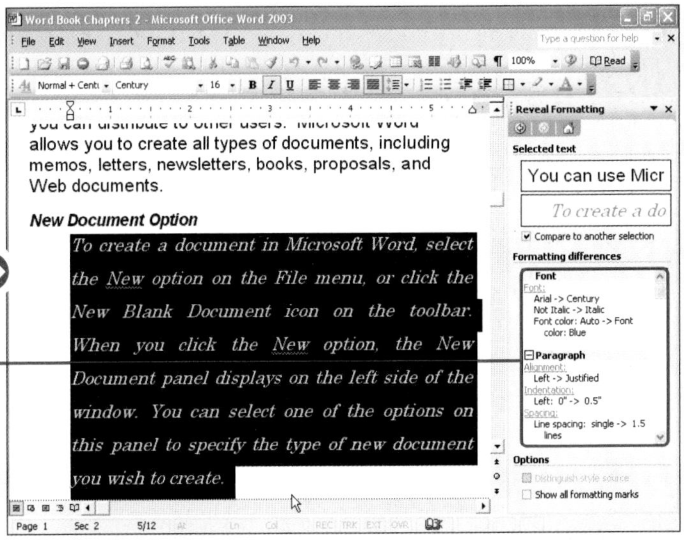

- A second Preview windows appears.

5. Select the text of the second section.

- Word indicates the formatting differences between the first and second selections.

Insert a DROP CAP

You can create a drop cap effect for a paragraph in your document. By using a drop cap effect, you can emphasize the start of a particular paragraph.

There are actually two types of drop cap formatting that you can apply. The Dropped format inserts the drop cap letter directly into the paragraph. The text in the paragraph is repositioned to make room for the drop cap. The In Margin format inserts the drop cap letter in the left margin. With the In Margin format, no changes are made to the flow of the paragraph.

You do not have to use the same font as the surrounding text for the drop cap. If you want to use a different font, you can select it from the Font field.

With a drop cap, you do not specify a font size. Instead, the size of the drop cap letter is based on the number of lines of text it covers. If you specify three lines, the drop cap will be as large as three lines of text.

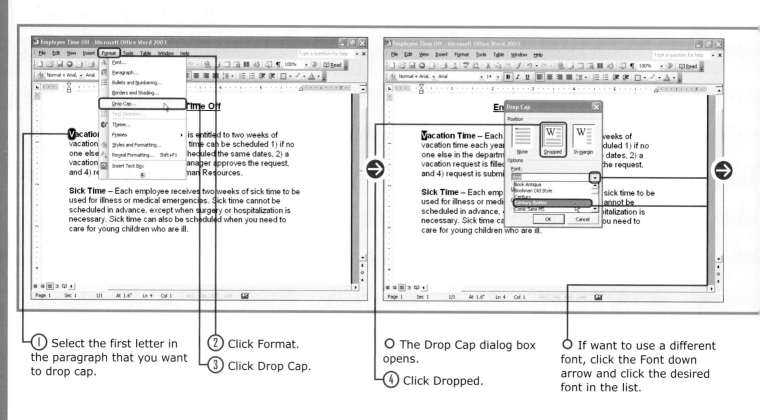

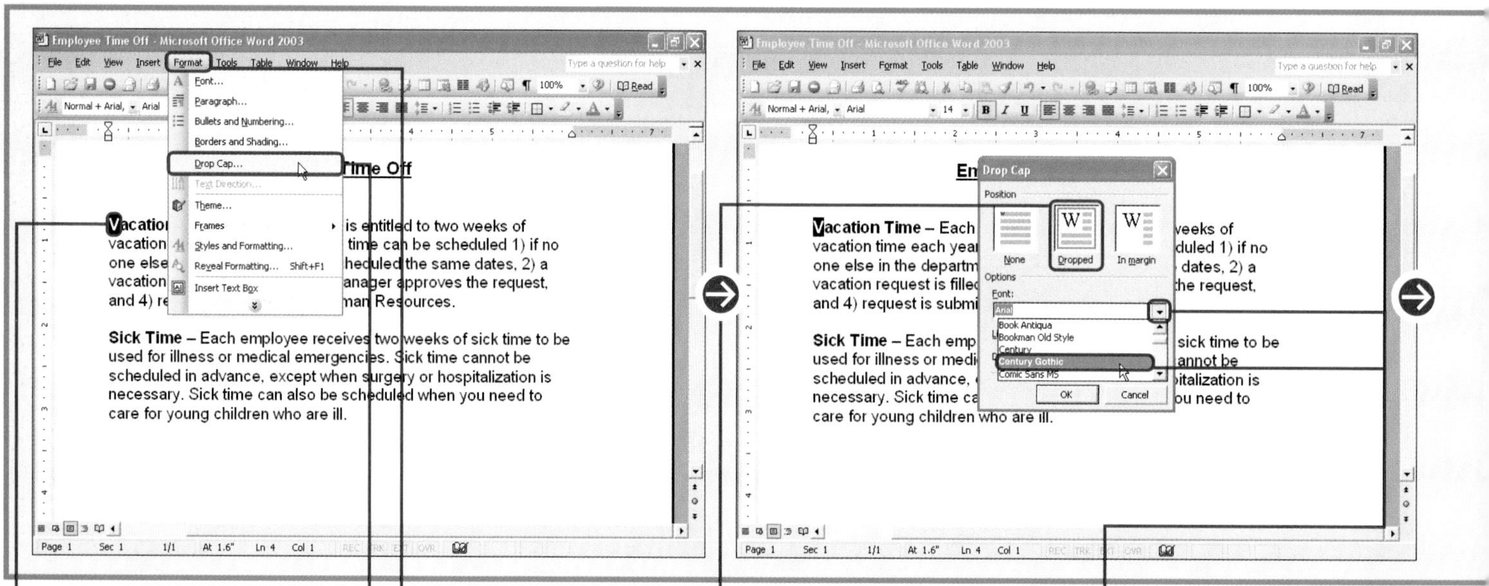

① Select the first letter in the paragraph that you want to drop cap.

② Click Format.

③ Click Drop Cap.

○ The Drop Cap dialog box opens.

④ Click Dropped.

○ If want to use a different font, click the Font down arrow and click the desired font in the list.

DIFFICULTY LEVEL

Did You Know?

You can have more than one letter drop capped for your paragraph, as long as the letters are all part of the first word in the paragraph. To drop cap more than the first letter, select the letters you want to emphasize before performing the steps to create a drop cap.

Did You Know?

If you select the In Margin option, depending on the size of the drop cap, Word may not be able to fit it all in the margin. If not, Word will move the text of the paragraph to accommodate the drop cap letter.

Did You Know?

After creating the drop cap letter, you can apply other text effects to it, such as changing the font color.

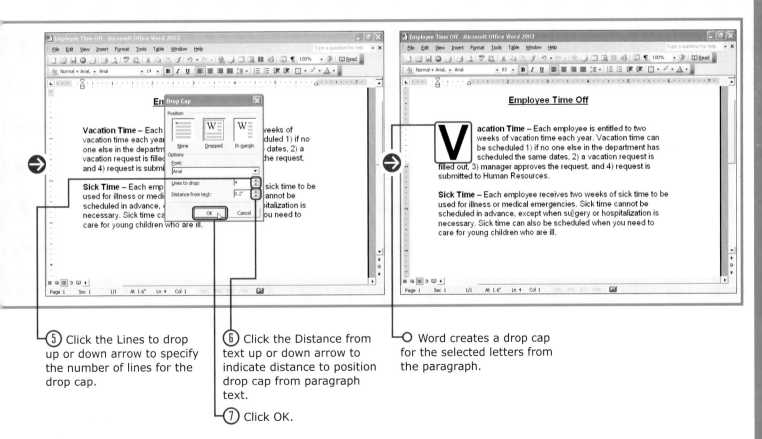

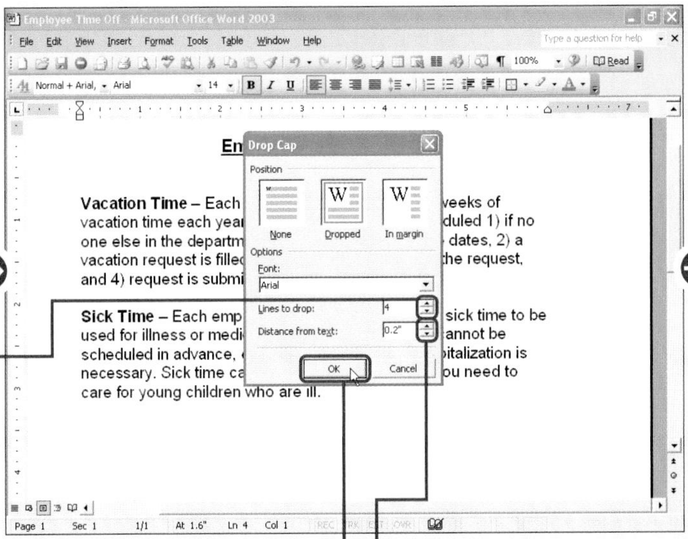

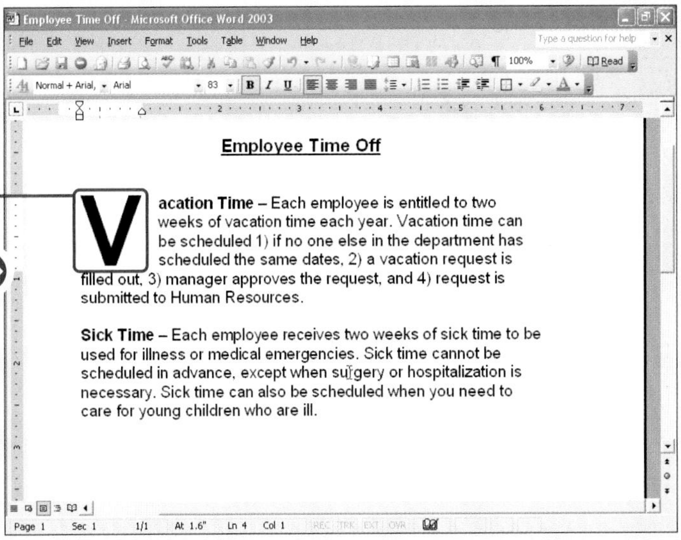

5. Click the Lines to drop up or down arrow to specify the number of lines for the drop cap.
6. Click the Distance from text up or down arrow to indicate distance to position drop cap from paragraph text.
7. Click OK.

- Word creates a drop cap for the selected letters from the paragraph.

Sort text based on a DIFFERENT LANGUAGE

You can sort a list of words using the rules associated with a different language than the default system language. For example, although your default language is English, you may want to add a list of Spanish words. Because Spanish has different rules for sorting, you would use those rules to sort a list instead of English rules.

When you sort a list of items, you use the Sort option available on the Table menu. Word automatically determines that the selection is a list instead of a table, and the dialog box that opens is for sorting text.

In the Sort Options dialog box, you specify the language you want to use to sort the list. Although Word lists several different language options, you must set up the specific language to be supported by Microsoft Office in order for the sort to work properly.

Word automatically changes the language of each word in the list to the selected language. Therefore, if you look up a list word in the dictionary, Word uses the corresponding dictionary from that language.

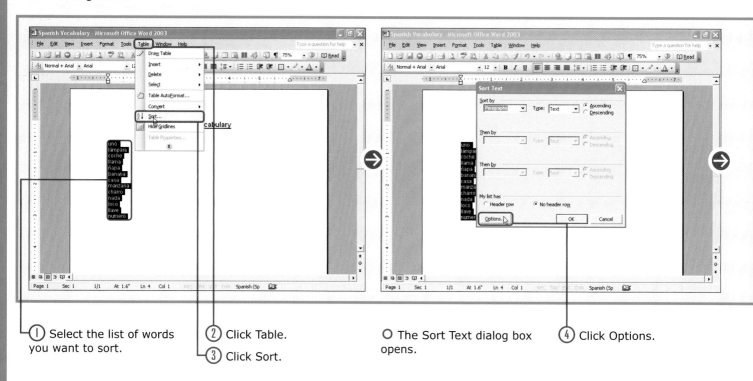

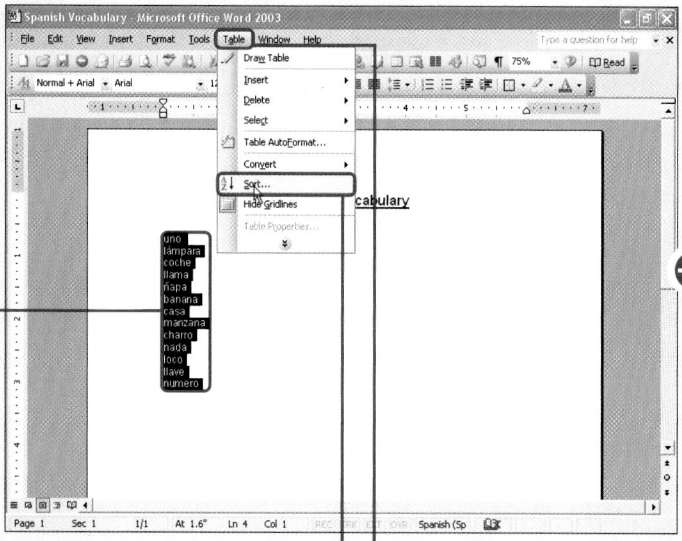

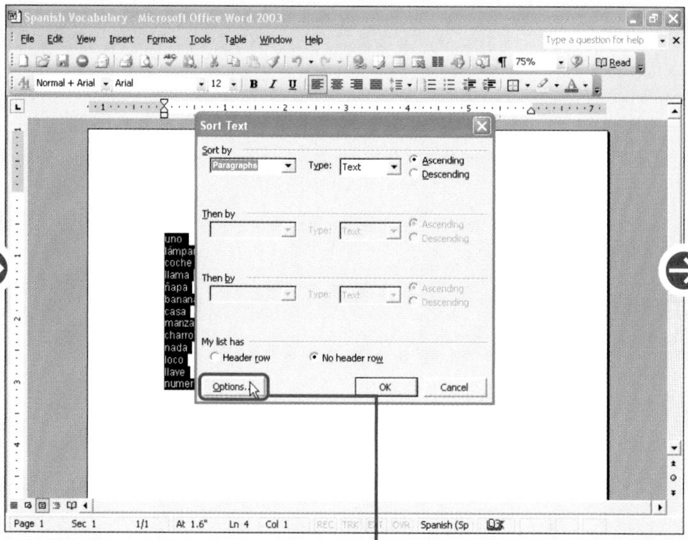

1. Select the list of words you want to sort.
2. Click Table.
3. Click Sort.

- The Sort Text dialog box opens.

4. Click Options.

DIFFICULTY LEVEL

Put It Together!

If you want to use multiple languages in Word, you need to enable those languages in Microsoft Office. To do so, click the Start Menu button and then click All Programs ➪ Microsoft Office Tools ➪ Microsoft Office 2003 Language Settings. In the Microsoft Office Language Settings dialog box, click the Enabled Languages tab. Select the desired language and click Add to add them to the Enabled Languages list.

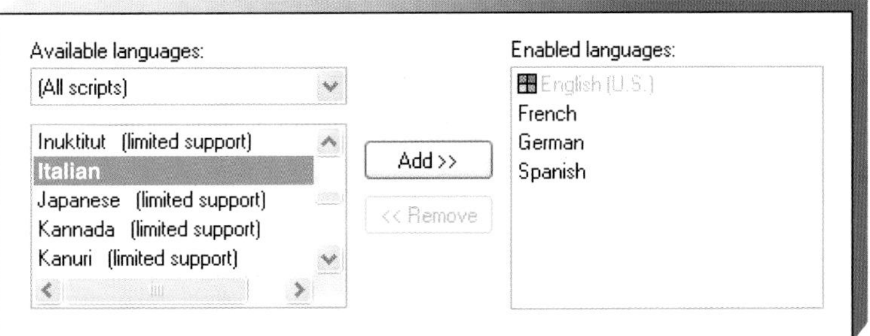

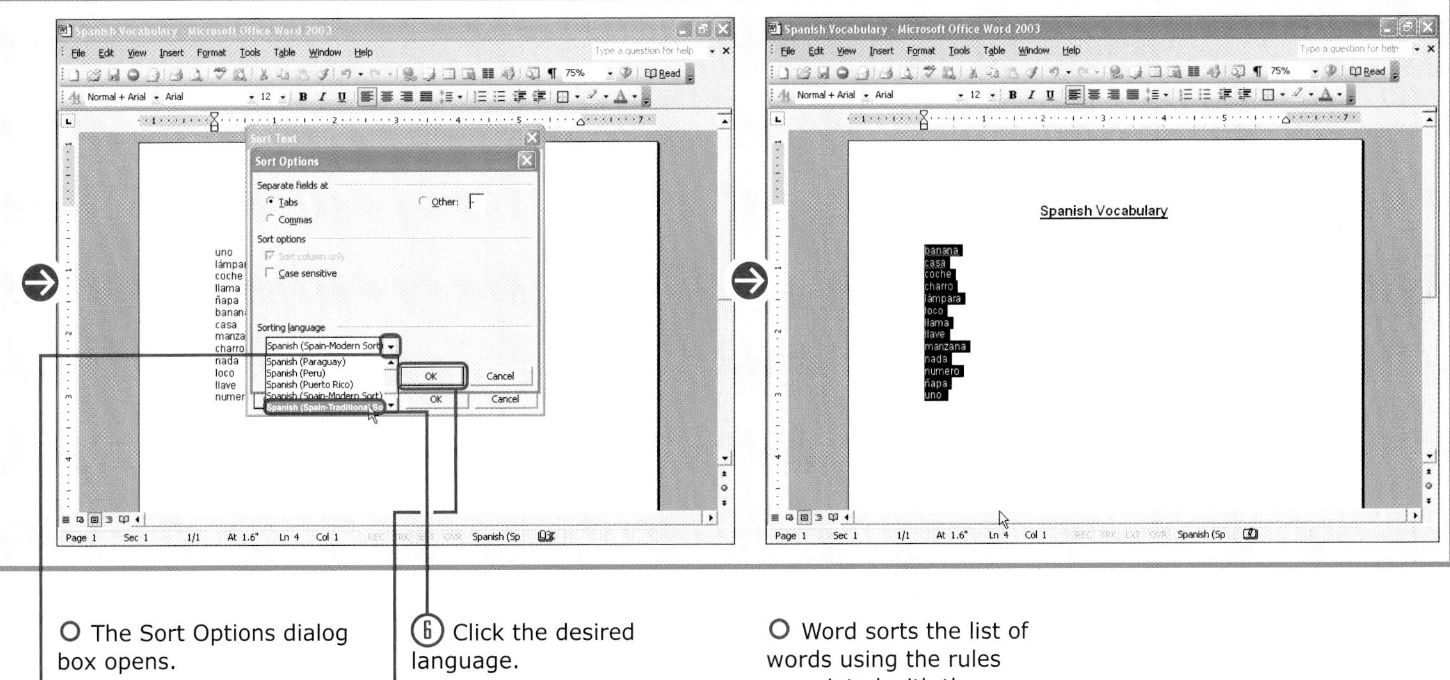

- The Sort Options dialog box opens.

5 Click the Sorting language down arrow to display a list of languages.

6 Click the desired language.

7 Click OK.

- Word sorts the list of words using the rules associated with the selected language.

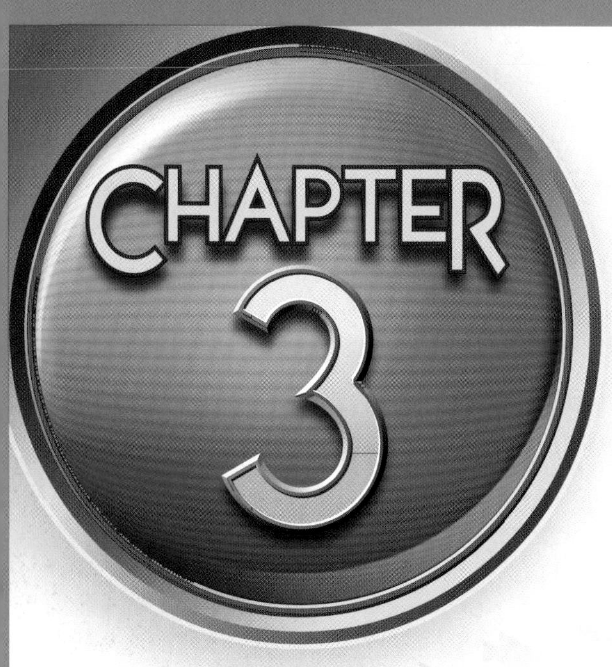

Work with Tables and Columns

Word provides several different options for organizing your information in a document. Two common methods are the use of tables and columns.

Tables consist of a series of rows and columns. You can custom design the layout of your table. Although typically tables have a consistent number of rows and columns, you can create complex tables where the number of rows and columns are not consistent. For example, one row may have four columns while the next only has three columns. You can also nest tables by inserting one table inside of another. Word also allows you to perform calculations using values within a table. The various features available with Word tables make them very similar to the worksheets you can create in Excel.

Columns allow you to lay out your document in a newspaper fashion. Using columns, you can set up the document to have text flow from one column to the next on the page. Typically, Word fills the entire column before moving to the next column, but by inserting continuous breaks you can control the flow.

The tasks presented in this chapter offer tips for working with tables and columns in Word. Using these tasks, you will be able to control the flow of text in both columns and tables, improving the layout of your document in Word.

TOP 100

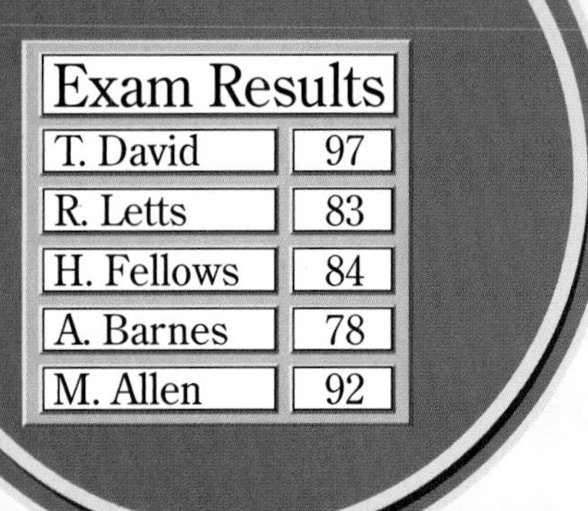

Exam Results	
T. David	97
R. Letts	83
H. Fellows	84
A. Barnes	78
M. Allen	92

Draw a COMPLEX TABLE

You can use the options on the Tables and Borders toolbar to create a complex table in Word. A *complex table* is any table that does not have a consistent number of rows and columns. For example, your table may have 2 columns, but one column may have 3 rows. Because the Insert Table option creates a table with a specific number of rows and columns, to create a complex table, you need to draw it manually.

When you use the Tables and Borders toolbar options, you can totally customize the look of the table. You use the Draw Table button to draw the outside borders of the table. When you click the button, the cursor changes to a pencil. You use the same option to draw lines within the borders to indicate the locations of each of the cells.

After you have created your table, you can add text to the cells by clicking the desired cell and typing text. You can use the Tab key to move between cells within the table.

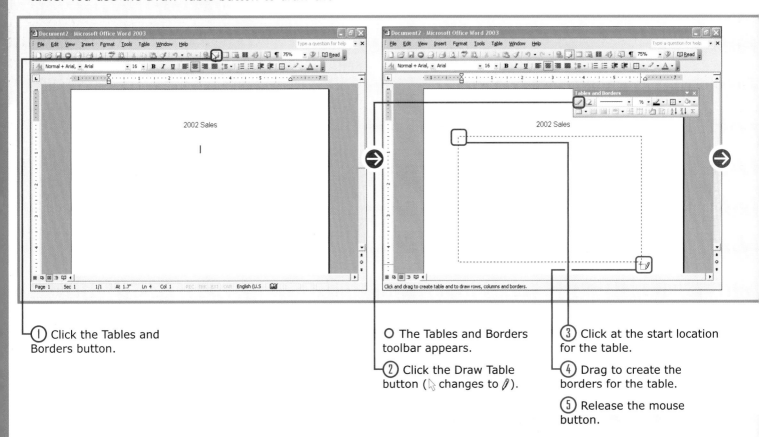

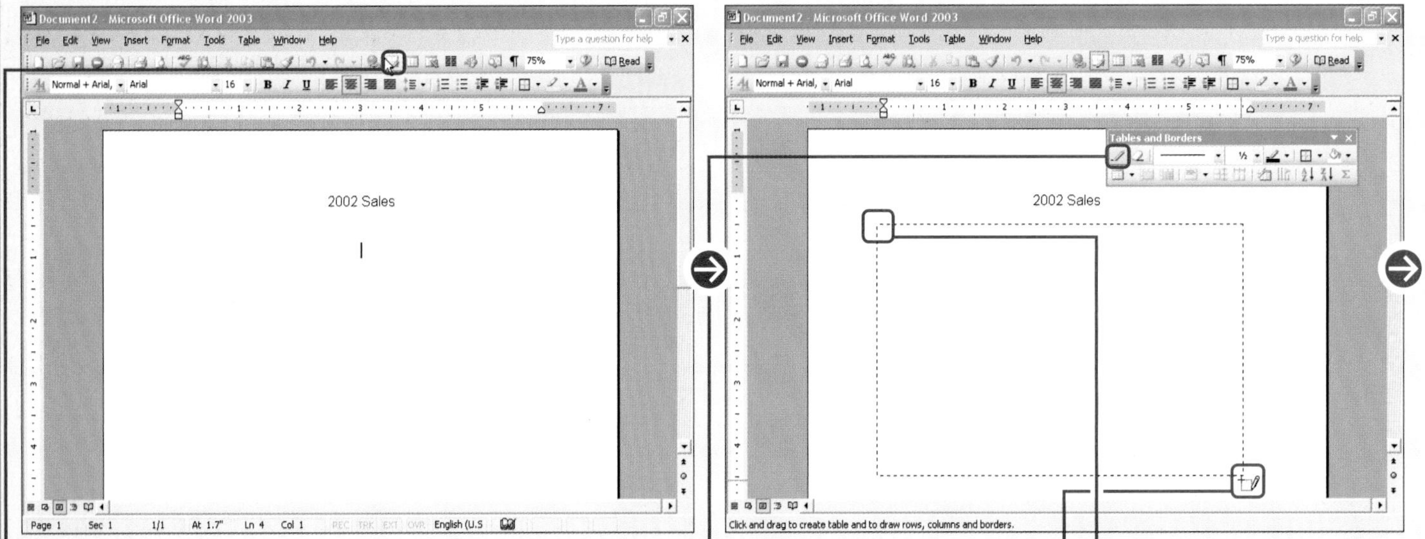

1 Click the Tables and Borders button.

○ The Tables and Borders toolbar appears.

2 Click the Draw Table button (↖ changes to ✎).

3 Click at the start location for the table.

4 Drag to create the borders for the table.

5 Release the mouse button.

#21

DIFFICULTY LEVEL

Did You Know?

You can use the Eraser option ( ) on the Tables and Borders toolbar to remove lines from your table. When you click , the cursor changes to . To remove a line, move the cursor over the line and click. You can remove lines from all tables using this option. When you remove a line between two cells, Word combines the text from the two cells.

Customize It!

If you do not want Word to automatically resize a column to fit the text you type, you need to turn off that feature. To turn off column resizing, click Table ⇨ Table Properties to display the Table Properties dialog box. On the Table tab, click Options. In the Options dialog box, click Automatically Resize to Fit Contents (changes to).

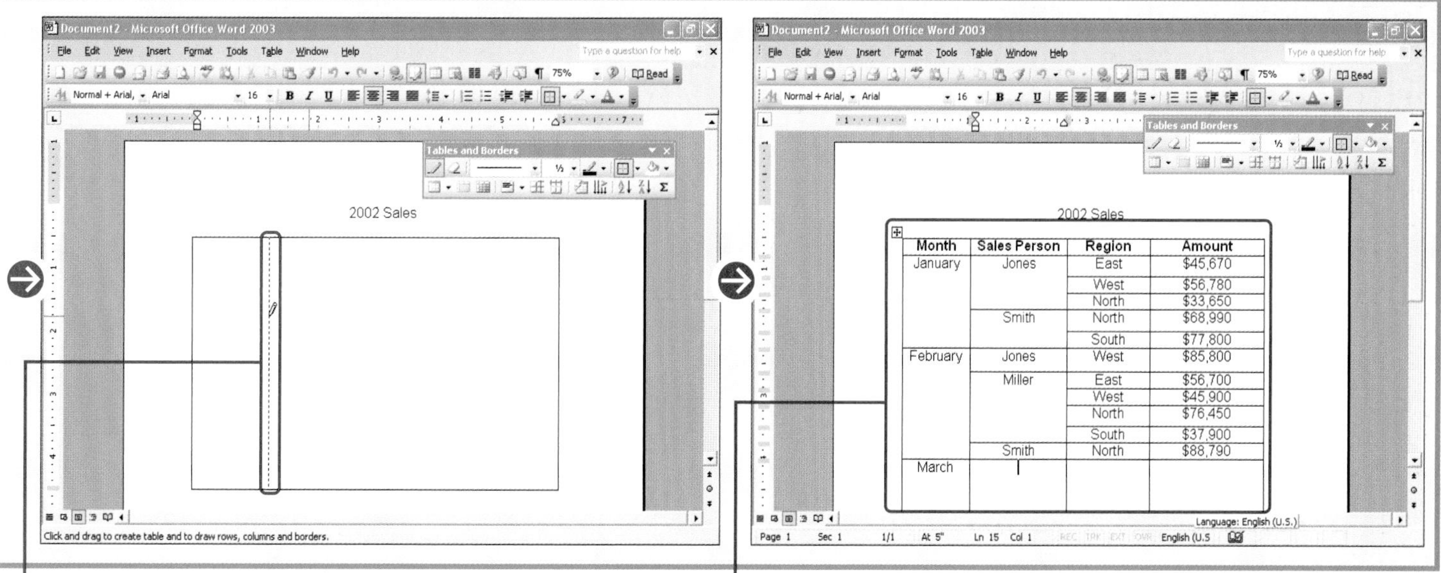

- Word creates the borders for the table.
- ⑥ Click a line and drag toward another line to create the first line in the table.
- ⑦ Repeat step **6** for each line of the table.
- ⑧ Add the text of the table.

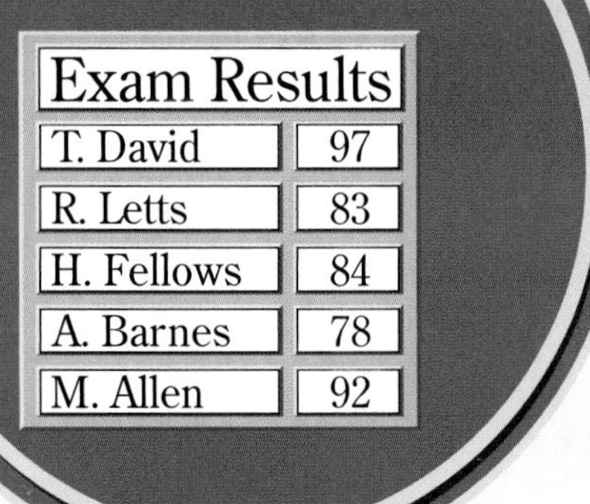

Create NESTED TABLES

You can insert a table inside the cell of another table to create nested tables. *Nested tables* are frequently used to lay out documents such as Web pages or newsletters. By creating one large table for the entire page, you can insert graphics and additional tables in cells to lay out the document within the outside table.

When you nest tables, the inserted table size is limited by the size of the cell of the table in which it is nested. If you want the nested table to be larger, you need to expand the size of the cell.

Even though you have a table nested within another table, you can still set the properties for each table separately. You can also position the nested table at the desired location within the cell. Microsoft Word allows you to click on a nested table and drag it to the desired position in the cell. You can also resize the nested table by clicking on the lower-right corner.

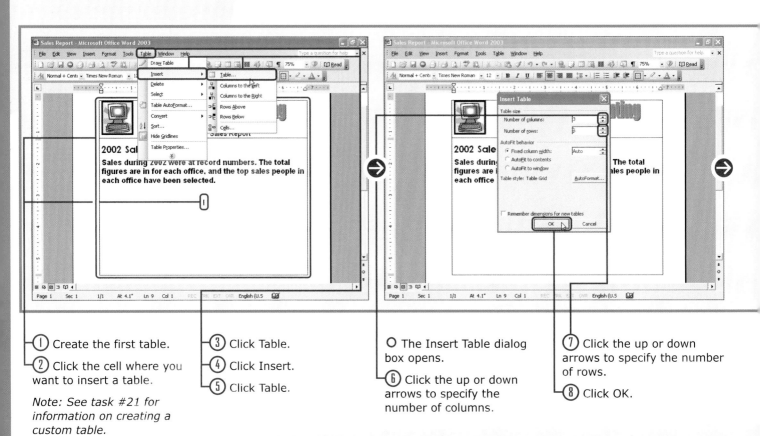

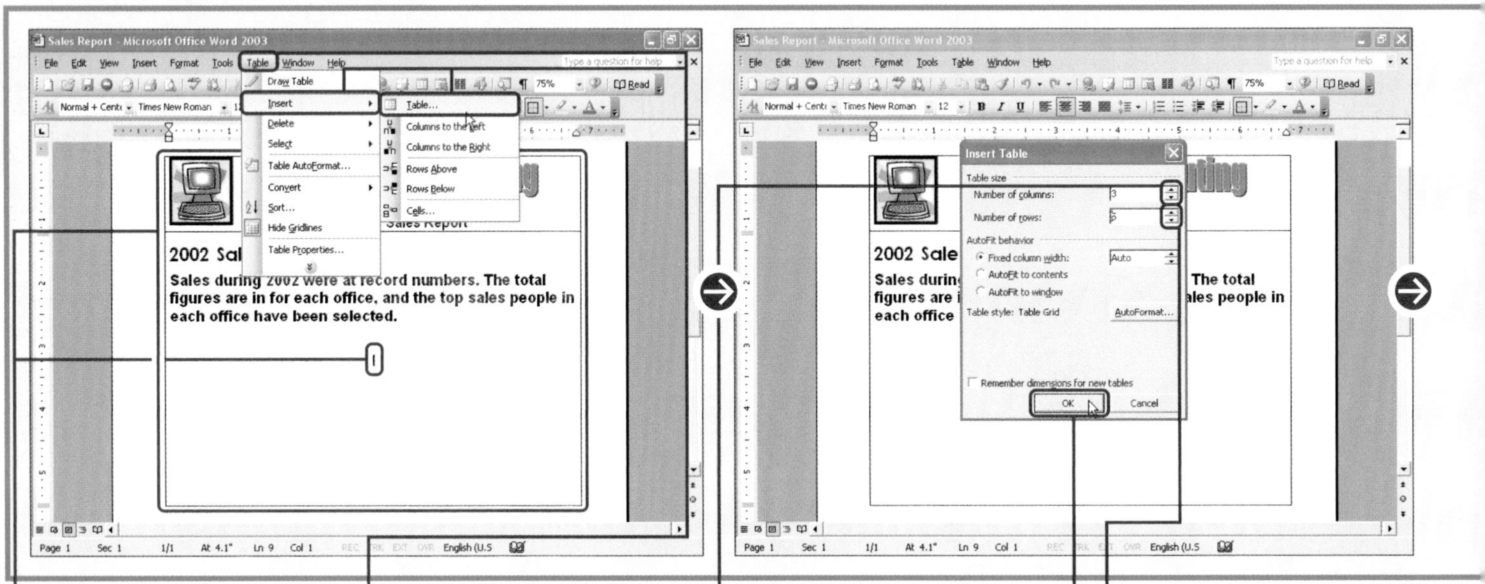

① Create the first table.

② Click the cell where you want to insert a table.

Note: See task #21 for information on creating a custom table.

③ Click Table.

④ Click Insert.

⑤ Click Table.

○ The Insert Table dialog box opens.

⑥ Click the up or down arrows to specify the number of columns.

⑦ Click the up or down arrows to specify the number of rows.

⑧ Click OK.

DIFFICULTY LEVEL

Did You Know?

You can apply an AutoFormat style to a table by selecting one of the built-in table styles. To apply an AutoFormat style during the table creation, click AutoFormat in the Insert Table dialog box. To format an existing table, select the table and click Table ➪ Table AutoFormat. In the Table AutoFormat dialog box you can click a style in the Table Styles list to see a preview.

Did You Know?

You can control the size of the table you nest by specifying the column widths in the Insert Table dialog box. Click the Fixed Column Width radio button and specify the desired width.

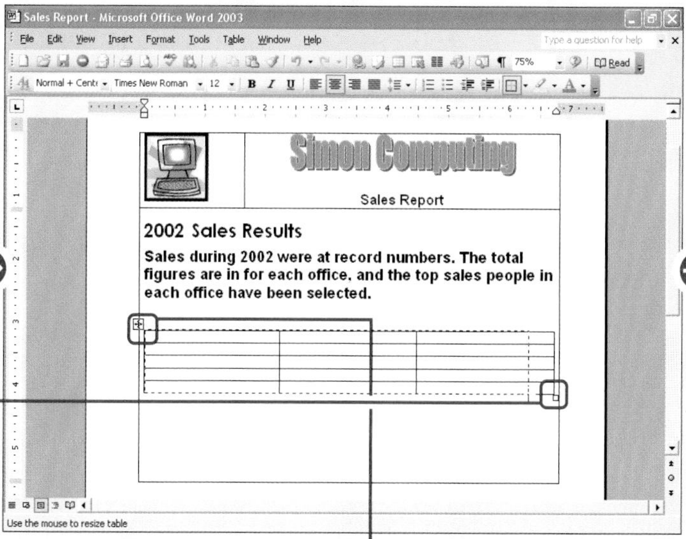

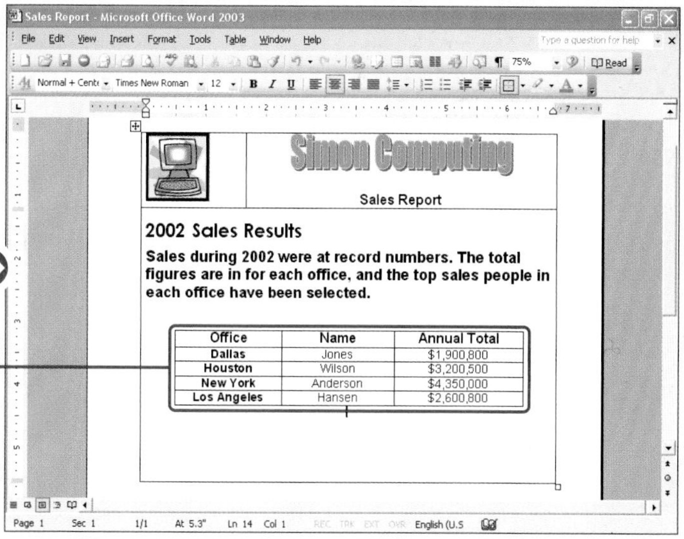

○ Word inserts a table in the selected cell.

9 Click the bottom-right corner of the table and drag to resize.

○ If desired, click the top-left corner and drag to reposition the table.

10 Type the table text.

○ The nested table remains in the selected position.

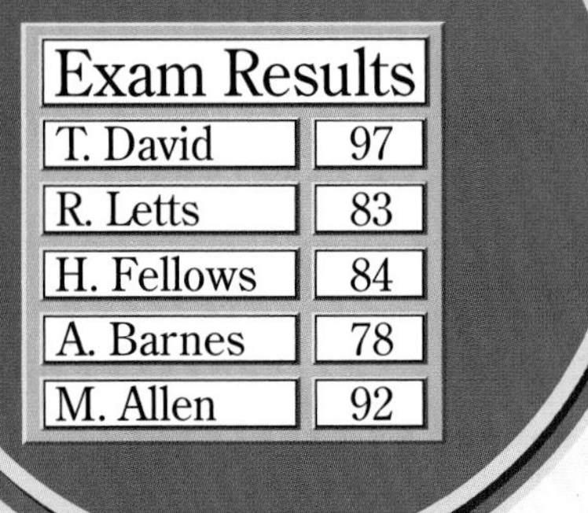

CONTROL TABLE BREAKS

across multiple pages

You can control the way that Word breaks up a table over multiple pages. By default, Word automatically breaks up a table when it fills a page. At times, this means that a row with multiple lines of text may be broken in the middle.

You may find that Word's methods for breaking up tables do not suit your requirements, so you need to control where the page breaks occur. To do so, you first need to remove the ability to break a table in the middle of a row. When you do this, you indicate that if the entire row does not fit on the page, that row should be placed on the next page. Typically this will make your tables easier to read because it is easier for the reader to tie the information together.

You can also manually indicate where you want a table to be broken. When doing this, you should create the entire table and then manually insert breaks at the appropriate locations. By creating the table first, you can see where the natural page breaks will occur.

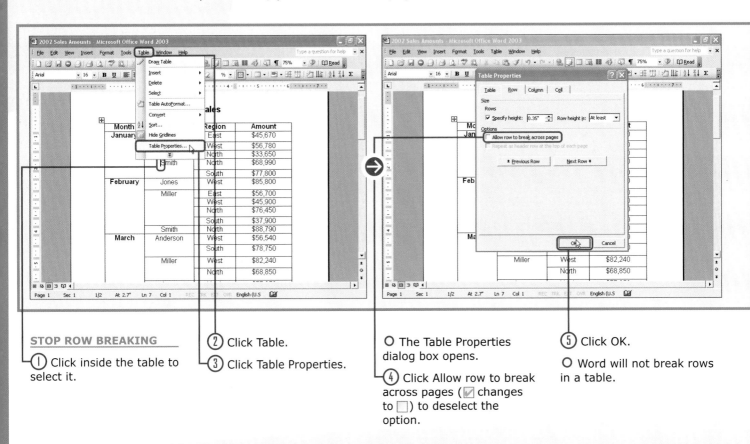

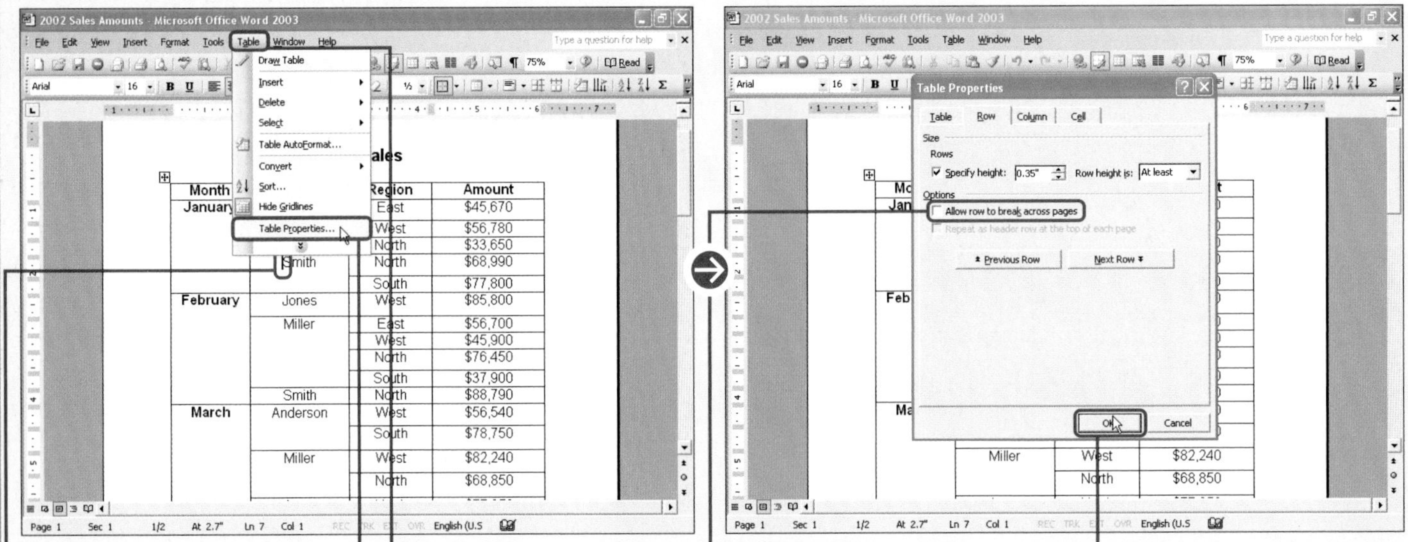

STOP ROW BREAKING

1. Click inside the table to select it.
2. Click Table.
3. Click Table Properties.

- The Table Properties dialog box opens.

4. Click Allow row to break across pages (☑ changes to ☐) to deselect the option.
5. Click OK.

- Word will not break rows in a table.

DIFFICULTY LEVEL

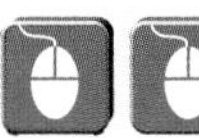   

Did You Know?

You can remove breaks that you insert in a table. This may become necessary if you add or remove information from the table. To remove the break, click at the end of the table on the first page and click Delete. You will probably need to click Delete twice to have the rows join back together.

Did You Know?

Keep in mind that it can be difficult to follow a table that spans several different pages. If you have an extremely large table, consider breaking it into smaller tables on separate pages. That way you can insert headings for the tables on every page, making the table easier to read.

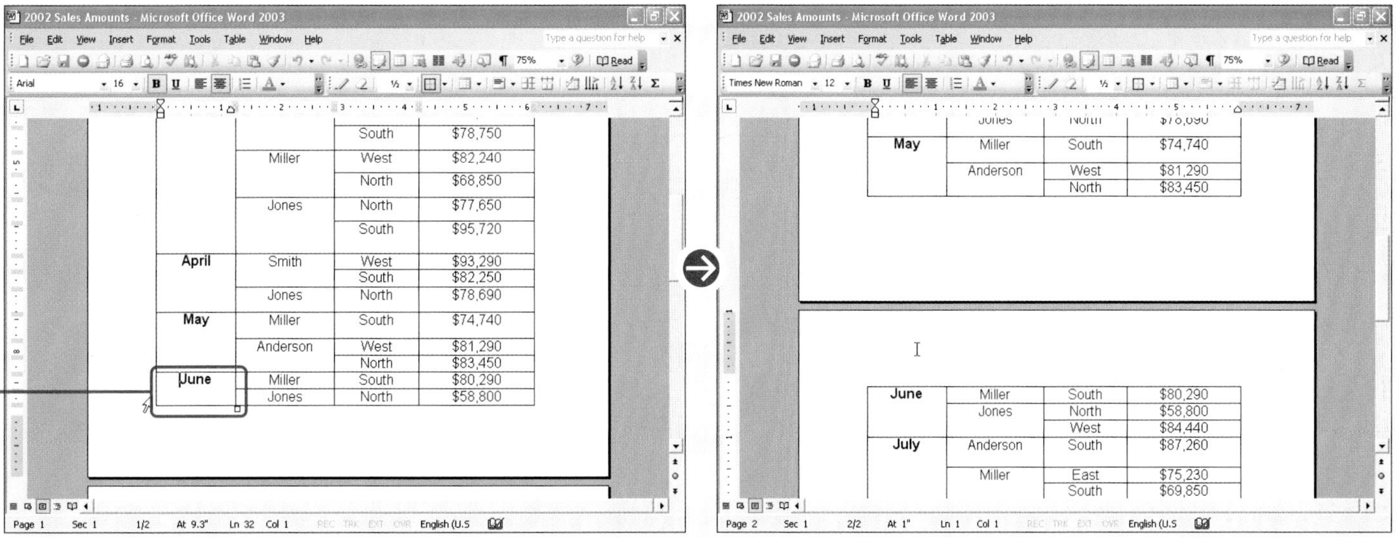

INSERT TABLE BREAK

1. Click the row in the table to place on the next page.

2. Press Ctrl+Enter.

- Word breaks the table at the specified row.

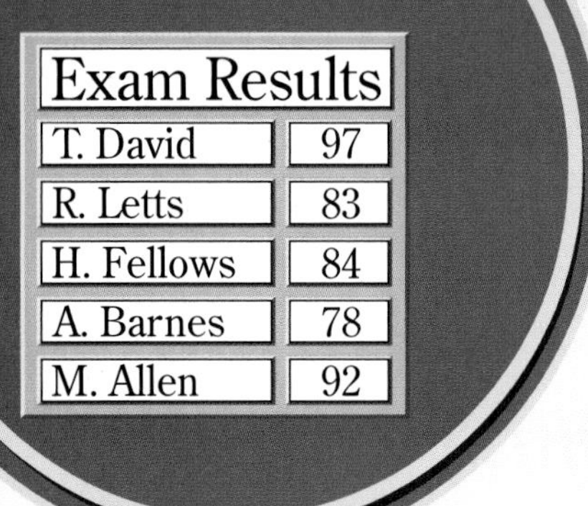

Use a DATA FORM to edit a table

You can simplify the process of adding and modifying data within a large table by using the Data Form dialog box. The Data Form dialog box is designed for tables storing lists of data, such as a telephone contact list. Using the Data Form dialog box makes the process of editing tables much easier because you only have to deal with the values from one row at a time.

In order to use the Data Form option, you must have a header row with column names at the top of your table. Word uses those header names to identify the columns when you view the document. A separate field on the Data Form dialog box represents the values from each column in the selected row. For example, the first record displayed on the Data Form dialog box is the second row of data in your table.

Any changes you make in the Data Form dialog box are applied to the actual table.

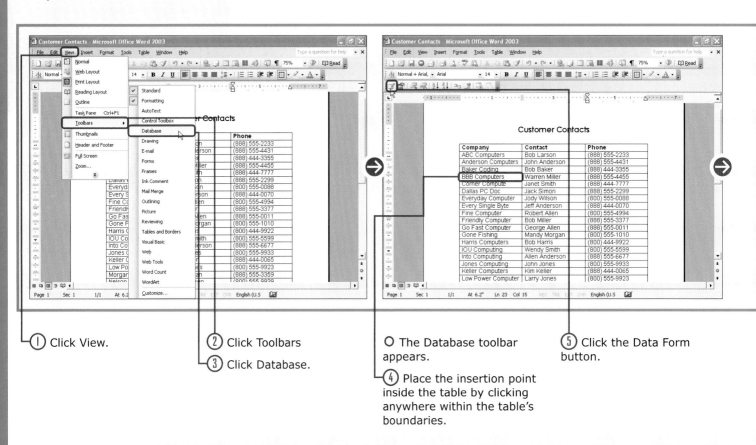

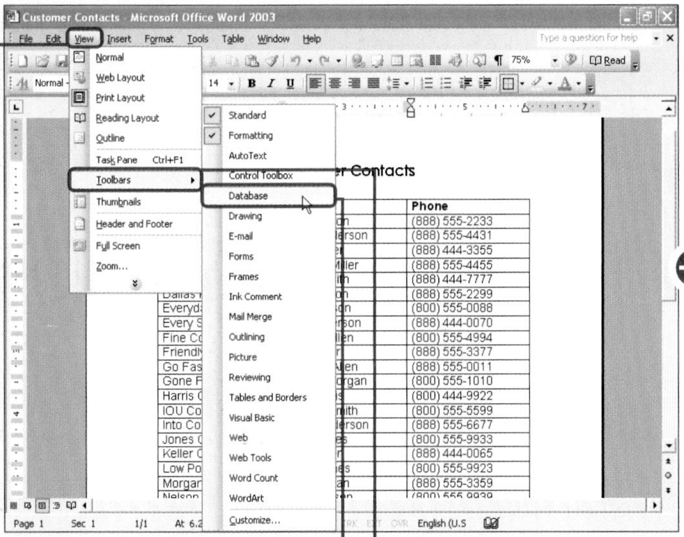

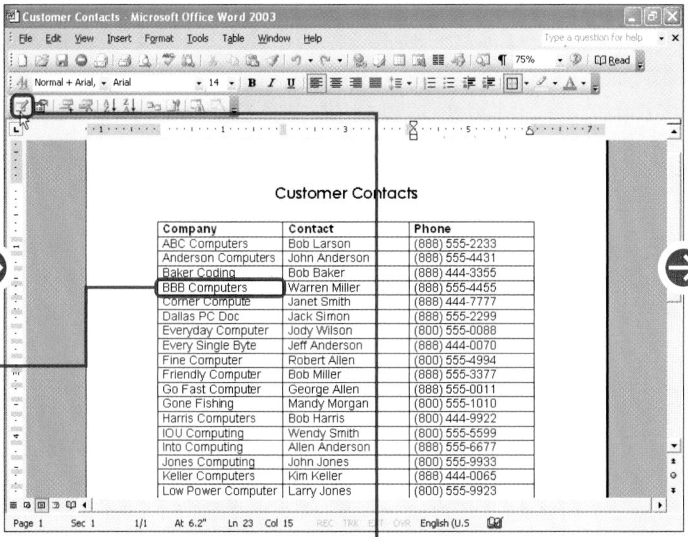

1. Click View.
2. Click Toolbars
3. Click Database.

- The Database toolbar appears.

4. Place the insertion point inside the table by clicking anywhere within the table's boundaries.
5. Click the Data Form button.

DIFFICULTY LEVEL

Did You Know?

To find specific values in a table, you can use the Find option in the Data Form dialog box. When you click Find, the Find in Field dialog box opens. Type the value you want to find in the Find What field and select the name of the table column to search in the In field drop-down list. Word displays the row that contains the specified field in the Data Form dialog box.

Did You Know?

You can add a new row to a table by using the Data Form dialog box. To create a new row, click Add New. Word creates a new row in the table and displays black fields for you to fill in.

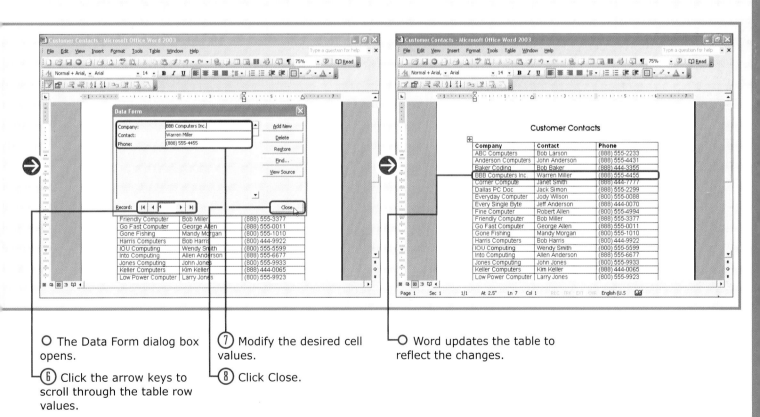

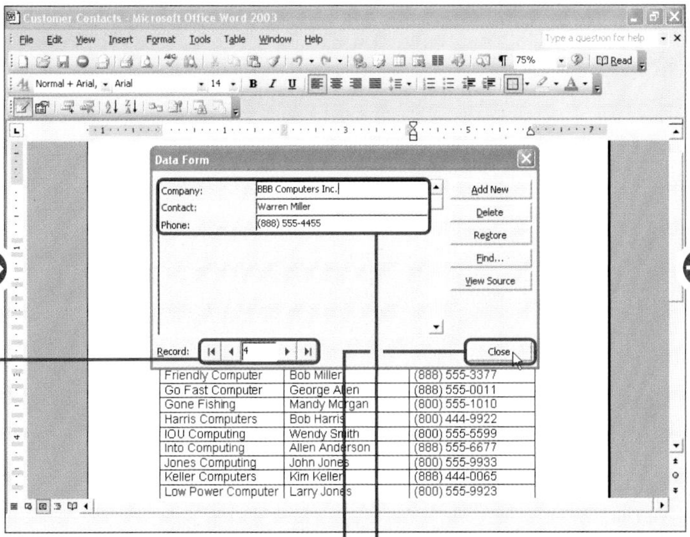

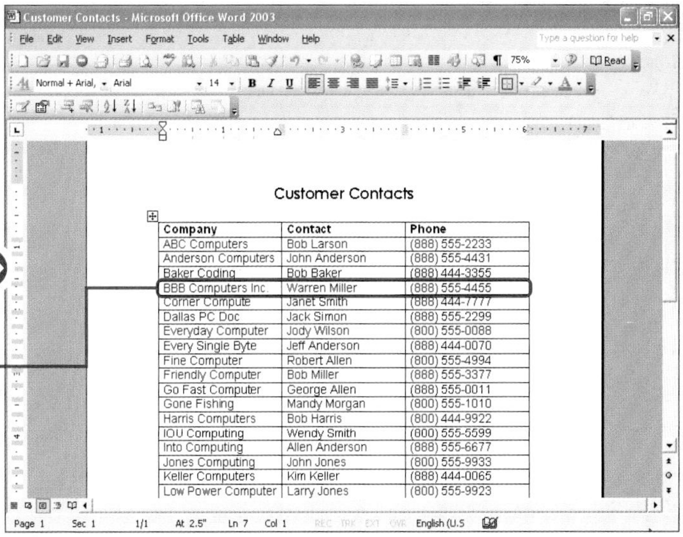

- The Data Form dialog box opens.
6. Click the arrow keys to scroll through the table row values.
7. Modify the desired cell values.
8. Click Close.

- Word updates the table to reflect the changes.

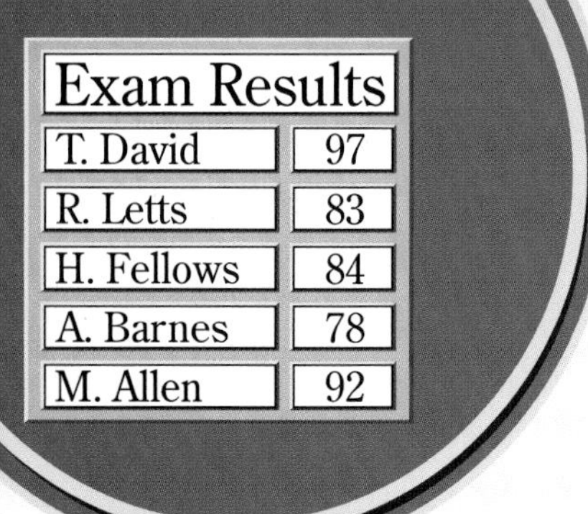

Exam Results	
T. David	97
R. Letts	83
H. Fellows	84
A. Barnes	78
M. Allen	92

PERFORM CALCULATIONS

on cells in a table

You can perform calculations, such as summing a list of numbers, on a row or column of cells within a table. This feature works well for totaling values in a table.

In order to perform a calculation on cells in a table, you need to use one of the built-in functions available in Word. You can select one of 18 different functions in the Formula dialog box.

After you select the desired function, you need to add a reference to the cells that you want to use in the calculation. For example, if you want to add the cells in a column, you need to reference those cells. Word provides some direction arguments you can use to identify the cells you want to use. To use the cells in the column above the cell, you type ABOVE as the argument for the selected function. You can use LEFT for cells located in the row to the left of the selected cell. You can also use RIGHT and BELOW as arguments.

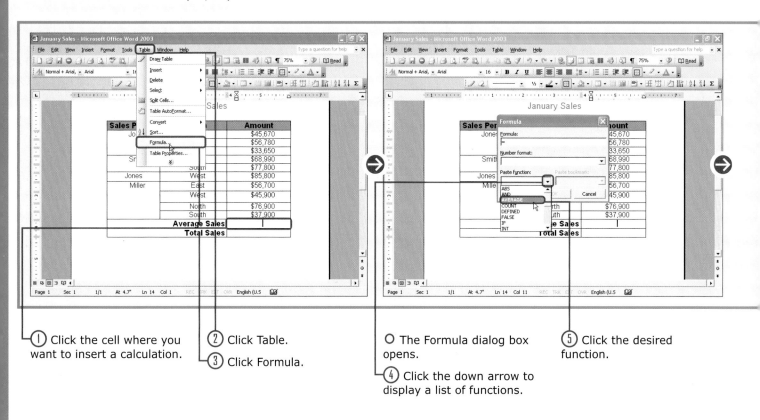

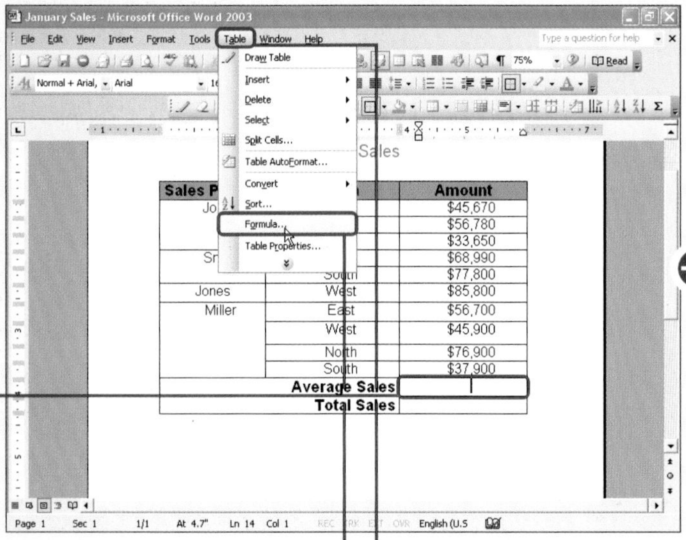

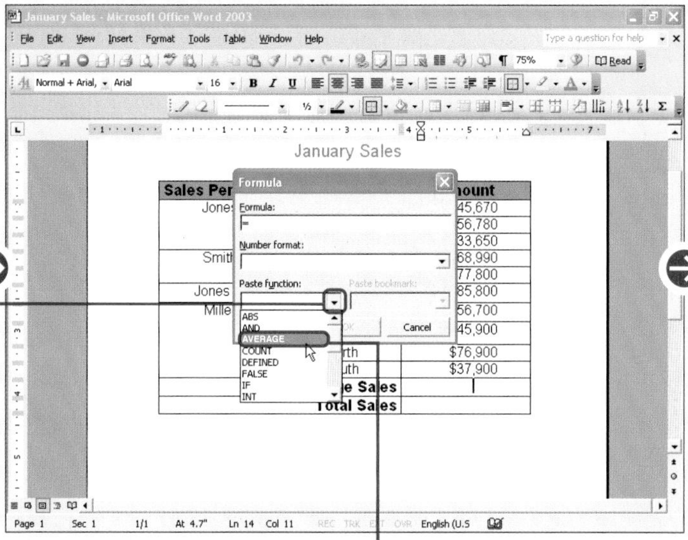

1. Click the cell where you want to insert a calculation.
2. Click Table.
3. Click Formula.

- The Formula dialog box opens.

4. Click the down arrow to display a list of functions.
5. Click the desired function.

DIFFICULTY LEVEL

Did You Know?

You can use cell references within the table to identify the cells you want to use in a calculation. Columns have alphabet references starting with the first column, and rows are numbered, so the first cell in a table is always A1. To sum the cells in the third column, you could have the formula =SUM(C2:C11). You use the column to indicate that you want to use the cells starting with the first reference through the last reference.

Did You Know?

If you just want to add the cells in a column, you can use the AutoSum button (Σ) located on the Tables and Borders toolbar. When you click this button, Word automatically inserts the results of the formula =SUM(ABOVE) in the selected cell.

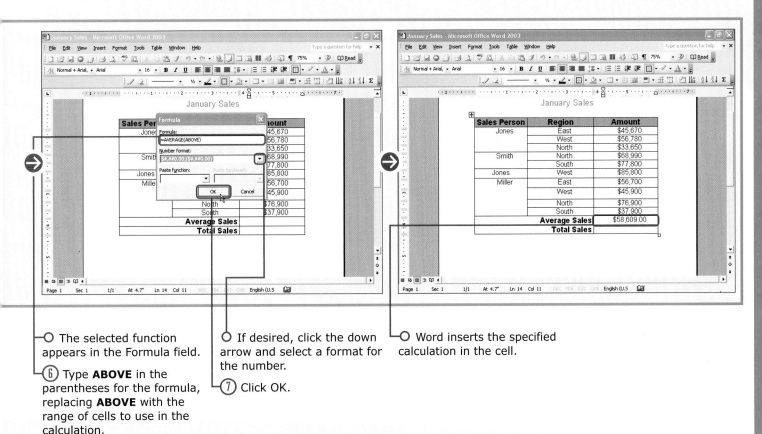

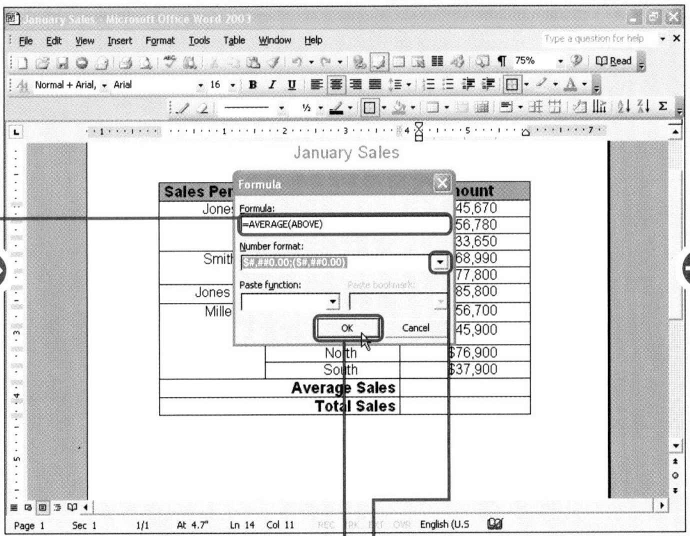

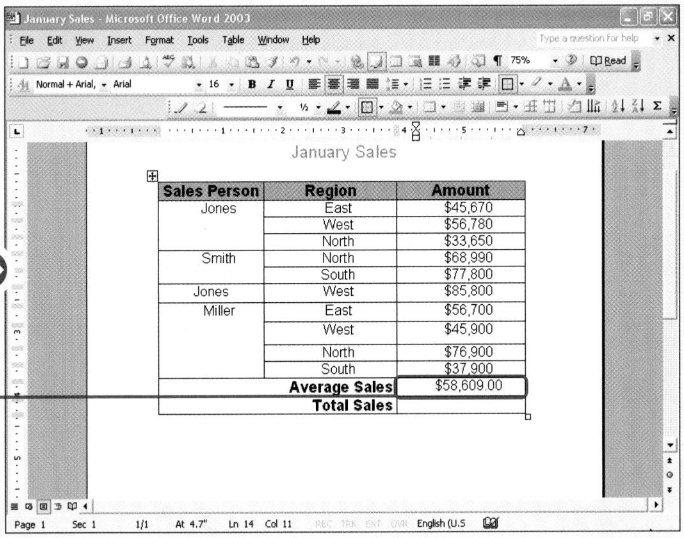

- The selected function appears in the Formula field.

6. Type **ABOVE** in the parentheses for the formula, replacing **ABOVE** with the range of cells to use in the calculation.

- If desired, click the down arrow and select a format for the number.

7. Click OK.

- Word inserts the specified calculation in the cell.

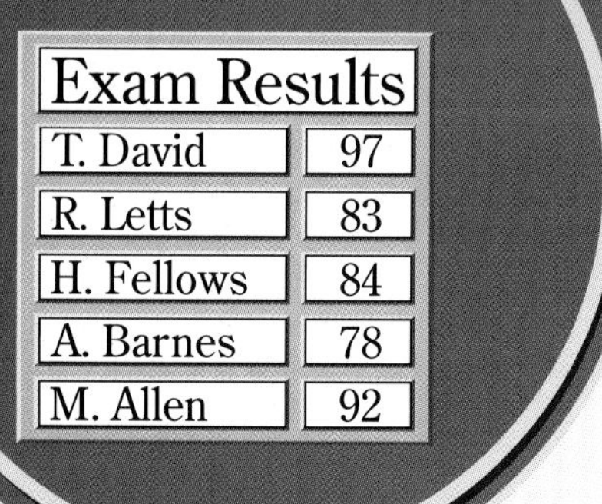

Exam Results	
T. David	97
R. Letts	83
H. Fellows	84
A. Barnes	78
M. Allen	92

SORT COLUMNS
in a table

You can sort a table based upon the values in specific columns. For example, you may want to sort a table alphabetically using the customer names in the second column.

When you perform a sort, Word keeps the values in a row together, treating each row as a separate record. If you are sorting by the value in the second column, Word moves the entire contents of the row during the sort, not just the values in the second column.

To perform a sort, you use the Sort dialog box. Word allows you to specify up to three different sort criteria. Word applies the criteria in the specified order: If you indicate that you want to sort by the first column in Ascending order, Word performs that sort and then uses the next sort criteria for any duplicates. For example, if the first sort criteria is by name and there are two John Smith names, Word uses the next sort, by location, to place the row with the John Smith from Dallas before the John Smith from Miami.

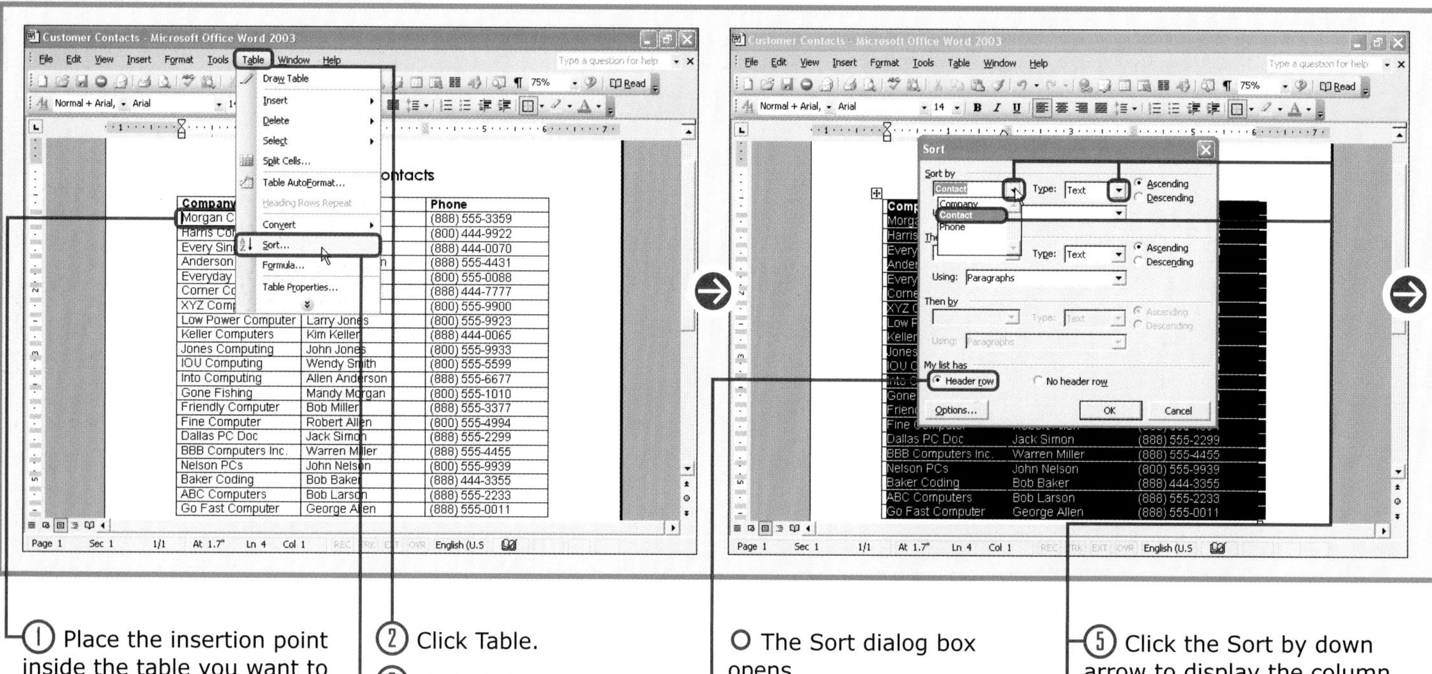

1. Place the insertion point inside the table you want to sort and click to select the table.
2. Click Table.
3. Click Sort.

- The Sort dialog box opens.

4. If the table has a header row, click Header row (○ changes to ◉).
5. Click the Sort by down arrow to display the column names.
6. Click the desired column for the sort.
7. Click the Type down arrow to select the desired sort type.

#26

DIFFICULTY LEVEL

Did You Know?

You have three different types of sorts to select when sorting a table. Select the sort that matches the type of data in the selected column. Select Number if the entire column contains numeric values. If some cells contain text or numeric strings such as phone numbers or ID numbers, select a Text sort. Select the Date sort option if all cells in the column contain dates; Word sorts the table in chronological order based upon the dates.

Did You Know?

You can sort a table using another language, such as Spanish or French. To use another language sort, you must set up the language using the Microsoft Office 2003 Language Settings. See task #20 for more information about sorting using another language.

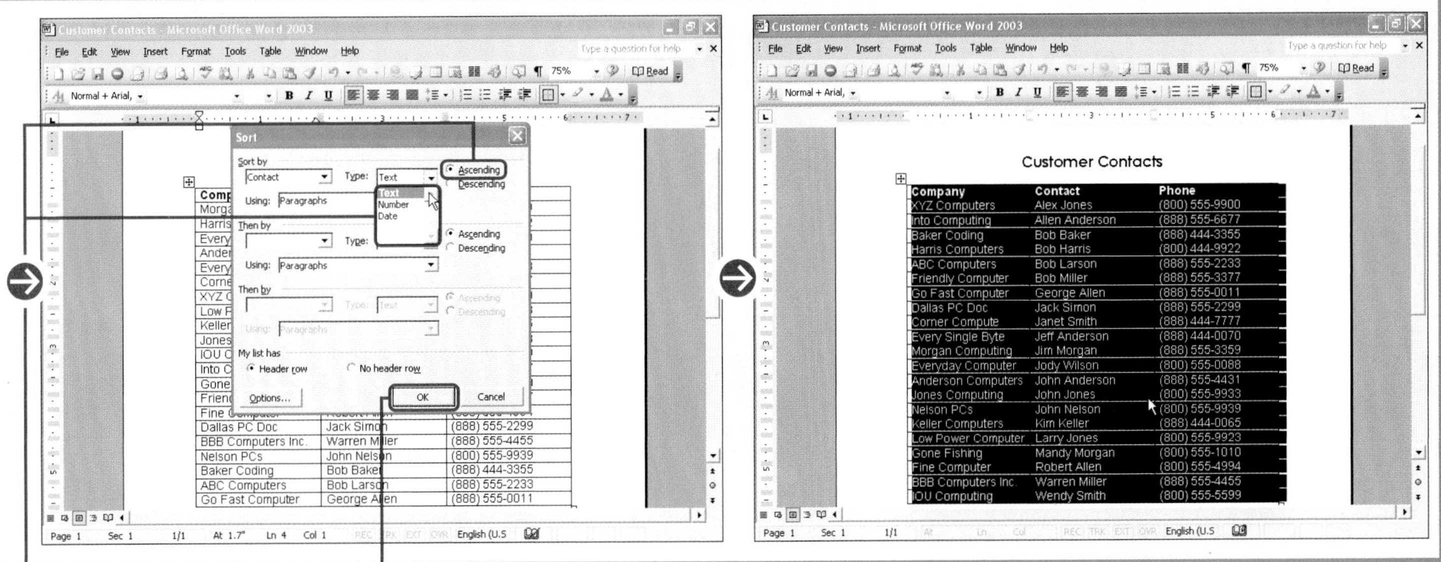

- The three sort types appear.

8. Click the sort that matches the type of values in the column.

9. Click Ascending to sort in ascending order (○ changes to ◉).

- If desired, you can sort the column in descending order.

10. Repeat steps **5** to **9** to create a second and third sort criteria.

11. Click OK.

- Word sorts the table based upon the sort criteria specified.

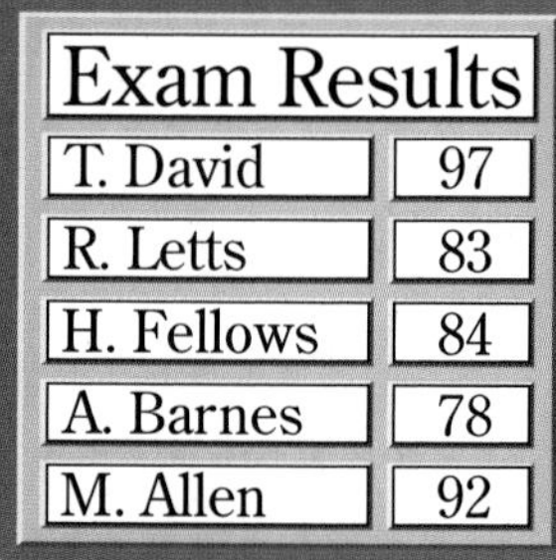

Exam Results	
T. David	97
R. Letts	83
H. Fellows	84
A. Barnes	78
M. Allen	92

REPEAT TABLE HEADINGS
on new pages

DIFFICULTY LEVEL

If you have a long table that requires multiple pages, you can have Word repeat the heading rows on each new page. For example, usually the first row of any table contains the column headings for the table, such as Month, Sales Person, Region, and Amount, which are labels to identify value types in specific columns.

Typically when a table breaks due to a page break, the table just continues on without any headers. By selecting the Heading Rows Repeat option, you can identify the specific rows that you want to repeat when the table breaks. You can specify any number of rows as the header, but they must be the first rows in the table.

Unfortunately, Word only applies the headers if there is a natural page break in the table. If you manually insert a page break, the headers will not be applied to the new page. See task #23 for more information on page breaks. If you want a heading on that page, you will need to copy the header rows and paste them manually.

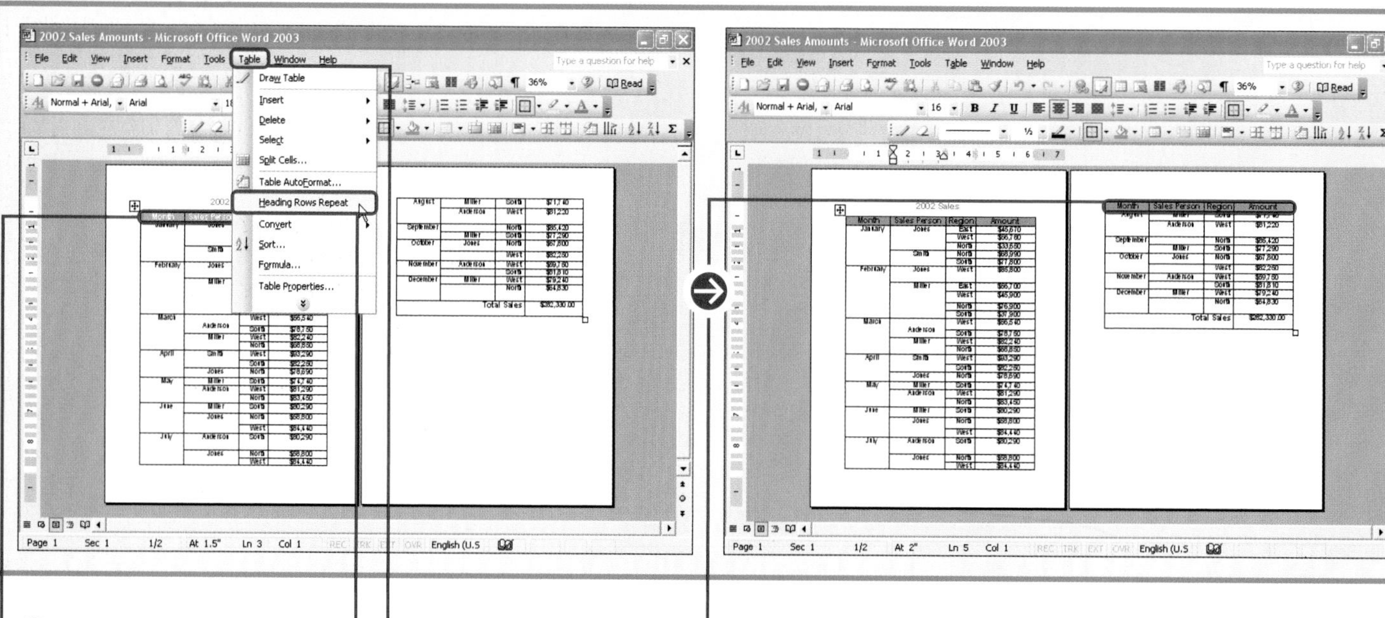

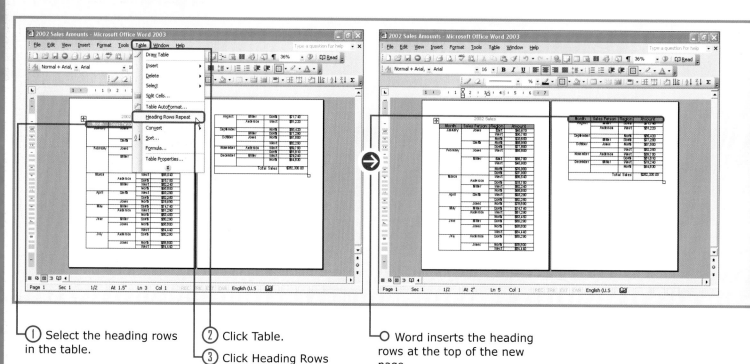

① Select the heading rows in the table.

② Click Table.

③ Click Heading Rows Repeat.

○ Word inserts the heading rows at the top of the new page.

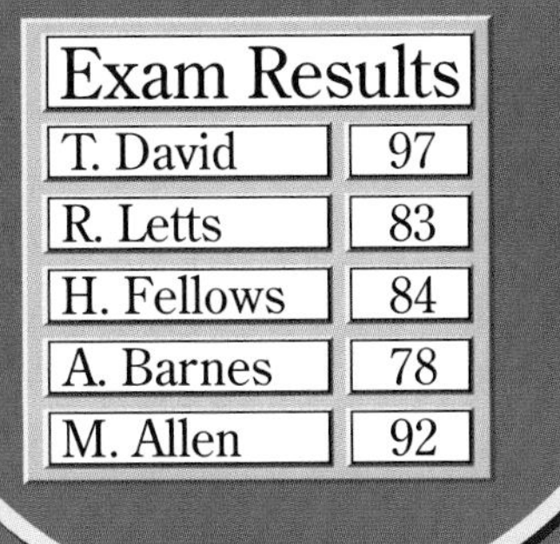

Make rows in a table the SAME SIZE

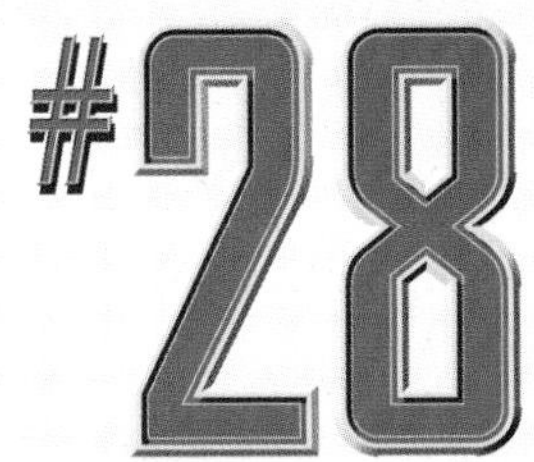

DIFFICULTY LEVEL

You can have Word automatically resize multiple rows in your table so that the cells are all the same height. This is very useful when you draw your table.

To resize the rows to be the same size, make sure you only select the rows that should be the same size. For example, if a cell spans two rows in one column, you only want to select other cells that span two rows.

By resizing rows using the Distribute Rows Evenly option, you avoid the need to manually resize each row using the Table Properties dialog box. Keep in mind that you can perform the same steps shown here to resize cells in a column to be the same width.

Did You Know?

You can have Word automatically change the width of a column as you add text. With this option, the column is adjusted to fit the widest cell. To have Word adjust the width automatically, click Table ➪ Autofit ➪ AutoFit to Contents.

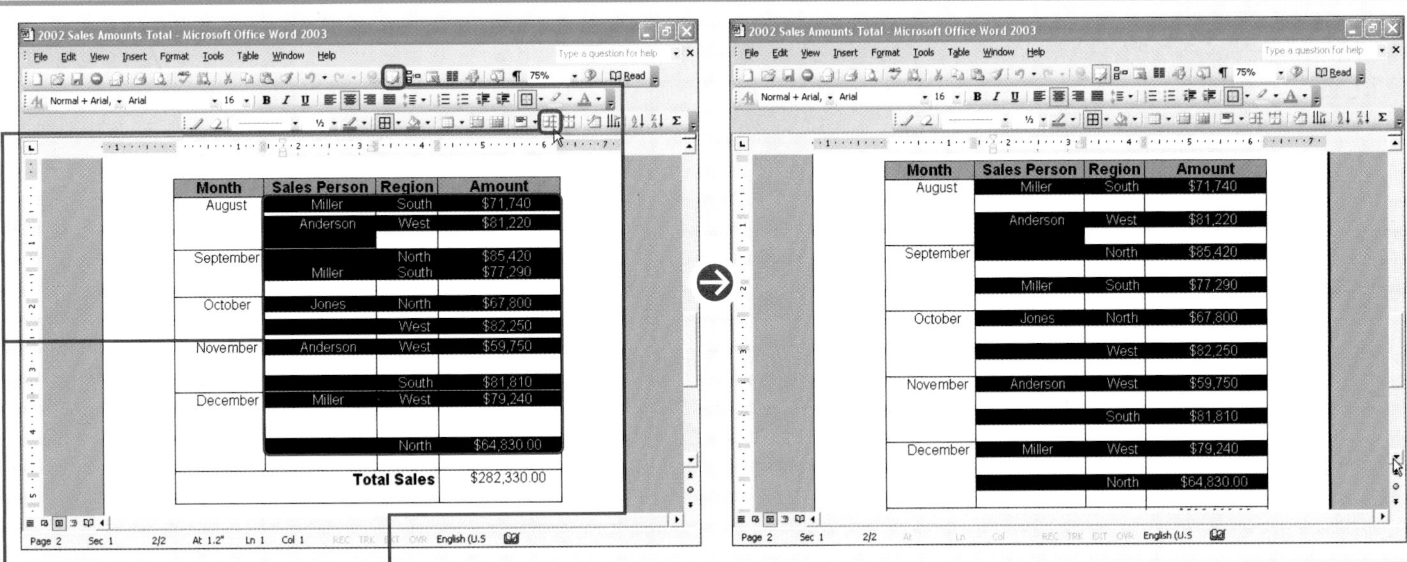

① Select the rows of the table you want to resize.

② Click the Distribute Rows Evenly button.

○ The Tables and Borders toolbar appears when you click the Tables and Borders button.

○ Word resizes the rows to be the same size.

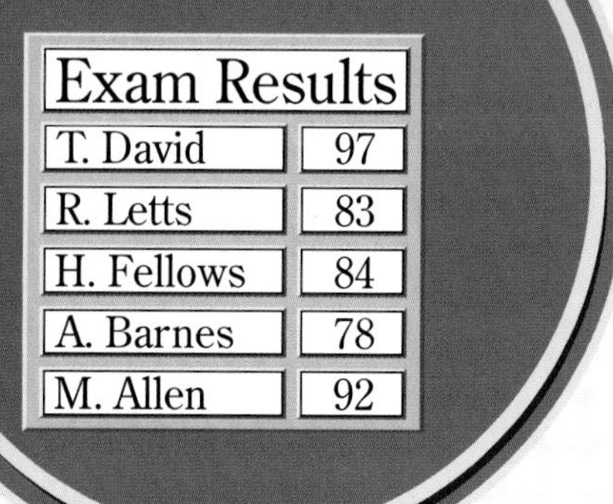

WRAP TEXT around a table

You can have Word wrap text around a table in your document, with the text wrapping either to the left or the right.

If you want to have a table wrapped with text, you need to make sure the table is sized small enough to allow text to be placed on either side. Word will keep everything within the margins, so if the table fills the page there will be no room for text on the side.

You specify that you want to wrap text by selecting the Around option. When you do so, you can drag the table to position it within the text of a paragraph.

If you drag the table to the left side of the paragraph, Word wraps the text so that it displays on the right side of the table.

You can drag a table by clicking the Move handle that appears in the upper-left corner of the table when you select it. The Move handle allows you to place the table in the desired position on the page.

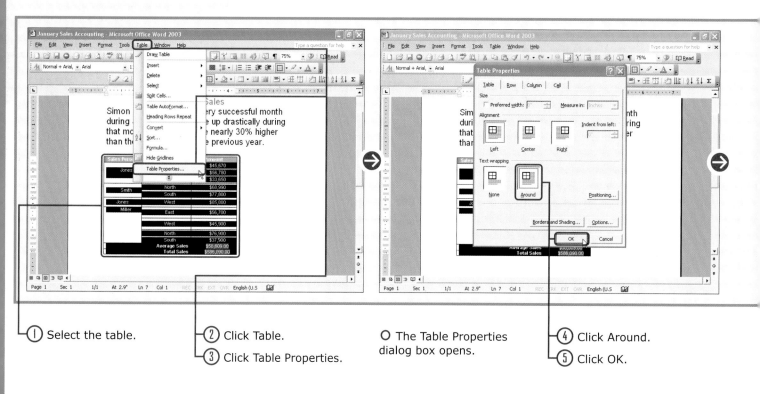

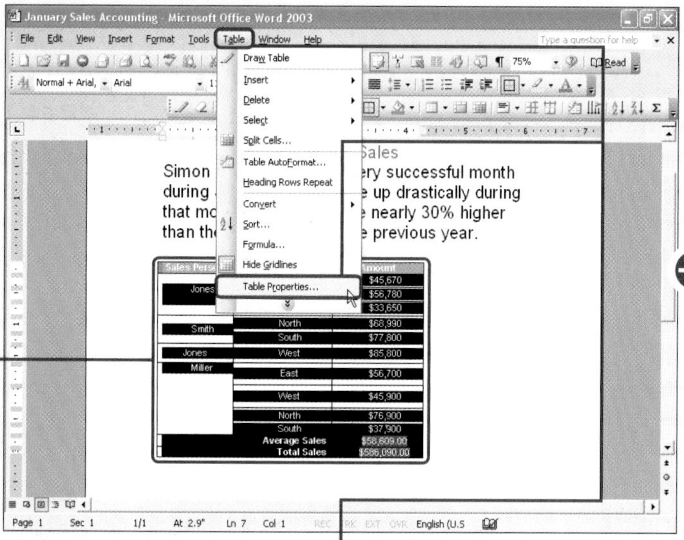

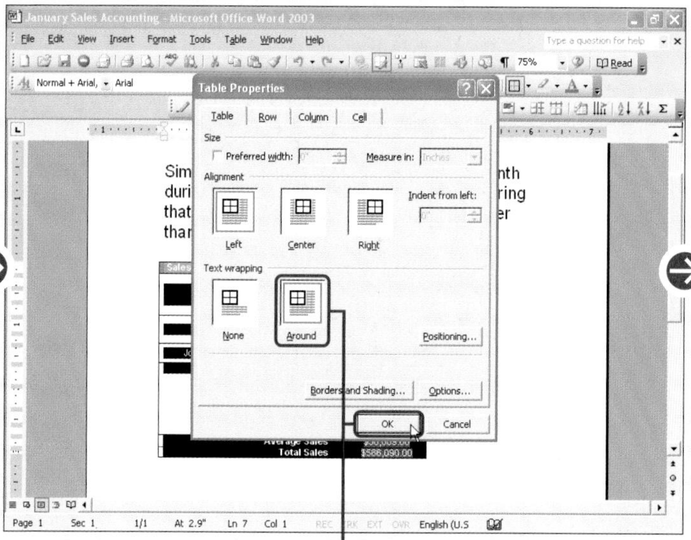

1 Select the table.

2 Click Table.

3 Click Table Properties.

○ The Table Properties dialog box opens.

4 Click Around.

5 Click OK.

DIFFICULTY LEVEL

Customize It!

You can specify the positioning of the table more precisely by selecting the Positioning button in the Table Properties dialog box. In the Positioning dialog box, indicate the desired positioning for the table in relation to the page and the surrounding text. For example, to place the table near the right margin, select a horizontal position of Right and a relative position of Margin.

You can place two tables next to each other by using columns. To do so, create two tables with one table preceding the other vertically on the page. Select both tables and click Format ➪ Columns to display the Columns dialog box. Click the Two option.

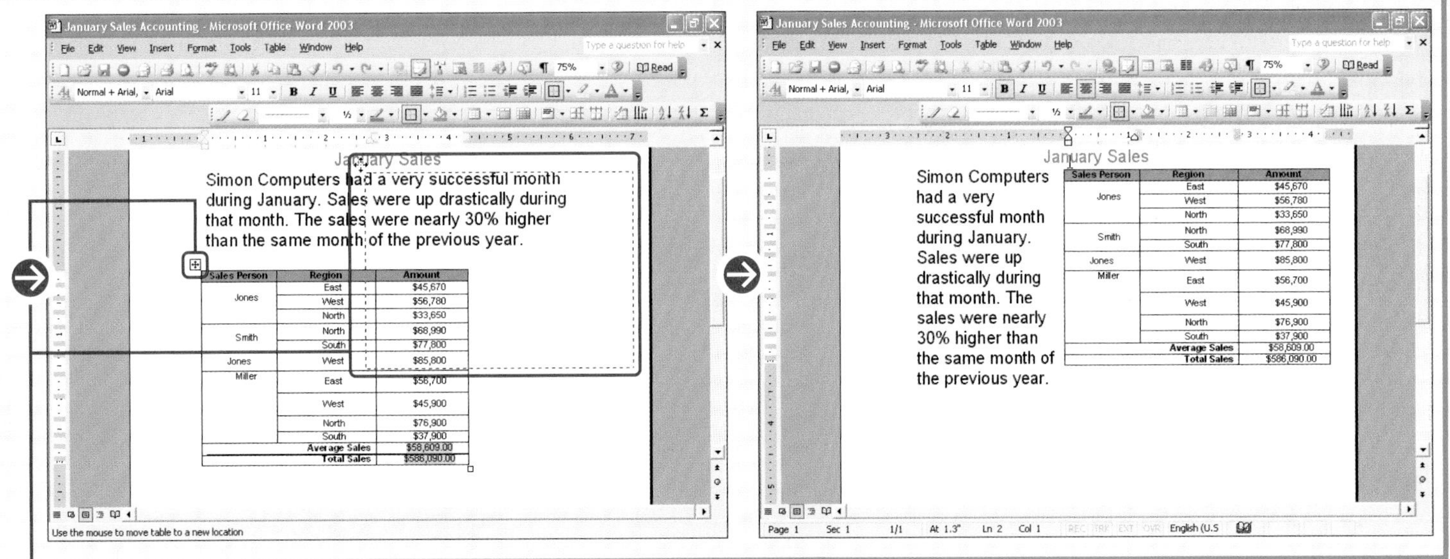

⑥ Click the Move handle.

⑦ Drag the table to the desired position.

⑧ Release the mouse button.

○ Word places the table and wraps the text around it.

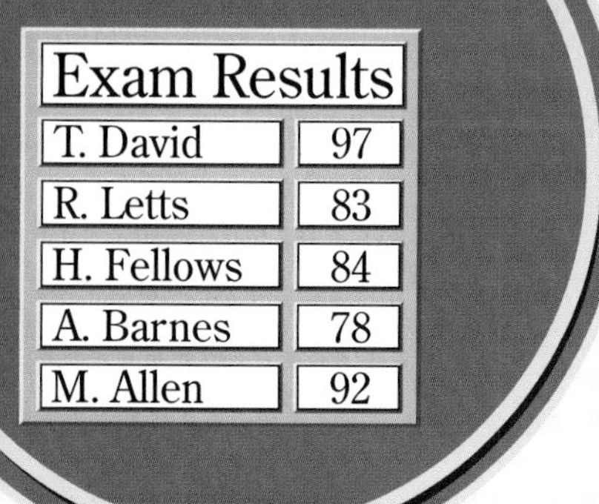

Create BALANCED COLUMNS on a page

You can have Word automatically balance the text on a page between the different columns. By doing so, you avoid having one column full while another one is only partially full.

When you use the columns feature, Word creates what is commonly referred to as *newspaper columns.* With these types of columns, the text flows down the first column and then to the next column on the page. Word allows you to create up to eight different columns on a page, although two or three columns are most common.

When you convert the text of a document to columns, Word automatically fills the first column with text before moving to the next column. You can avoid this unbalanced look by inserting a continuous break. You add this break to the end of the last column that you want to balance. Then, as you add text to any of the columns, Word automatically adjusts the columns so that they take up equal space.

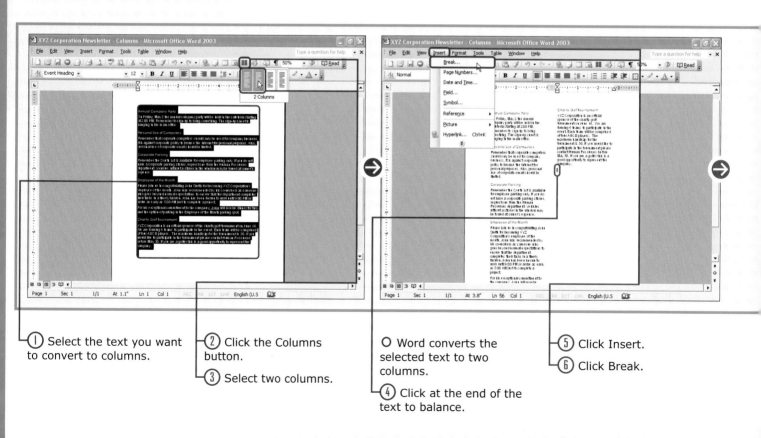

1. Select the text you want to convert to columns.
2. Click the Columns button.
3. Select two columns.

- Word converts the selected text to two columns.

4. Click at the end of the text to balance.
5. Click Insert.
6. Click Break.

DIFFICULTY LEVEL

Did You Know?

You can make modifications to column sizes in the Columns dialog box, which you access by clicking Format ⇨ Columns. You can specify the width for each column and the spacing between two columns. You can also change the number of columns by specifying a different number in the Number of Columns field.

Did You Know?

You can force columns to break at a specific location by inserting a column break. To do so, select the location where you want the break and click Insert ⇨ Break. In the Break dialog box, click Column Break. Keep in mind that if you insert a manual column break, Word will not be able to balance the columns correctly with a Continuous page break.

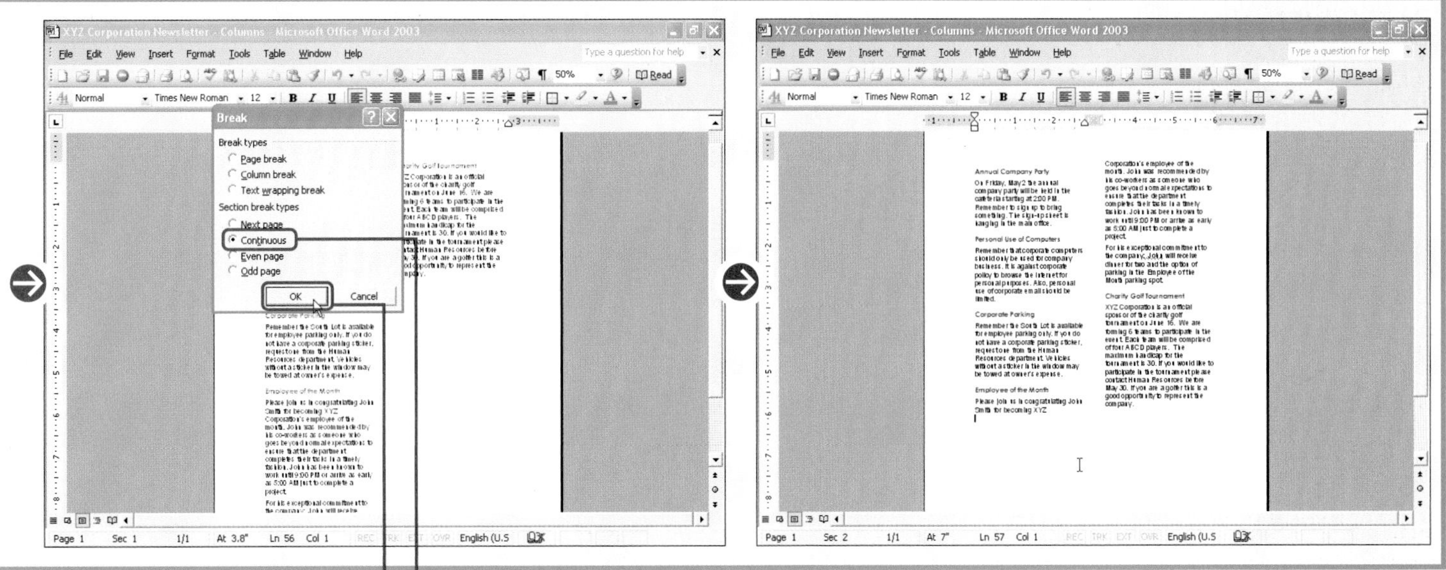

- The Break dialog box opens.

7. Click Continuous (○ changes to ◉).
8. Click OK.

- Word balances the text between the two columns.

Add Graphics and Objects

You can create more interest in your Word documents by incorporating different graphic images. Microsoft Office comes with several clip art images that you can add to your documents, but you can also use pictures you have gathered from other sources. You can also add your own graphics to the Clip Organizer to provide one central location for your graphic images.

Although Word is not a graphics editor, it does provide several options for making minor modifications. Not only can you resize a graphic image, but you can also crop it to remove unwanted portions. You can specify the exact location of a graphic and place graphics behind text as watermarks.

When you insert a graphic image, you can either have the graphic placed inline or floating in your document. If a graphic is inline, it is placed at the insertion point within the text, and the graphic moves with the text on the page. In most situations, the floating option works best because you have the ability to move the graphic freely on the page and position it in the desired location. You can also have text flow around the graphic.

Word enables you to insert several different types of objects into your documents. For example, you can embed an Excel worksheet directly into your document. When you select the worksheet, you are able to edit it directly in Word using Excel options.

Another useful object is the Microsoft Equation editor. You can create equations to display within your Word documents.

TOP 100

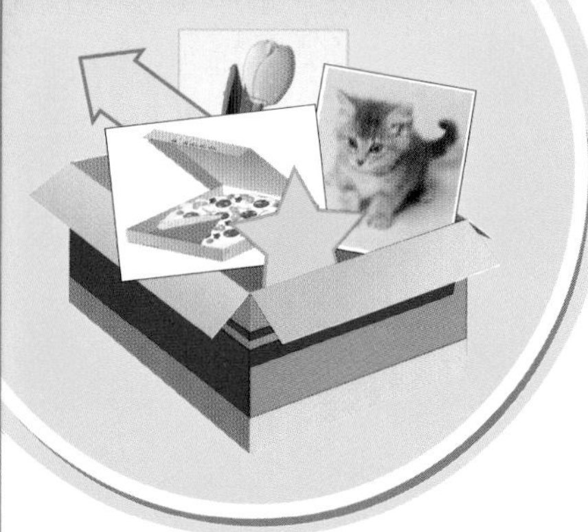

CROP A PICTURE

to focus attention

You can crop a picture that you have pasted into Word. This feature is useful when you have a picture that you want to trim to eliminate part of it. By cropping a picture, you can make sure that the attention is focused on a specific portion of the picture. Cropping also enables you to resize the picture without reducing the size of the subject.

To crop pictures, you need to use the Crop button on the Picture toolbar. The toolbar should appear when you click a picture that has been inserted into your document. You can also display the toolbar by clicking Insert ➪ Toolbar ➪ Picture. You crop the picture by clicking one of the cropping handles and dragging. The portion of the picture that is not within the dotted lines is cropped out of the picture.

When you crop a picture that you have inserted into Word, the cropping affects only the pasted image. The original graphic image is not altered. If you paste the image again, it will not be cropped.

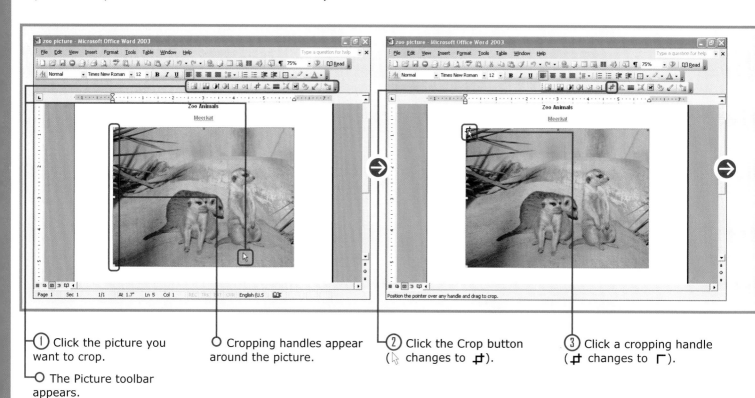

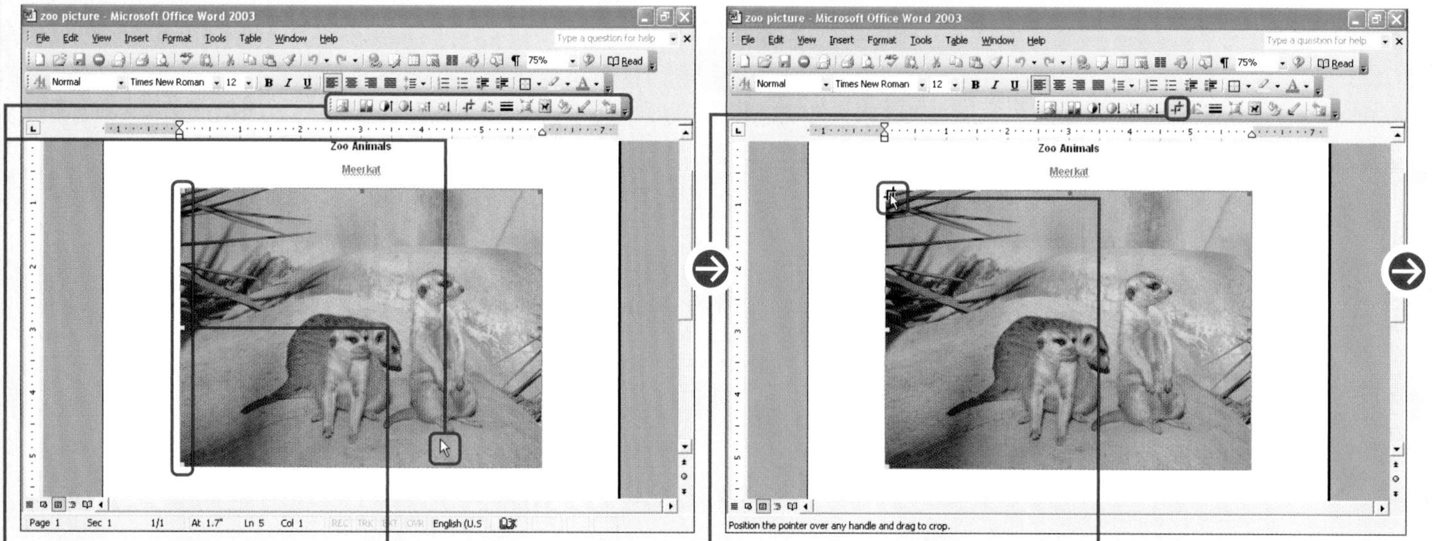

① Click the picture you want to crop.

○ The Picture toolbar appears.

○ Cropping handles appear around the picture.

② Click the Crop button (↖ changes to ⌗).

③ Click a cropping handle (⌗ changes to ┌).

Did You Know?

When you crop a picture, Word retains the entire picture. If you want to uncrop the picture, you can click the Crop tool and drag outward. You must click on the side of the picture that was cropped.

Did You Know?

If you want to crop a picture evenly from all four corners, crop all four corners at once. To do so, press Ctrl and click a corner cropping handle. Drag the corner handle toward the center. Word crops the same amount from all four sides of the picture.

Did You Know?

Word does not allow you to crop animated GIF images. If you want to crop an animated GIF, you have to use an animated GIF editing package before loading the animated GIF into Word.

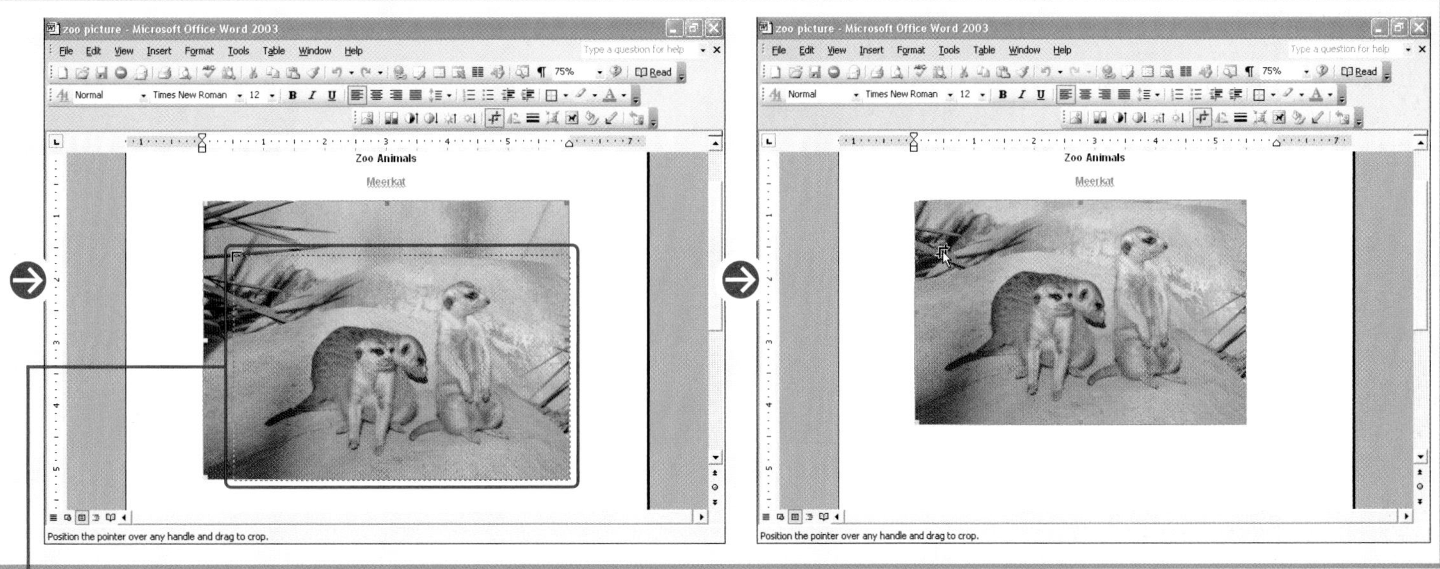

4 Drag to select the portion of the picture that you want to crop.

5 Release the mouse button.

- Word crops the picture as indicated.

ALIGN MULTIPLE OBJECTS

on a page

You can have Word align floating objects in your document. You can align objects either vertically or horizontally on the page. For example, you can align objects along the left side of the page, or at the top.

To set the alignment, you need to select the objects that you want to align and then indicate the type of alignment to apply. Keep in mind that Word aligns the objects by moving them in the direction necessary for the alignment. For example, if you have two objects and you select Align Top, Word may place one object on top of the other object. This happens because each object is a floating object.

You also need to specify whether to align the objects to each other or to the page. For example, if you want to align the objects relative to the page, when you select the Align Top option, Word aligns the objects across the top of the page. If you do not align to the page, Word aligns them across the top based on the top of the highest-placed object on the page.

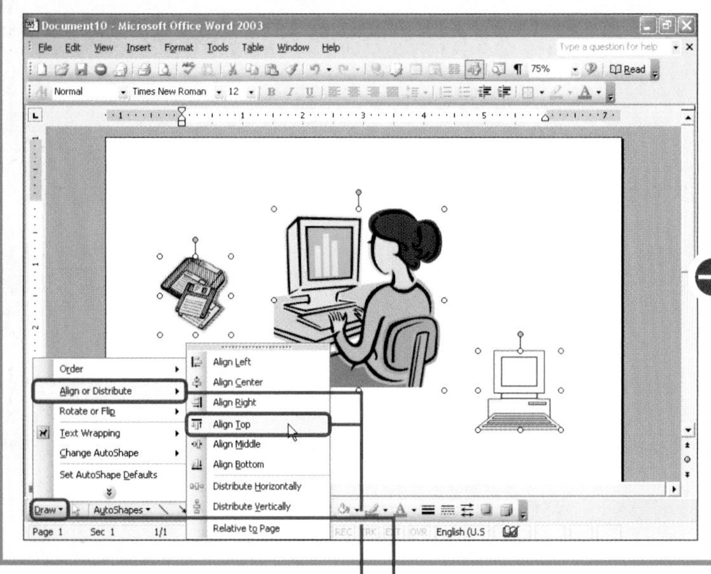

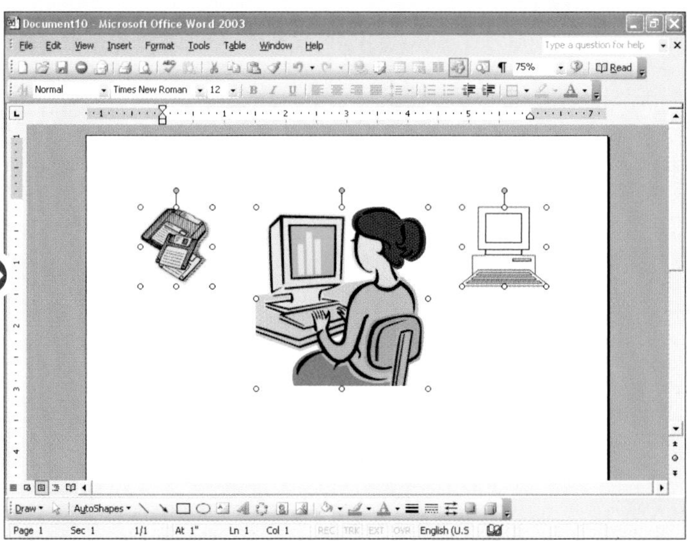

ALIGN TO TOP OF OBJECTS

1. Select the objects.

- If the Drawing toolbar is not displayed, click View ➪ Toolbars ➪ Drawing to display it.

2. Click Draw.
3. Click Align or Distribute.
4. Click Align Top.

- Word aligns the objects based on the top object.

Did You Know?

You can align the objects horizontally across the page by selecting the Distribute Horizontally option. You can arrange the objects vertically from top to bottom by selecting the Distribute Vertically option.

Caution!

Avoid using the Relative to Page option for documents that you want to print. This option moves the objects toward the specified edge of the page. In most cases, the printer cannot print all the way to the edge of the paper, which means that part of the images will be cut off.

Did You Know?

To align objects, you must select at least two different objects. If you do not do so, the options on the Align and Distribute menu will be grayed out.

ALIGN TO TOP OF PAGE

1. Select the objects.
2. Click Draw.
3. Click Align or Distribute.
4. Click Relative to Page.
5. Click Align Top.

- Word aligns the objects to the top of the page.

USE GRID LINES

to align shapes

You can turn on grid lines, called the *drawing grid,* in your Word document to help control the placement of shapes on the page. Grid lines are horizontal and vertical lines designed to help you place graphics on a page. You can align shapes by making them line up on a particular line in the grid.

By default, Word turns on the Snap Objects to Grid option. This means that as you move objects, Word automatically places them at the next set of grid lines.

You customize the drawing grid by specifying the distance between the horizontal and vertical lines. When you specify the grid size, you can indicate how frequently you want the lines to display on the screen. For example, you can create a grid with lines spaced at .25 inches, but you may only want the lines to display for every other grid, or at .5 inches. Keep in mind that Word will still snap to the closest grid lines, even if they are not visible.

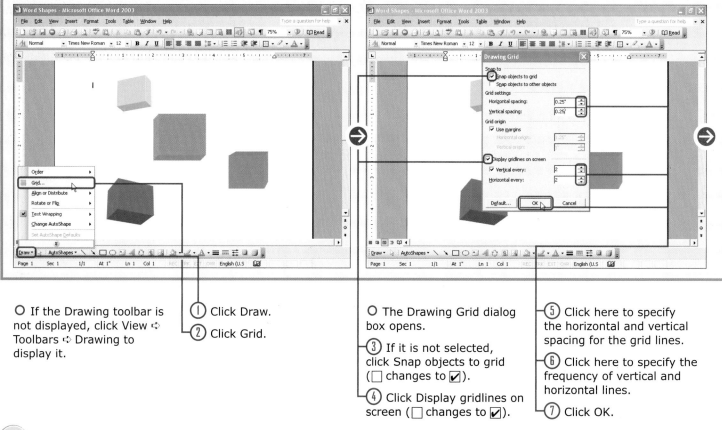

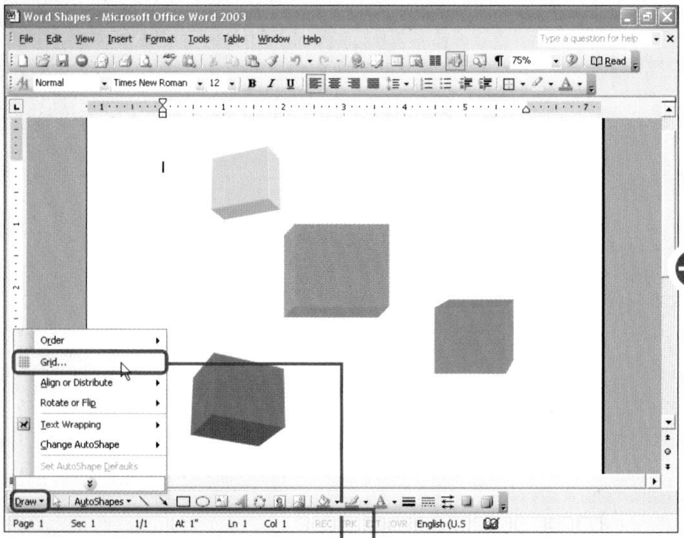

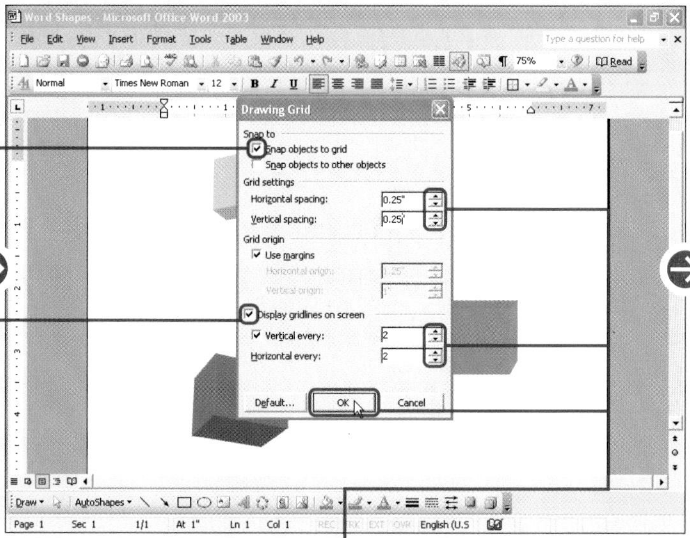

- If the Drawing toolbar is not displayed, click View ➪ Toolbars ➪ Drawing to display it.

1. Click Draw.
2. Click Grid.

- The Drawing Grid dialog box opens.

3. If it is not selected, click Snap objects to grid (☐ changes to ☑).
4. Click Display gridlines on screen (☐ changes to ☑).
5. Click here to specify the horizontal and vertical spacing for the grid lines.
6. Click here to specify the frequency of vertical and horizontal lines.
7. Click OK.

Did You Know?

Word creates the grid within the page margins. To change the grid size, deselect the Use Margins option. In the Horizontal Origin field, specify the distance for the grid from the left edge of the page. In the Vertical Origin field, indicate the location for the grid from the top of the page.

Did You Know?

When you move 3D shapes, Word bases the placement of the object on the front of the object.

Customize It!

To always use the same grid size when you move shapes on the page, specify your grid settings as the default settings by clicking Default. Keep in mind that these settings are active whether or not you display the grid on the page.

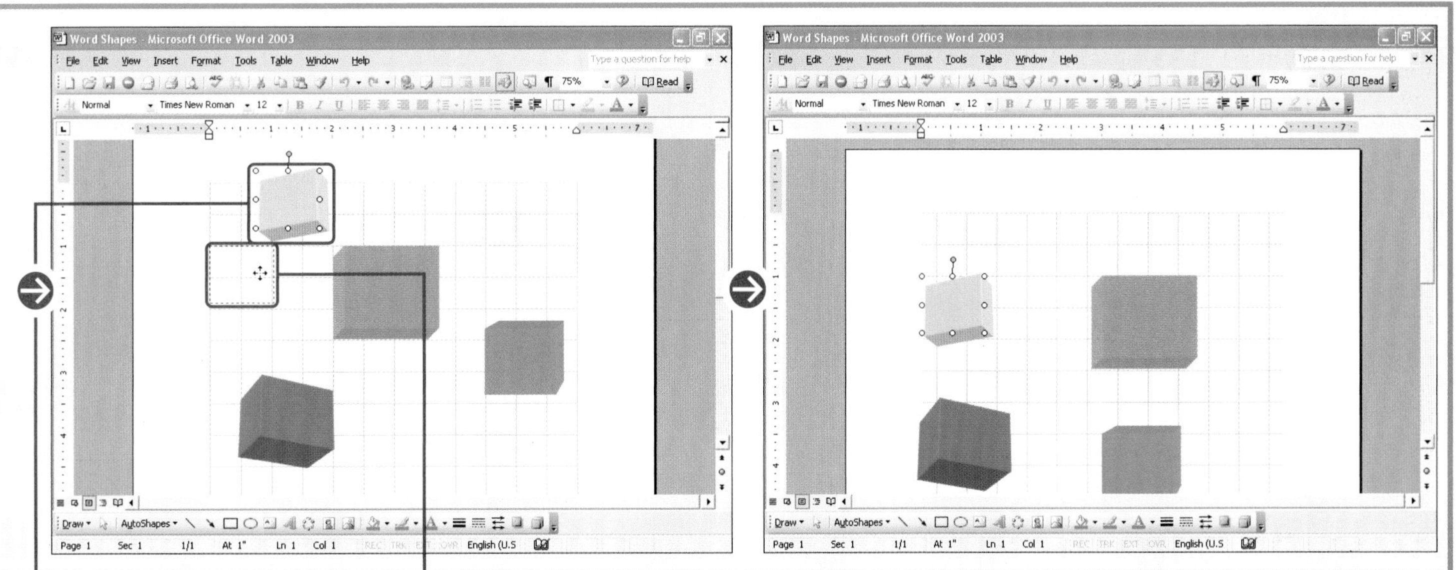

- A grid appears on the page.

8 Click a shape.

9 Drag it to the desired location on the grid.

10 Repeat steps **8** and **9** for each shape.

- Word places the shapes on the page based on the grid settings.

INSERT CAPTIONS

for tables, equations, and graphics

You can create captions for tables, equations, and graphic images in your documents. When you use the caption option, you can later create a table of figures using the captions from the document. See Chapter 6 for more information about creating a table of figures.

When you create a caption for an object in your document, Word creates a text label with the Caption style. The numbered portion of the caption is inserted using the SEQ field. The SEQ field is used to make sure that the objects are numbered sequentially. For example, all figures are numbered sequentially starting with Figure 1.

You need to select the text to use for the caption. Word provides three different captions from which to select. You also need to select the location of the caption in respect to the object. You can place the caption either above or below the object.

You can select the numbering style used for the caption. By default, captions are numbered starting with 1, but you can also used alphabetic characters or Roman numerals.

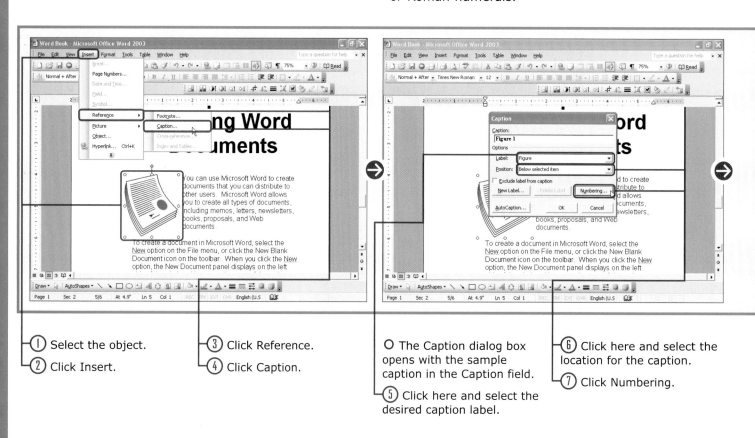

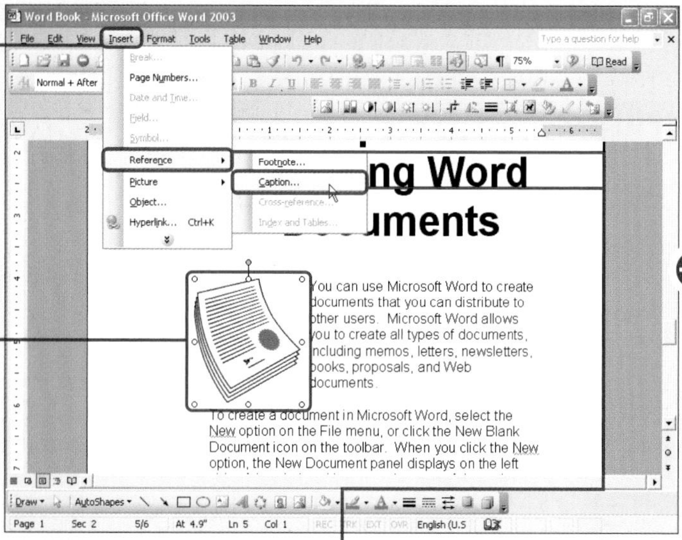

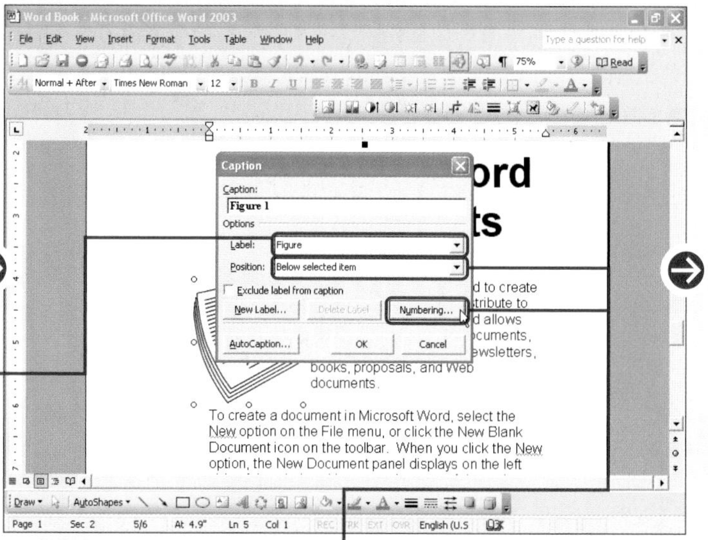

1. Select the object.
2. Click Insert.
3. Click Reference.
4. Click Caption.

- The Caption dialog box opens with the sample caption in the Caption field.

5. Click here and select the desired caption label.
6. Click here and select the location for the caption.
7. Click Numbering.

#34

DIFFICULTY LEVEL

Did You Know?

You can create your own caption label by clicking the New Label button in the Caption dialog box. When you type a new label in the New Label dialog box, the new label is added to the Label list in the Caption dialog box.

Did You Know?

You can have Word automatically place captions on specific types of objects by clicking the AutoCaption button. In the AutoCaption dialog box, select the types of objects that you want to have captioned.

Caution!

You should avoid changing the numeric portion of the caption. Word uses sequential numbering for the caption numbers. If you alter a number manually, the numbering for the remaining captions in the document will not be correct.

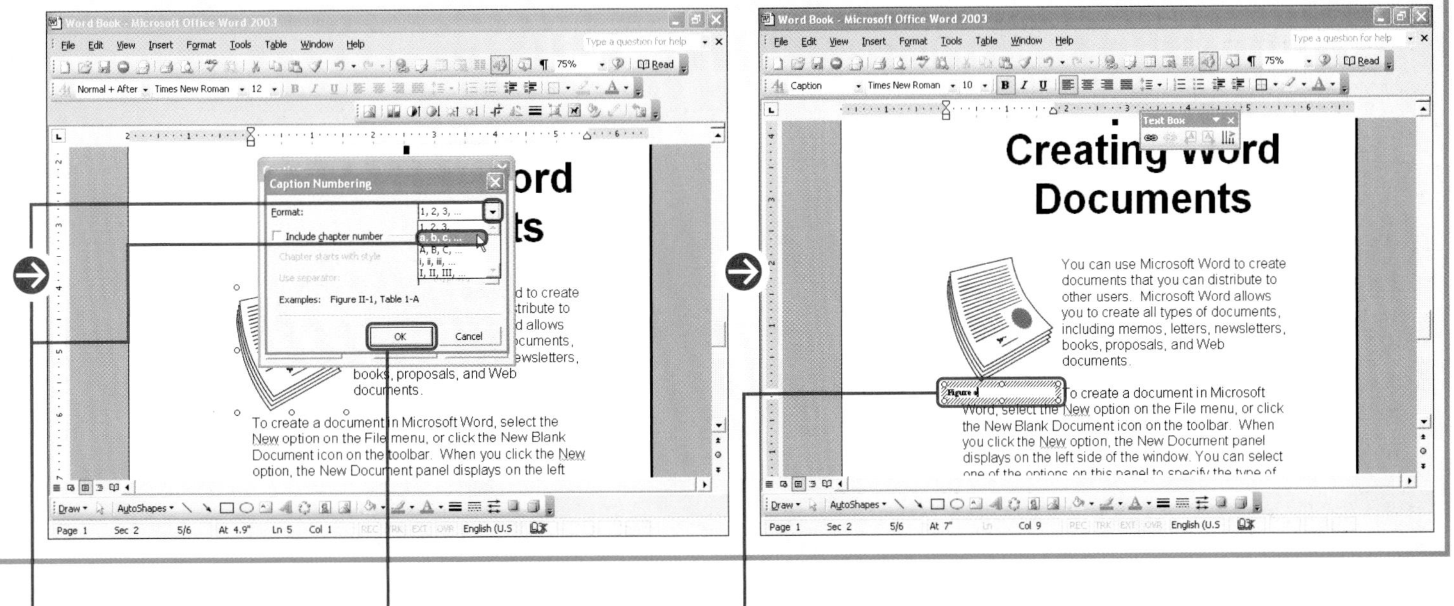

- The Caption Numbering dialog box opens.
- 8 Click here to display the available number formats.
- 9 Select the format that you want.

Note: You can also include the chapter number. See Chapter 1 for more information on numbering.

- 10 Click OK.

- Word creates a caption for the object.

Turn a graphic object into a WATERMARK

You can convert any graphic image to a watermark in Word. You can use watermarks when you want to have a background graphic or text on the page.

The most common method of watermarking with a graphic image is to click Format ⇨ Background ⇨ Printed Watermark. With this option, however, you can only create one watermark for the document, and it repeats on every page.

A more flexible method enables you to specify the watermark location on the page and place multiple watermarks. You have to add the watermarks to each page where you want them to appear. You can use this method for any object that you add, including Word clip art images and Excel worksheets. See task #39 for more information about embedding Excel worksheets.

You make a graphic object into a watermark by changing the properties of the object to place it behind the text. You can also make the object appear washed out.

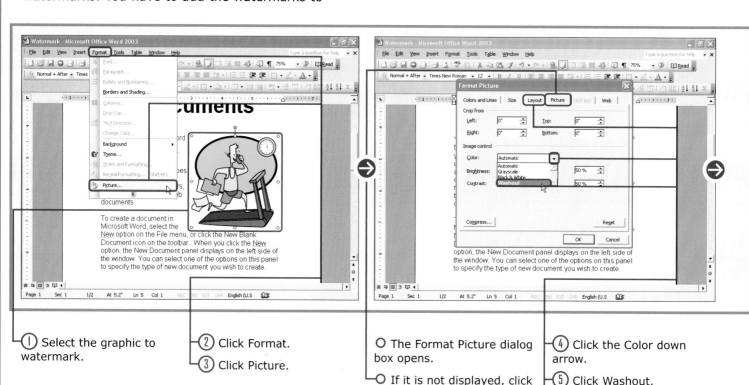

1. Select the graphic to watermark.
2. Click Format.
3. Click Picture.

- The Format Picture dialog box opens.
- If it is not displayed, click the Picture tab.

4. Click the Color down arrow.
5. Click Washout.
6. Click the Layout tab.

Did You Know?

You can change the location of the watermarked image by clicking and dragging it to the desired new location.

Apply It!

If the Washout option makes your graphic too light, you can fade it by changing the brightness and contrast settings on the Picture tab. The brighter you make the image, the more washed out it will appear. The higher the Contrast value, the more visible the image will be.

Put It Together!

You can combine both types of watermarking on the same page. For example, to place a watermark image on all the pages, use the Format ➪ Background ➪ Printed Watermark option. To add another watermark to a specific page, insert the graphic and watermark it as described in this section.

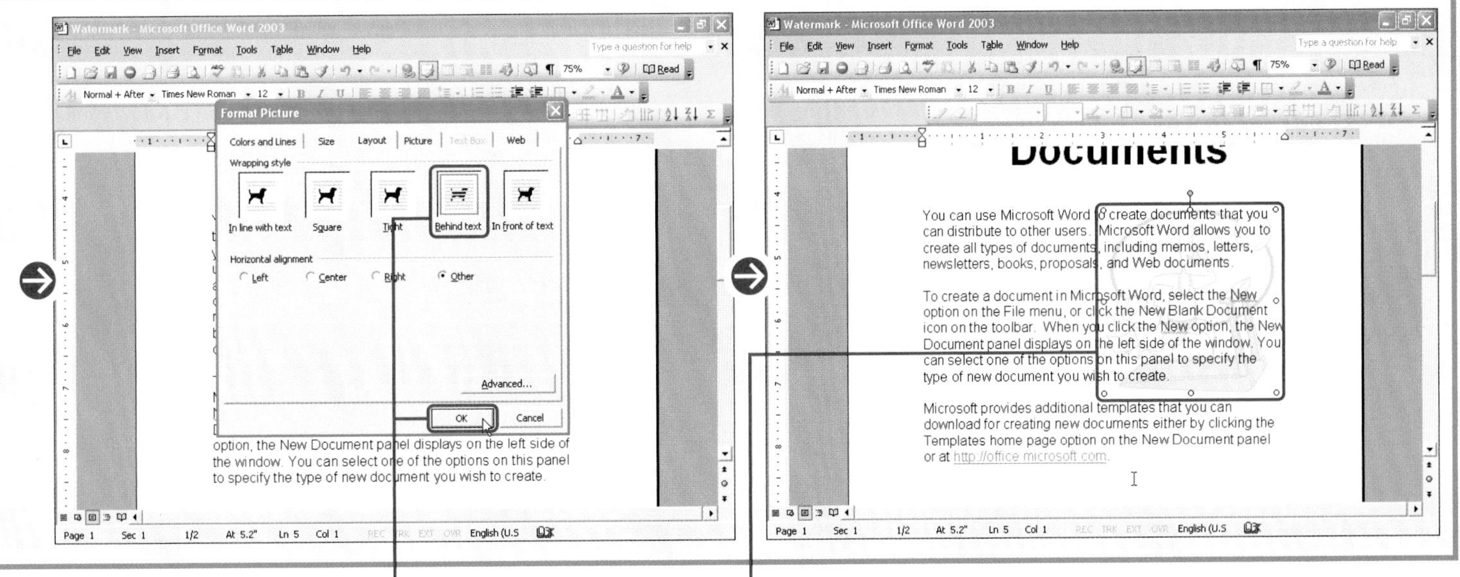

- The Layout tab appears.

7. Click Behind text.
8. Click OK.

- Word places the image in the background and allows text to flow over it.

WRAP TEXT

around a graphic

You can have Word *wrap* text around a graphic image in your document, which means that you can place a graphic within a paragraph and have the text flow around its sides. If you do not wrap the text, Word places the text either above or below the graphic.

To wrap text around a graphic, you need to select the appropriate text wrapping style. Typically, you use the Square option. This style wraps the text around the square bounding box that surrounds the graphic image.

You need to indicate the sides of the image where you want the text to wrap around the image. For example, you may want the text to wrap only on the right side of the image; if so, you select Right only.

You can also indicate the amount of space that you want between the graphic image and the text. You can specify space for each side of the image. Keep in mind that you also need to be aware of the amount of space between the text that precedes and follows the graphic.

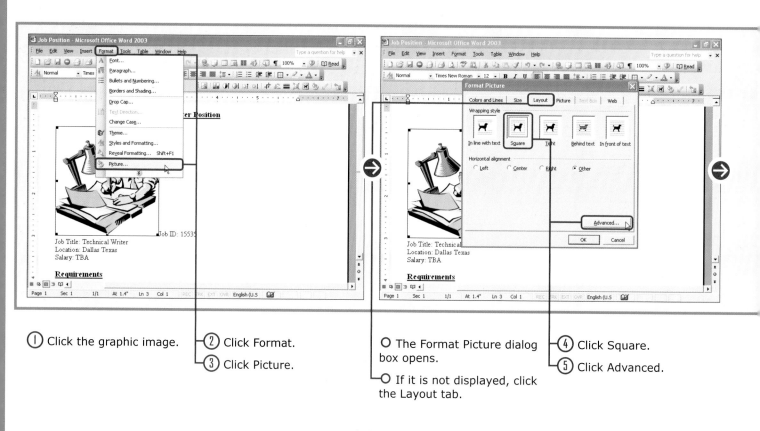

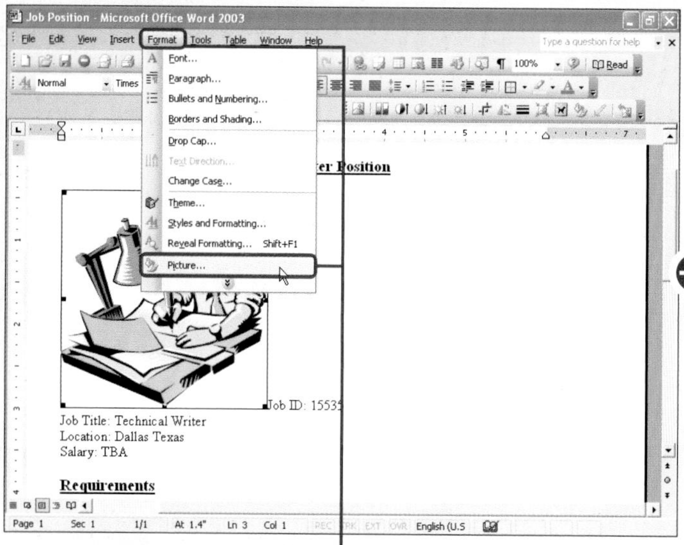

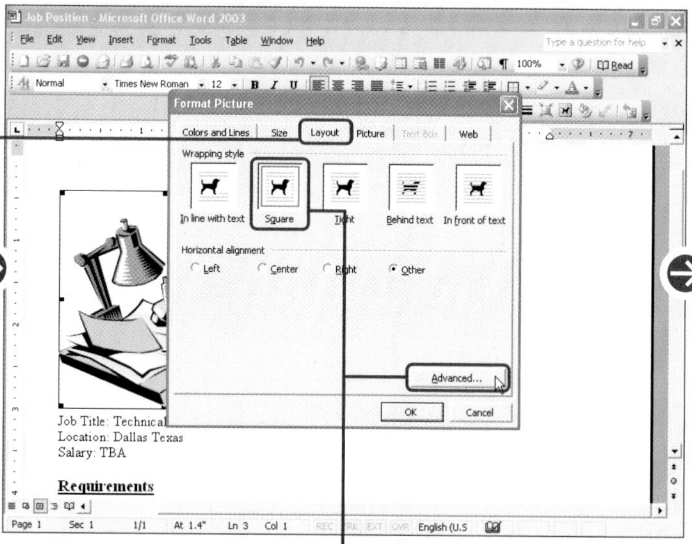

1. Click the graphic image.
2. Click Format.
3. Click Picture.

- The Format Picture dialog box opens.
- If it is not displayed, click the Layout tab.

4. Click Square.
5. Click Advanced.

#36

DIFFICULTY LEVEL

Did You Know?

The Horizontal Alignment radio buttons enable you to specify the location of the graphic with respect to the page. If you manually specified a location for the graphic, select Other.

Did You Know?

You can select from five different text wrapping styles, as shown in the following table.

Style	Description
In Line with Text	Inserts graphic at the insertion point in a line of text. Text flows above and below the graphic.
Square	Wraps text around the bounding box of the graphic.
Tight	Wraps text around the actual edges of the graphic.
Behind Text	Places graphic on a layer behind the text.
In Front of Text	Places graphic on a layer in front of the text.

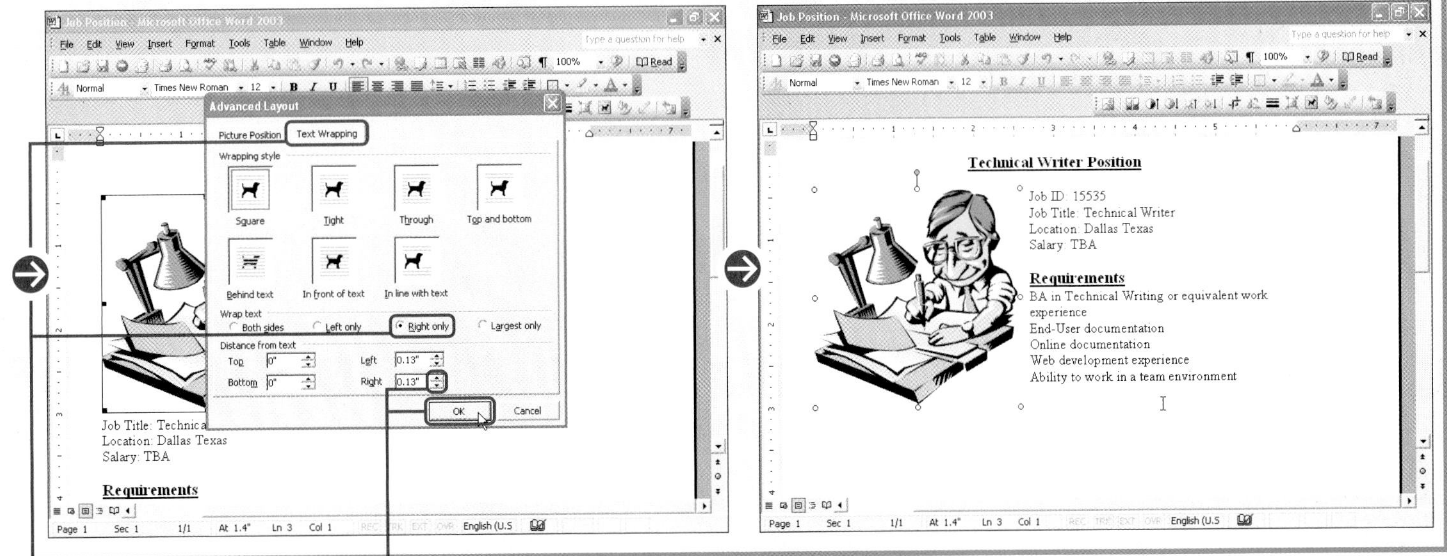

- The Advanced Layout dialog box opens.
- If it is not selected, click Text Wrapping.

6. Click Right only to wrap the text on the right side of the graphic (○ changes to ⦿).

Note: You can also select Left only, Both sides, or Largest only.

7. Click here to specify the distance between the graphic and the text.
8. Click OK.

- Word wraps the text on the specified side of the graphic.

Make areas of a graphic TRANSPARENT

You can make areas of a graphic transparent within your Word document. When you do so, the background color is displayed in the transparent portion of the picture. You can use this option when you want to replace a color in a graphic image. You make the original color transparent and then replace it with a color that you assign to the background.

You can set only one transparent color for a graphic image in Word. You do so using the Set Transparent Color button on the Picture toolbar. Because you can apply only one transparent color to a graphic image, if you select a different color, the previous selection reverts back to the original color.

If you want the color that is displayed behind the transparent selection to be different than the page color, you need to set a background color for the picture. When you set a background color, it is applied behind the picture and is displayed in all transparent locations. You set the background color in the Format Picture dialog box.

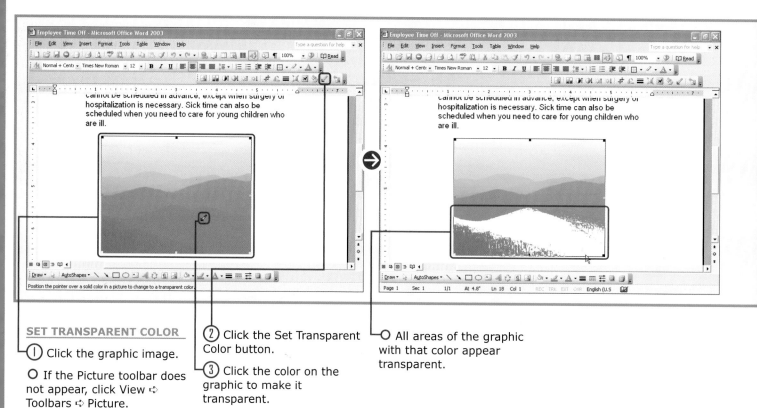

SET TRANSPARENT COLOR

① Click the graphic image.

○ If the Picture toolbar does not appear, click View ⇨ Toolbars ⇨ Picture.

② Click the Set Transparent Color button.

③ Click the color on the graphic to make it transparent.

○ All areas of the graphic with that color appear transparent.

Did You Know?

If you want to set more than one transparent color in the graphic, you need to use an external graphics package. You cannot create transparent colors on animated GIFs; you need to use an external animated GIF editing package.

Did You Know?

When you print a graphic that has transparent color, the transparent portion remains the color of the paper that you print it on if no background color was applied.

Did You Know?

If you no longer want a transparent color, you can restore the original image by clicking the Reset Picture button ( ). Keep in mind that clicking this button restores all original settings for the graphic, including the size.

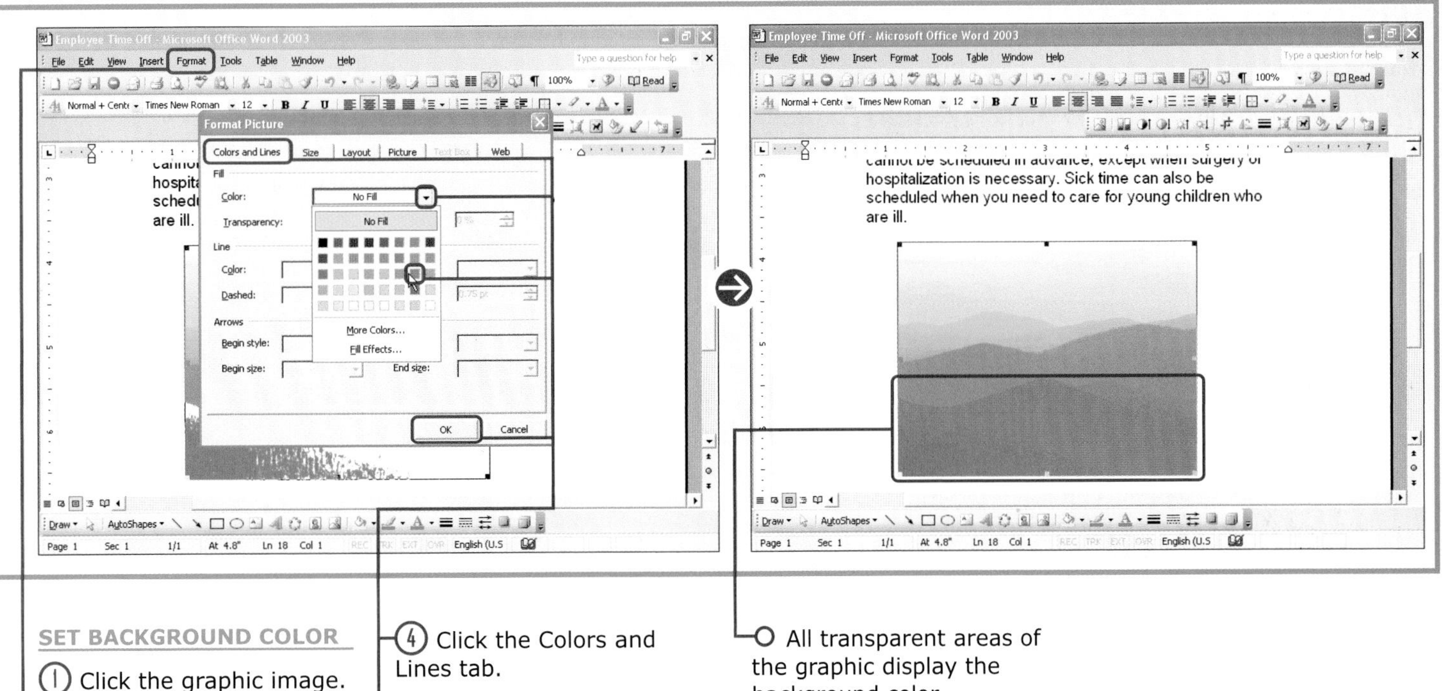

SET BACKGROUND COLOR

1. Click the graphic image.
2. Click Format.
3. Click Picture.

- The Format Picture dialog box opens.

4. Click the Colors and Lines tab.
5. Click the down arrow.
6. Click the desired background color.
7. Click OK.

- All transparent areas of the graphic display the background color.

Add new graphics to the CLIP ORGANIZER

You can add graphic images that you use frequently to the Clip Organizer. When you do so, you no longer have to remember where the graphic files are located. You can select the images from the Clip Organizer using the same steps that you use to select other clip art images.

When you add graphics to the Clip Organizer, Word creates collection lists under the My Collections folder. This process keeps the clips that you create separate from the clip art available with Microsoft Office or for download from the Internet.

The Clip Organizer enables you to view thumbnail images of all the clip art images to which you have access. The images provided with Office and on the Web are sorted into folders based on different categories.

After you add an image to the clip art collection, when you search for a clip in the Clip Art dialog box the added image will also appear in the list.

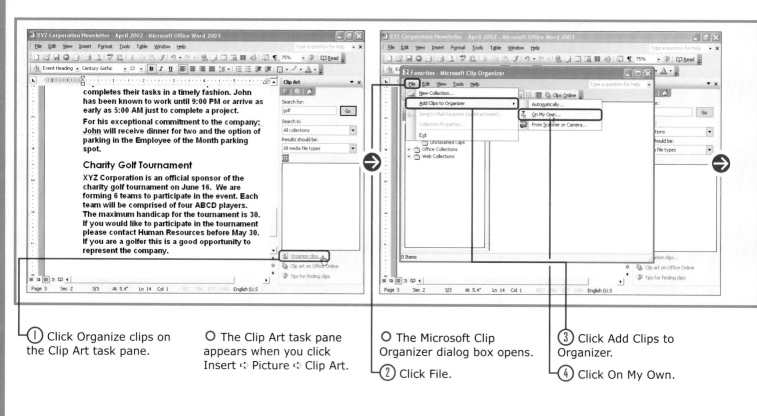

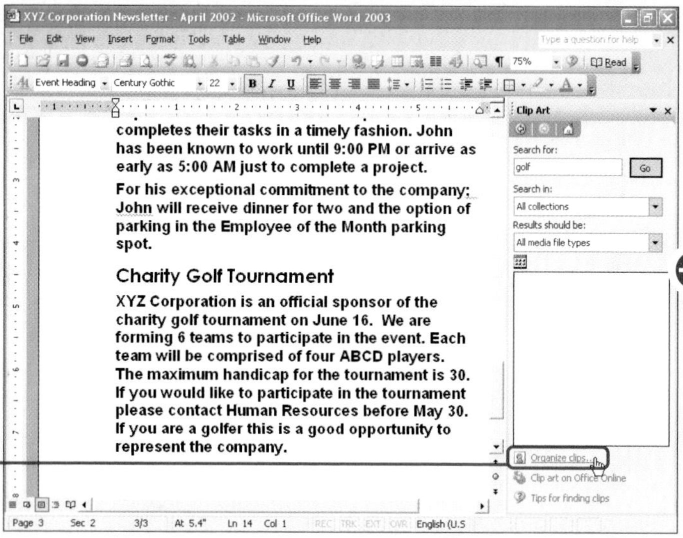

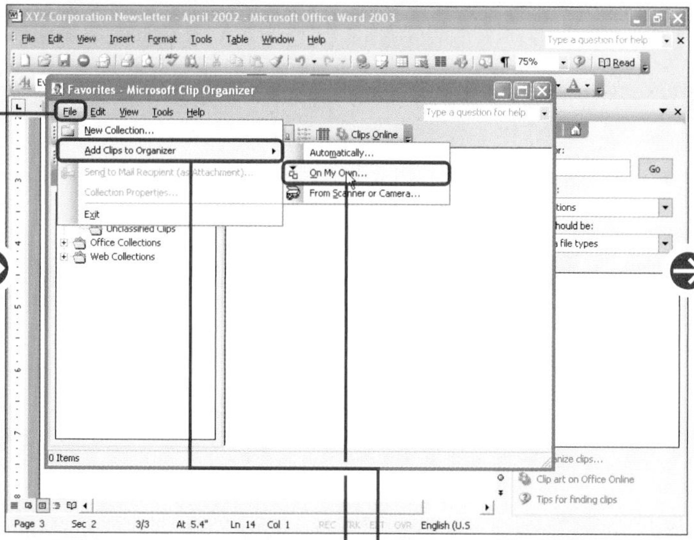

1 Click Organize clips on the Clip Art task pane.

- The Clip Art task pane appears when you click Insert ⇨ Picture ⇨ Clip Art.

- The Microsoft Clip Organizer dialog box opens.

2 Click File.

3 Click Add Clips to Organizer.

4 Click On My Own.

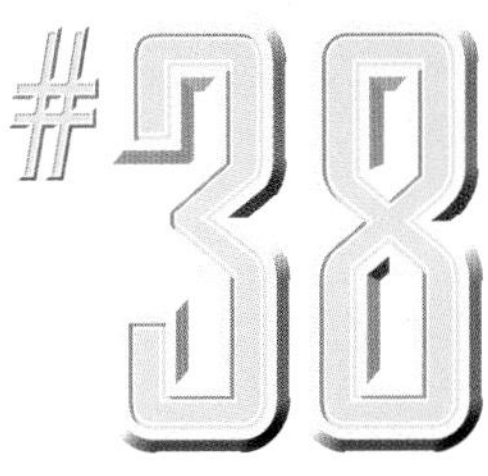

Did You Know?

You can create folders to organize the images that you add. You create a folder in the Microsoft Clip Organizer dialog box by clicking File ➪ New Collection. Type the name of the folder in the New Collection dialog box. After you create the collection folder, you can click an image and drag it to the folder.

Did You Know?

Word uses the keywords associated with the graphic image to locate the clip art images that match your search criteria. You can specify the keywords to use as search criteria for the new clip art images that you add. To specify keywords, right-click on the image and click the Preview/Properties option. Type the desired keywords in the Keywords list box.

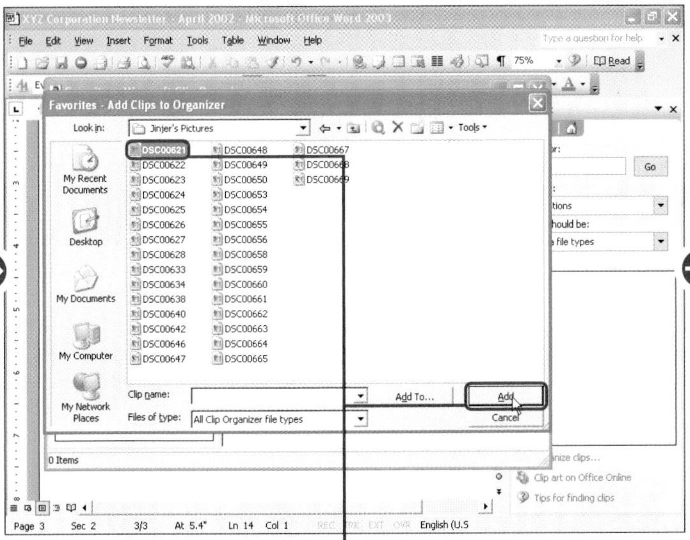

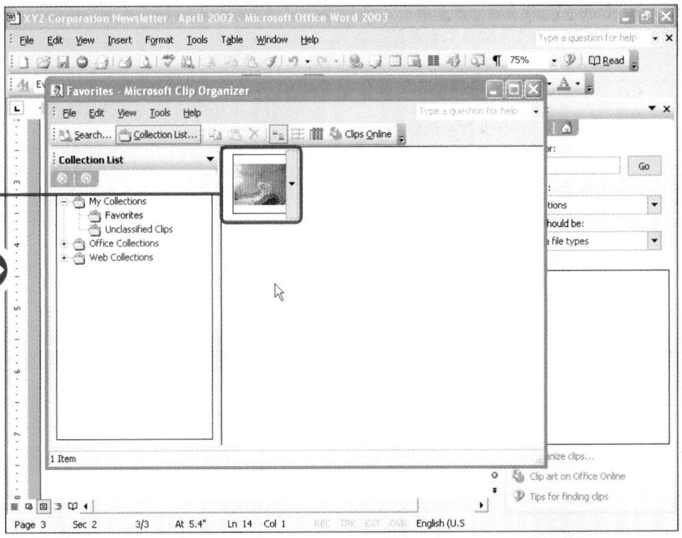

- The Add Clips to Organizer dialog box opens.

⑤ Select the desired graphic files.

⑥ Click Add.

- Word adds the graphic to the My Collections folder.

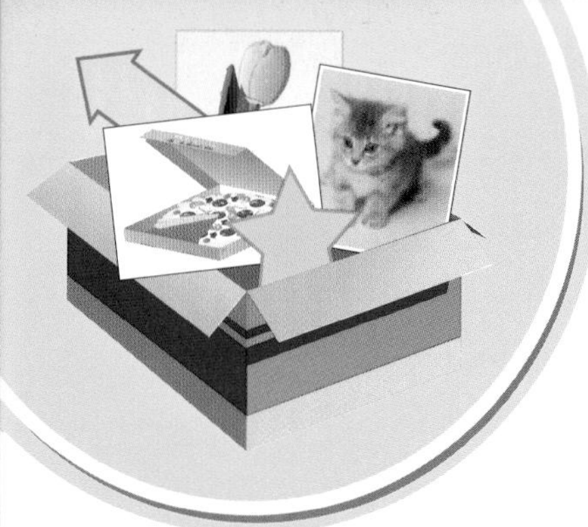

Embed an EXCEL WORKSHEET

You can place an Excel worksheet directly in a Word document. When you do so, a copy of the original Excel file becomes part of the Word document. Any changes that you make to the embedded file do not affect the original source file.

When you embed an Excel worksheet, Word actually embeds it as an object. You have the option of either creating a new object or embedding an object that you already have created.

You can view and modify the worksheet, which means that you essentially have the capabilities of Excel while working within Word. To do so, however, you must have Excel loaded on your computer. This same limitation is true for other object types.

You embed an Excel worksheet by locating it with the Browse dialog box. When you select it, Word embeds the entire workbook in the document. However, you can only display the active sheet within your document. To change the sheet, select the object and select a new active sheet.

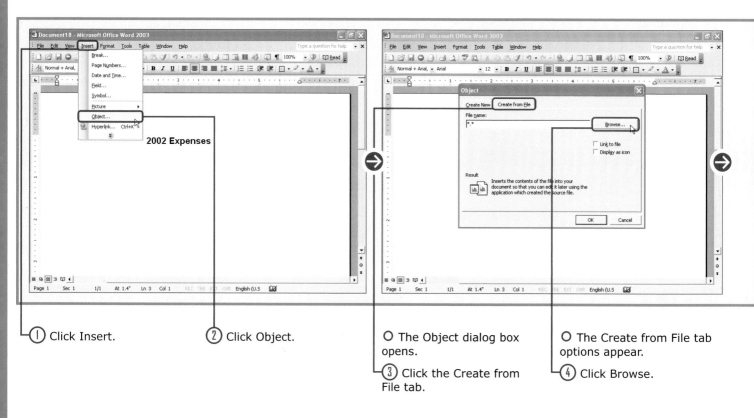

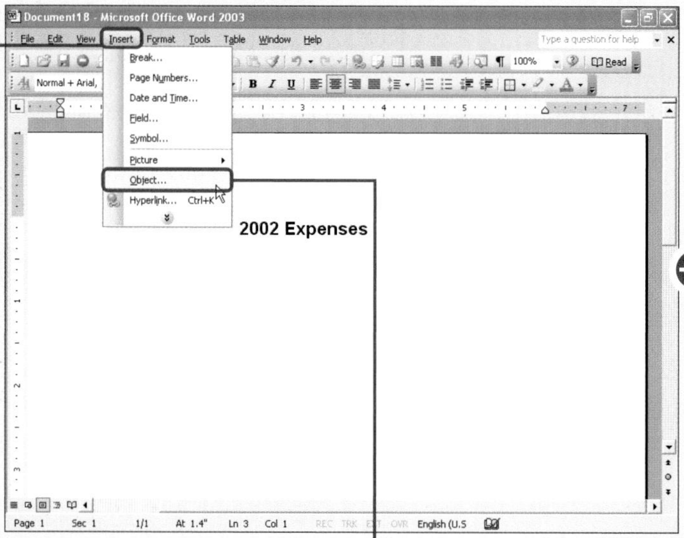

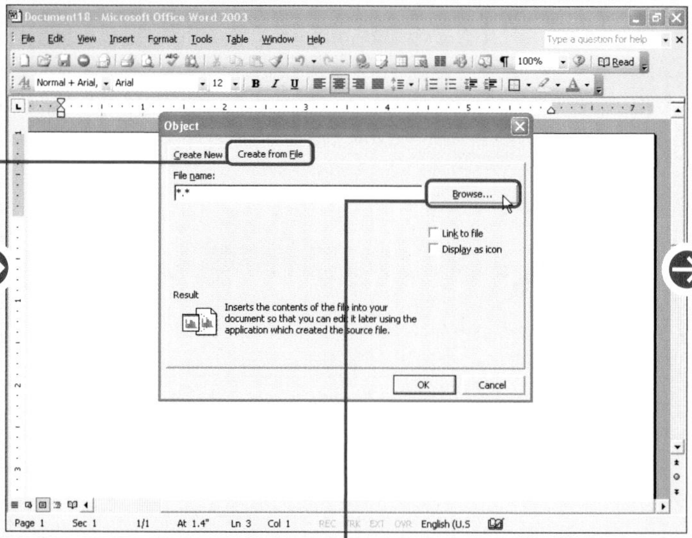

1. Click Insert.
2. Click Object.

- The Object dialog box opens.

3. Click the Create from File tab.

- The Create from File tab options appear.

4. Click Browse.

Did You Know?

You can add objects to a document by embedding or linking them. With an embedded file, all data is stored in the Word document. With a linked object, the Word document stores only a link to the source file. Any changes made to the source are updated in your Word document. To create a linked file, click Link to File in the Object dialog box. Word must be able to locate the file whenever you open the Word document. To update a linked object at any time click Edit ➪ Update Link.

Put It Together!

If you plan to share a document with an embedded worksheet, you can lock it to prevent someone from altering it by clicking Tools ➪ Protection ➪ Protect Sheet and specifying a password.

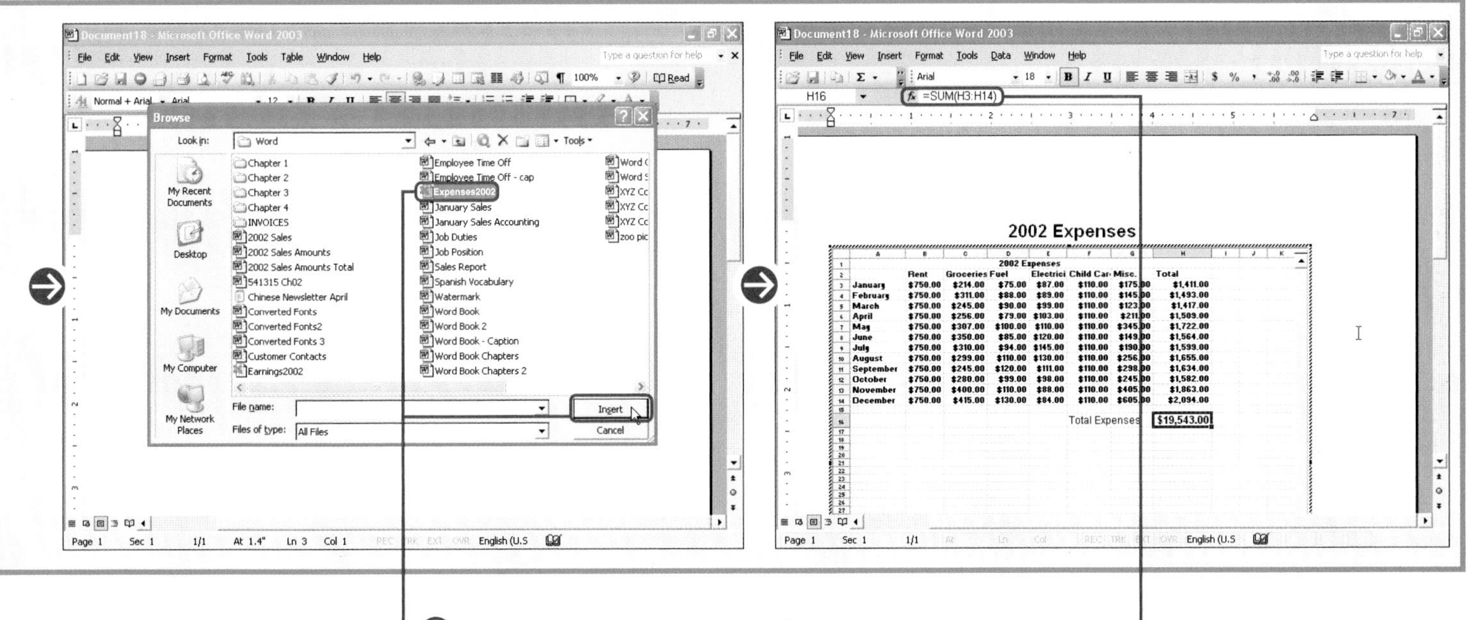

- The Browse dialog box opens.

5. Locate the Excel workbook file that you want to embed.
6. Click Insert.

- Word embeds the selected workbook in your document.
- When you select the workbook object, the menu options change to reflect Excel options.

CREATE AN EQUATION

to show a mathematical computation

You can create equations within your Word document to illustrate a mathematical computation. This option is useful when you need to use an equation to provide additional information in your document.

You create equations using Microsoft Equation. The program launches a toolbar that provides over 150 different symbols and templates that you can use to create an equation. Just like other Word objects, when you are editing the equation, the Microsoft Equation menus appear at the top of the window.

You can use any of the options from the menus to customize the look of the equation.

Microsoft Equation helps you create the equation by adjusting the font size and number placement based on the size of the object. The placement and size of the symbols and numeric values in the equation are based on mathematical typesetting conventions.

If you want the equation to be larger, you can simply resize the bounding box for the equation within Word. When you do so, the sizing changes proportionately.

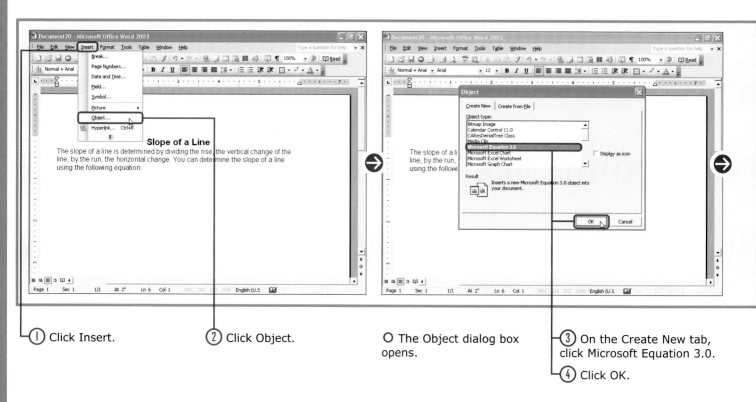

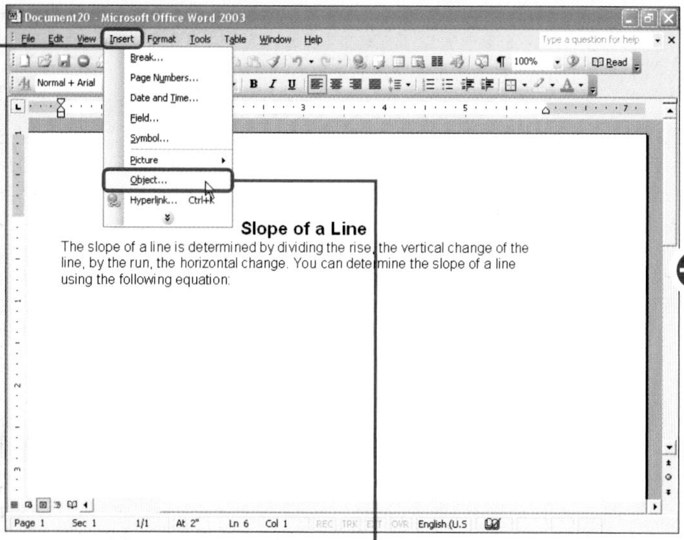

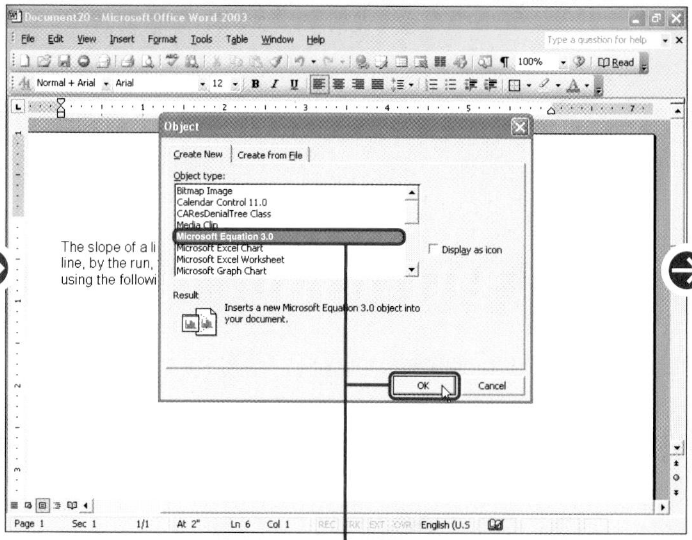

1. Click Insert.
2. Click Object.

- The Object dialog box opens.

3. On the Create New tab, click Microsoft Equation 3.0.
4. Click OK.

#40

DIFFICULTY LEVEL

Did You Know?

The equation that you create is for display purposes only. The equation does not actually perform any calculations. If want to perform a calculation, you need to use one of the mathematical fields. See Chapter 3 for more information on using fields.

Put It Together!

If the Equation Editor is not available, you can load it using the Add/Remove Programs option on the Windows Control Panel. Make sure the Microsoft Office CD is inserted in the drive, select the Microsoft Office option, and click Change. Click Add or Remove Features and then click Next. Click Choose advanced customization of applications and then click Next. Expand the Office Tools menu and click the down arrow next to the Equation Editor. Select Run from My Computer and then click Update.

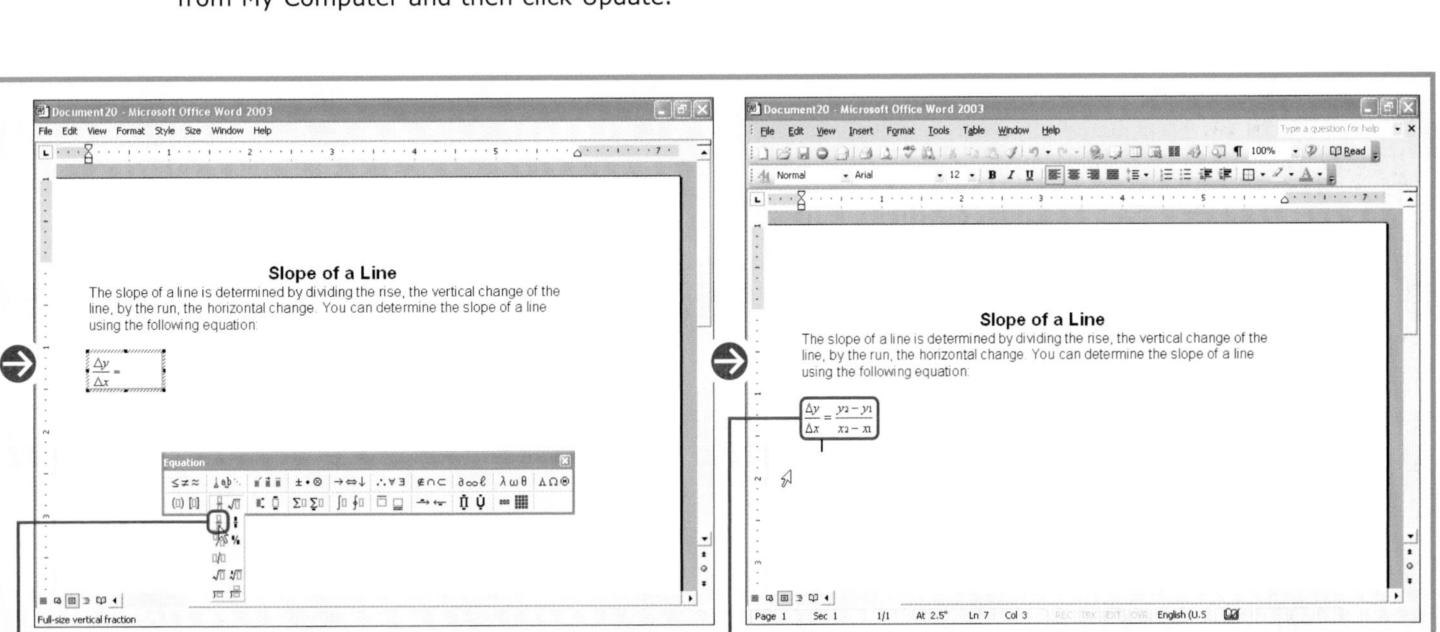

- The Equation toolbar and Equation menu appear.

5. Click the desired symbols and templates on the Equation toolbar.

Note: You can combine your equation symbols with any text or numeric values.

6. When complete, click to the side of the equation.

- Word displays the equation object.

Using Macros and Fields

You can use macros and fields in your documents to automate specific tasks. Macros enable you to have Word automatically perform a series of steps. Fields enable you to automatically insert specific text into the document.

You can create macros either by recording tasks that you perform in Word or manually by creating Visual Basic for Applications (VBA) code to execute. When you create macros, you can choose to either have the macro activated when you press a specific key sequence or when you click a button on a toolbar.

Where you store a macro is important. If you want the macro available for all documents, you need to store it in the Normal.dot template file. This file opens whenever you run Microsoft Word, and any macros in the file are available for all open documents. If you store the macro in a specific document, it is only available when you have that document open.

You can use fields in your document to insert specific text. For example, if you have repeated text that needs to be frequently updated, you can insert an AutoText field. This enables you to update the corresponding AutoText entry and then update its references when you refresh the fields.

This chapter provides some useful tips for creating and working with macros and fields in your document. It also looks at how the two can be combined to execute a macro when a field is selected.

TOP 100

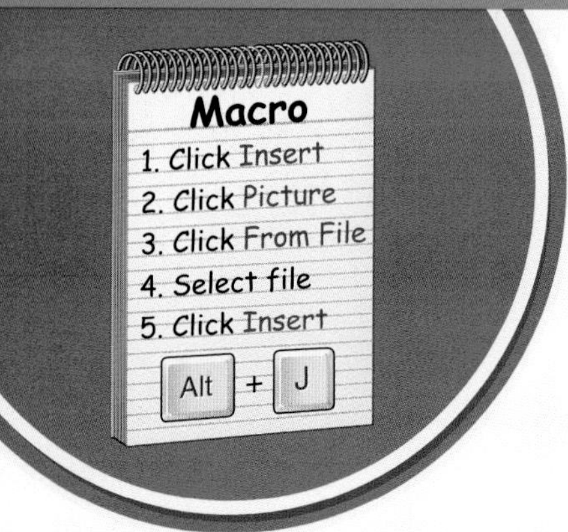
Macro
1. Click Insert
2. Click Picture
3. Click From File
4. Select file
5. Click Insert
Alt + J

Adjust MACRO SECURITY

You can specify the security level for Word to use when opening any document that contains macros. This option enables you to control the loading of macros, thus eliminating potential computer viruses often contained in macros.

Word has three different security settings for opening documents that contain macros: Low, Medium, and High. You should typically avoid using the Low security because it allows Word to load all documents without checking the macros. The High security option allows macros to load only from trusted sources. If you want the option of loading all macros with your verification, select the Medium setting.

When you open a document that contains a macro, Word displays the Security Warning dialog box. If the macros have a *digital signature,* a verification from the macro creator to verify the safety of the macro, the digital signature information appears in the dialog box. If you are willing to open all macros from that source, you can make the macro creator a trusted source. If you do so, the Security Warning dialog box no longer appears when you open macros from that source.

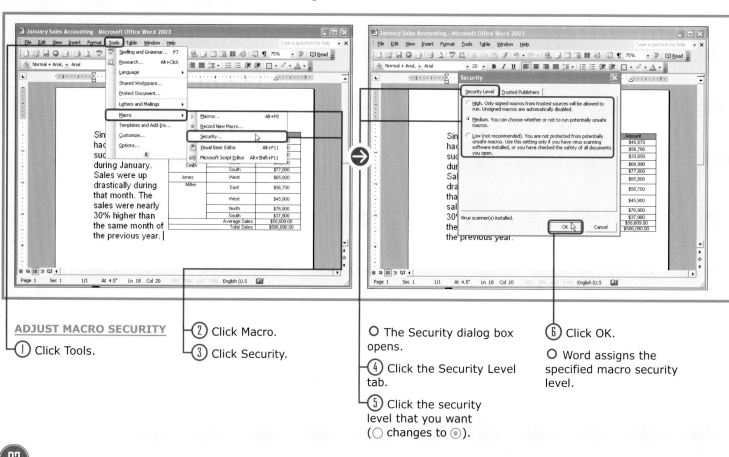

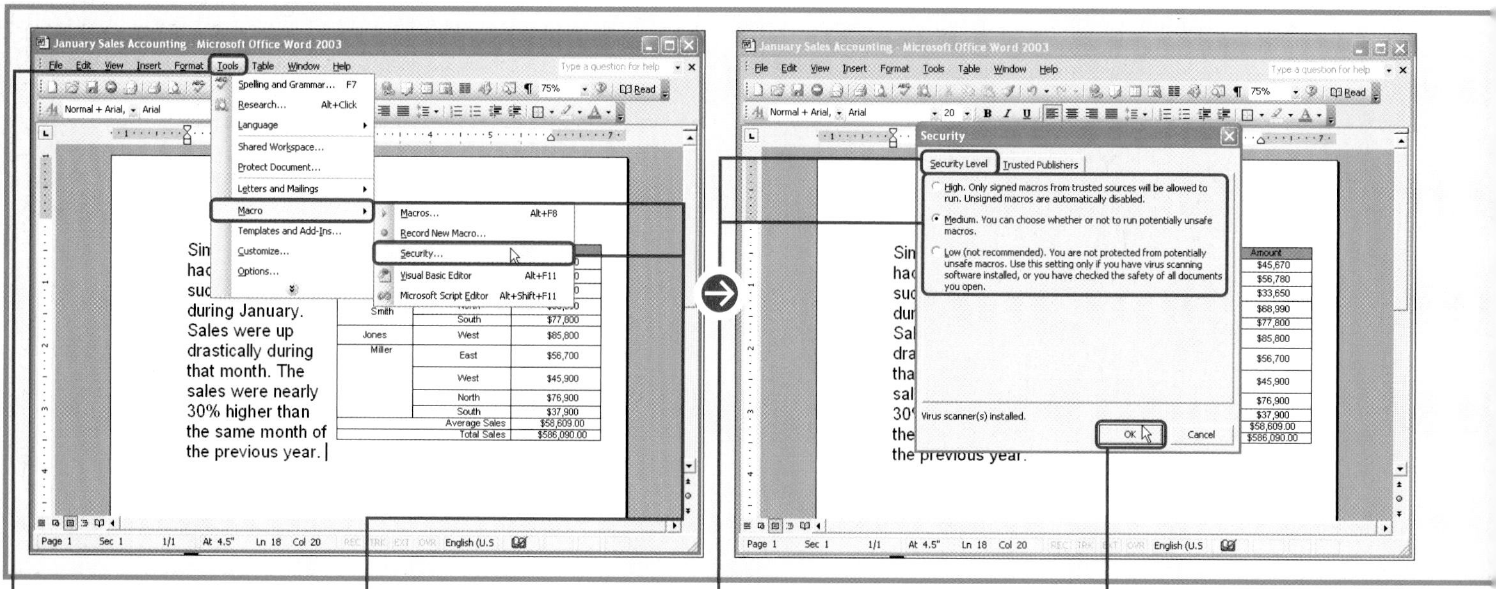

ADJUST MACRO SECURITY

1. Click Tools.
2. Click Macro.
3. Click Security.

- The Security dialog box opens.

4. Click the Security Level tab.
5. Click the security level that you want (○ changes to ◉).
6. Click OK.

- Word assigns the specified macro security level.

DIFFICULTY LEVEL

Did You Know?

If you no longer want to trust macros from a source listed on the Trusted Publishers tab, you can highlight the name of the publisher and click Remove. The next time you open a document containing macros from that source, Word prompts you to accept the macros by displaying the Security Warning dialog box.

Did You Know?

To get more information about a trusted source, highlight the source on the Trusted Publishers tab and click View. Word displays the Certificate dialog box, which provides details about the creation of the digital certificate.

Did You Know?

If you modify a document that contains a digital certificate, the digital certificate is removed when you save the document. This ensures that only unaltered documents are digitally signed.

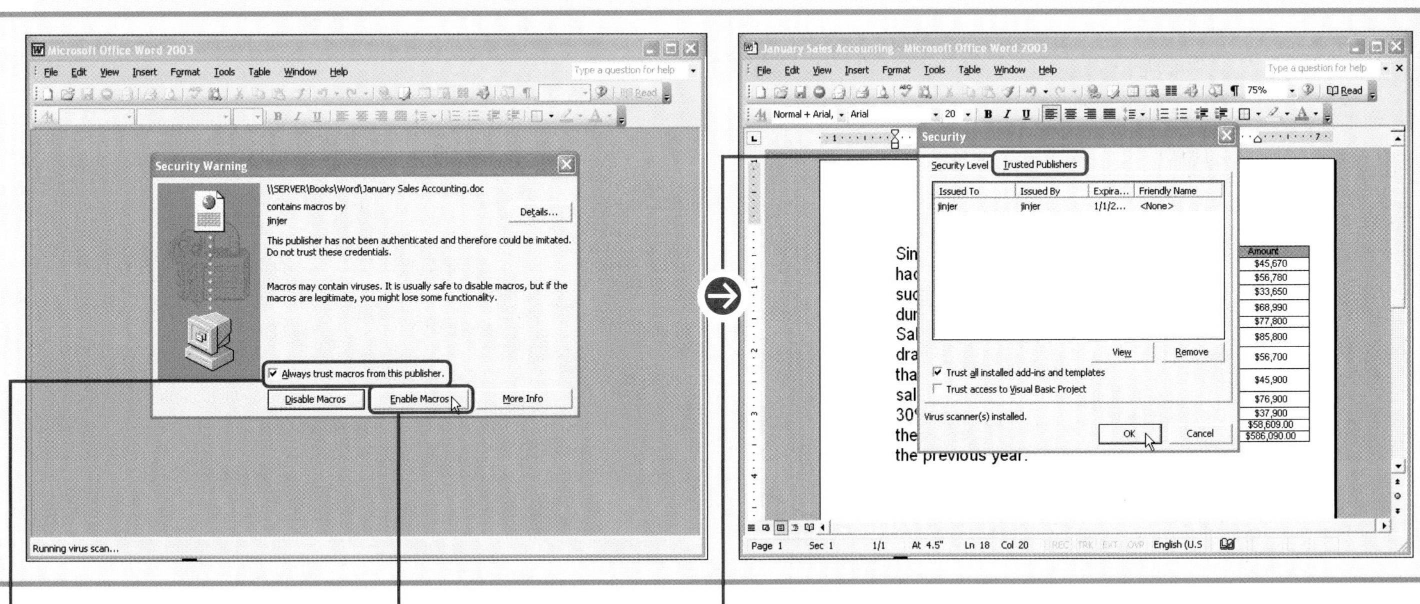

SET TRUSTED SOURCE

1. Open the document containing macros.
2. Click Always trust macros from this publisher.
3. Click Enable Macros.

- Word adds the digital certificate to the Trusted Sources list.
- Word opens the document and enables the macros.

4. In the Security dialog box, click the Trusted Publishers tab.

- The Security dialog box opens when you click Tools ⇨ Macro ⇨ Security.
- The tab lists the trusted macro publishers.

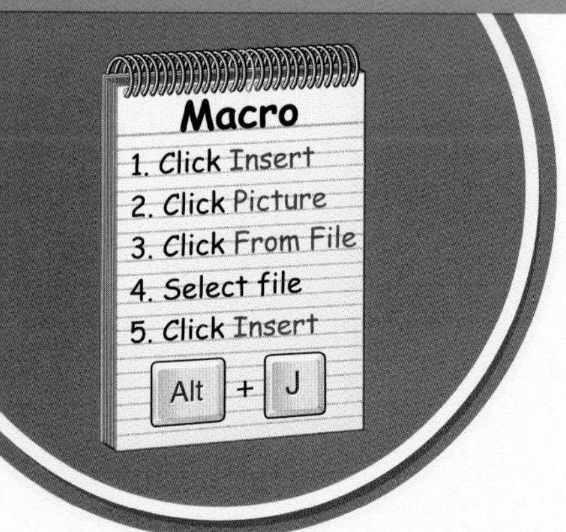
Macro
1. Click Insert
2. Click Picture
3. Click From File
4. Select file
5. Click Insert
Alt + J

RECORD A MACRO

to automate your work

You can use a macro to automate a series of steps in Word, such as applying special formatting. The easiest method for creating a macro is to use the Record New Macro option. When you select this option, Word captures every selection and keystroke that you make and creates a macro of those steps. You can repeat the same steps by running the recorded macro.

Before recording a macro, you should plan out the steps that you want to perform in the macro. This eliminates the recording of excess steps and makes the macro run more efficiently.

You need to decide where you want to store the macro that you create. If you want the macro available only to the current document, you should store it in that location. To make the macro available for all documents that you open, store the macro in the Normal.dot template file. You should assign a macro name that corresponds to the steps the macro performs.

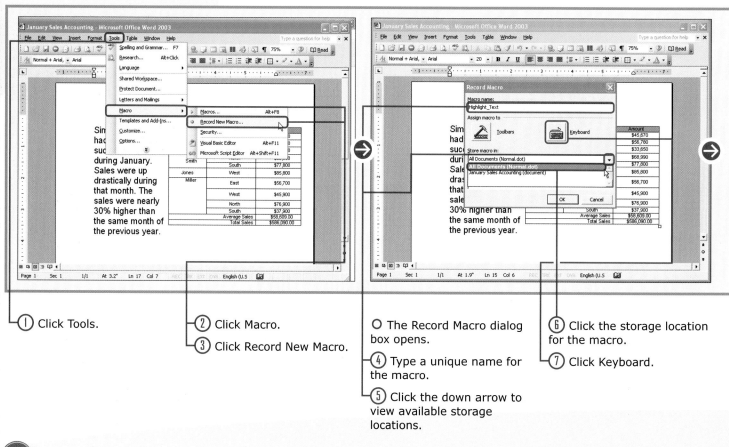

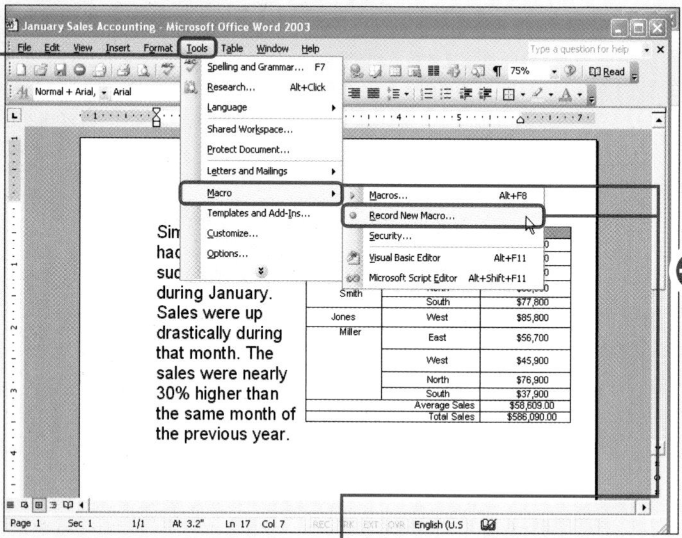

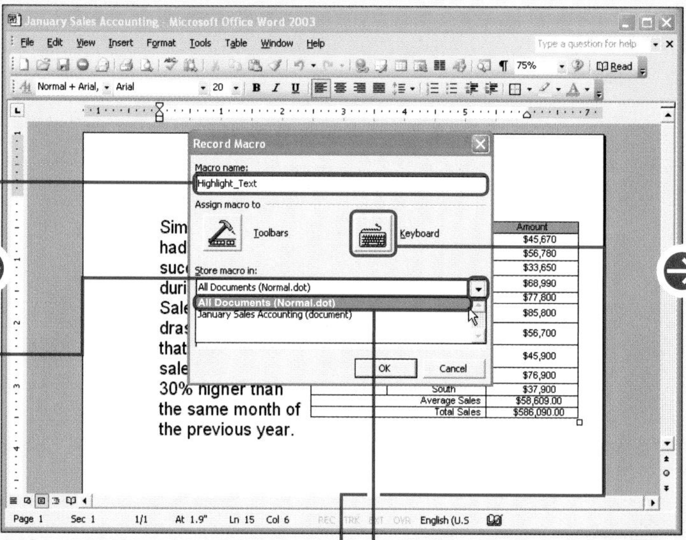

① Click Tools.

② Click Macro.

③ Click Record New Macro.

○ The Record Macro dialog box opens.

④ Type a unique name for the macro.

⑤ Click the down arrow to view available storage locations.

⑥ Click the storage location for the macro.

⑦ Click Keyboard.

DIFFICULTY LEVEL

Did You Know?

You can create multiple keyboard commands to execute the same macro by clicking Assign after specifying each key sequence. Word displays each key sequence in the Current Keys field.

Did You Know?

If you specify a keyboard sequence for your macro that matches another Word command, the new keyboard sequence overrides the Word command. For example, if you assign the keyboard sequence Ctrl+B, your macro executes instead of bolding text.

Did You Know?

You cannot use the mouse to select text when recording a macro. You need to use the corresponding keyboard commands. For example, to select the entire document, press Ctrl+A. To select an entire row, press F8 and End. Use the up and down arrows to select multiple lines of text.

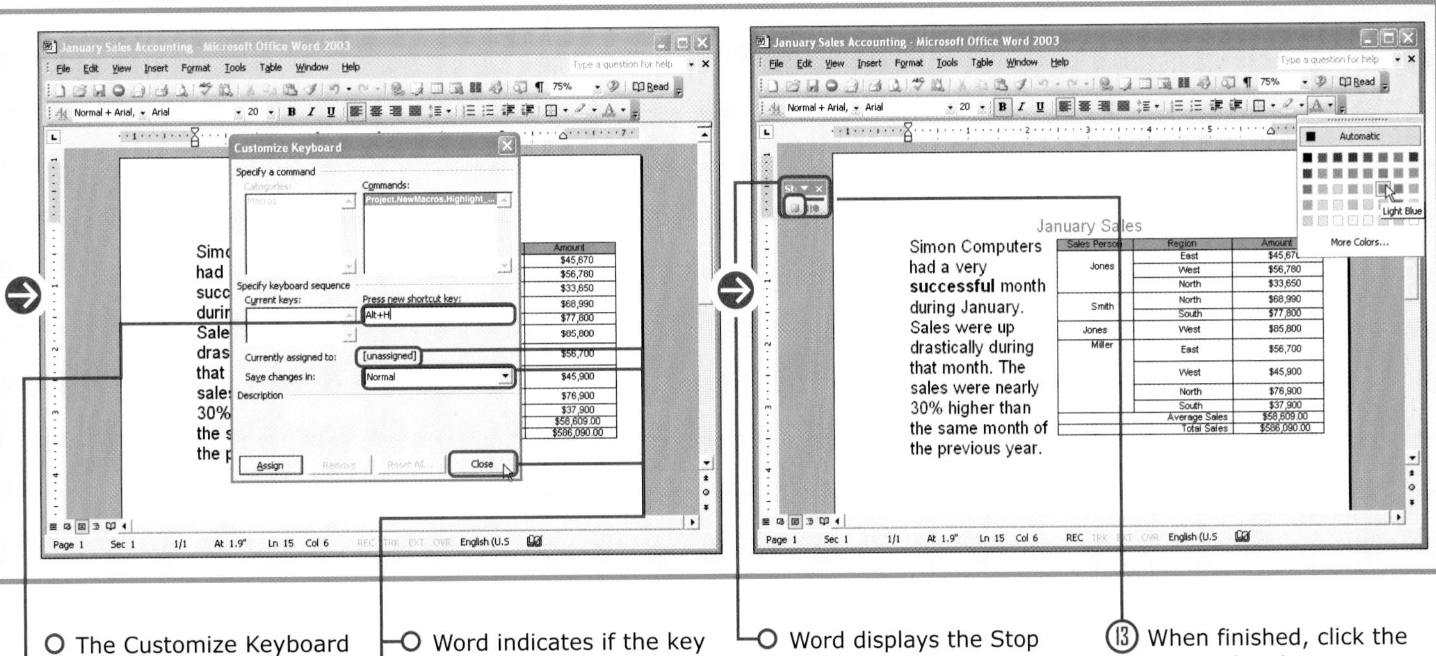

- The Customize Keyboard dialog box opens.
- (8) Click in the Press new shortcut key field.
- (9) Press the key sequence that you want to use to activate the macro.
- The key sequence appears in the field.
- Word indicates if the key sequence is used by another command.
- (10) Click the down arrow and select the location for the keyboard command.
- (11) Click Close.
- Word displays the Stop Recording toolbar.
- (12) Press the appropriate keystrokes to record the macro.
- (13) When finished, click the Stop Recording button.
- Word creates the macro and closes the Stop Recording toolbar.

Macro
1. Click Insert
2. Click Picture
3. Click From File
4. Select file
5. Click Insert
Alt + J

ADD A MACRO BUTTON

to a toolbar

You can add any macro you create to a toolbar. By placing a macro button on a toolbar, you eliminate the need to remember a specific key sequence whenever you want to activate the macro.

You can place a macro on a toolbar both during the creation of the macro or anytime afterwards. To place the macro on the toolbar during the macro-creation process, click the Toolbars button. If you do so, however, you do not have the option of assigning a key sequence. Therefore, you should consider creating the macro and then adding it to the toolbar as described in this section.

You add a macro button to a toolbar by dragging the macro onto the toolbar. If you want the macro available to all documents, it needs to be stored in the default template, Normal.dot. If you specify that you want to view the button only when the current document is open, the button will not appear when you view other documents in Word.

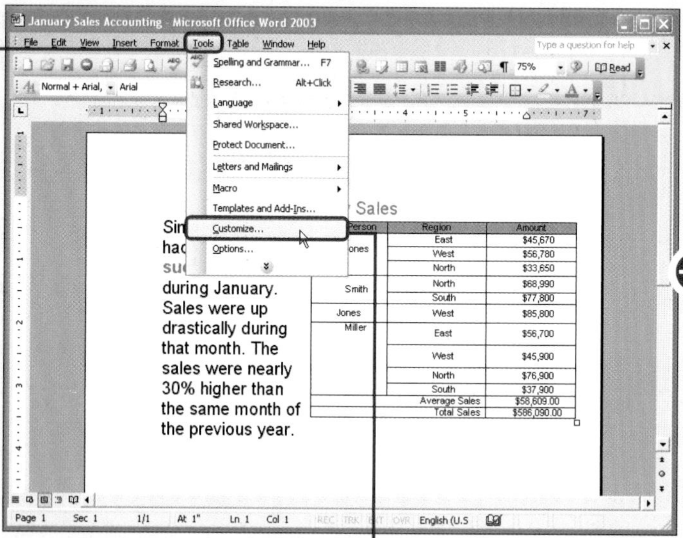

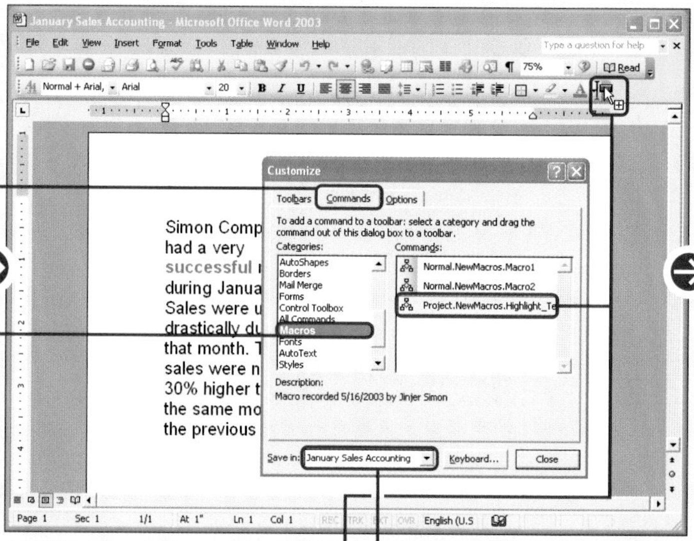

1 Click Tools.

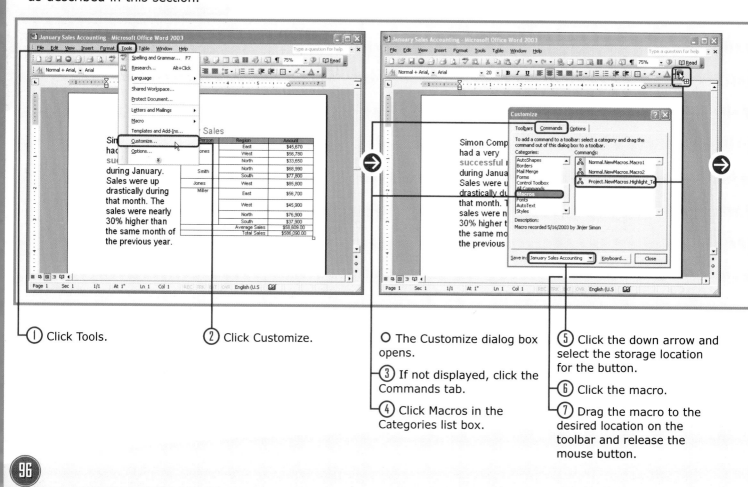

2 Click Customize.

- The Customize dialog box opens.

3 If not displayed, click the Commands tab.

4 Click Macros in the Categories list box.

5 Click the down arrow and select the storage location for the button.

6 Click the macro.

7 Drag the macro to the desired location on the toolbar and release the mouse button.

DIFFICULTY LEVEL

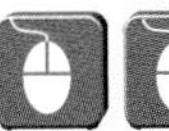

Customize It!

You can create a new toolbar to store your macro buttons. To do so, click the Toolbars tab in the Customize dialog box. Click New. In the New Toolbar dialog box, type the name of the new toolbar in the Toolbar Name field. Select Normal for the Make Toolbar Available To field to use the toolbar for all documents. If you want the toolbar available only for a specific document, click that document name.

Did You Know?

You can set or change the key sequence for a macro in the Customize dialog box. Click Keyboard to display the Customize Keyboard dialog box. In the Categories list box, click Macros and then select the desired macro name. Press the desired key sequence for executing the macro.

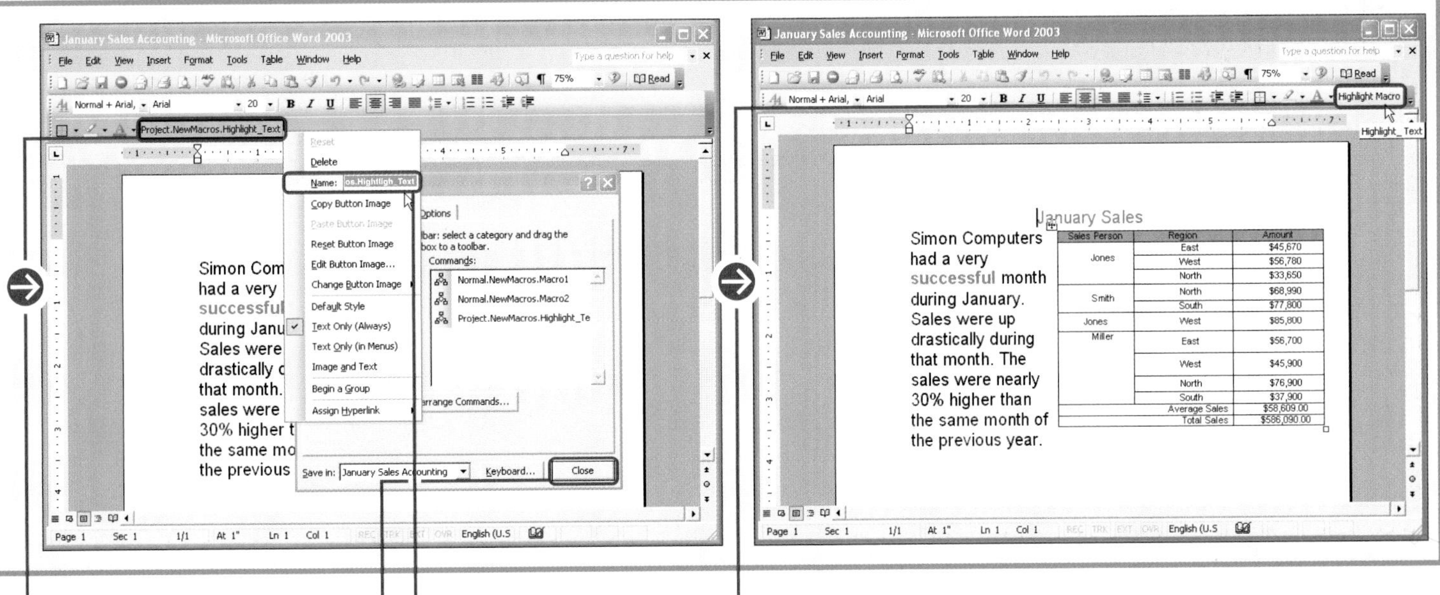

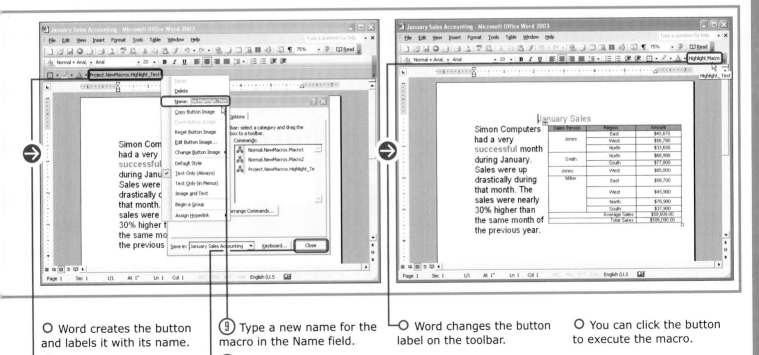

- Word creates the button and labels it with its name.
- (8) Right-click on the macro button to display a menu.
- (9) Type a new name for the macro in the Name field.
- (10) Click Close.
- Word changes the button label on the toolbar.
- You can click the button to execute the macro.

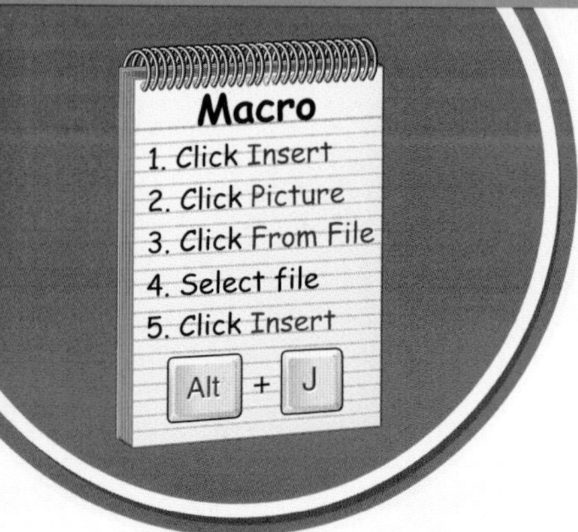
Macro
1. Click Insert
2. Click Picture
3. Click From File
4. Select file
5. Click Insert
Alt + J

REMOVE STEPS

from a recorded macro

You can make modifications to any of the macros that you record in Word. To modify a recorded macro, you need to modify the VBA code used by Word to create the macro. You modify macro code using the Visual Basic Editor, available for use with all Microsoft Office applications.

You can select macros to run, modify, or delete from the Macros dialog box, which lists all the macros that you have created. When you click Edit in the Macros dialog box, the Visual Basic Editor displays the code for the selected macro in a Code window.

Each macro that you create is actually a subroutine in VBA. The Sub statement identifies the start of the macro code, and the End Sub statement indicates the end. The name of the macro follows the Sub statement. If you alter the name of the subroutine, the name changes will appear in the Macros dialog box.

The macro code appears in black between the Sub and End Sub statements. Any changes that you make to the code affect the execution of the macro.

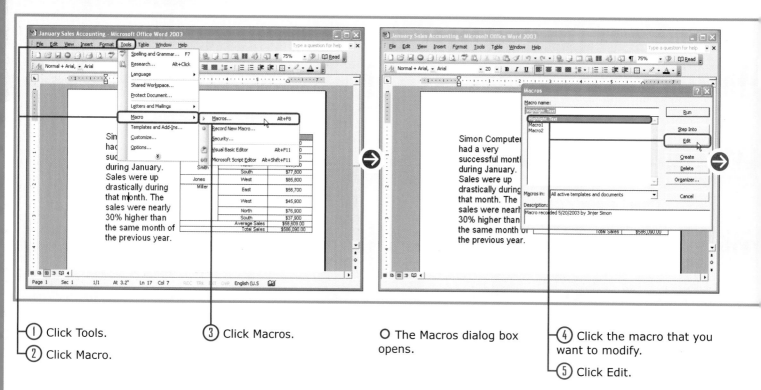

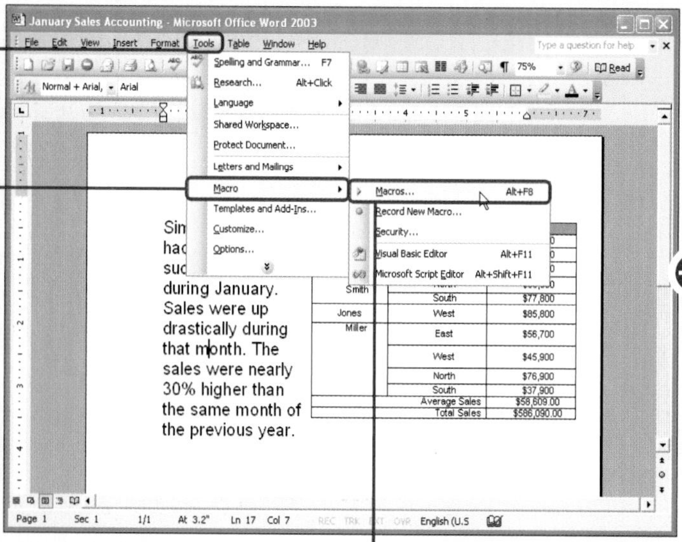

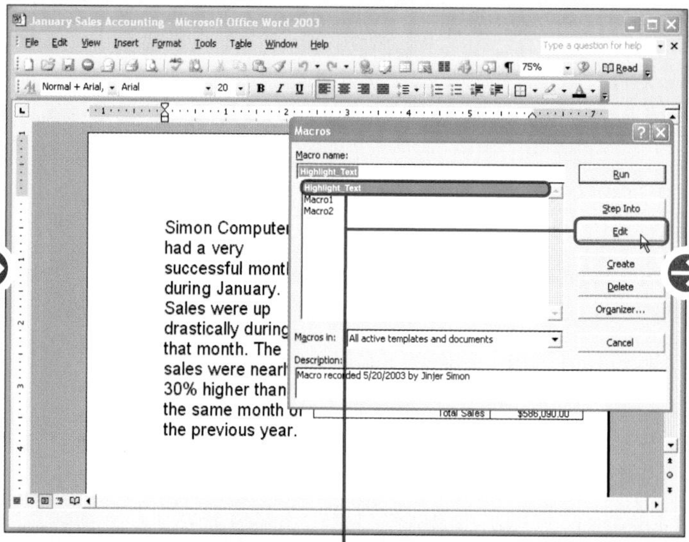

① Click Tools.

② Click Macro.

③ Click Macros.

○ The Macros dialog box opens.

④ Click the macro that you want to modify.

⑤ Click Edit.

DIFFICULTY LEVEL

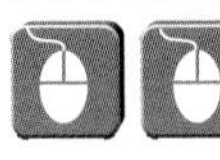

Did You Know?

If you are not sure which code lines to delete, you can have Word ignore code lines by commenting them out. To do so, insert the comment symbol (an apostrophe) in front of a line of code. The text changes to green.

Put It Together!

Because modifying a macro requires you to work with VBA code, a quick method for updating a macro is to record a second macro containing the steps you want to add and then using the Copy and Paste options to copy the new code to the original macro. See task #42 for more information on recording a macro. After copying the code to the macro, you can delete the extra macro in the Macros dialog box.

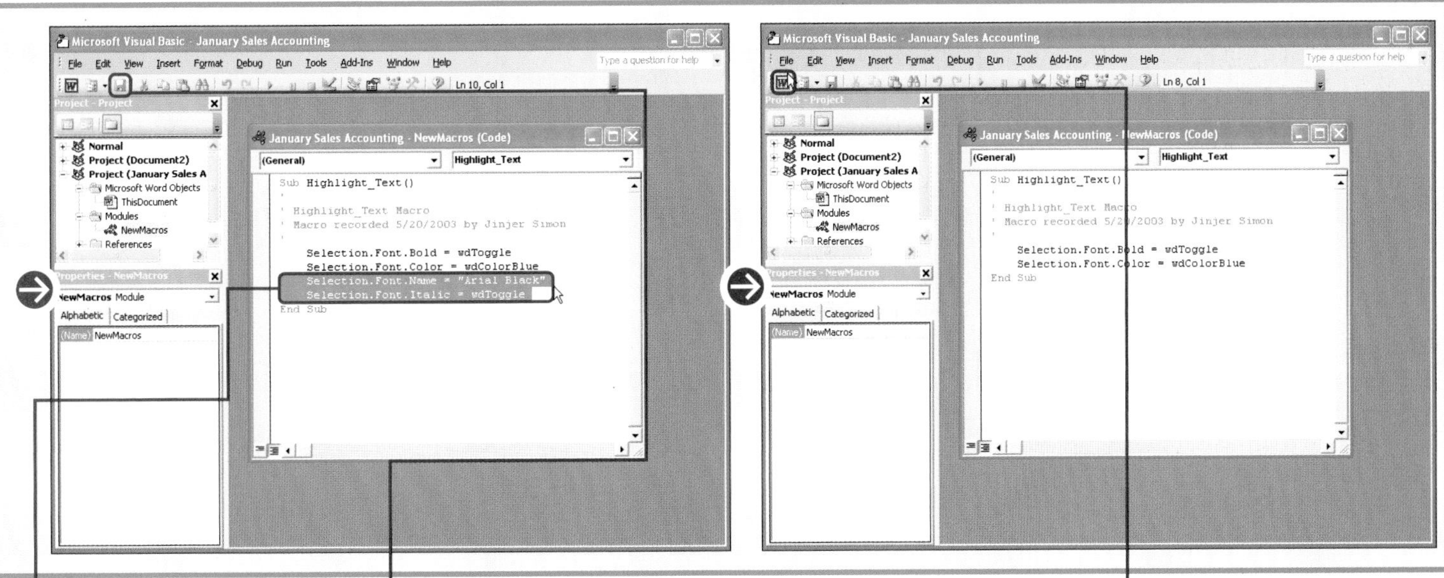

- The Visual Basic Editor displays the code for the selected macro.
- ⑥ Highlight the code that you want to remove.
- ⑦ Press the Delete key.
- ⑧ Click the Save button.
- Word updates the macro.
- You can click the View Microsoft Word button to return to Word.

Macro
1. Click Insert
2. Click Picture
3. Click From File
4. Select file
5. Click Insert
Alt + J

AUTOMATICALLY RUN A MACRO

when a document opens

You can have Word automatically run a particular macro whenever a specific document loads. This works well for any tasks that you perform consistently when you open a document. For example, you may want to make sure that specific toolbars are visible, change the font for the document, or even display a message box.

To create a macro that executes whenever you open a document, you need to create a subroutine within the Visual Basic Editor named Document_Open as part of the ThisDocument object for the selected document. The ThisDocument object is located in the Microsoft Word Objects folder under the selected document project in the Projects window. Any macros that exist in the ThisDocument object for a document are executed automatically by Word; to have the macro execute when a document opens, it must be called Document_Open. You can create another macro, Document_Close, that would execute as you close a document.

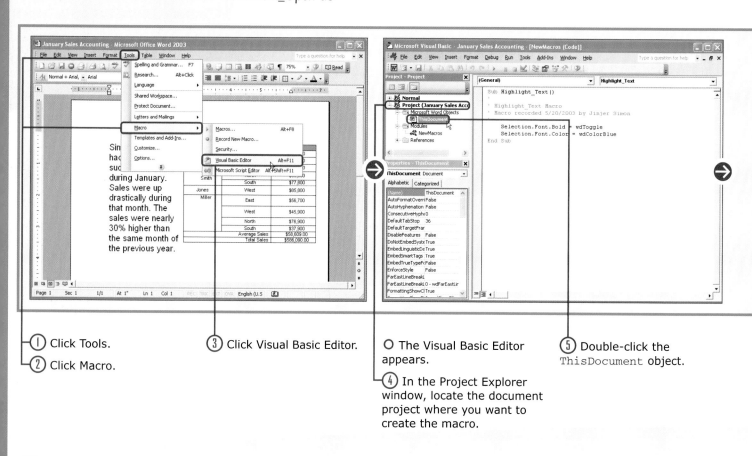

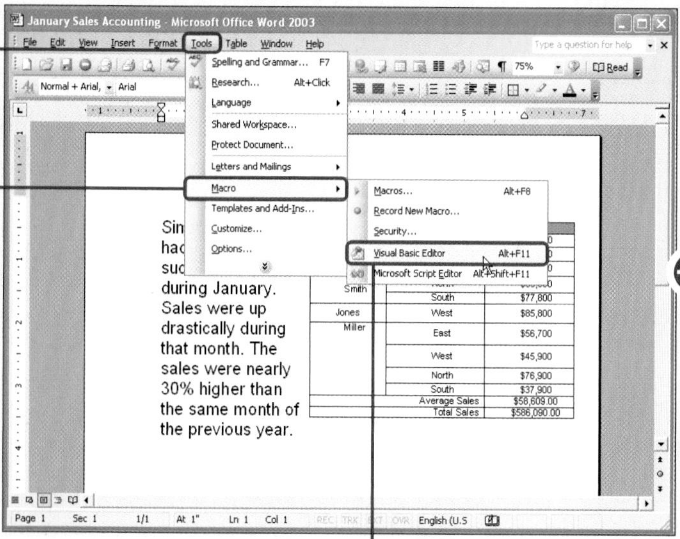

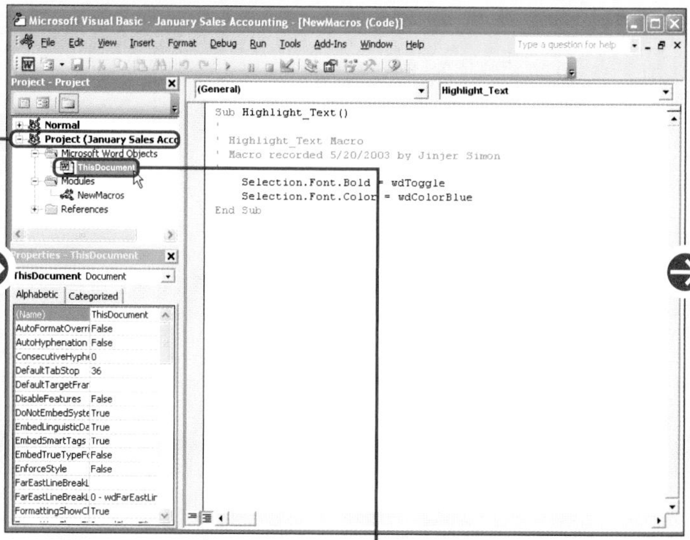

① Click Tools.

② Click Macro.

③ Click Visual Basic Editor.

○ The Visual Basic Editor appears.

④ In the Project Explorer window, locate the document project where you want to create the macro.

⑤ Double-click the `ThisDocument` object.

DIFFICULTY LEVEL

Did You Know?

You can prevent a macro from executing when a document opens by pressing the Shift key. Press the Shift key immediately after selecting the document and hold it until the document is completely open.

Did You Know?

Type Private before the subroutines you add to the ThisDocument object to hide the subroutines so they will not display in the Macros dialog box.

Apply It!

If you want to execute an already existing macro when Word opens a document, you can simply copy the macro code from the existing macro and paste it into the Document_Open macro subroutine. You can also record a macro and then copy the desired code. See task #42 for more information on recording macros.

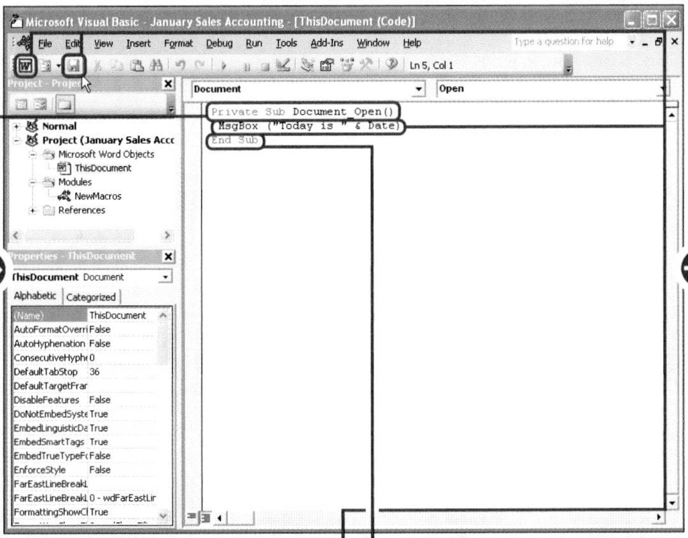

```
Private Sub Document_Open()
MsgBox ("Today is " & Date)
End Sub
```

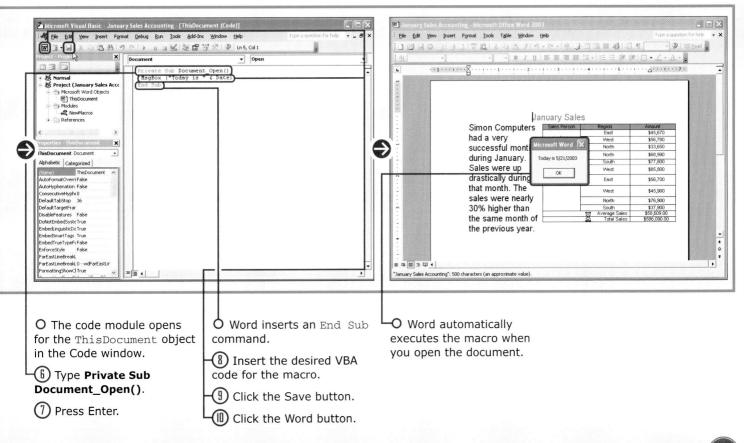

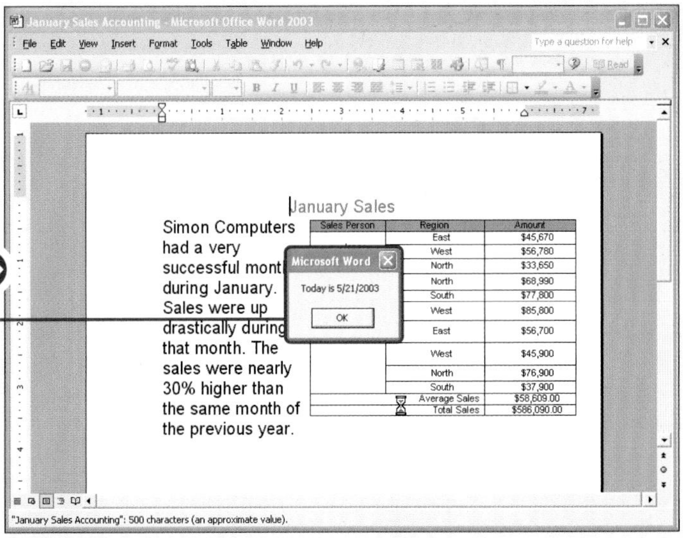

- The code module opens for the `ThisDocument` object in the Code window.

6 Type **Private Sub Document_Open()**.

7 Press Enter.

- Word inserts an `End Sub` command.

8 Insert the desired VBA code for the macro.

9 Click the Save button.

10 Click the Word button.

- Word automatically executes the macro when you open the document.

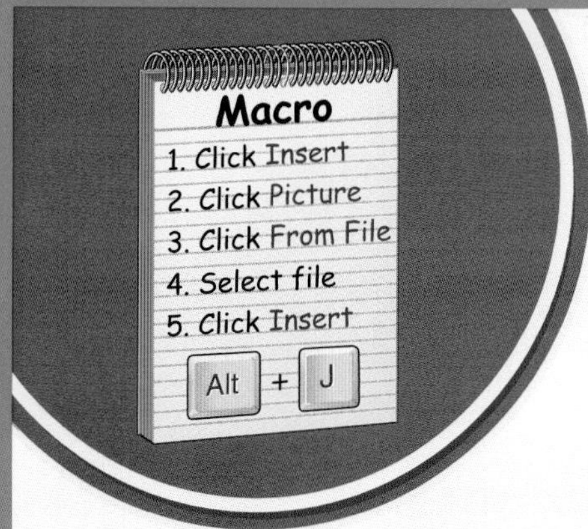

1. Click Insert
2. Click Picture
3. Click From File
4. Select file
5. Click Insert
Alt + J

Create a macro that CHANGES A FORM FIELD

You can create a macro that executes when a specific action occurs on a form, such as selecting specific text or clicking a button. This process enables you to create an interactive document in which values change based on the selections made by the user.

A fairly simple example of this type of macro is one that changes selected text based on the current value of the selection. For example, you may want to scroll through a list of selections. You reference the selected text in a document using the Selection object. You can change the value of a field in a document using the Fields property. For example, if you select a field, Selection.Fields(1) refers to the selected field. By using the Fields property, you can insert a field in your Word document that changes based on your macro. See task #47 for more information.

To change the value of a field on a document, you need to determine the field value. The best method for doing so is to use a Select Case statement to look for different values in the field.

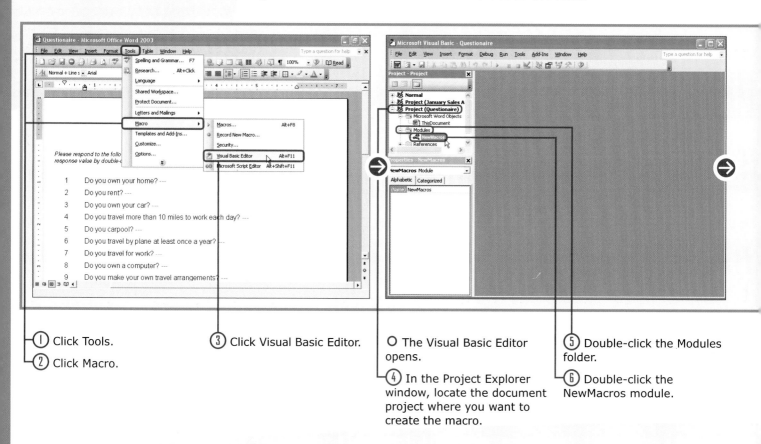

1. Click Tools.
2. Click Macro.
3. Click Visual Basic Editor.

- The Visual Basic Editor opens.

4. In the Project Explorer window, locate the document project where you want to create the macro.
5. Double-click the Modules folder.
6. Double-click the NewMacros module.

#46

DIFFICULTY LEVEL

Did You Know?

When you use the Fields property, you need to indicate the value in the field that you want to modify. For example, if you are changing the value of the MACROBUTTON field, it has to have the following format: {MACROBUTTON MacroName text}. You indicate the character position in the field you want to change. For example, the *t* in text is located in the twenty-third position within the string, so the code to change that character is

Selection.Fields(1).Code.Characters(23) = "b".

Apply It!

You use the Selection object to modify any selected text in a document, using the Text property. For example, to change the value of the selected text to "Microsoft Word," you type the following in your macro:

Selection.Text = "Microsoft Word"

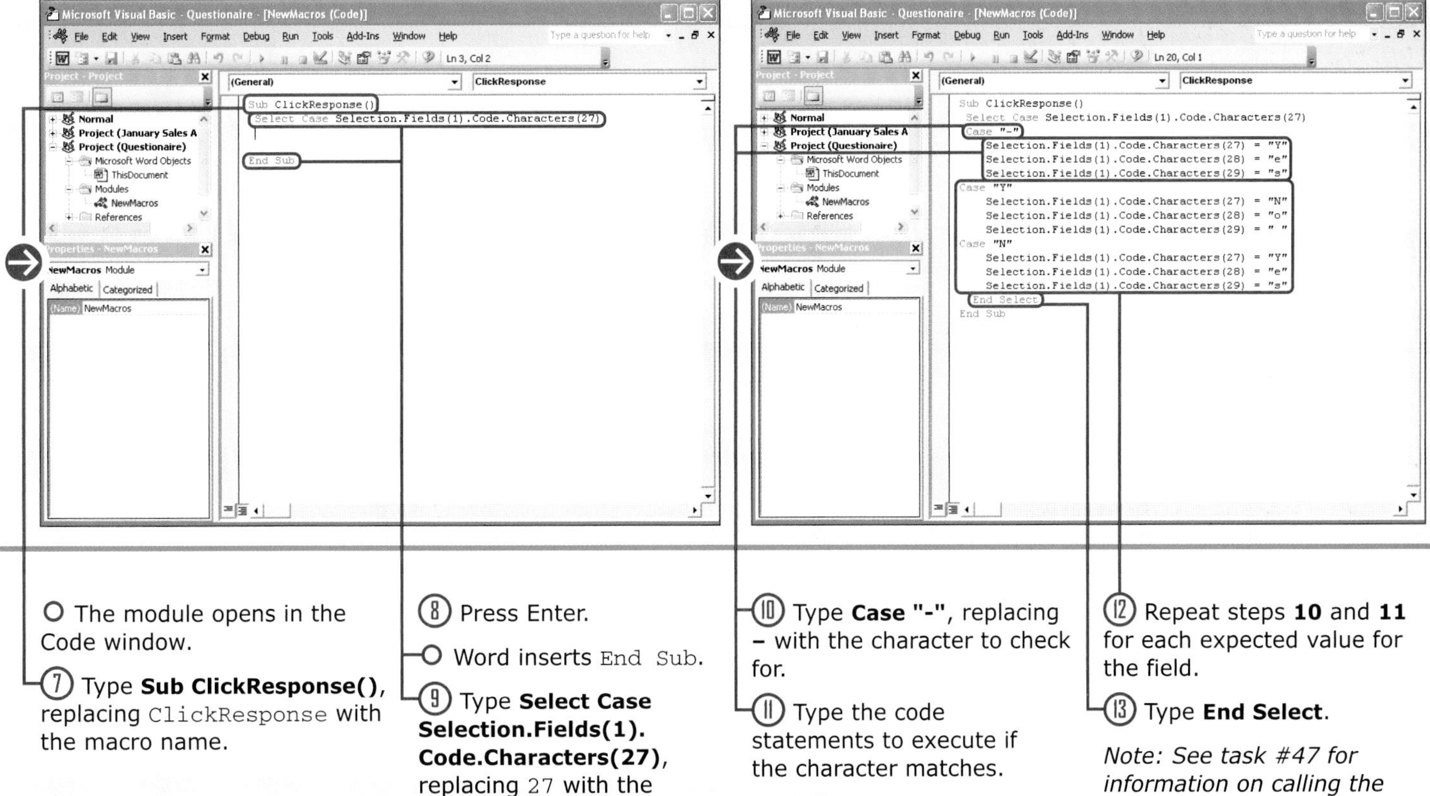

- The module opens in the Code window.

7. Type **Sub ClickResponse()**, replacing ClickResponse with the macro name.

8. Press Enter.

- Word inserts End Sub.

9. Type **Select Case Selection.Fields(1). Code.Characters(27)**, replacing 27 with the character to check in the field.

10. Type **Case "-"**, replacing – with the character to check for.

11. Type the code statements to execute if the character matches.

12. Repeat steps **10** and **11** for each expected value for the field.

13. Type **End Select**.

Note: See task #47 for information on calling the macro.

Macro
1. Click Insert
2. Click Picture
3. Click From File
4. Select file
5. Click Insert
Alt + J

ASSIGN A MACRO

to a document field

You can have a macro run when an action occurs on any field on a document. To do so, you can use the MacroButton field to call a macro. When you use this field, you indicate the macro to run whenever the user clicks the field. This works well when you want to call a macro that changes a value in a field when the field is clicked.

The MacroButton field allows you to specify two parameters: the name of the macro to run and the text or graphic to display for the field. You insert the field using the field curly brackets that you create by pressing Ctrl+F9 or by using the Field dialog box. The MacroButton field has the following format:

{MACROBUTTON MacroName FieldValue}

In the Field dialog box, you select the MacroButton field and then select the name of the macro to run. Remember to type the value you want to display as the button for the field in the Display Text field. If left blank, the field will not be visible in your document.

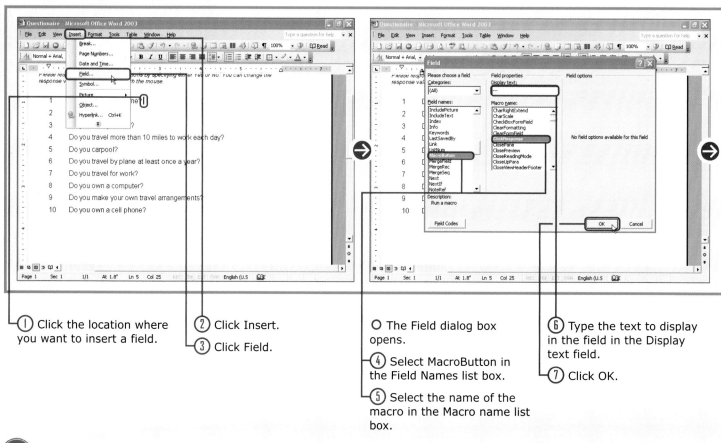

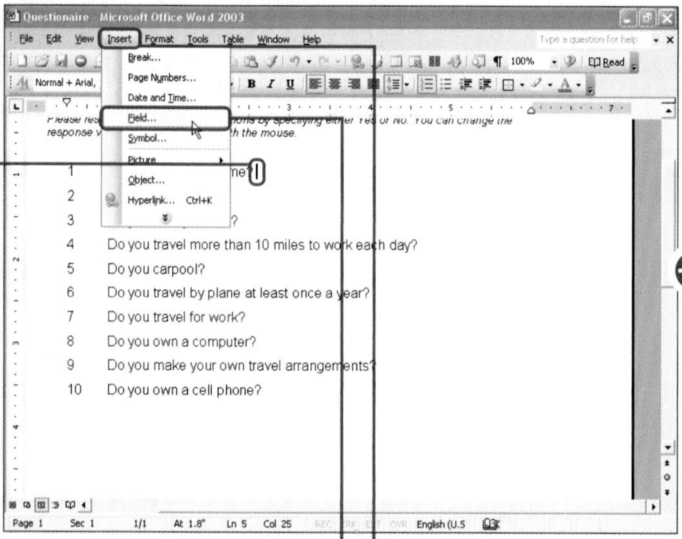

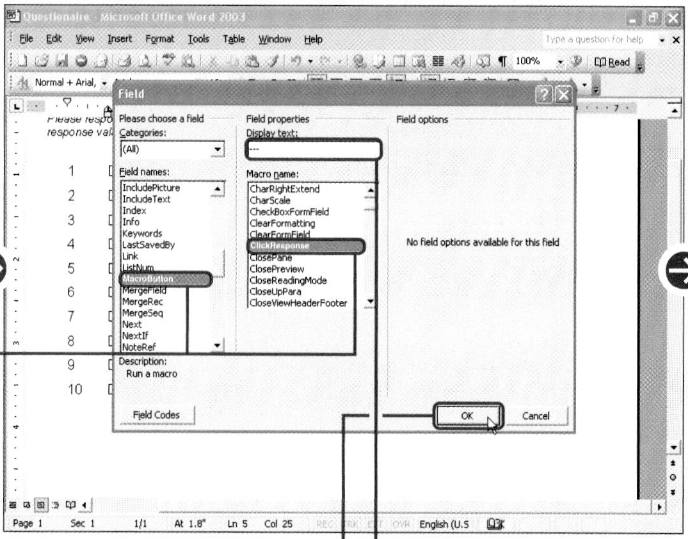

① Click the location where you want to insert a field.

② Click Insert.

③ Click Field.

○ The Field dialog box opens.

④ Select MacroButton in the Field Names list box.

⑤ Select the name of the macro in the Macro name list box.

⑥ Type the text to display in the field in the Display text field.

⑦ Click OK.

DIFFICULTY LEVEL

Did You Know?

You can view the codes that will be inserted for the field by clicking Field Codes in the Field dialog box. When you select this option, Word displays the parameters for the selected field under the Field Codes field.

Apply It!

You can repeat a field in a document either by reinserting it or using the Copy and Paste options.

Did You Know?

When you use the MacroButton field, you can format the text of the field using any of the text formatting commands. To format the text, select the entire field and apply the desired formatting. Any formatting that you apply remains with the field. Therefore, if the value of the field changes, the formatting remains the same.

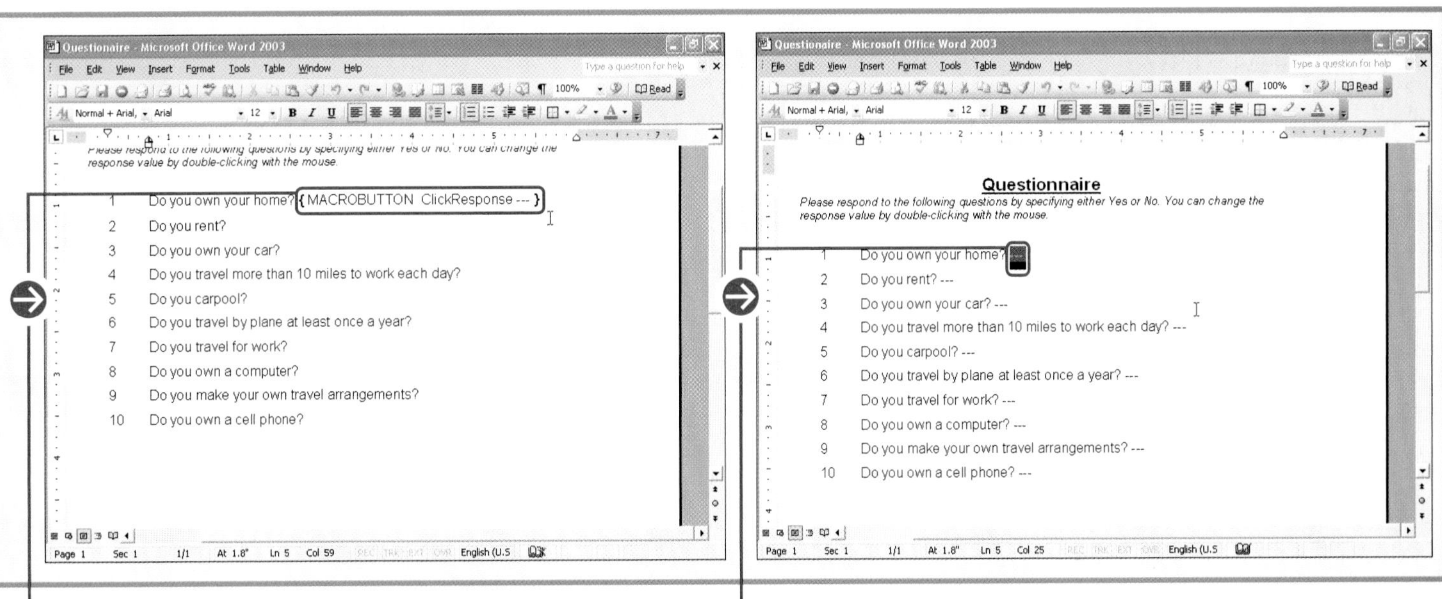

- Word inserts the field in the document.

8. Press Alt+F9 to hide the field codes.

- Word displays the text specified in the Display text field of the Field dialog box.
- You can double-click the field to activate the macro.

Macro
1. Click Insert
2. Click Picture
3. Click From File
4. Select file
5. Click Insert
Alt + J

CREATE AN AUTOTEXT FIELD

for frequently repeated text

You can insert a field that adds the contents of an AutoText entry to your document. Although this task may appear more cumbersome than just inserting the AutoText entry directly, the difference is that you can have Word update the field when you use this option. This means that if you decide to modify the AutoText entry, you simply need to update the fields to have the changes made in your document.

You should consider using this option for important text that is used frequently within your document and may change. For example, if a company name changes, you simply update the AutoText entry and then select the field update option, and Word does the rest.

When you insert an AutoText field, you need to specify whether you want to also apply the formatting from the AutoText field or maintain the formatting of the surrounding text. Keep in mind that if you decide to use the formatting of the AutoText entry, the formatting will change whenever you update the field.

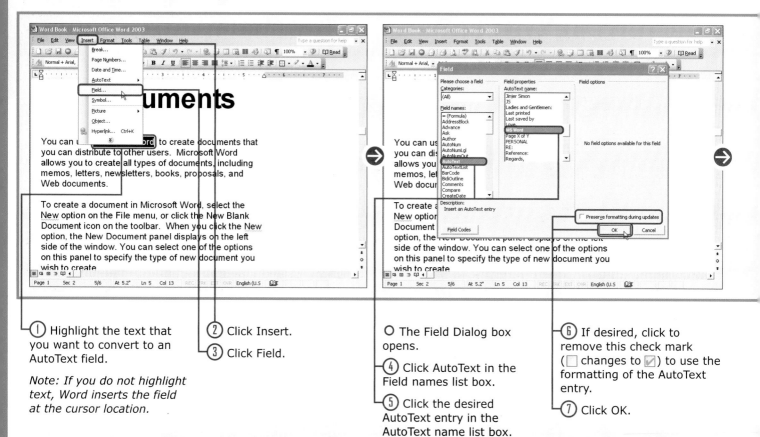

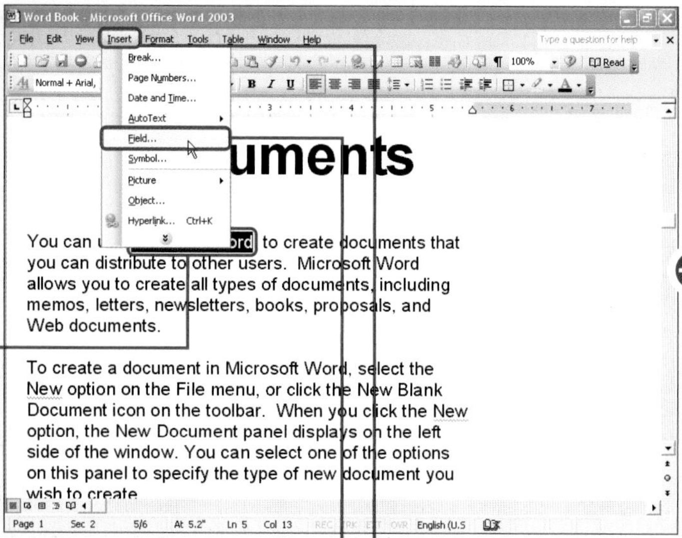

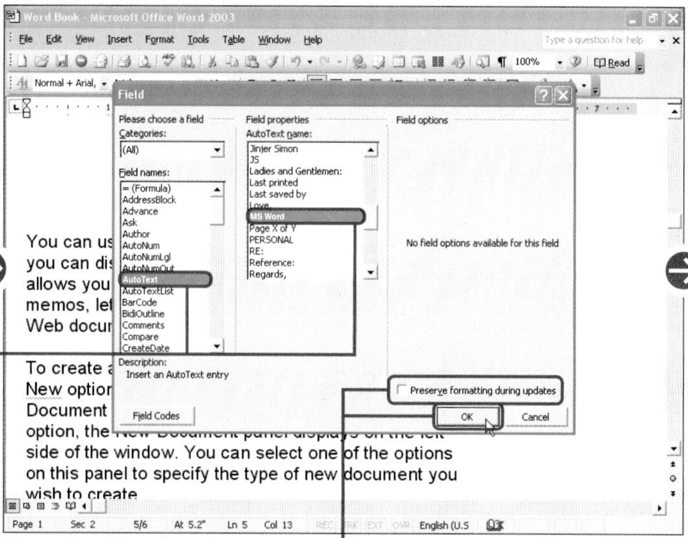

1. Highlight the text that you want to convert to an AutoText field.

Note: If you do not highlight text, Word inserts the field at the cursor location.

2. Click Insert.
3. Click Field.

- The Field Dialog box opens.

4. Click AutoText in the Field names list box.
5. Click the desired AutoText entry in the AutoText name list box.
6. If desired, click to remove this check mark (☐ changes to ☑) to use the formatting of the AutoText entry.
7. Click OK.

DIFFICULTY LEVEL

Apply It!

You can update the fields in your document by clicking Edit ➪ Select All and then pressing F9. When you do so, if you have modified any AutoText entries, they are updated within the document. If you want to update only a single field, select that field and press F9.

Put It Together!

You can update the fields in a document before printing. This ensures that you are printing the most current information. To update the fields, click the Update Fields option in the Print Options dialog box. See Chapter 7 for more information on printing.

Did You Know?

If you manually insert the AutoText field using Ctrl+F9 to insert the brackets, you must place the AutoText entry name in double quotes.

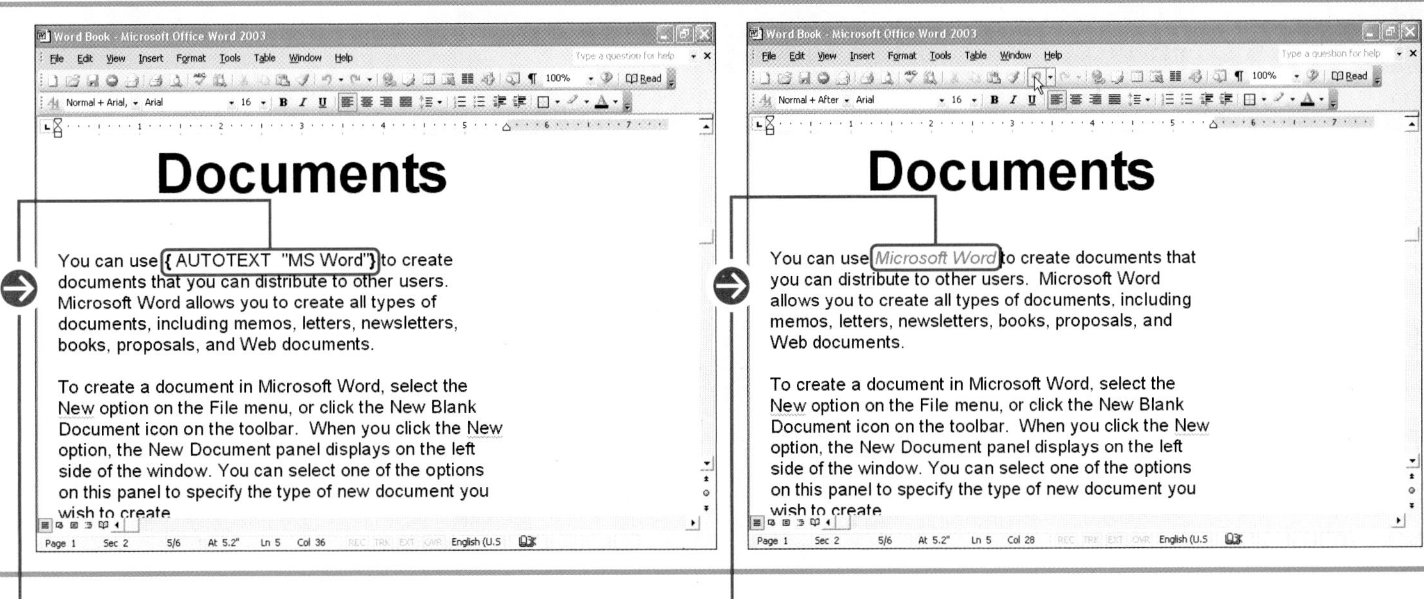

- Word inserts the AutoText field in the document at the selected location.

8. Repeat steps **1** to **7** for each occurrence of the text.
9. Press Alt+F9 to hide the fields.

- Word displays the AutoText field using the specified formatting.

Macro
1. Click Insert
2. Click Picture
3. Click From File
4. Select file
5. Click Insert
Alt + J

Add fields to AUTOMATICALLY REQUEST A RESPONSE

You can have Word request specific information from the user by creating a fill-in field. This type of field works well when you have a document that contains a form that you want the user to fill out. You can use these fields to request information, such as name and address.

When you use a fill-in field, a pop-up dialog box appears as you insert the field requesting the text for the field. The dialog box appears again each time that you update the fields by pressing F9. If your document contains multiple fill-in fields, the dialog boxes display in the order they appear in the document.

If you want to have the dialog boxes appear automatically when the document opens, you need to create a macro. The easiest method is to create a Document_Open macro that Word runs each time you open the document. In this macro, you need to insert the code to select the document and reset the fields. See task #45 for more information.

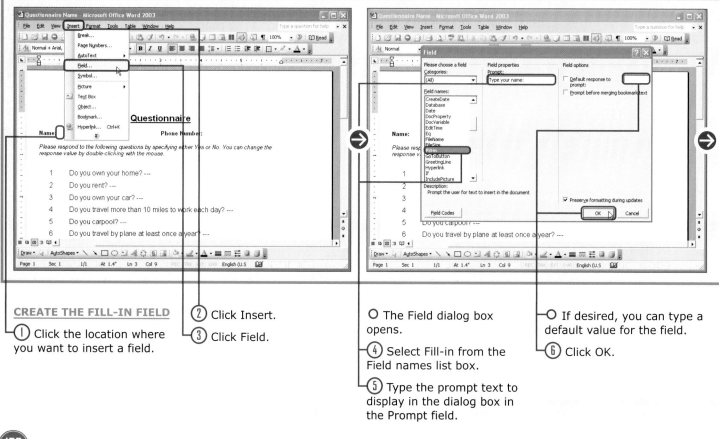

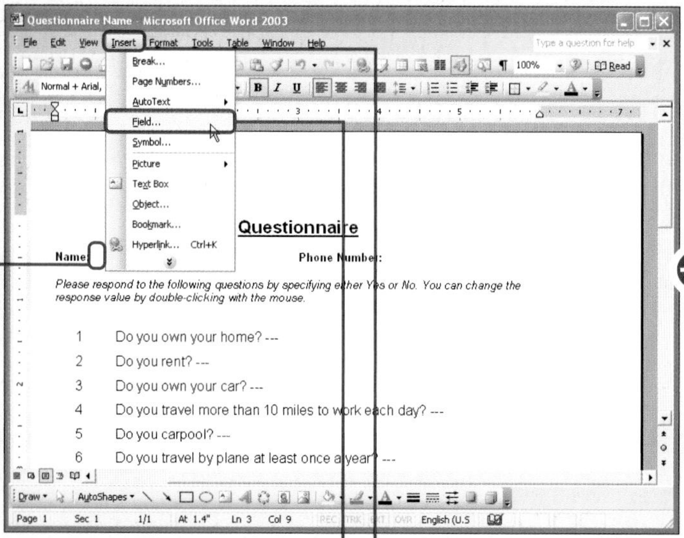

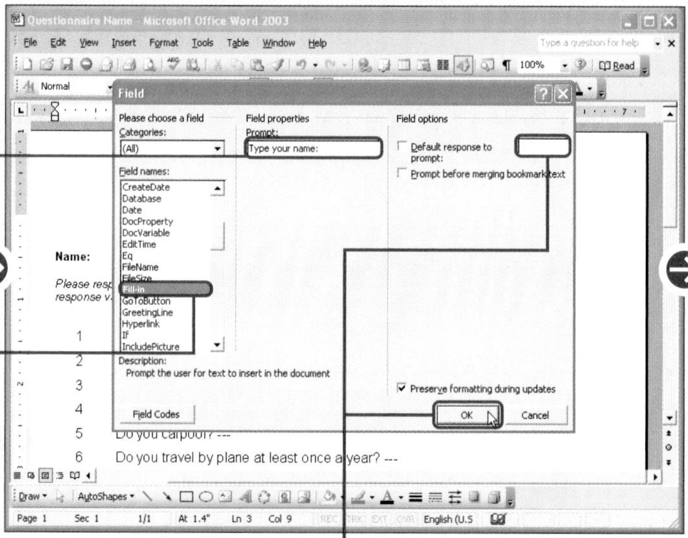

CREATE THE FILL-IN FIELD

1. Click the location where you want to insert a field.
2. Click Insert.
3. Click Field.

- The Field dialog box opens.

4. Select Fill-in from the Field names list box.
5. Type the prompt text to display in the dialog box in the Prompt field.

- If desired, you can type a default value for the field.

6. Click OK.

DIFFICULTY LEVEL

Put It Together!

Instead of creating a macro that refreshes the fields as the document opens, you can use a MacroButton field to allow the user to restart the form at any point. To do so, simply create a macro that refreshes the form and then insert a MacroButton field to run it. See task #47 for more on the MacroButton field.

Did You Know?

You can record the macro that refreshes the fields in the document by clicking Edit ➪ Select All and then pressing F9. You deselect the text of the document by pressing Ctrl+Home.

Caution!

Avoid typing directly over a field. If you type on top of a field, Word replaces the field with the text you type.

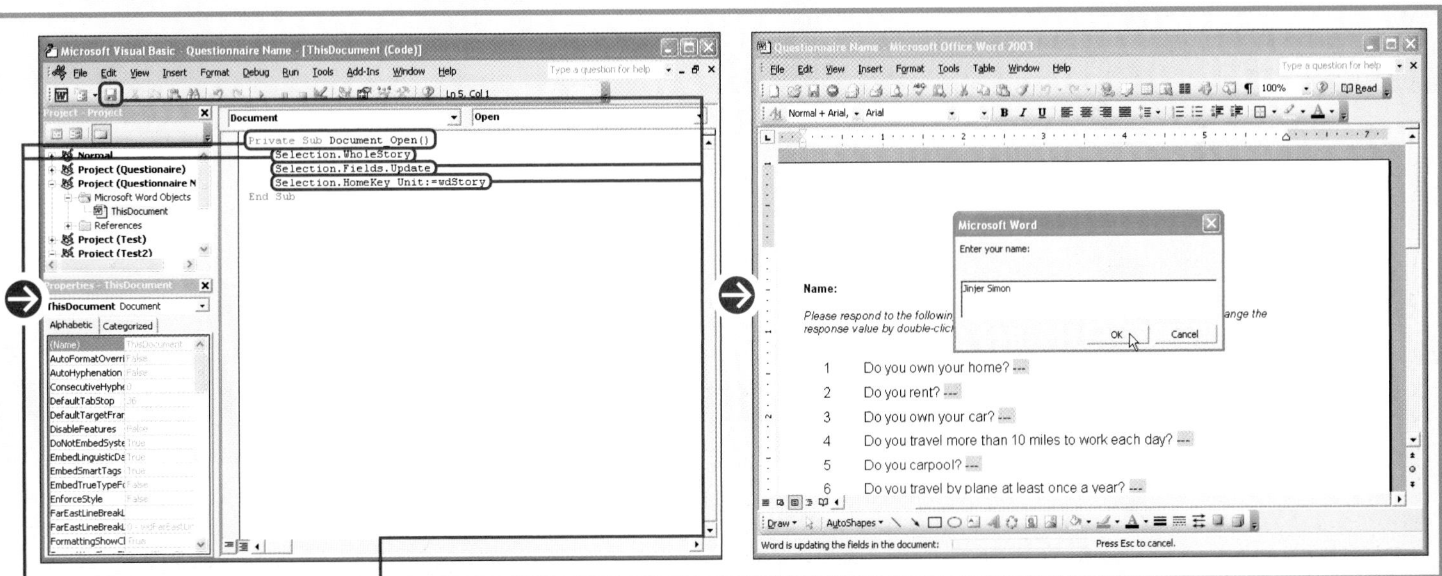

CREATE THE MACRO

⑦ In the `ThisDocument` object module, type **Private Sub Document_Open()**.

Note: See task #45.

⑧ To have Word select the entire document, type **Selection.WholeStory**.

⑨ Type **Selection.Fields.Update**.

⑩ Type **Selection.Homekey Unit:=wdStory**.

⑪ Click the Save button.

○ Word displays the corresponding dialog boxes each time that you open the document.

Macro
1. Click Insert
2. Click Picture
3. Click From File
4. Select file
5. Click Insert
Alt + J

Create DICTIONARY-STYLE page headers

You can create dictionary-style page headers in your Word documents. With dictionary headers, Word indicates the first and last paragraph on the page. This type of header works well when you are creating an alphabetized list, such as a directory or list of terms.

You insert dictionary-style headers using the StyleRef field. You can insert the StyleRef fields either manually or using the Field dialog box. When you select the StyleRef field, the Style Name list box lists all the available styles for your document.

You need to specify the style to use to locate the text that displays for the field. For example, if you use the Normal style for the text in your document, you need to select that style so that Word can find the first word with that style.

To insert both the first and last word on the page, you need to use the StyleRef field twice — once for each word. To get the last word on the page, add the \l switch to the field, as in the following:

{STYLEREF Normal \l}

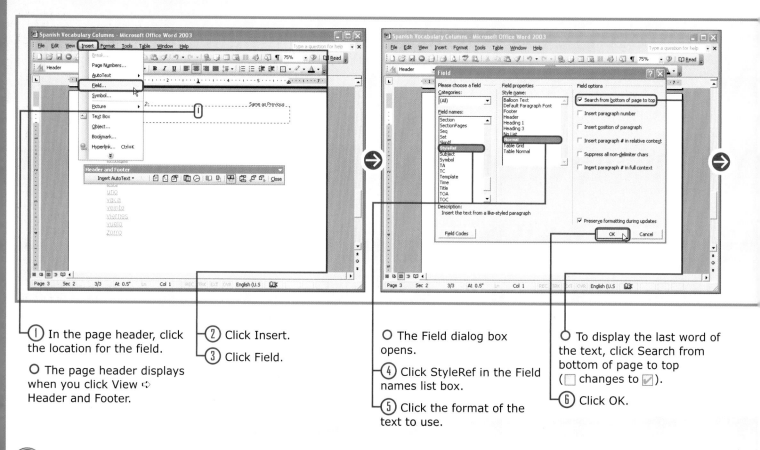

1. In the page header, click the location for the field.

- The page header displays when you click View ➪ Header and Footer.

2. Click Insert.
3. Click Field.

- The Field dialog box opens.

4. Click StyleRef in the Field names list box.
5. Click the format of the text to use.

- To display the last word of the text, click Search from bottom of page to top (☐ changes to ☑).

6. Click OK.

DIFFICULTY LEVEL

Did You Know?

If you use the Normal style as the Style name, Word may not find the last word on the page. This occurs if the text on the last page does not fill the entire page. If the blank part of the page is formatted using the same style, Word determines that the final word on the page is blank. To correct this problem, create a style specific to the text you want to use for the text that is placed in the header. Apply that style to the text and select that style in the Style name list box in the Field dialog box.

Did You Know?

If Word cannot locate a word on the page with the specified style, it continues looking on the next page.

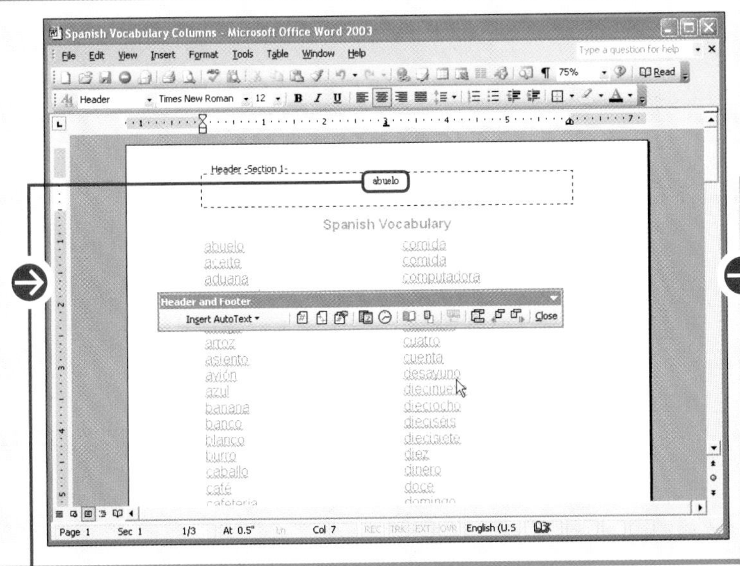

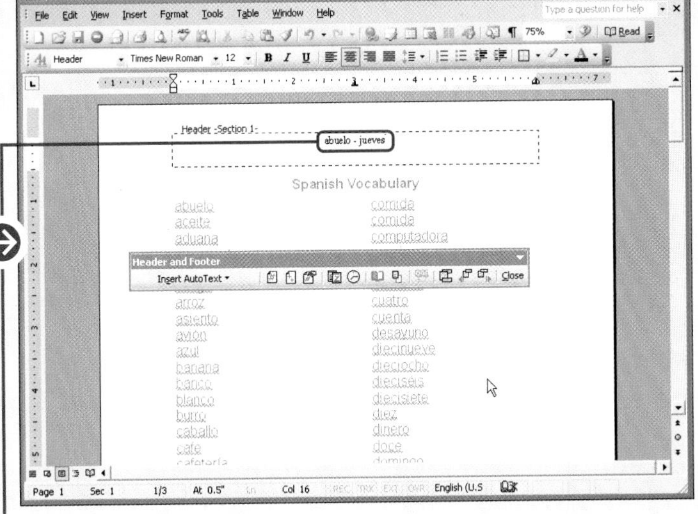

○ Word inserts the first word of the specified style in the header.

⑦ Repeat steps **2** to **6** to add the last word on the page.

○ Word displays the first and last words on the page.

Work with Large Documents

You can create and work with large documents such as brochures or even books in Word. Word provides several features for large documents, including the ability to create indexes and tables of contents (TOCs).

When creating a large document, you should consider creating several smaller documents, called *subdocuments,* and then use a master document to tie the smaller documents together. This method gives you the freedom of editing each of the subdocuments separately but bringing them all together to print, index, and create tables, such as a table of contents.

Another convenient feature of a master document is that it allows other users to modify the subdocuments simultaneously. Each user can modify a different subdocument, and then modifications can be brought together in the master document. Keep in mind that you can still only have a file open for modification on one computer at a time. If another computer accesses an open Word document, it opens in read-only mode.

Within a master document, you can reorder the subdocuments and create additional document elements, such as an index or a table of contents.

You can manually mark index entries or create an index using a concordance file that lists all the desired entries.

You can also flag text that you want to reference in your document by using the Bookmark feature. Bookmarked text can be referenced using a cross-reference. You can also cross-reference other document elements, such as headings or figures.

TOP 100

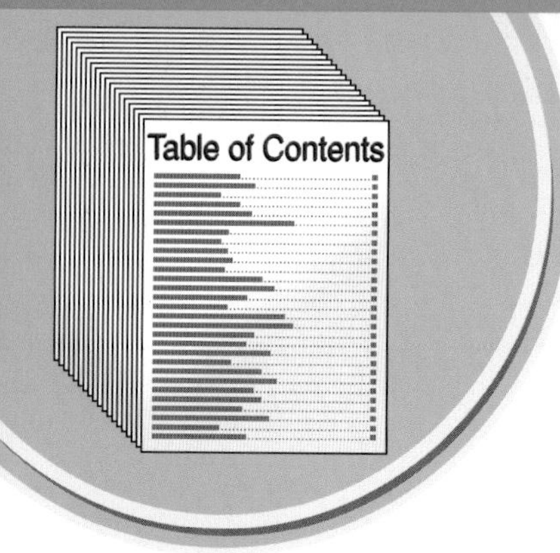

Create a MASTER DOCUMENT

You create a master document in Word to organize a series of smaller files, such as chapters in a book. By using a master document, you bring together related files, called *subdocuments,* to create items such as a common table of contents or an index. The master document contains only links to the subdocuments; all content is stored in the individual subdocuments.

You can create a master document by working in the Outline view mode. You can add existing files into the master document, or you can create the subdocuments from the master document. If you create the subdocuments from the headings in the master document, Word names the subdocuments to match the heading of the text you select for the subdocument. For example, if the heading is "Create Tables," Word creates a Create Tables.doc file in the same folder as the master document.

When Word creates a subdocument, it inserts a section break in the master document both before and after the text in the subdocument.

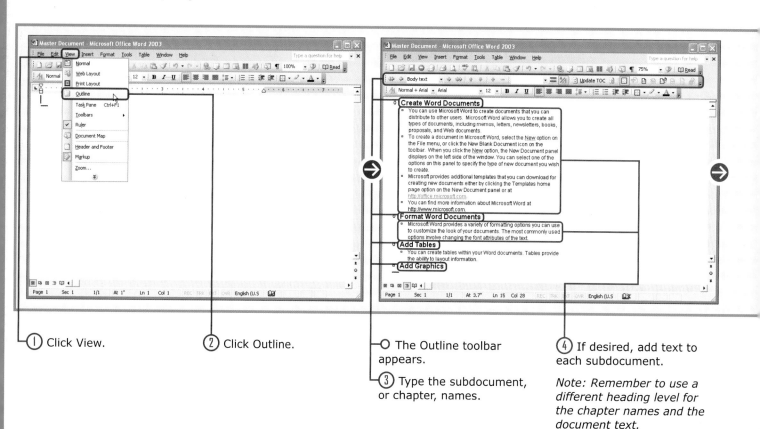

1. Click View.
2. Click Outline.

- The Outline toolbar appears.

3. Type the subdocument, or chapter, names.
4. If desired, add text to each subdocument.

Note: Remember to use a different heading level for the chapter names and the document text.

DIFFICULTY LEVEL

Did You Know?

You can keep all the documents related to the master document together by placing everything in the same folder. You should create a folder for the project before creating the subdocuments in the master document. Word inserts a link to the subdocument in the master document. If you move or rename a subdocument, Word will no longer be able to locate it for the master document.

Apply It!

If you already have documents created that you want to use as subdocuments, click the location in the master document where you want to insert the subdocument and then click the Insert Subdocument button ( ). Word opens the Insert Subdocument dialog box in which you can select the desired document.

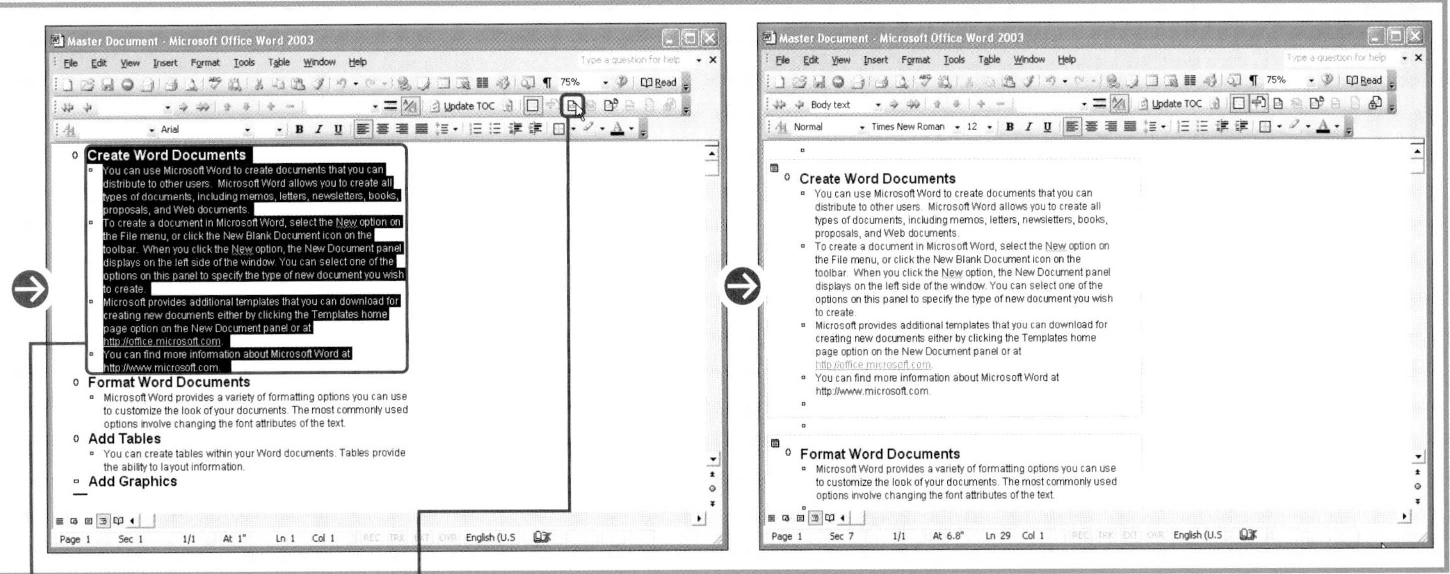

5 Highlight the text of the first subdocument.

6 Click the Create Subdocuments button.

7 Repeat steps **5** and **6** for each subdocument.

○ Word creates the specified subdocument. In Outline view, Word draws a box around each subdocument.

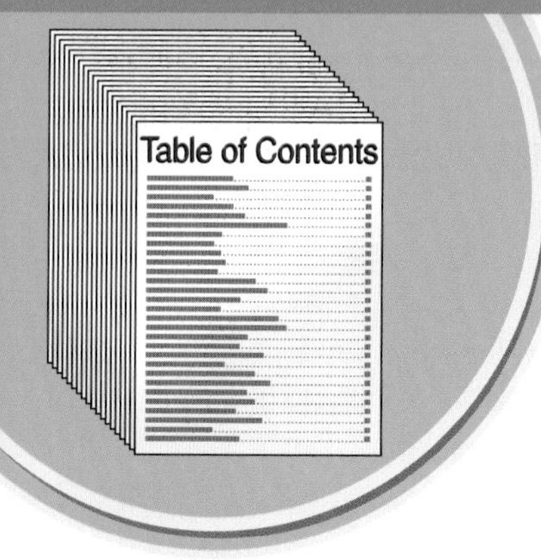

REORDER SUBDOCUMENTS

in a master document

You can change the order of the subdocuments in your master document. For example, if you decide to change the order of the chapters in a book, you will need to reorder the documents within the master document so that the page numbering is correct and the chapters are listed in the correct order in the table of contents.

You cannot reorder subdocuments if they are locked. Word automatically locks the subdocument if it is open on another machine. Subdocuments can also be locked to prevent changes. You need to unlock the subdocument before you move it.

You can move a subdocument when it is collapsed or expanded. However, it is easier to move subdocuments if you have only the first level, typically the subdocument title, displayed. This eliminates the need to scroll through a long document when moving a subdocument. You can specify the level to display using the Show Level list box.

You select the subdocument using the Subdocument icon. This ensures that the entire document is selected so that you can move it.

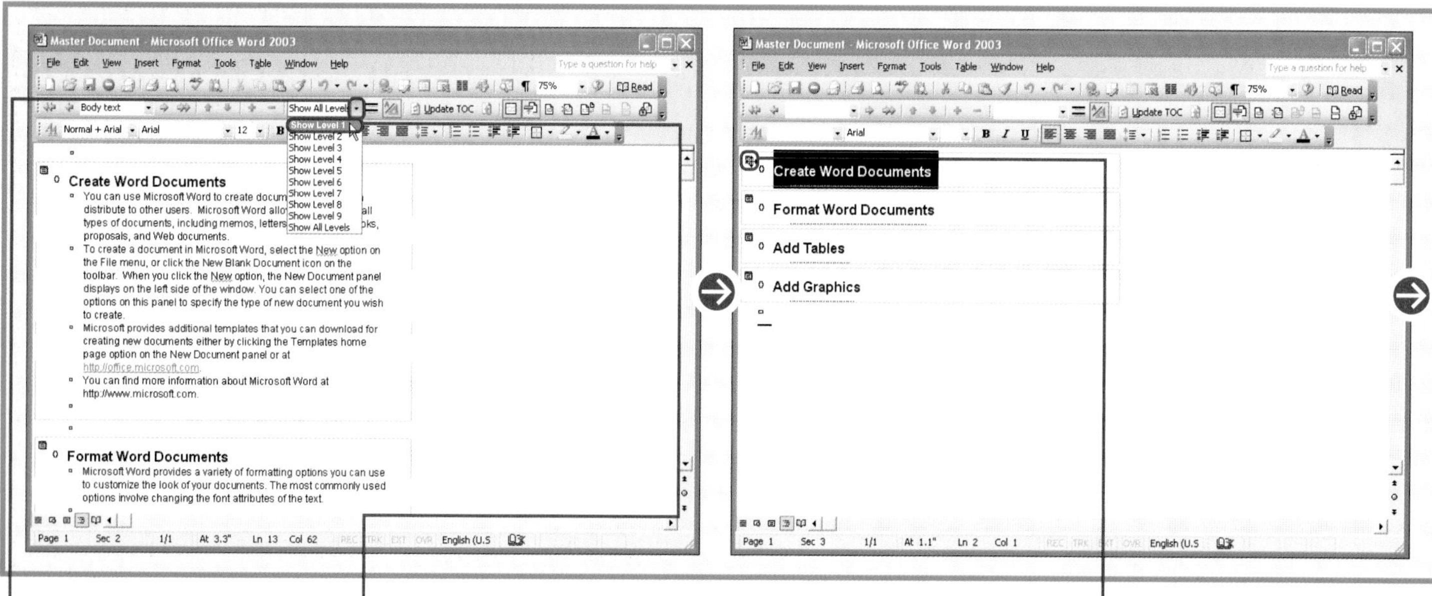

1. Click the down arrow to display a list of levels.

Note: You can click View and then Outline to display the Outline toolbar.

2. Click Show Level 1.

- Word collapses all the subdocuments and displays only the first level text.

3. Click the icon next to the desired subdocument.
4. Drag the subdocument icon to the desired location.

Did You Know?

You can lock a subdocument to prevent changes to the document while working with the master document. When a subdocument is locked, a lock icon displays next to the subdocument in Outline view, and the formatting buttons are grayed out. To lock a subdocument, click the Lock Document button.

Did You Know?

You can move multiple subdocuments within a master document at the same time. To do so, first make sure that the desired subdocuments are located together in the master document. Then click the first subdocument icon, hold down the Shift key, and click the last subdocument. Word highlights the selected subdocuments, enabling you to move them both.

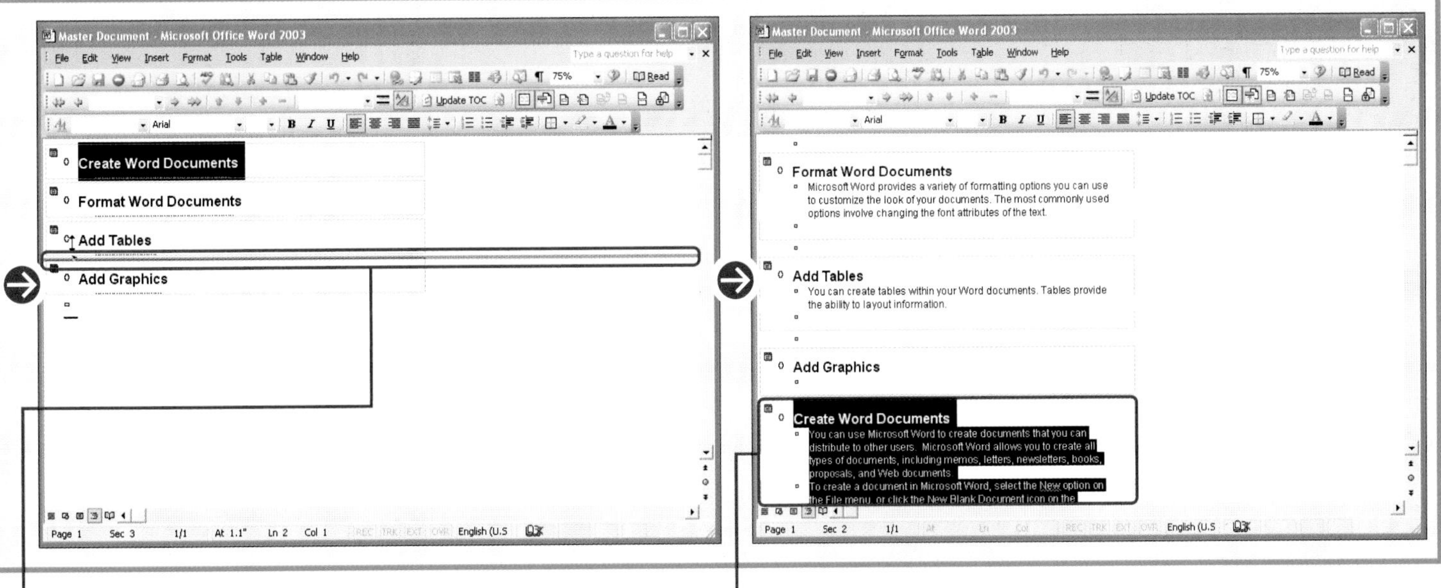

- As you drag, Word displays a vertical line, indicating the location of the subdocument.

5. Release the mouse button.

- Word moves the entire subdocument to the new location.

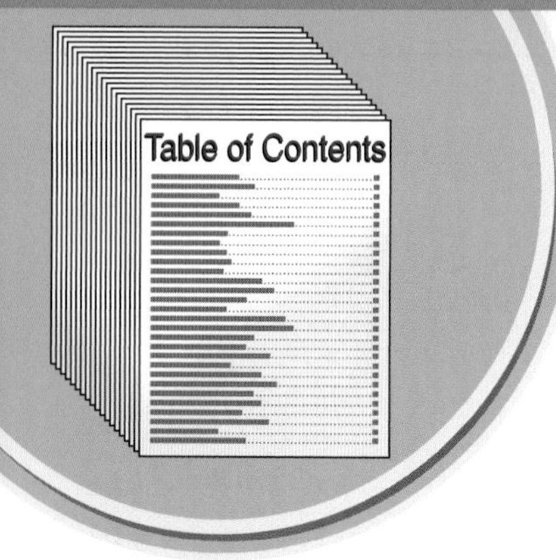

COMBINE OR SPLIT
subdocuments

You can change the layout of your master document by combining multiple subdocuments into one subdocument or splitting a subdocument into two subdocuments. You may want to do this if you decide to combine multiple short chapters into one chapter or split a long chapter into multiple chapters.

To combine multiple subdocuments, you need to make sure that they are located together in your master document. You should also make sure that they are listed in the order you want them to be in the new subdocument. When you combine the subdocuments, Word saves the combined subdocument with the same name as the first subdocument.

When you split a subdocument, Word creates a new subdocument and names it to match the heading text where you split the document. The original document is updated so that it no longer contains the split text. Before you split the document, you need to insert a heading at the location where you intend to split the subdocument.

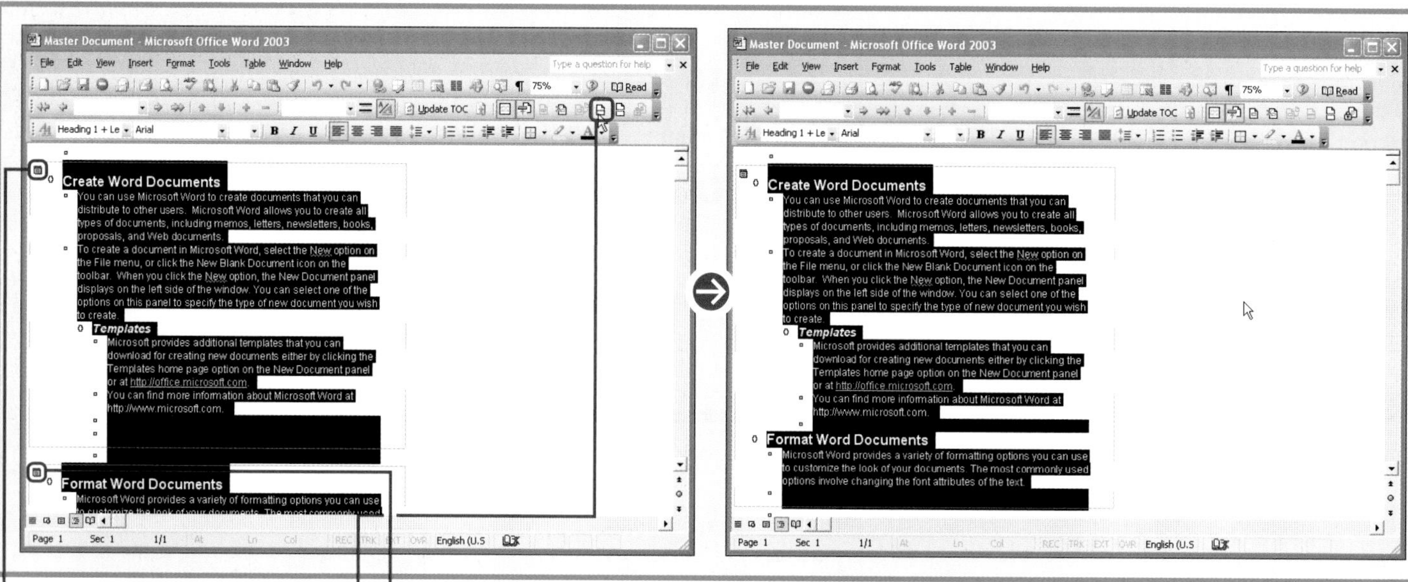

COMBINE SUBDOCUMENTS

① Click the icon of the first subdocument to combine.

② Press Shift.

③ Click the icon of the last subdocument to combine.

④ Click the Merge Subdocument button.

○ Word combines the selected subdocuments.

Did You Know?

Word does not create subdocument files until you save the master document file. Therefore, if you split a subdocument, the new subdocument file is not created until you save.

Did You Know?

If you combine two subdocuments and then later split the combination back to the original subdocuments, Word creates new subdocuments. For example, if the original subdocument is format documents.doc, the new subdocument could be named format subdocument1.doc. This happens because Word does not recognize the correlation between the new subdocument and the original version, and therefore creates a new one to avoid overwriting any existing documents.

Did You Know?

When you combine subdocuments, the combined subdocument is saved in the first subdocument. The other subdocument files remain unchanged.

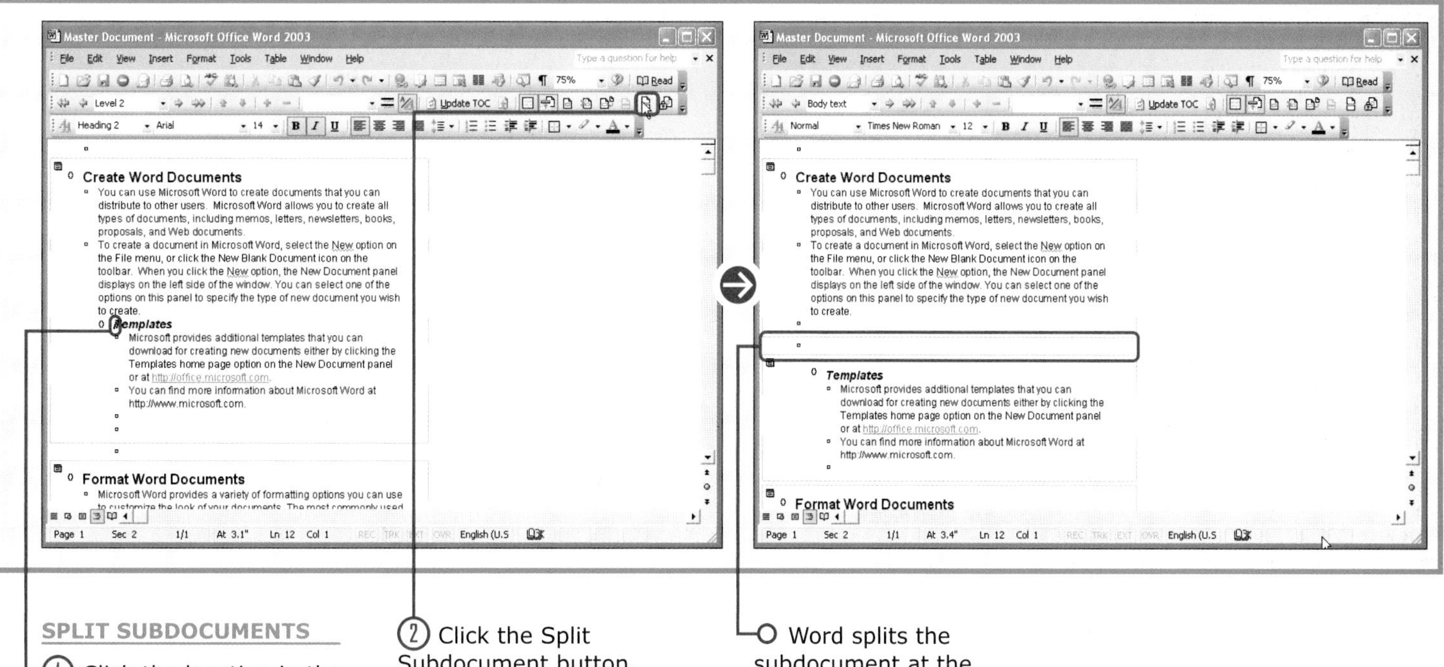

SPLIT SUBDOCUMENTS

1. Click the location in the subdocument where you want to split it.
2. Click the Split Subdocument button.

- Word splits the subdocument at the specified location.

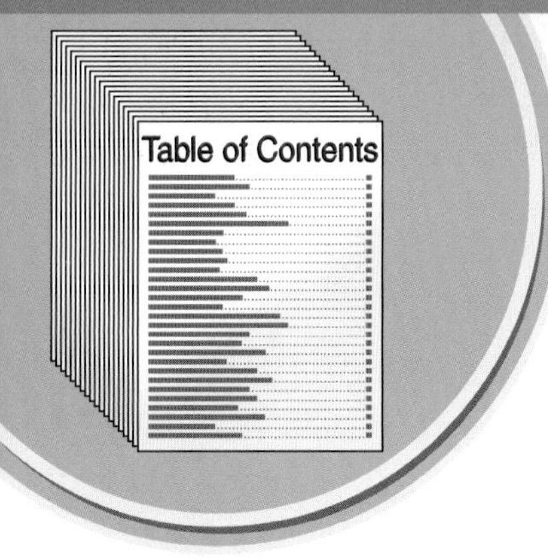

Mark INDEX ENTRIES

You can create an index for any of your documents. Indexes typically appear at the end of large documents, especially books, to provide an alphabetical listing of the topics covered.

To create an index, you must first identify the index entries. The most common method is to manually mark each entry in your document. To do so, highlight the text and then select the Mark Entry option in the Index and Tables dialog box.

In the Mark Index Entry dialog box, you indicate how you want the index entry to appear in the index. You need to specify the main entry text and any subentry text. For example, if you are adding an entry for creating documents, you have several options. You can create a main index entry of *Create,* or you can have a main entry of *Document,* with a subentry of *Create.* When you specify a subentry, the subentry text appears under the main entry. For example, an index entry of *Document* can have several subentries under it.

You can create multiple index entries for the same text in your document.

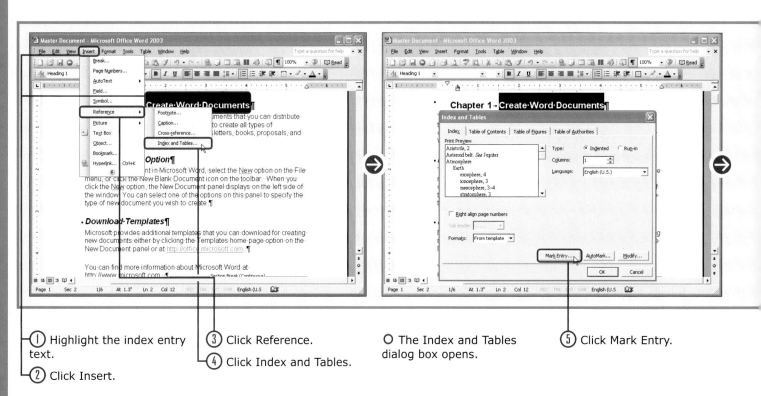

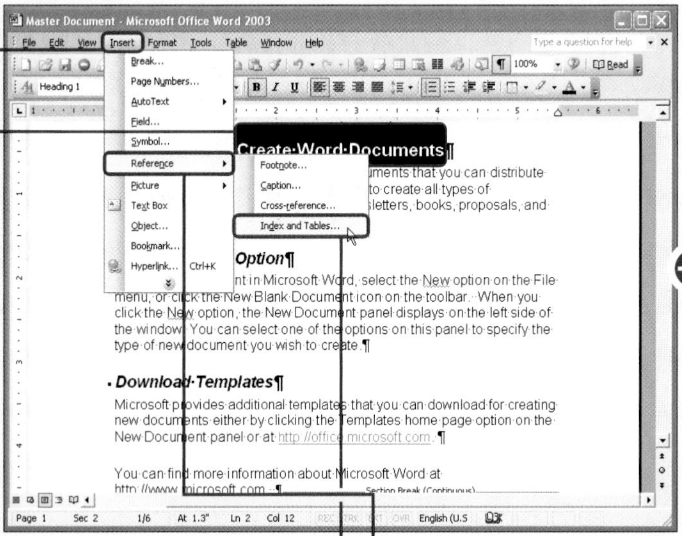

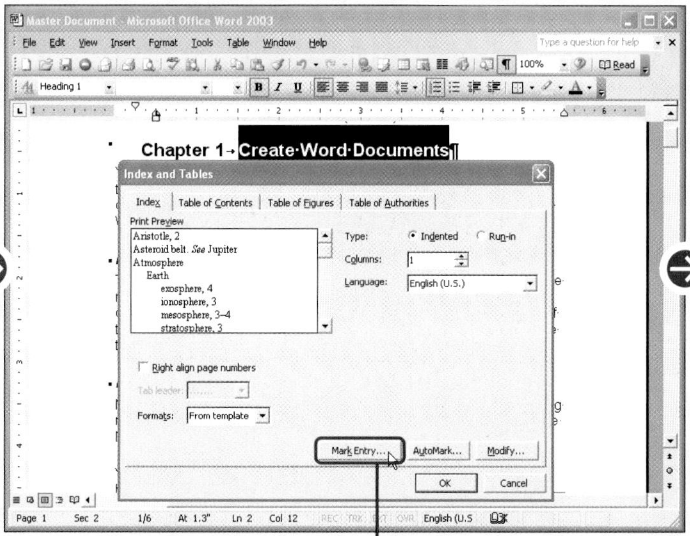

① Highlight the index entry text.

② Click Insert.

③ Click Reference.

④ Click Index and Tables.

○ The Index and Tables dialog box opens.

⑤ Click Mark Entry.

DIFFICULTY LEVEL

Did You Know?

You can press Alt+Shift+X to display the Mark Index Entry dialog box.

Did You Know?

If you have a large document, marking each index entry can be somewhat tedious. Instead, you can create a *concordance* file to create the index. With a concordance file, the index entries you want are specified in a Word table. Word uses the concordance file and locates all occurrences of the specified entries. The nice thing about a concordance file is that you can reuse it to index other related documents. To use the concordance file, click AutoMark in the Index and Tables dialog box. When you do so, Word uses the selected concordance file and automatically inserts index fields at each location in the document.

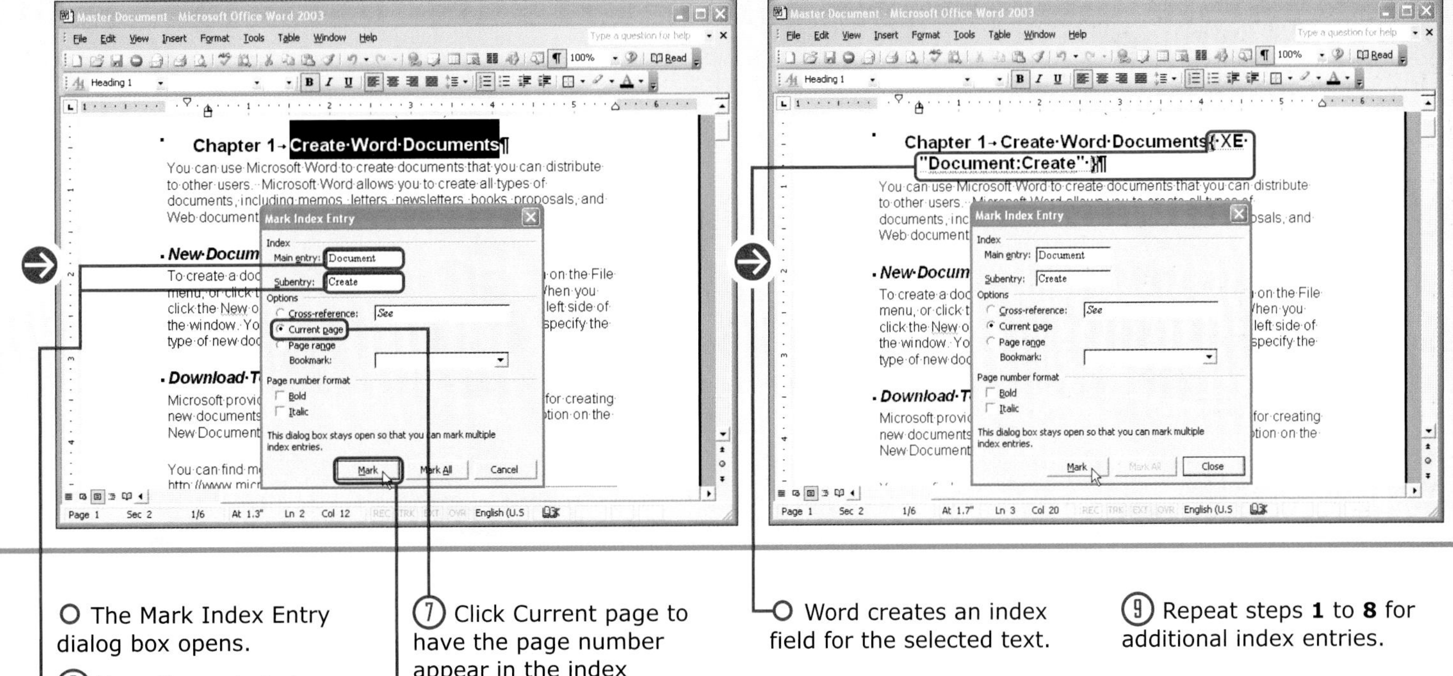

- The Mark Index Entry dialog box opens.

6 Type the main index entry text in the Main entry field.

- If desired, type subentry text in the Subentry field.

7 Click Current page to have the page number appear in the index (○ changes to ◉).

8 Click Mark.

- Word creates an index field for the selected text.

9 Repeat steps **1** to **8** for additional index entries.

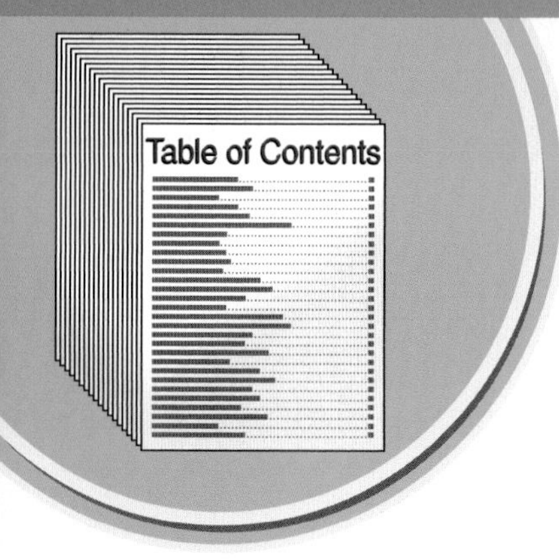

CREATE AN INDEX

from marked entries

You can create an index in any Word document. You create an index from previously marked index entries. See task #54 for more information on marking index entries in a document.

When Word creates an index, it looks for all the index fields in the document. When it finds a field, Word creates a reference by indicating the page number. You can create the index by selecting one of the built-in index formats. You also have the option of specifying the number of columns to use to display the index. Creating a two-column index is common, but if you have a smaller document, you may want to use a single-column index.

After you create the index, you can use any of the text-formatting options to customize the appearance of the index text. The only thing that you should not change is the page number reference.

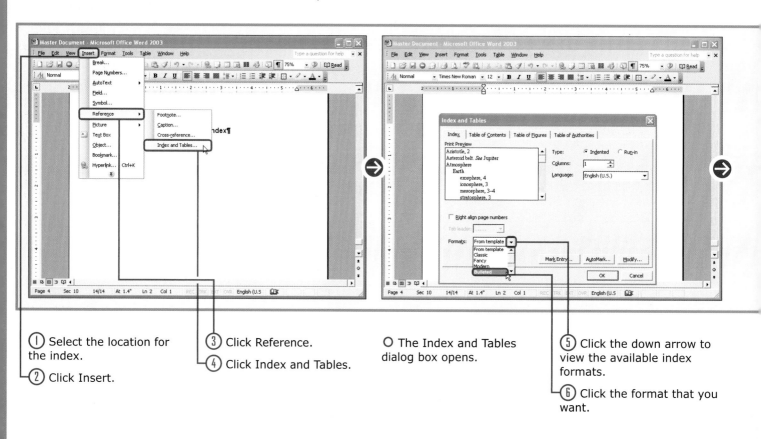

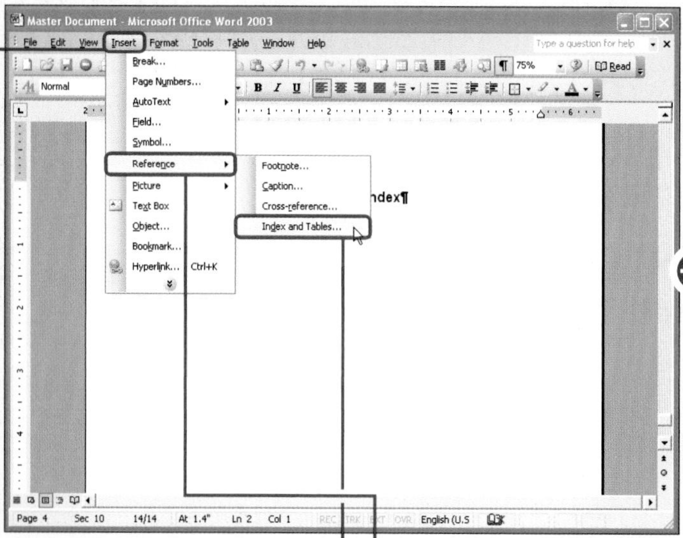

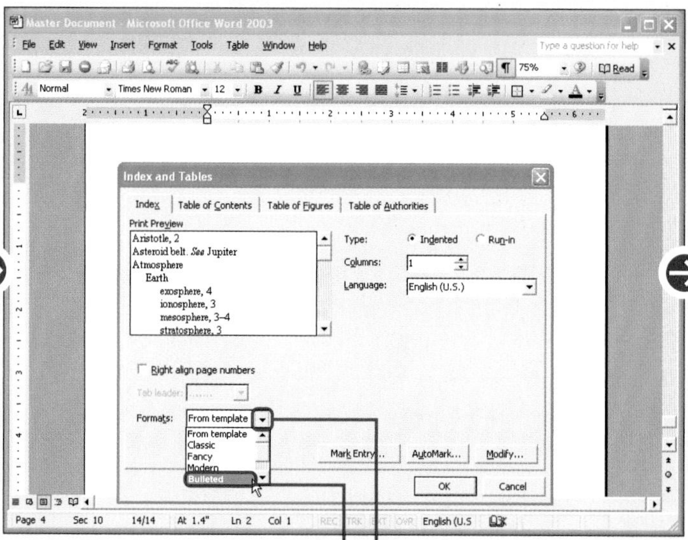

1. Select the location for the index.
2. Click Insert.
3. Click Reference.
4. Click Index and Tables.

- The Index and Tables dialog box opens.

5. Click the down arrow to view the available index formats.
6. Click the format that you want.

DIFFICULTY LEVEL

Apply It!

Before creating an index, make sure that the page numbering is correct. If you have the Reveal Codes option turned on, the page numbering may not be accurate. To hide the formatting and field codes, click the Show/Hide button (¶) on the toolbar.

Apply It!

If you are creating an index in a master document, make sure that all subdocuments are expanded correctly. To expand documents, click Show All Levels in the Show Level list box on the Outline toolbar. See task #51 for more information on working with a master document.

Caution!

If you make any changes to the formatting or layout of the index, those changes will be overwritten anytime you update the index.

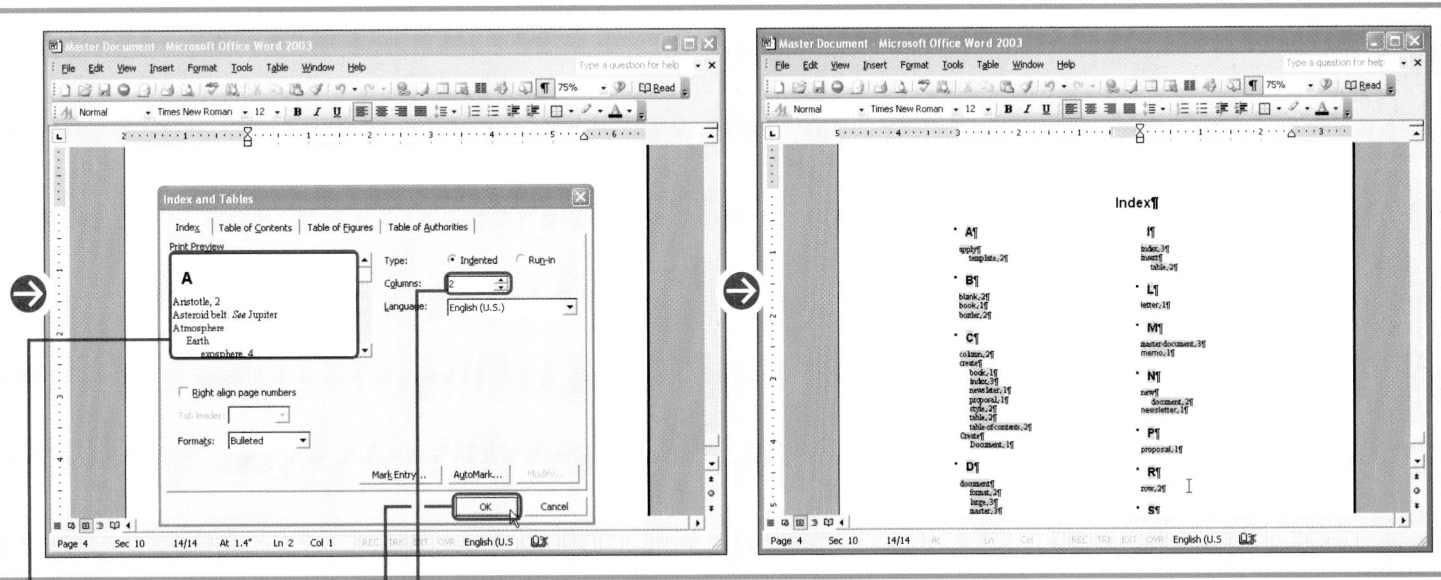

○ The Print Preview window updates to show a sample of the selected index format.

⑦ Click the up or down arrows to select the desired number of columns.

⑧ Click OK.

○ Word creates an index using all the index entries within the document.

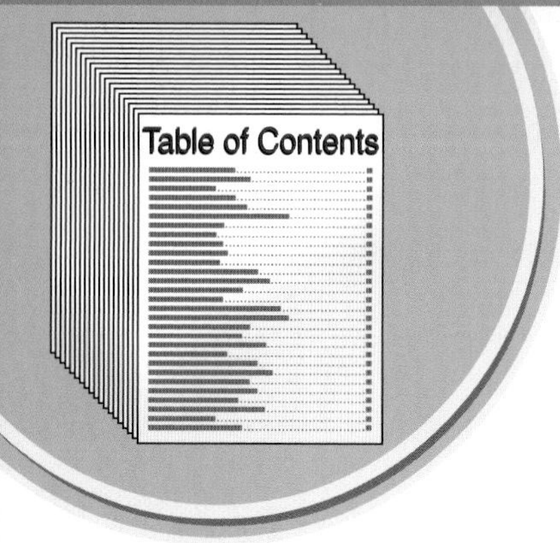

Create a TABLE OF CONTENTS

You can create a table of contents for any Word document. You can use a table of contents to provide an outline of the document for the reader. The table of contents also provides page numbers to identify the location of specific sections in the document.

You use the Index and Tables dialog box to create a table of contents. You can select the layout of the table of contents by selecting one of the available formats. You can indicate the number of levels that you want to display in the tables of contents. For example, if you have three levels of headers in your document, you indicate that you want to show three levels.

If you have custom heading styles, you need to select those styles and indicate the TOC levels in the Table of Contents Options dialog box. When you type a level next to a style, Word automatically selects the style. Keep in mind that Word will use only the styles selected in the dialog box to create the table of contents.

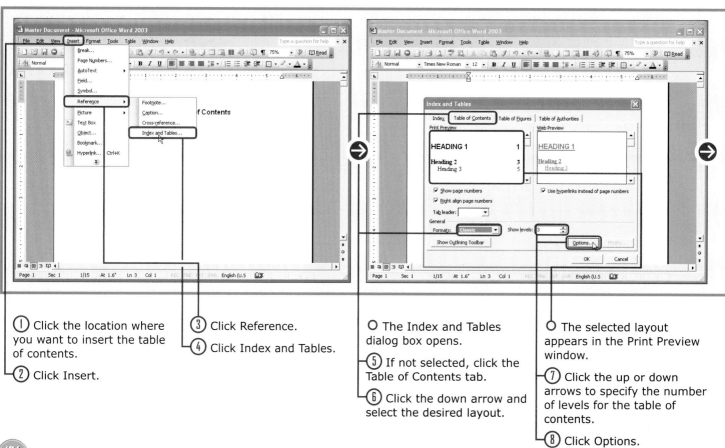

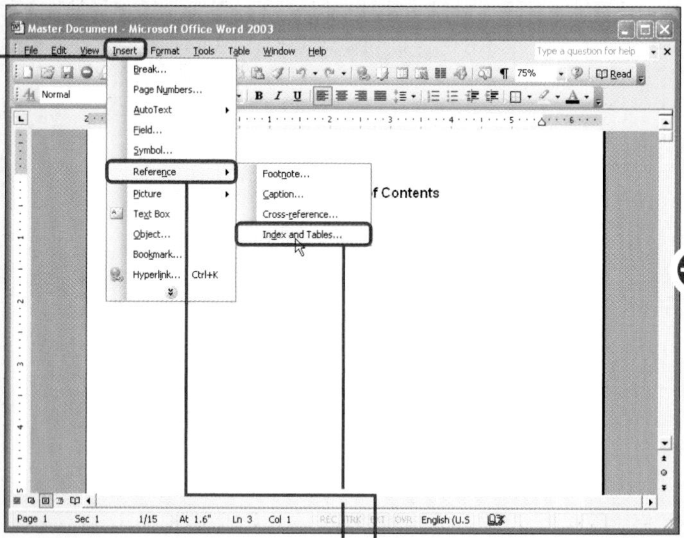

1. Click the location where you want to insert the table of contents.
2. Click Insert.
3. Click Reference.
4. Click Index and Tables.

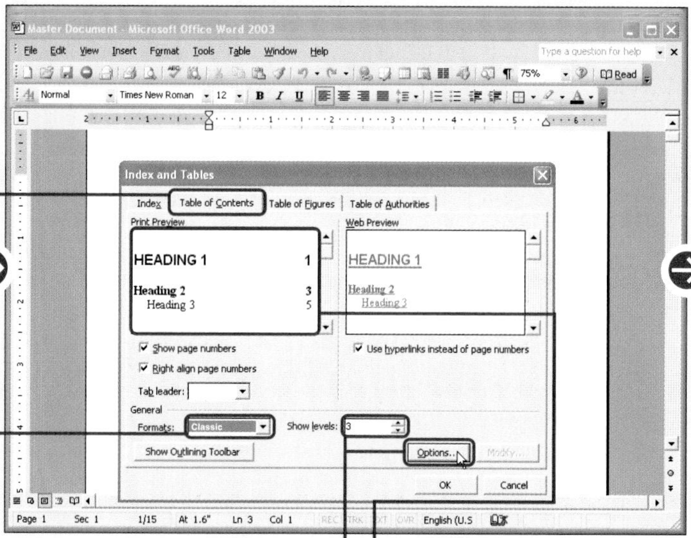

- The Index and Tables dialog box opens.

5. If not selected, click the Table of Contents tab.
6. Click the down arrow and select the desired layout.

- The selected layout appears in the Print Preview window.

7. Click the up or down arrows to specify the number of levels for the table of contents.
8. Click Options.

#56

DIFFICULTY LEVEL

Apply It!

If you create a table of contents for a Web document, you can have hyperlinks appear for each entry instead of page numbers. To create hyperlinks, click the Use Hyperlinks Instead of Page Numbers check box in the Index and Tables dialog box.

Did You Know?

If you make changes to the document that affect the table of contents, such as modifying a title or page numbering, you can update the table of contents. To do so, right-click on the table of contents and select the Update Field option from the menu to display the Update Table of Contents dialog box. You can update just the page numbers or the entire table of contents.

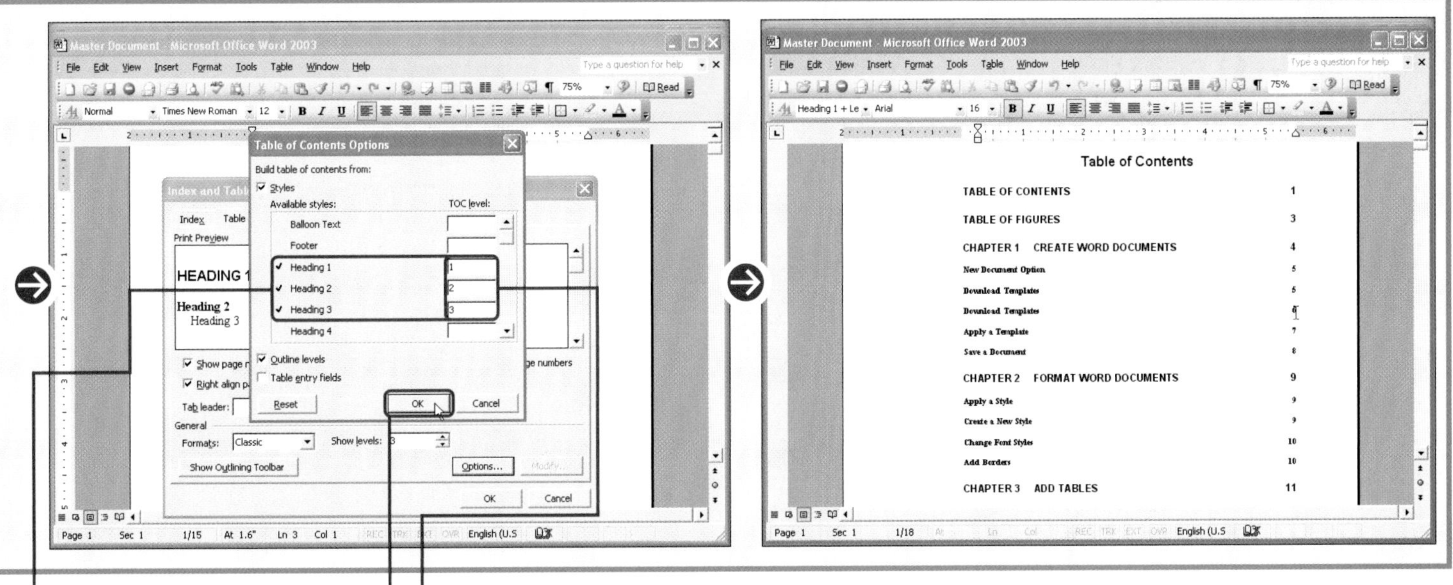

- The Table of Contents Options dialog box opens.

9 Locate the styles that you want to use for the table of contents.

10 Type a number between **1** and **9** to indicate the table of contents level.

11 Click OK.

- Word creates the table of contents using the specified settings.

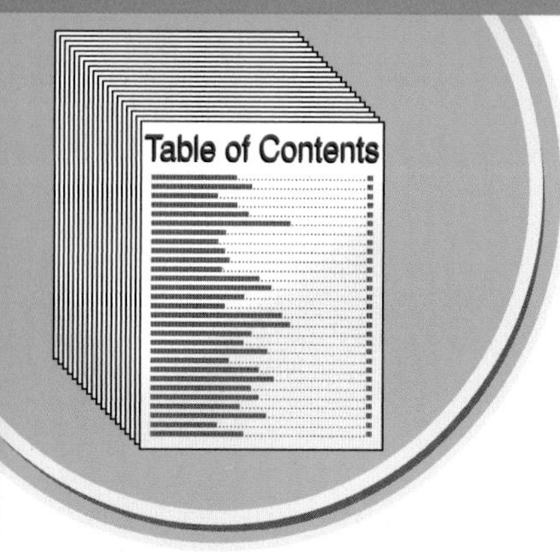

Create a TABLE OF FIGURES

You can create a table of figures for your Word document. You can use a table of figures to provide the reader with a reference to the location of pictures, tables, and equations within your Word document.

In the Index and Tables dialog box, select the format that you want to apply to the table of figures. You can select one of the provided layout formats for the table of figures.

If you want to create a table for only one type of figure, such as tables, you select that type of figure from the Caption Label field. For example, you may want to separate the figures and tables into two different tables. To do so, you would create two different tables and specify the desired type in the Caption Label field for each table.

If you want the table to include all three types of figures, you need to specify the style used to create the captions for all the figures in the Tables of Figures Options dialog box.

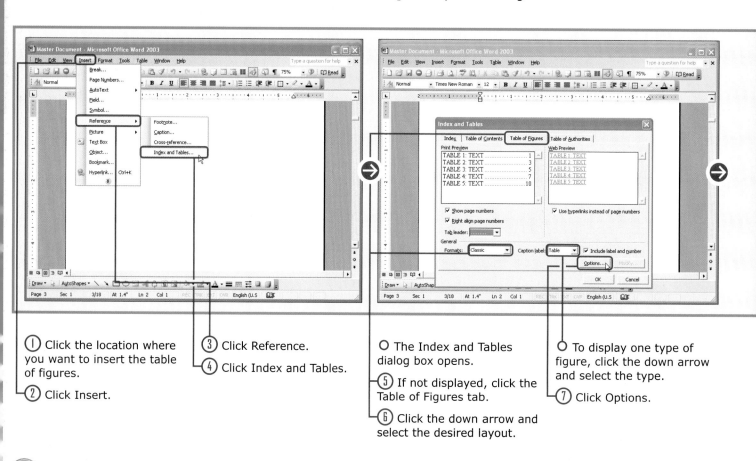

1 Click the location where you want to insert the table of figures.

2 Click Insert.

3 Click Reference.

4 Click Index and Tables.

- The Index and Tables dialog box opens.

5 If not displayed, click the Table of Figures tab.

6 Click the down arrow and select the desired layout.

- To display one type of figure, click the down arrow and select the type.

7 Click Options.

Did You Know?

When you add a caption to a floating object, Word automatically places the caption in a text box. Unfortunately, when you create a table of figures, Word does not find captions that are inserted in text boxes. To correct this, select the text box containing the caption and click Format ➪ Text Box to display the Format Text Box dialog box. In the Text Box tab, click Convert to Frame. Word converts the text box around the caption to a frame so that it can be added to the table of figures.

Apply It!

If you add new figures to your document, the figure captions may not be in numeric order. You can update the figure numbering by pressing Ctrl+A to select the entire document and then pressing F9.

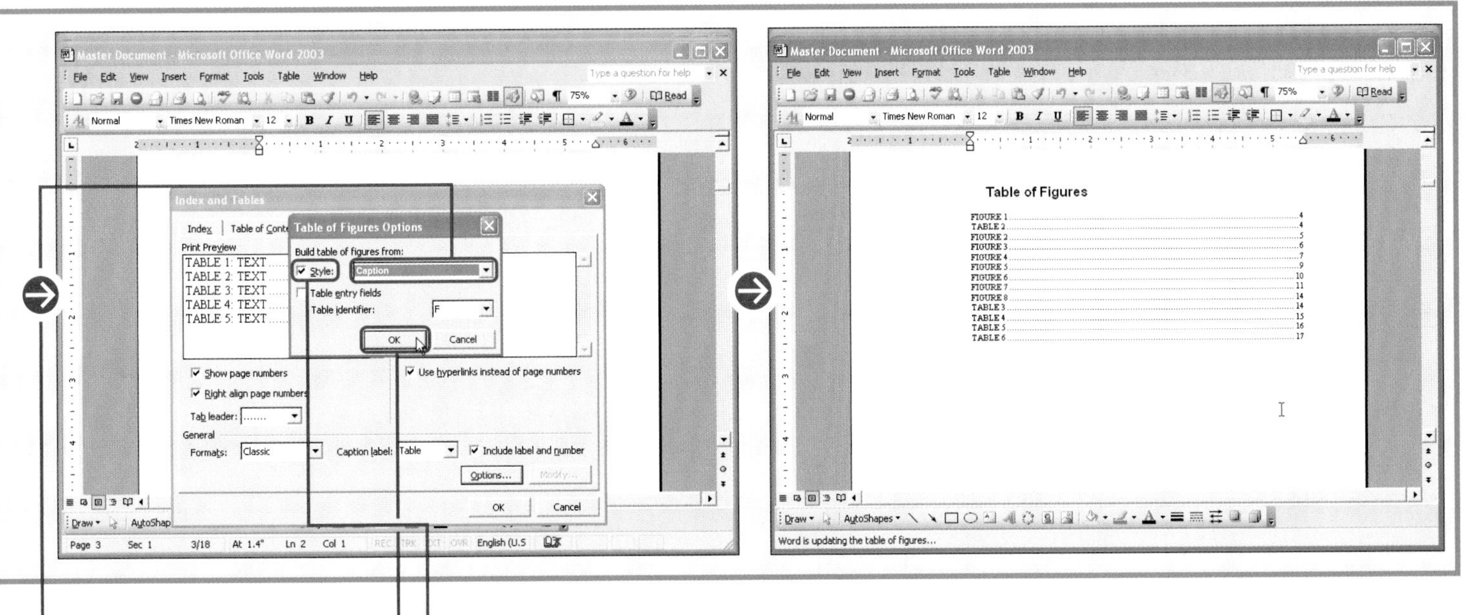

- The Table of Figures Options dialog box opens.

8. Click the down arrow and select the style of the caption text.

- Word automatically selects the Style field (☐ changes to ☑).

9. Click OK.

- Word creates a table of figures that contains all figures, tables, and equations in the document, or just one of these, if you selected only one type.

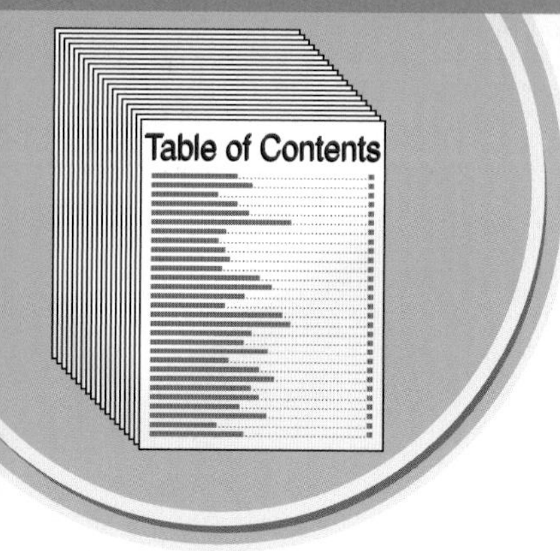

Create a TABLE OF AUTHORITIES

You can create a table of authorities to list the citations in your document. *Tables of authorities* are typically used in legal documents to list the cases and other legal documents that are referenced in the document. You can also use a table of authorities to list any type of citations in your documents, such as quotes from other books.

You create a table of authorities using the Index and Tables dialog box. You can create a table of authorities that includes citations for all categories or just a specific category. For example, you may want to display only the citations related to cases.

If your document includes the same citation five or more times, you can insert the word *passim* instead of the actual page numbers. If you prefer to display all the page numbers, make sure that the Use Passim option is not selected.

You can select only the formats available in the Index and Tables dialog box for laying out the table of authorities. As you select the layout, a sample appears in the Print Preview window.

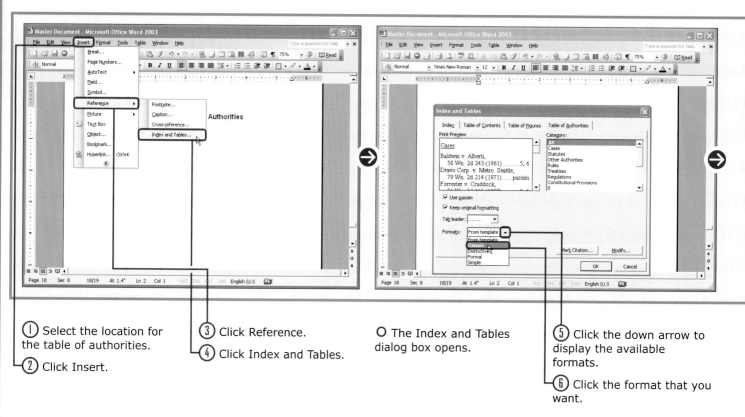

1. Select the location for the table of authorities.
2. Click Insert.
3. Click Reference.
4. Click Index and Tables.

- The Index and Tables dialog box opens.

5. Click the down arrow to display the available formats.
6. Click the format that you want.

DIFFICULTY LEVEL

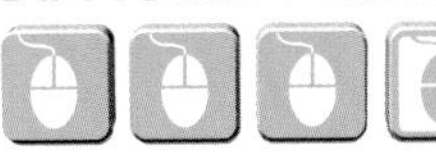

Did You Know?

You can create citations anywhere in your document. To create a citation, highlight the text and press Alt+Shift+I to display the Mark Citation dialog box. Select the category to assign to the citation. Click Mark to mark the text as a citation in your document.

Did You Know?

You can create your own citation categories in the Mark Citation dialog box, which opens when you click Alt+Shift+I. Click Category to display the Edit Category dialog box and select the category name you want to modify. You can change the name of any category, and you can have up to 16 different categories.

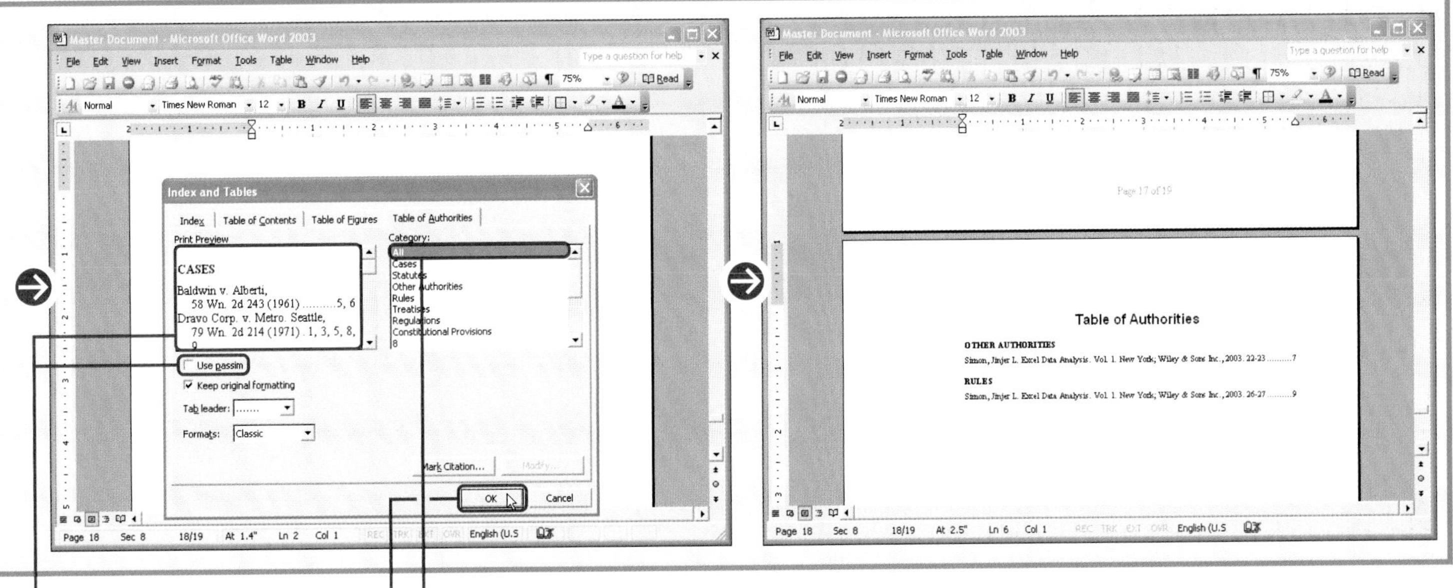

- The selected format appears in the Print Preview window.

7 Click Use passim to remove the check mark (☐ changes to ☑) and display all page numbers.

8 Click All to add all the citations to the table of authorities.

9 Click OK.

- Word creates the table of authorities with the specified options.

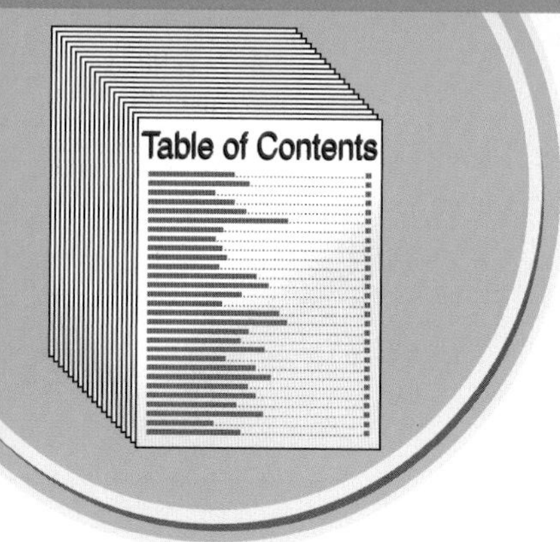

ADD CROSS-REFERENCES

to your document

You can insert cross-references to other locations in your Word documents. You use a cross-reference to specify another part of the document that covers the related information. You can also insert the page number of the cross-reference. Because the cross-reference is a field, when you update your fields in the document, Word also updates all cross-references. This ensures that the cross-references are current.

You create a cross-reference in the Cross-reference dialog box. You need to specify the type of item that you want to reference. You can create cross-references to specific headings or other Word elements, such as bookmarks, equations, and even tables. The type of element you select determines the available selections in the dialog box. For example, if you select Table, Word lists the captions for the tables in the document. Keep in mind that you must have captions assigned to tables, figures, and equations in order to create cross-references.

You need to indicate what type of reference you want to place in the document. You can reference the corresponding text or the page number.

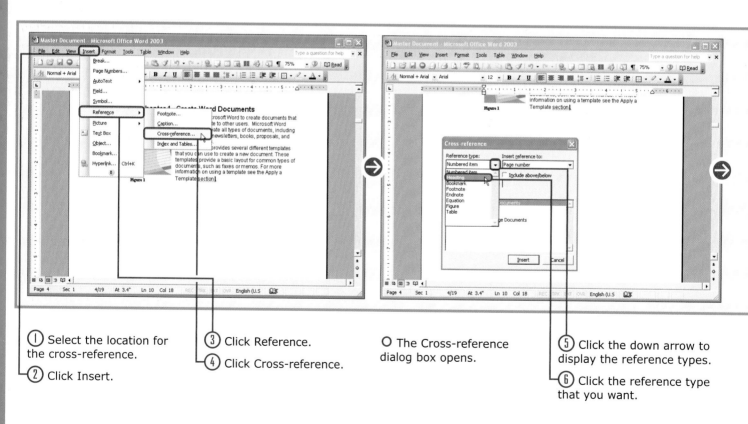

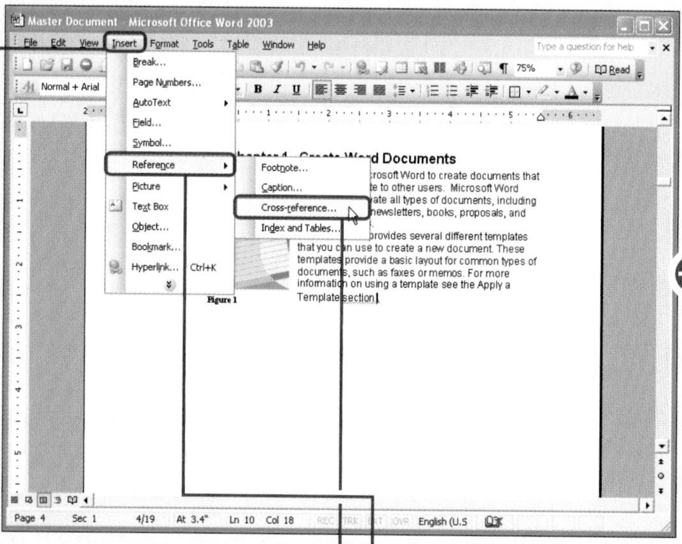

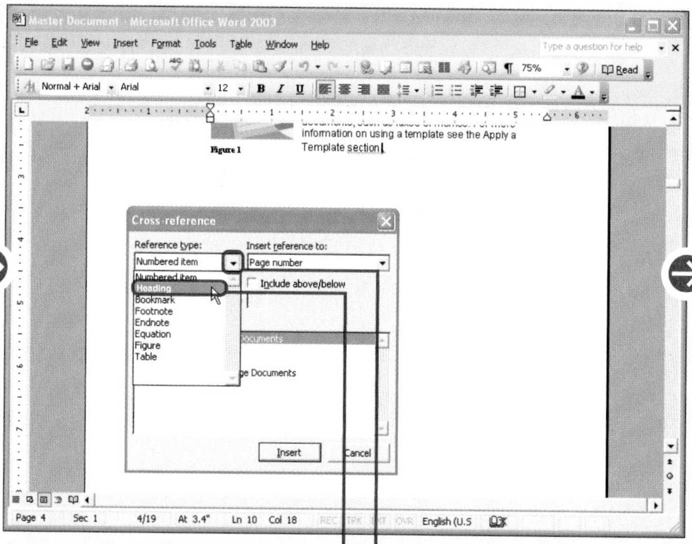

1. Select the location for the cross-reference.
2. Click Insert.
3. Click Reference.
4. Click Cross-reference.

- The Cross-reference dialog box opens.

5. Click the down arrow to display the reference types.
6. Click the reference type that you want.

DIFFICULTY LEVEL

Did You Know?

You can update the cross-references in a document by updating the fields. To do so, click Edit ➪ Select All to select the entire document and then press F9. Word verifies the reference locations of all the cross-reference fields and updates them.

If you do not see the heading that you want to cross-reference listed in the Cross-Reference dialog box, it probably does not have the correct style. You can cross-reference only headings with the built-in styles, such as Heading 1 and Heading 2. If you do not see your heading listed, try applying one of those styles.

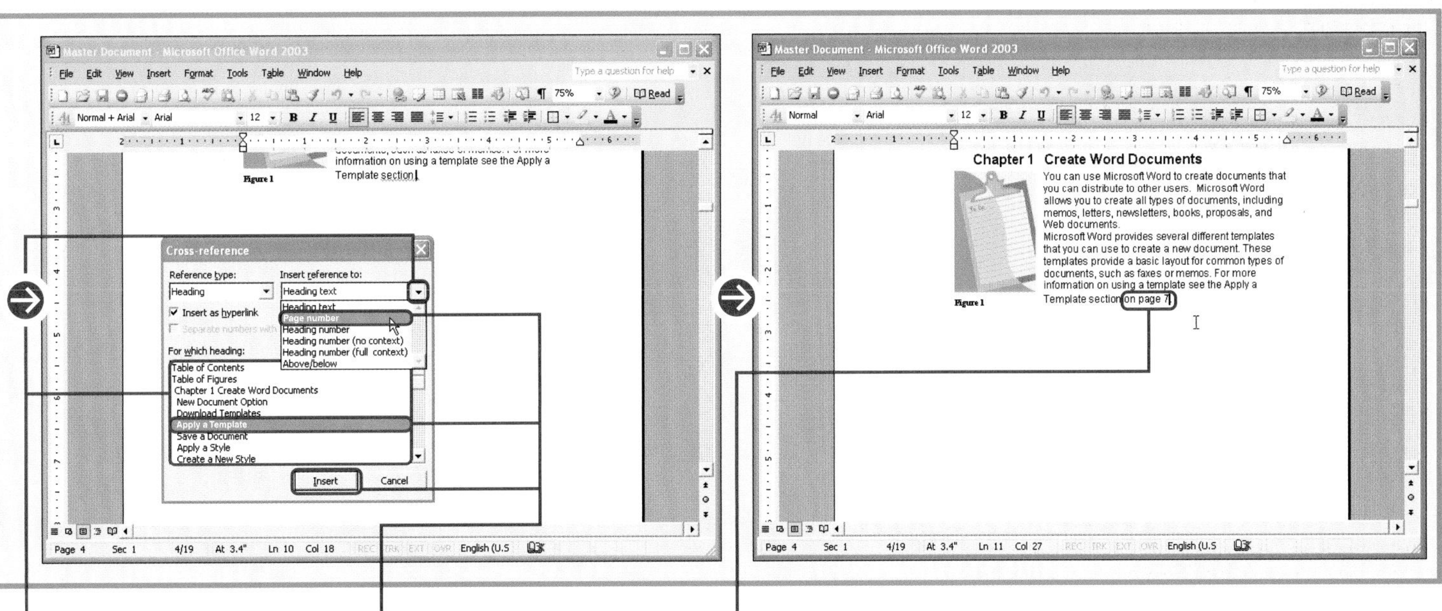

- The corresponding references appear in the list box.
- ⑦ Click the down arrow to display the reference types.
- ⑧ Click the reference type that you want.
- ⑨ Click the reference.
- ⑩ Click Insert.
- Word creates the specified cross-reference.

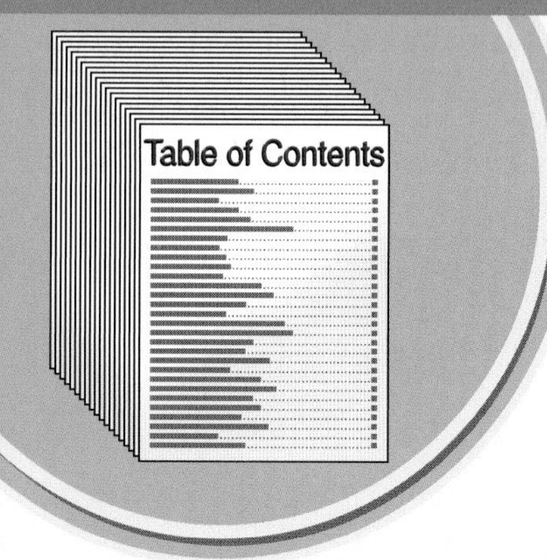

USE A BOOKMARK
in your document

You can create bookmarks in your Word documents to identify text that you want to reference at another time. For example, you can use bookmarked text to create a cross-reference. See task #69 for more information on creating a cross-reference. You can also use bookmarks to identify text that you want to revise.

You create a bookmark in the Bookmark dialog box. The dialog box lists all the current bookmarks in your document. You can assign any name to a bookmark, but the name must begin with a letter and cannot contain any spaces. You can, however, use an underscore character (_) to represent a space. For example, Create_bookmarks is a valid bookmark name.

When you insert a bookmark in your document, Word places square brackets ([ ]) around the text. If the bookmark brackets are not visible, you can turn them on by clicking Tools ⇨ Options ⇨ View and selecting the Bookmarks option.

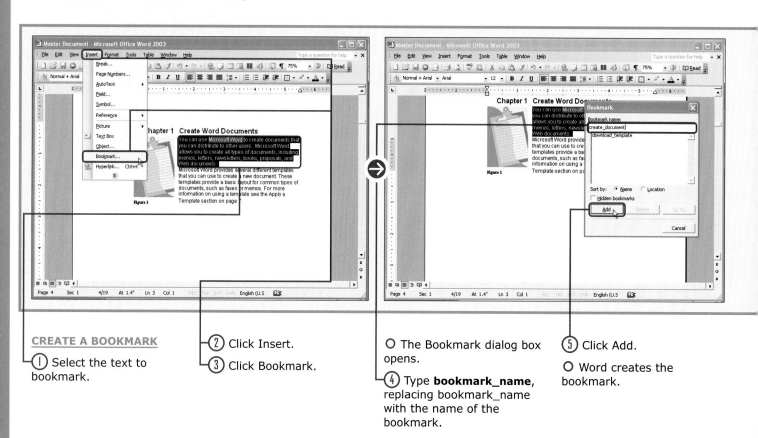

CREATE A BOOKMARK

1. Select the text to bookmark.
2. Click Insert.
3. Click Bookmark.

- The Bookmark dialog box opens.

4. Type **bookmark_name**, replacing bookmark_name with the name of the bookmark.
5. Click Add.

- Word creates the bookmark.

DIFFICULTY LEVEL

Apply It!

You can jump to a bookmark in your document from the Bookmark dialog box. The dialog box lists all the existing bookmarks in the document either in alphabetical order or sorted based on the order that they occur in your document. To change the sort order, click Name to sort alphabetically or Location to sort by the order. Click the bookmark that you want in the list and click Go To. Word jumps to the start of the selected bookmark.

Did You Know?

If you no longer need a bookmark, you can remove it from the document. Click Insert ➪ Bookmark to display the Bookmark dialog box. Click the bookmark that you want to remove and click Delete.

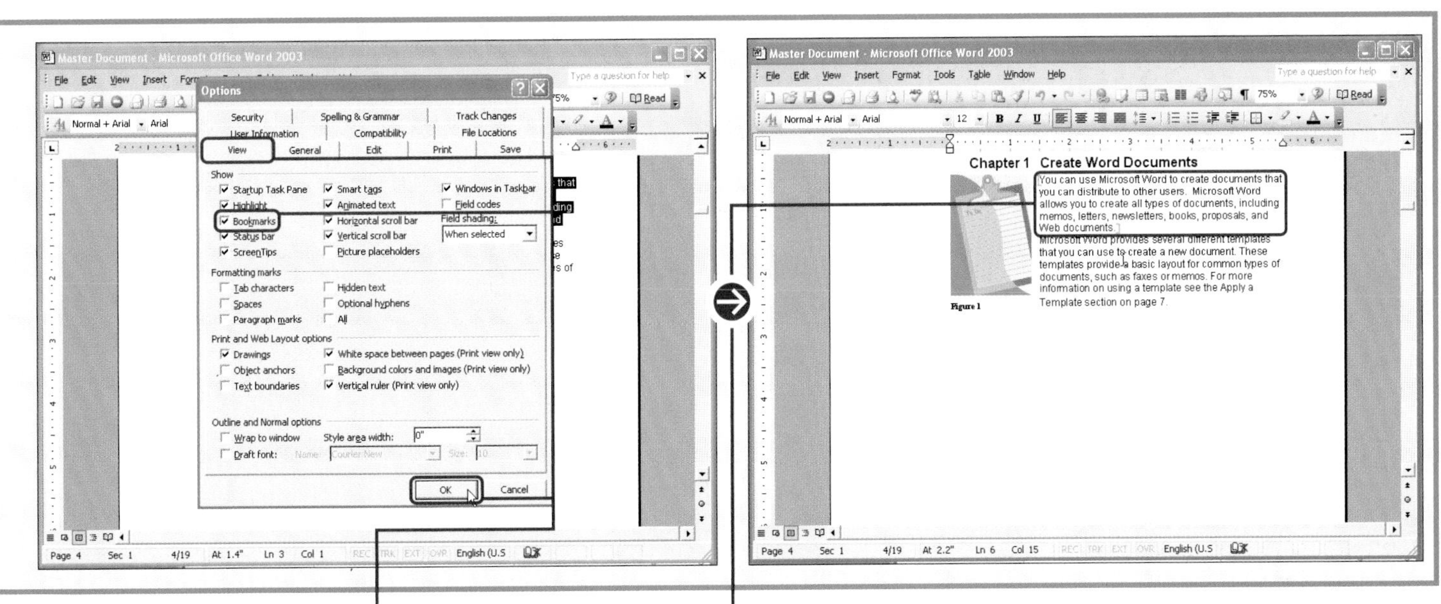

MAKE BOOKMARKS VISIBLE

① Click Tools.

② Click Options.

- The Options dialog box opens.

③ Click the View tab.

④ Click Bookmarks (☐ changes to ☑).

⑤ Click OK.

- Word displays [ ] around each of the bookmarks in the document.

CHAPTER 7

Printing Documents

Word provides a variety of print features that you can use to control the look of your printed documents. These features include setting the layout, controlling margin sizes, and even duplexing printouts.

When working with large master documents, you should always print from the master document to ensure the proper page numbering, even if you want only a small section of the document. You can specify a range of pages to print from a document, even when the range spans multiple sections. To do so, you specify not only the pages you want to print but also the sections for the pages.

Word provides both Print Preview and Print Layout views for working with documents before printing. You can use the Print Layout view to create the entire document and see exactly where text and objects will reside on the page. Before printing, select the Print Preview mode to preview the printout and see how the document lays out on multiple pages.

Word enables you to create different document types, including a folded booklet. With this type of book, Word prints two pages on each sheet of paper. You fold the paper in the center to create the binding.

This chapter looks at different features to simplify the process of printing documents in Word.

TOP 100

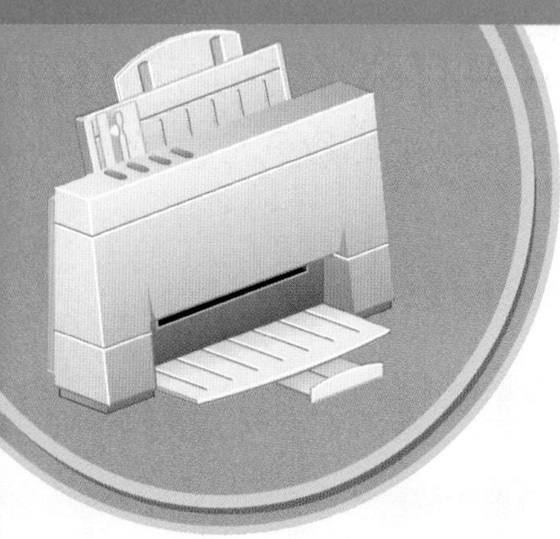

Print a MASTER DOCUMENT

You can print out an entire master document. *Master documents* enable you to link several subdocuments together into one large document. See Chapter 6 for more information on creating and working with master documents.

When you are ready to print the final document, you want to print from the master document instead of the subdocuments to ensure that elements of the master document such as page numbering, headers, and footers are correct.

To print an entire master document, you need to open or expand the linked subdocuments so that they appear in the master document. Word prints only in the expanded portions of your master document, so if the subdocuments are not expanded, they will not print. You expand the subdocuments from the Outline view. After the documents are expanded, you can switch to the Print Layout view to see what the document will look like.

After the master document is expanded, Word prints the specified range of pages. If you do not want to print the entire document, you can print specific ranges; See task #62 for more information.

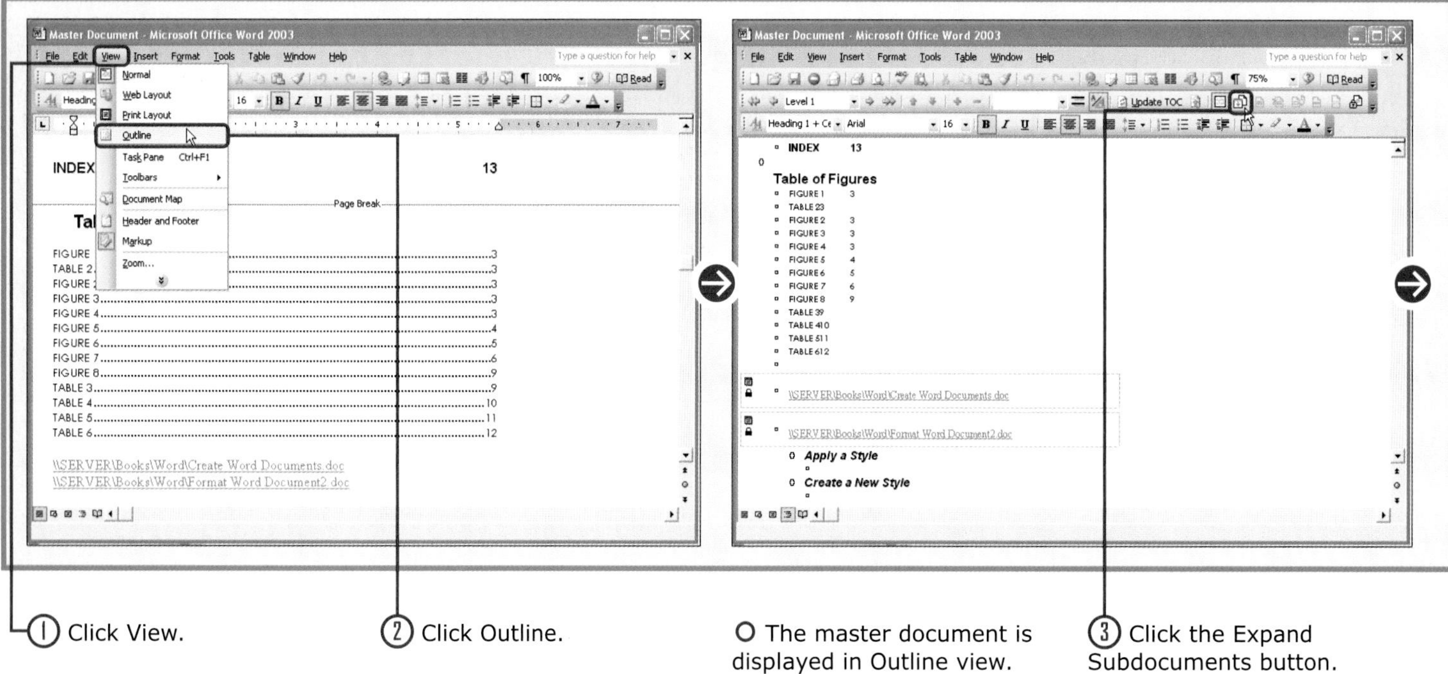

① Click View.

② Click Outline.

○ The master document is displayed in Outline view.

③ Click the Expand Subdocuments button.

#61

DIFFICULTY LEVEL

Did You Know?

You can print only specific portions of the document by collapsing the other heading levels. To expand and collapse the document, you need to be in Outline view, which you can access by clicking View ➪ Outline. If you want to display only the headers, you can select the desired heading levels.

Put It Together!

If the subdocuments have been modified and your master document includes a table of contents, index, or other type of table, you need to update the fields before printing. The fastest way to update the fields is to click Edit ➪ Select All to select the entire document and then press F9. Word displays a dialog box for each table to determine if you want to re-create the table or just update the page numbers.

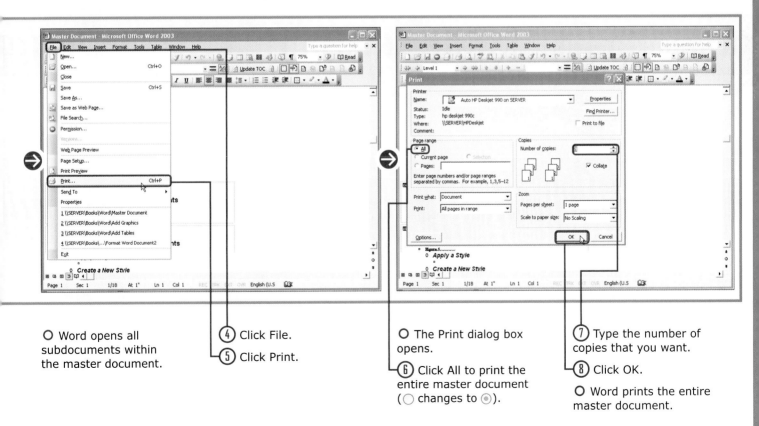

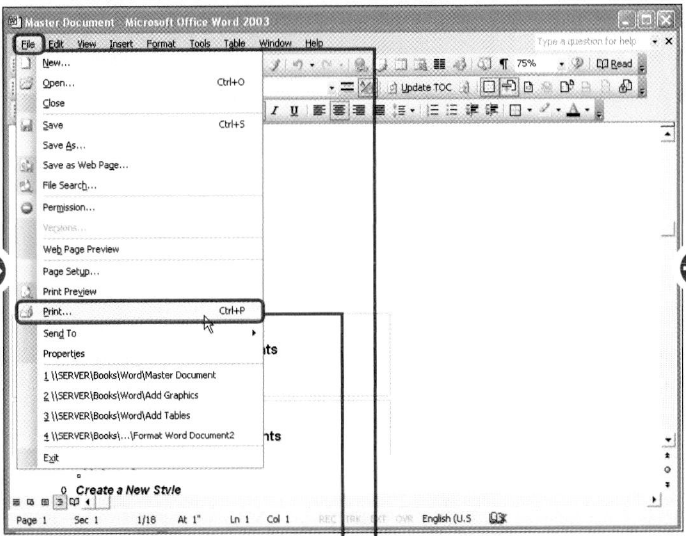

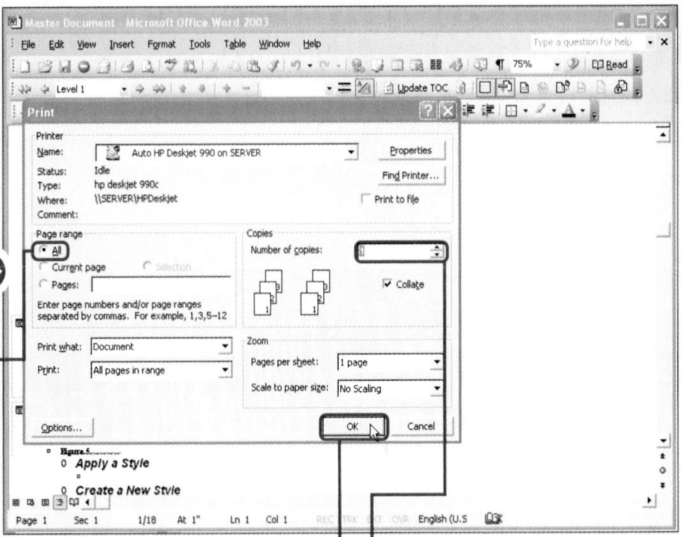

- Word opens all subdocuments within the master document.

4. Click File.
5. Click Print.

- The Print dialog box opens.

6. Click All to print the entire master document (○ changes to ◉).
7. Type the number of copies that you want.
8. Click OK.

- Word prints the entire master document.

Print a RANGE OF PAGES ACROSS SECTIONS

You can print a range of pages that spans multiple sections in a document. If you are printing from a master document, Word treats each subdocument as a separate section in the document. If you want to print only specific pages in the document, you need to identify the pages based on the section number and the page number within the section.

You can see the page number and section number by looking at the bottom-left corner of the status bar. For example, "Page 4 Sec 1" indicates that you are viewing the fourth page in the first section of the document.

When you print, you specify the page number by preceding it with a *p;* for example, for page 4, you type p4. You specify a section number with an *s,* such as s2 for section 2. Therefore, you type p4s2 for the fourth page in the second section. You specify the range of pages to print in the Pages field of the Print dialog box.

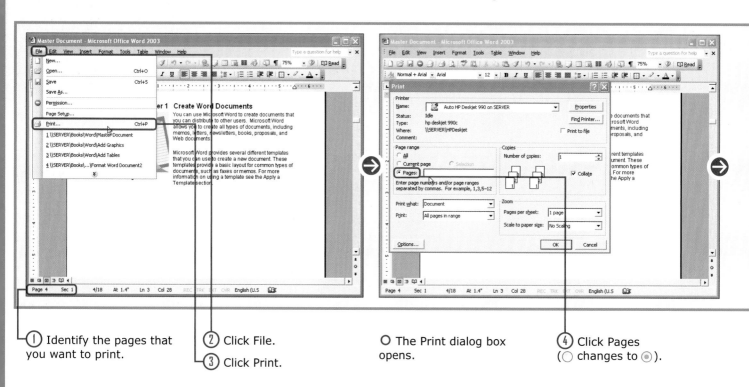

1. Identify the pages that you want to print.
2. Click File.
3. Click Print.

- The Print dialog box opens.

4. Click Pages (○ changes to ◉).

Apply It!

If the pages you want to print are not consecutive, you can specify each individual page number. For example, you can type p4s1, p2s2, p3s3 to print pages from multiple sections. You can also combine a range of pages with individual page numbers. For example, you can type p1s1-p15s1, p1s2, p3s4 to print a range of pages from section 1 and individual pages from other sections.

Did You Know?

You can print only the odd or even pages in a range. To do so, specify the desired range in the Print dialog box, and then select Even Pages or Odd Pages in the Print field to print only the even or odd pages in that range.

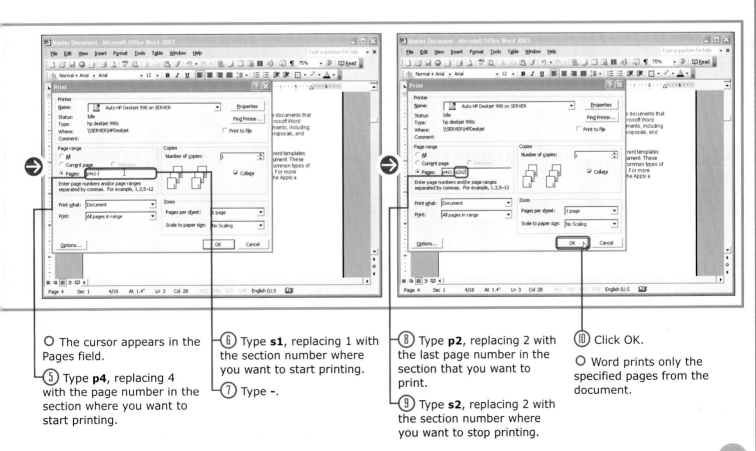

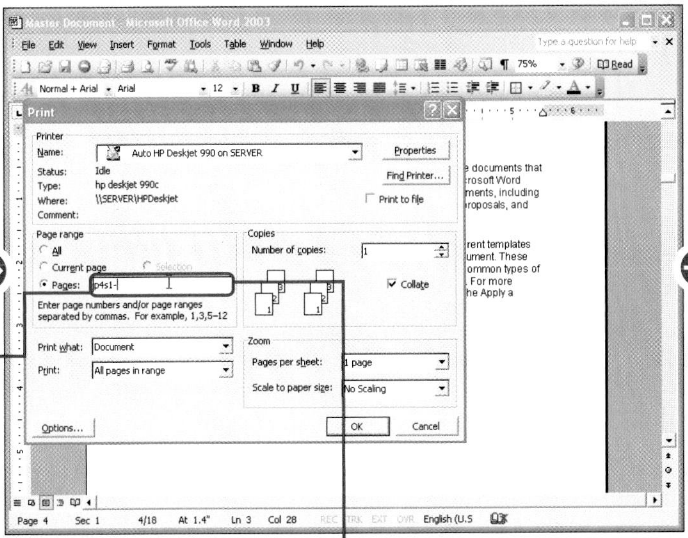

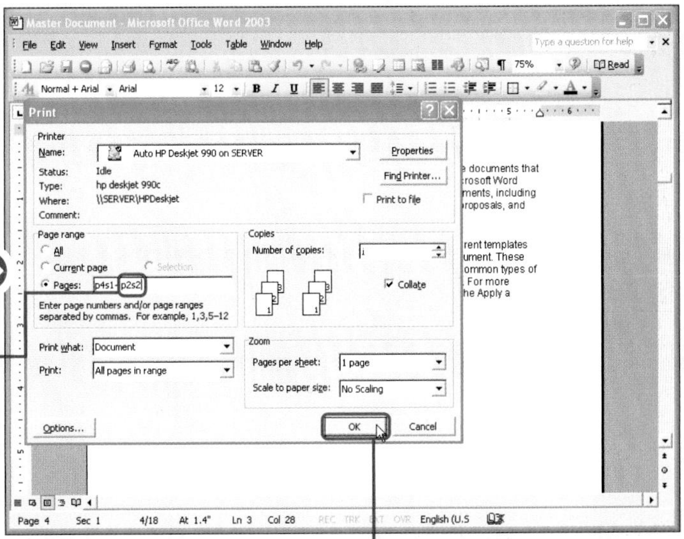

- The cursor appears in the Pages field.

5 Type **p4**, replacing 4 with the page number in the section where you want to start printing.

6 Type **s1**, replacing 1 with the section number where you want to start printing.

7 Type **-**.

8 Type **p2**, replacing 2 with the last page number in the section that you want to print.

9 Type **s2**, replacing 2 with the section number where you want to stop printing.

10 Click OK.

- Word prints only the specified pages from the document.

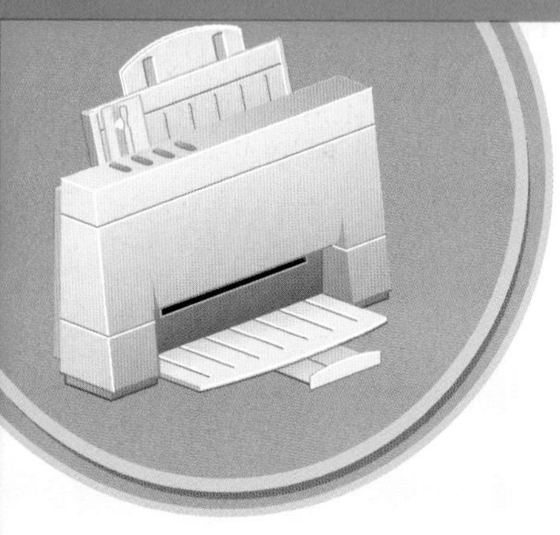

HIDE THE WHITE SPACE in Print Layout view

When you look at a document in Print Layout view, you can have Word hide the excess white space so that you can see more of the actual text. You can use this option when you need to review the text and graphics in the document and are not concerned about the extra spacing at the top and bottom of each page.

When you hide the white space in the document, Word still shows the page breaks by drawing heavy black lines between each page. You can quickly scroll through the document and see how everything is layed out. Keep in mind that Word still maintains the actual pages sizes, so edits to the document still have the same effect on the document flow.

When you hide the white space, Word also hides the headers and footers that normally appear in Print Layout view. The headers and footers are still there; you can view them by clicking View ⇨ Header and Footer.

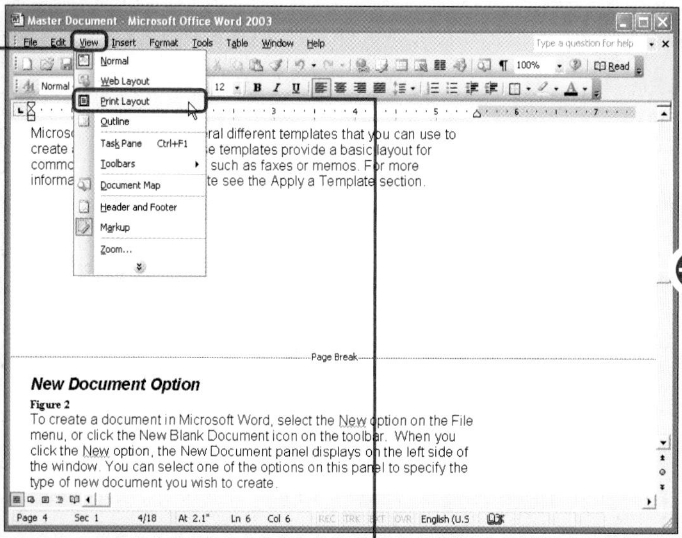

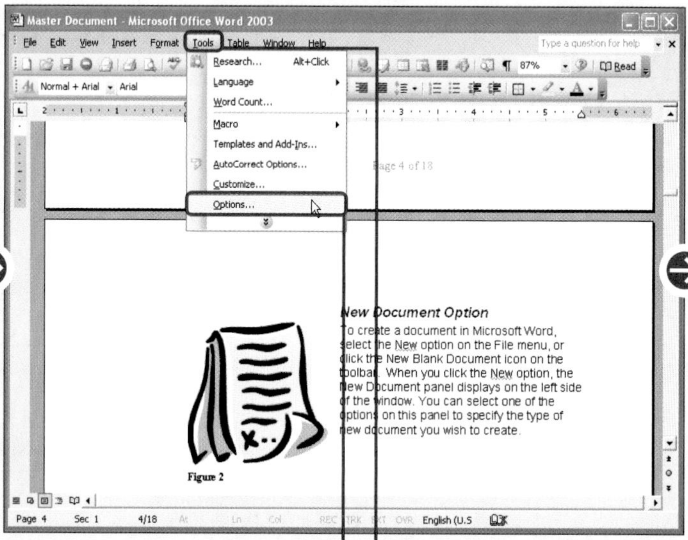

1. Click View.
2. Click Print Layout.

- The document is displayed as it will print.

3. Click Tools.
4. Click Options.

DIFFICULTY LEVEL

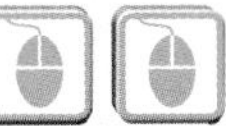

Did You Know?

You can specify whether to display background colors and images in Print Preview by clicking the Background Colors and Images option in the Options dialog box. If the option is not selected, any background colors or watermark images will not appear in Print Preview.

Did You Know?

You can quickly cancel the Hide White Space option by clicking the black line that divides the pages. By clicking on the page breaks you can toggle between hiding and showing the white space of the document.

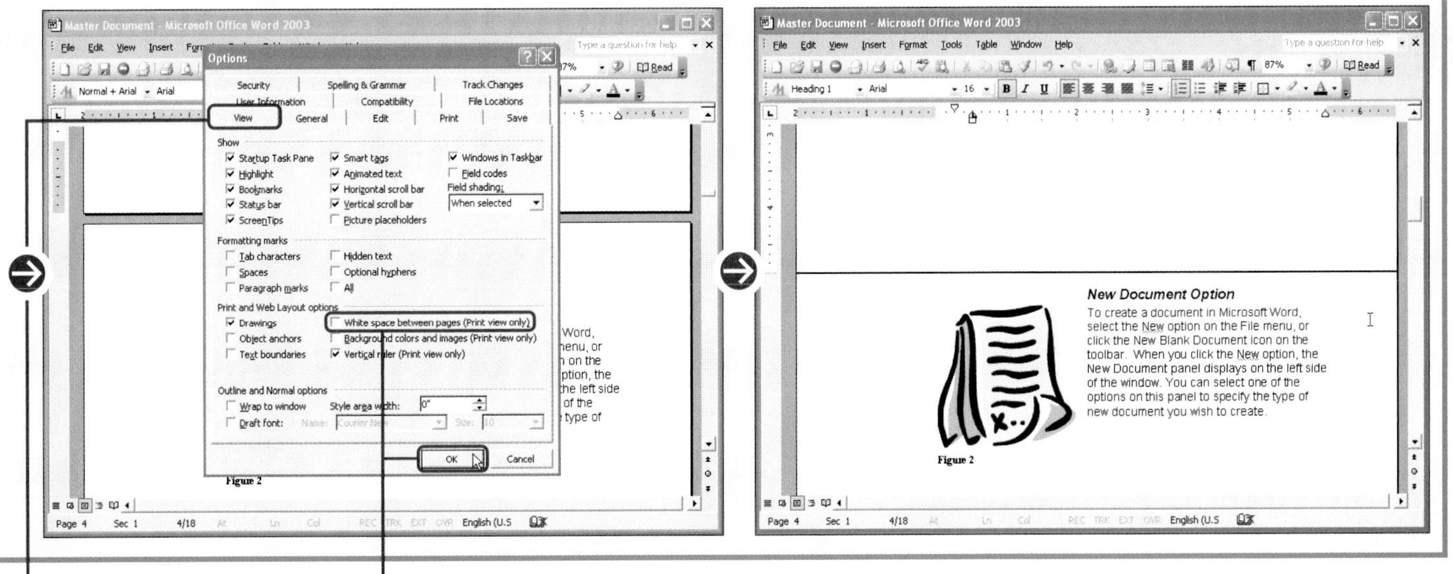

- The Options dialog box opens.

5. If it is not displayed, click the View tab.

6. Click White Space between pages to remove the check mark (☑ changes to ☐).

7. Click OK.

- Word removes the excess white space between pages.

Edit Text in PRINT PREVIEW

You can make several modifications to the text of the document when you are viewing it in Print Preview. This enables you to make minor adjustments before actually printing.

Print Preview displays the pages of your document as they will print on paper. For example, if you have specified that you do not want to print the graphic images, they will not show in Print Preview. See task #70 for more information.

When you display a document in Print Preview, the Magnification mode is automatically selected. To modify the text, you need to turn off that mode.

As you are looking for final edits to make, you may want to make sure that there are no single lines of text on a page. For example, you may have a table of contents that does not fit on a complete page. Select the Shrink to Fit button, and Word will reduce the font sizes of the text on the previous page to make the single line of text fit on the first page.

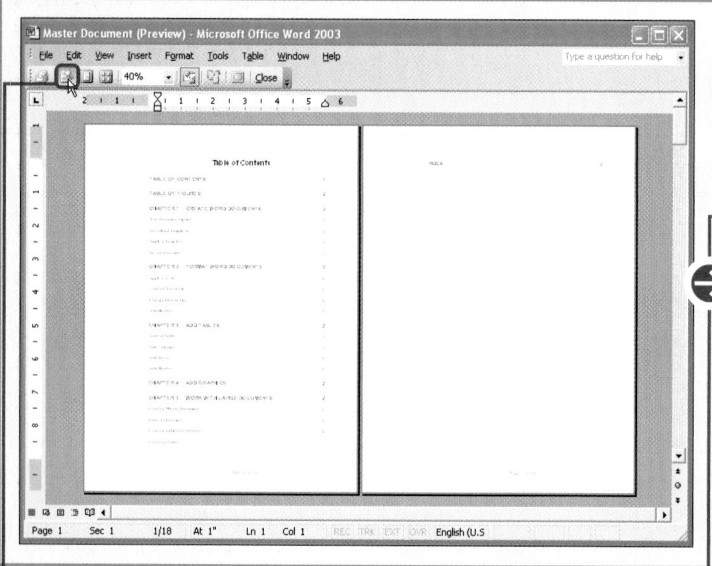

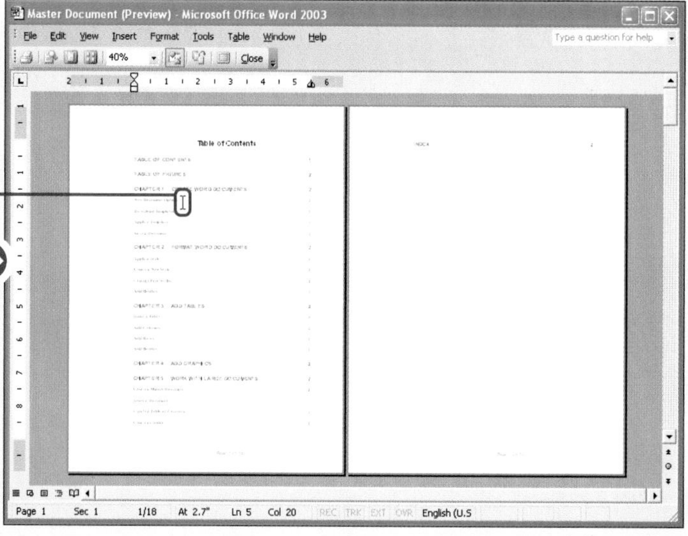

EDIT TEXT

1. In Print Preview, click the Magnifier button.

- You can click the Print Preview button (🖨) to switch to Print Preview.

- 🔍 changes to I.

2. Make the desired edits to the text.

Did You Know?

You can undo a Shrink to Fit command by clicking File ➪ Undo Shrink to Fit.

Did You Know?

If you select the Shrink to Fit option to adjust the paging for a table of contents or any other type of table, that edit remains only until you update the table. When you update the table, you will probably need to shrink the text again to make it fit on one page.

Did You Know?

You can click the Print button ( ) to print the document directly from Print Preview. Keep in mind that this prints the entire document without displaying the Print dialog box. If you want to make any changes to your print settings, you need to click File ➪ Print to display the Print dialog box.

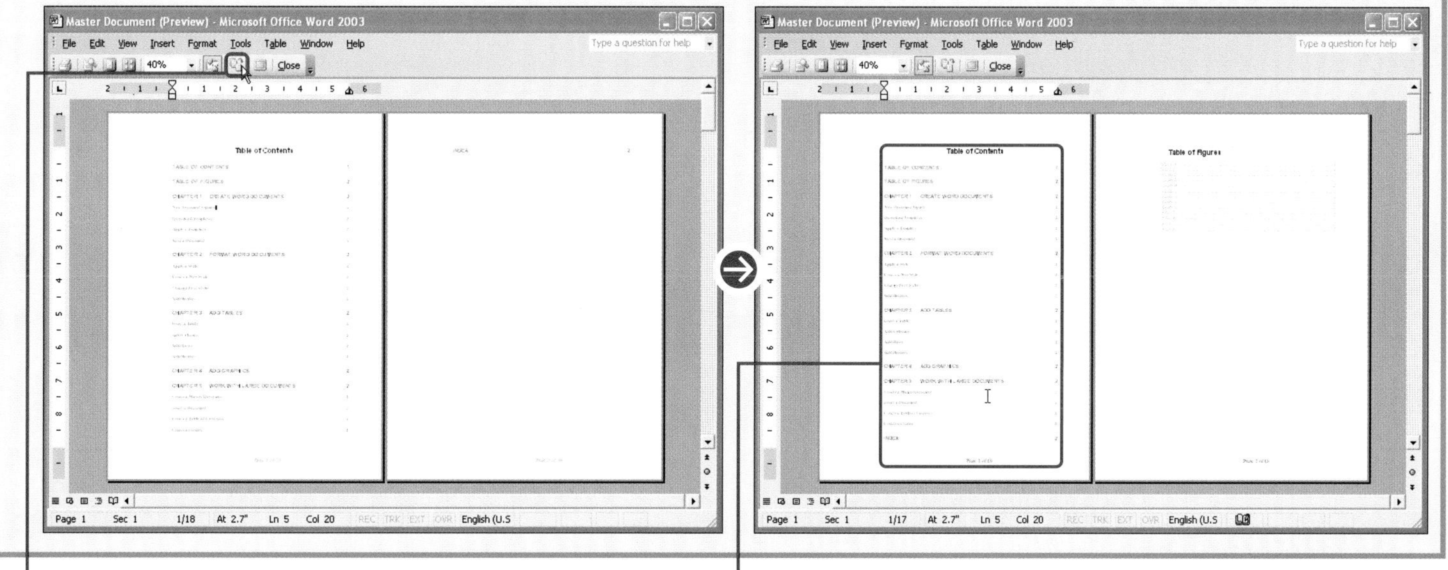

SHRINK TEXT

1. Click the Shrink to Fit button.

- Word shrinks the text size to make all the text fit on one page.

- You can click the Print button to print from Print Preview.

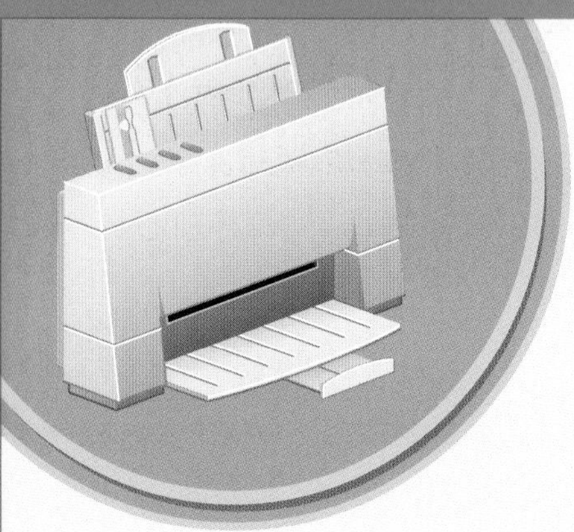

Change the DEFAULT PAGE SETTINGS for printing

You can change the default settings that Word uses each time that you print a document. For example, if you use the same margin settings for all your documents, you can make those the default page settings so that your pages always print that way. This eliminates having to make the same settings modifications for every document that you create.

You can change any of the page settings in the Page Setup dialog box. For example, if you require specific margin sizes for all your documents, you can specify those margin settings in the Margins tab. When changing the margin settings, remember that each printer has minimum margin sizes. Refer to your printer documentation for more information. You can also specify the amount of space allowed for binding, called the *gutter*.

When you save the new default settings, Word saves them to the default template, Normal.dot. This means that any documents that you create using the default template will use the new page settings.

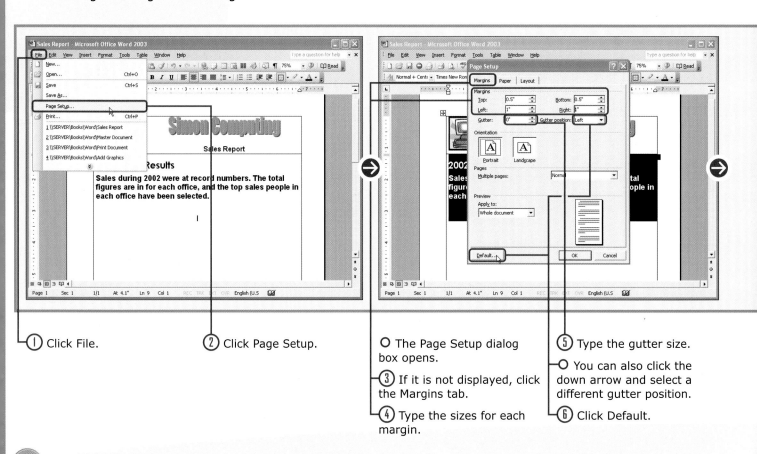

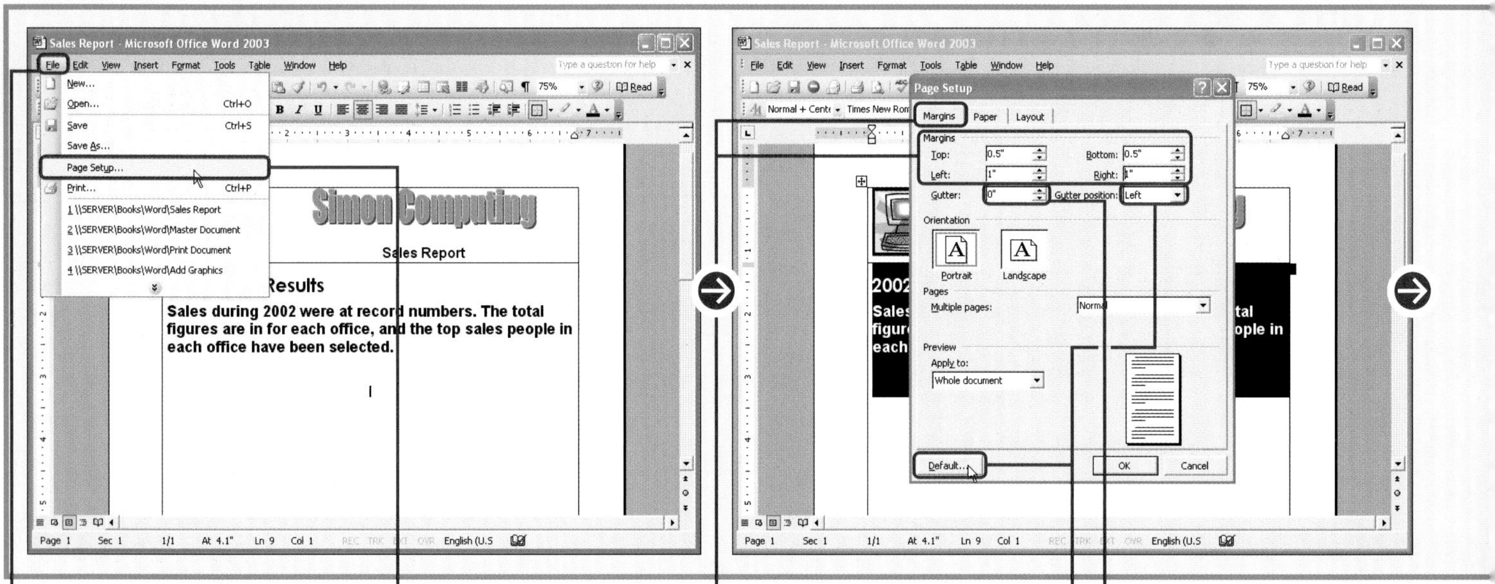

1. Click File.
2. Click Page Setup.

- The Page Setup dialog box opens.

3. If it is not displayed, click the Margins tab.
4. Type the sizes for each margin.
5. Type the gutter size.

- You can also click the down arrow and select a different gutter position.

6. Click Default.

Did You Know?

You can specify the type of paper that you typically use on the Paper tab. Word provides several default paper sizes from which you can choose. For example, if you select Legal, Word assumes that the paper is 8.5 inches wide and 14 inches long. If you cannot find a default paper size that matches your paper, you can type the appropriate paper sizes in the Width and Height fields.

Did You Know?

You can also save the layout information for the placement of headers and footers on the page. For example, if you always create a new header on the first page, you can select that option on the Layout tab.

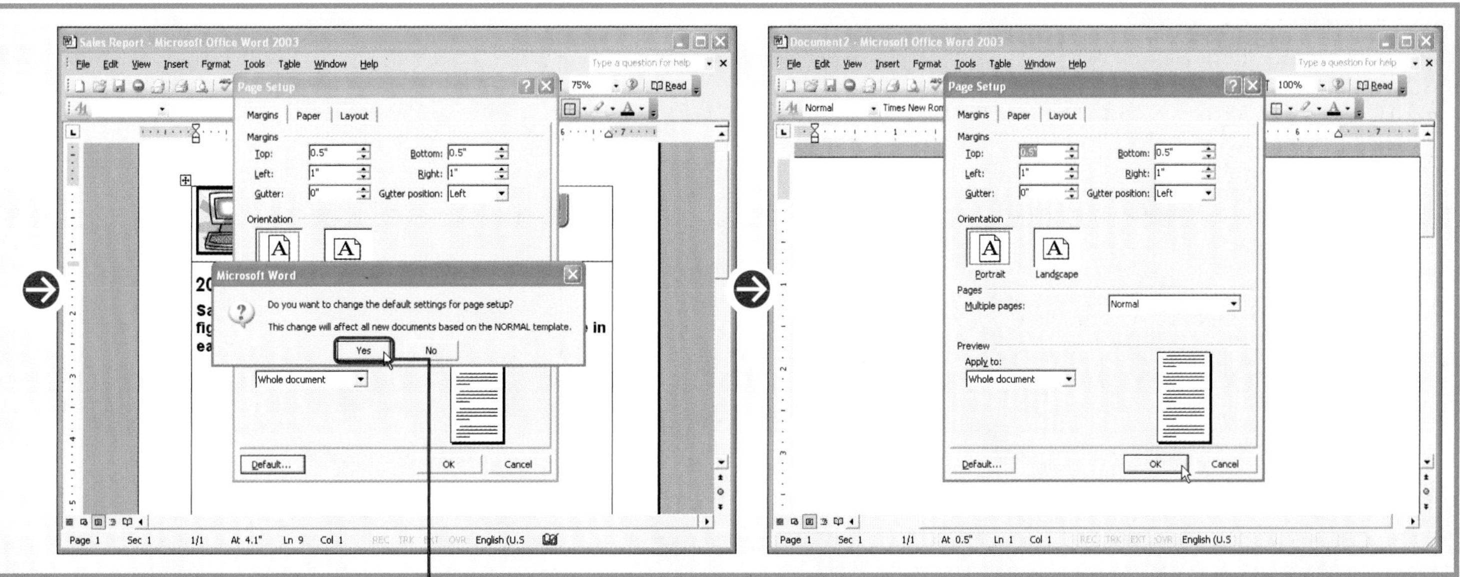

- A dialog box appears to verify that you want to change your default settings.

7 Click Yes.

- Word changes the default page settings for the selected template.
- Word now applies those same settings to each new document that you create.

Create a PRINT FILE

You can print a Word document to a file. You can later print it on a printer to which you are currently not connected. For example, you can create a print file on your machine and then print it from a different computer.

When you create a print file, it is created for a specific printer. Just like printing directly to a printer, you need to select the printer that will print the print file in the Print dialog box. The print file will work only on the selected type of printer, so you may want to name the print file to identify the printer type.

When you create the print file, Word creates a file with a .prn file extension. This is a binary file type in the format required by your printer. You cannot open and modify this file in Word. If you need to modify the file, you will have to print it to file again from the original Word file.

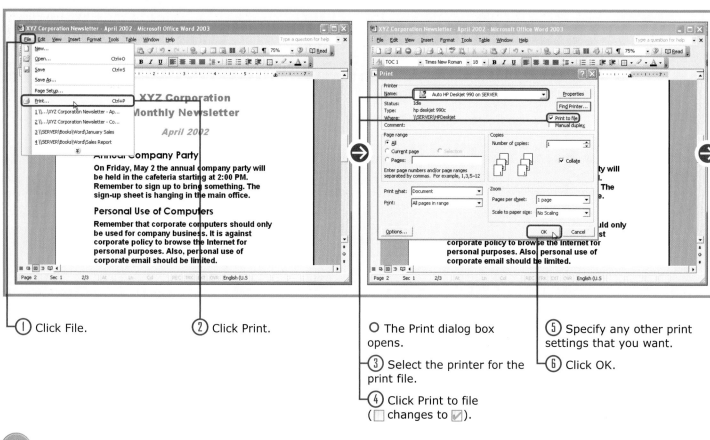

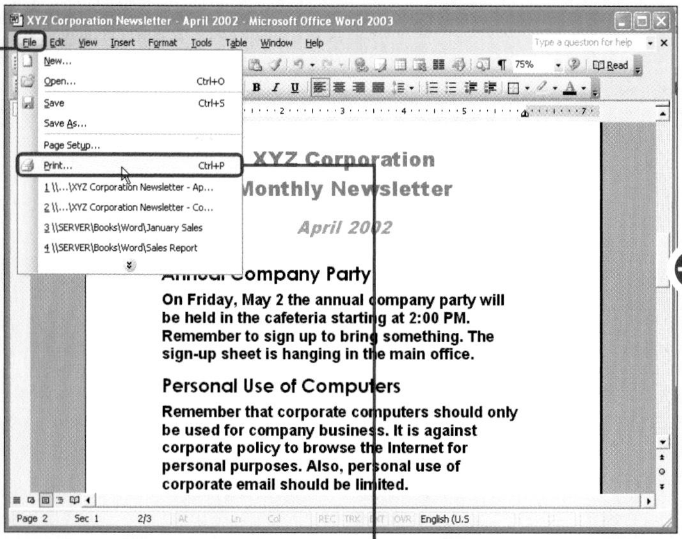

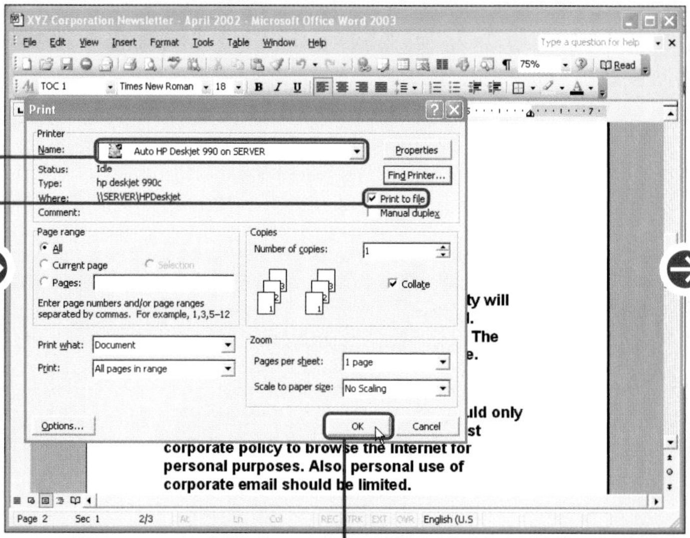

1. Click File.
2. Click Print.

- The Print dialog box opens.

3. Select the printer for the print file.
4. Click Print to file (☐ changes to ☑).
5. Specify any other print settings that you want.
6. Click OK.

Did You Know?

You print a .prn file on your computer from the DOS prompt in Windows. You open a DOS window by clicking Start ➪ All Programs ➪ Accessories ➪ Command Prompt. In the DOS window, switch to the folder containing the print file. Type CD \ to return to the root directory and then type CD path, replacing path with the folder location. To print the file, type Copy test.prn LPT1 /b, replacing test.prn with the name of the print file.

Did You Know?

You can send a print file to a network printer by redirecting a port on your computer to the network printer. To do so, you need to use the Net command in the DOS Command Prompt window:

```
Net use lpt1: \\SERVER\HPDeskjet
```

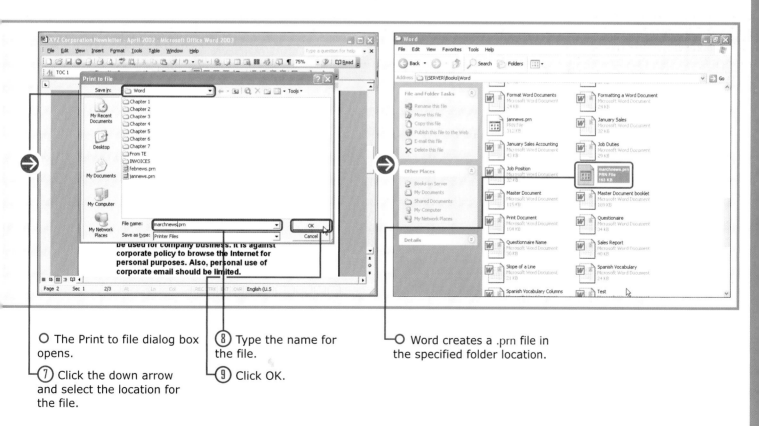

○ The Print to file dialog box opens.

⑦ Click the down arrow and select the location for the file.

⑧ Type the name for the file.

⑨ Click OK.

○ Word creates a .prn file in the specified folder location.

Print the AUTOTEXT ENTRIES

You can print out the AutoText entries that you have set up in Word. You can use AutoText entries for frequently used text and phrases. See Chapter 8 for more information on creating AutoText entries. By printing the AutoText entries, you create a sheet that you can use as a reference when creating documents.

When you print your AutoText entries, Word prints all the entries from every template that you have open. The printout includes the AutoText entry names in bold followed by the AutoText entries.

If any special formatting has been applied to an AutoText entry, the formatting is printed on the page. This enables you to see how an entry will appear when inserted in your document.

You select the option to print AutoText entries in the Print dialog box. When you select this option, most of the dialog box options become grayed out. The only options available are the printer selection and number of copies.

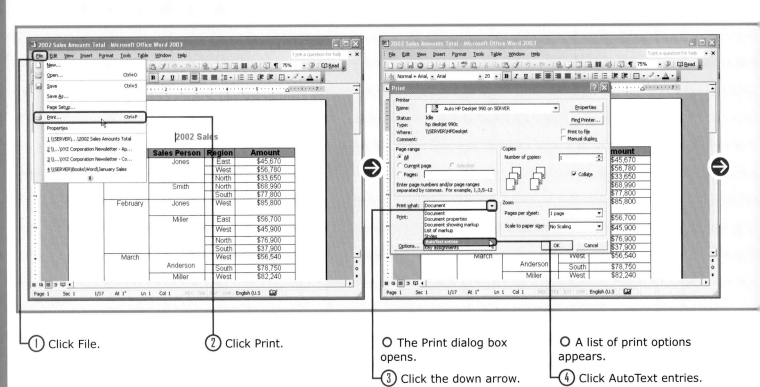

1. Click File.
2. Click Print.

- The Print dialog box opens.

3. Click the down arrow.

- A list of print options appears.

4. Click AutoText entries.

DIFFICULTY LEVEL

Did You Know?

You can print other information besides the AutoText entries about your document by using the options in the Print What field. The following table describes the available options:

Option	Description
Document	Prints the specified portion of the document
Document Properties	Prints information about the currently selected document, such as filename, directory, and word count
Document Showing Markup	Prints out the document showing any edits that have been made
List of Markup	Lists the modifications made to the document
Styles	Lists all the available styles
AutoText Entries	Lists the AutoText entries
Key Assignments	Lists the key assignments that were made in the document

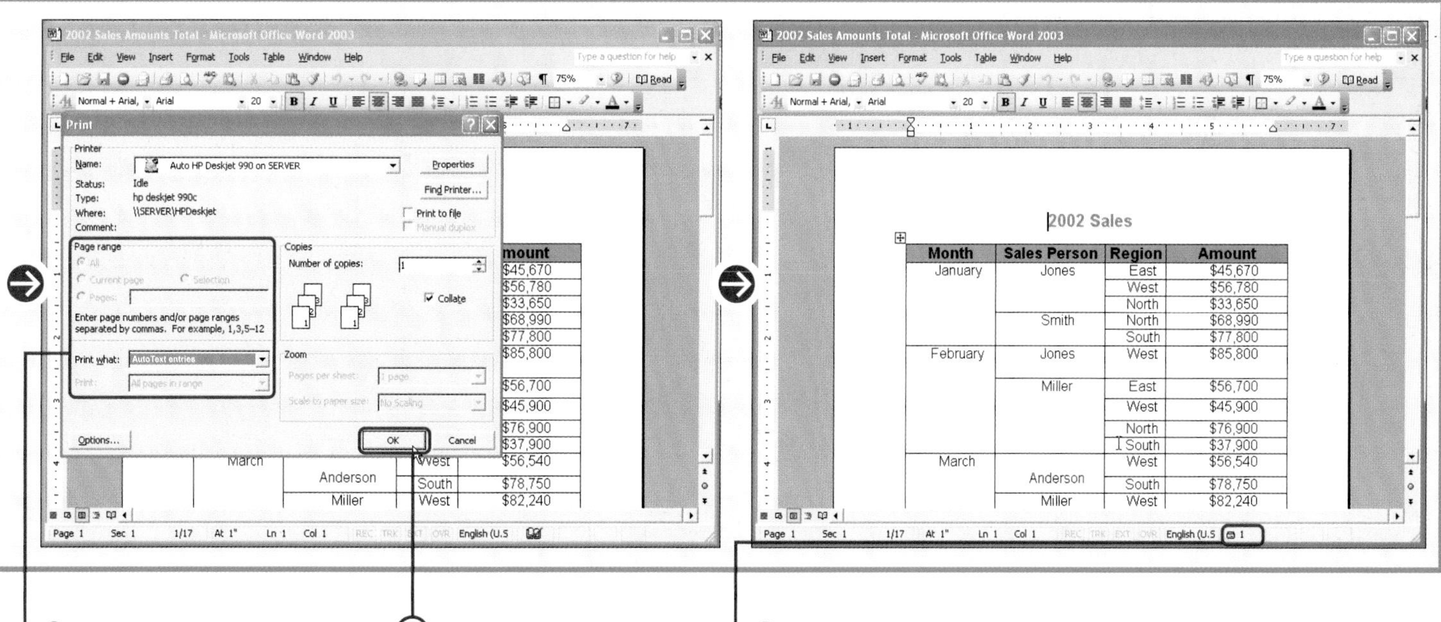

- Word grays out most of the options in the dialog box.

5 Click OK.

- Word prints all the current AutoText entries.

Create a FOLDED BOOKLET

You can print out a document so that it can be folded like a booklet. For example, you may have a pamphlet that you want to print with two pages on each sheet of paper so that you can fold and staple it down the middle.

To print a folded booklet correctly, you need to change the settings in the Page Setup dialog box. You select the Book fold option. When you do so, Word sets up the document to print in Landscape format. The Gutter option specifies the amount of space to allow for stapling or binding the book.

By default, the first page in your document becomes the cover of the booklet, and the last page prints as the back cover.

If possible, you should set up the document to print using the Book fold option before laying out pages. Typically, the pages will be shorter when you switch to book fold option, and you may want to change features such as the page formatting and table sizing.

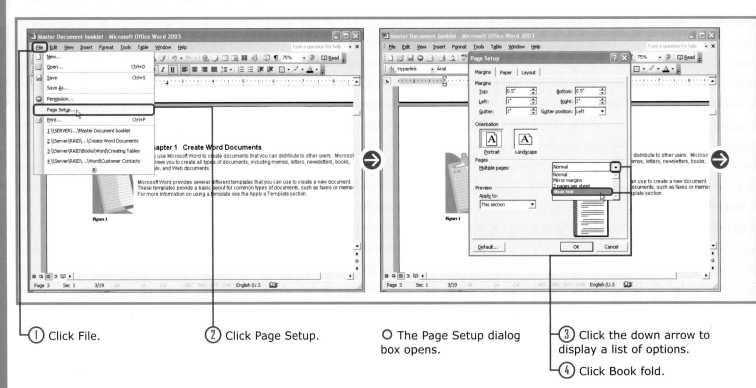

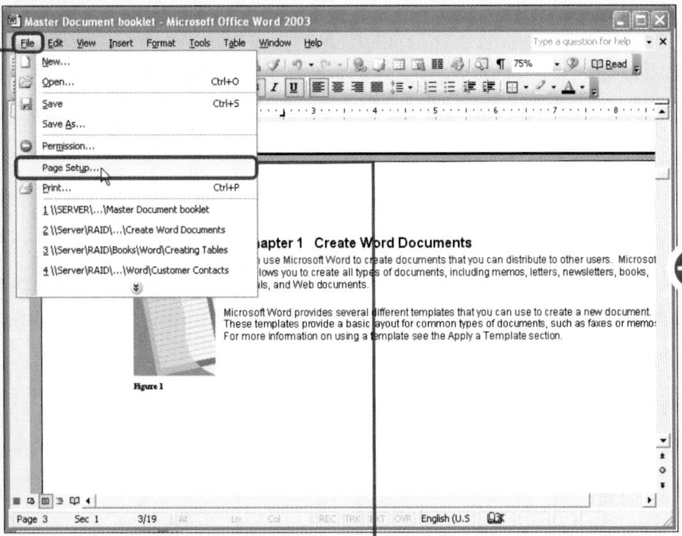

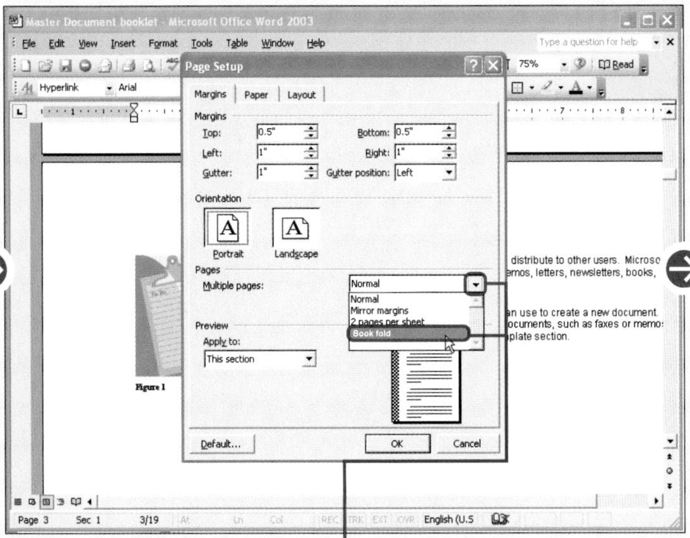

① Click File.

② Click Page Setup.

○ The Page Setup dialog box opens.

③ Click the down arrow to display a list of options.

④ Click Book fold.

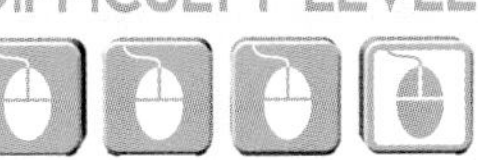

Did You Know?

The Book Fold option is designed to work with duplex printers. This is because booklets are normally printed on both sides of the paper. If your printer does not duplex, you will need to manually duplex by clicking the Manual Duplex option in the Print dialog box. Word automatically prints out the front side pages. Then you can turn the sheets over and place them back in the printer to print the back side.

Apply It!

Make sure that you allow enough space with the Gutter margin to accommodate your book's binding. You should print a test copy of the book and bind it with the appropriate binding to ensure that the spacing is correct.

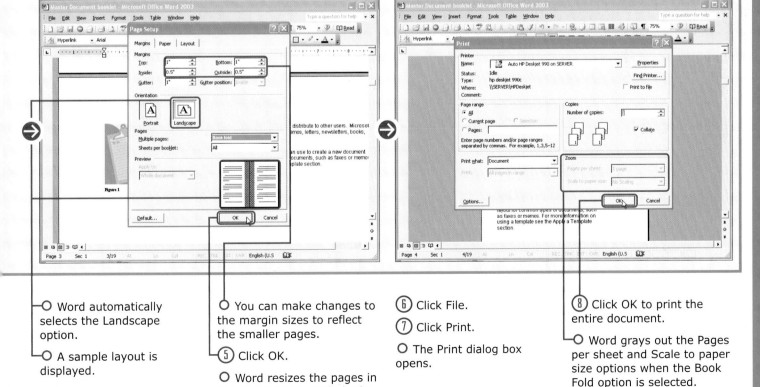

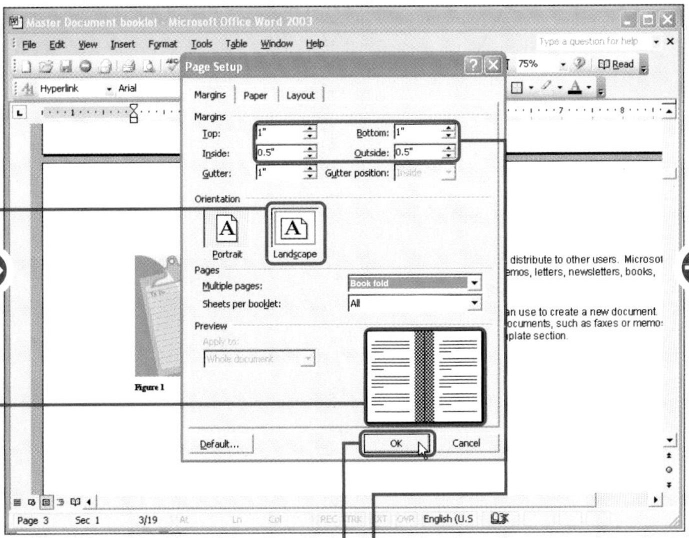

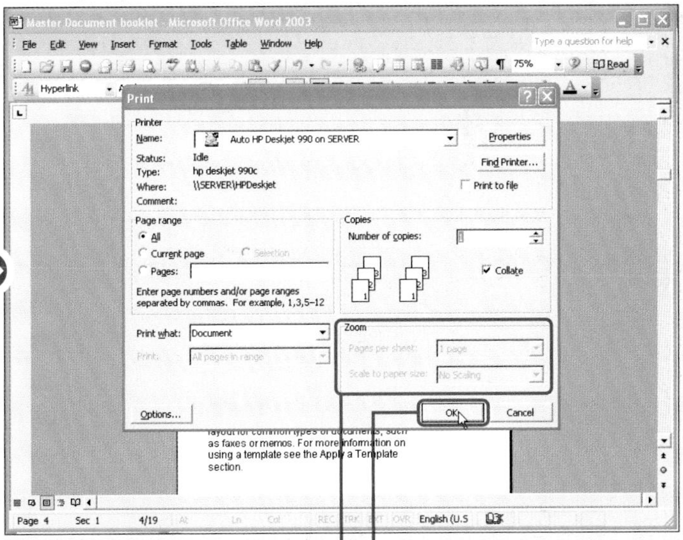

- Word automatically selects the Landscape option.
- A sample layout is displayed.
- You can make changes to the margin sizes to reflect the smaller pages.

5. Click OK.

- Word resizes the pages in the document to include the margin settings.

6. Click File.
7. Click Print.

- The Print dialog box opens.

8. Click OK to print the entire document.

- Word grays out the Pages per sheet and Scale to paper size options when the Book Fold option is selected.

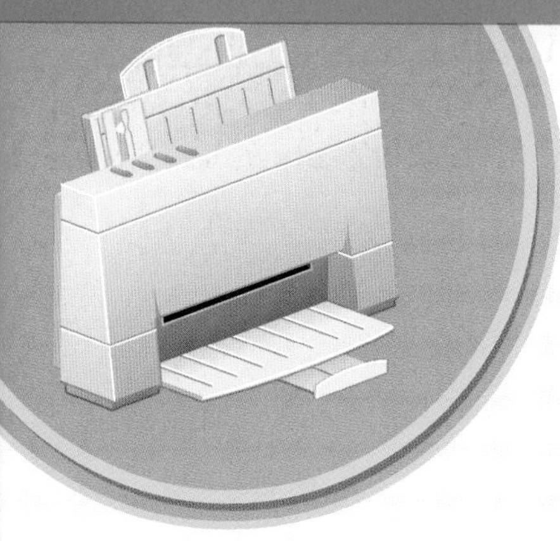

UPDATE LINKED CONTENT
before printing

You can ensure that the links in your document are current by updating them all before printing. You want to make sure that any linked information within the document contains the most current values. To ensure this, you should always update the links before printing.

You update the links in the document by selecting the Update Links option in the Print dialog box. Word updates any links to other files. For example, if you insert a link to an Excel worksheet in your document and later update the links, Word loads the most recent copy of the worksheet before printing.

If you have inserted different fields in your document, you should consider updating those before printing. You update field values by clicking the Update Fields options. For example, a table of contents creates links to specific headings in the document. By updating the fields, you ensure that the table of contents references the correct pages.

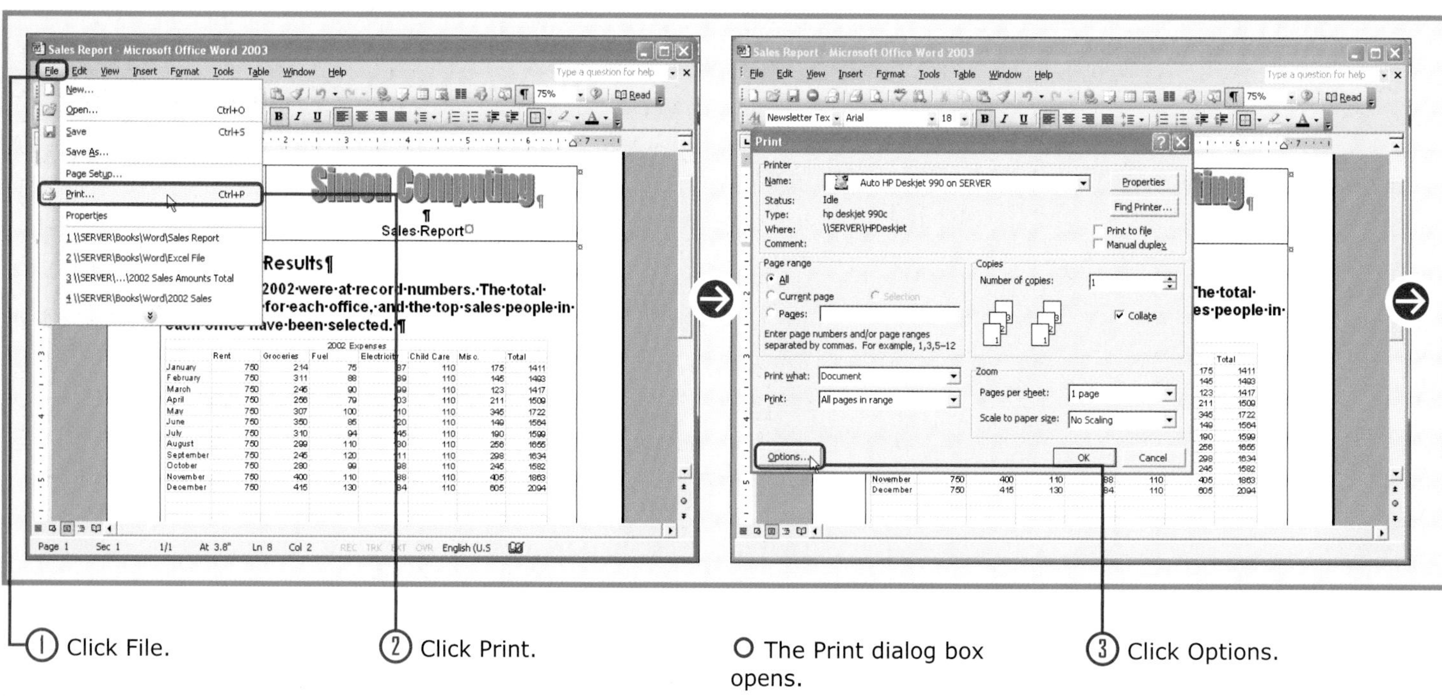

① Click File.

② Click Print.

○ The Print dialog box opens.

③ Click Options.

DIFFICULTY LEVEL

Did You Know?

You can also update links from the Links dialog box, which appears when you click Edit ⇨ Links. The Links dialog box provides a list of all linked objects in the document. To update a link, select the link and click Update Now.

Did You Know?

If you do not want a linked document to update when you click Update Links, you need to lock it in the Links dialog box, which appears when you click Edit ⇨ Links. Highlight the link that you want and click Locked (☐ changes to ☑).

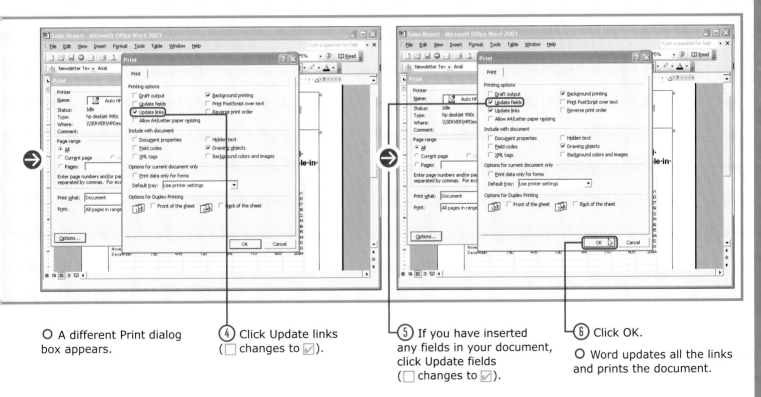

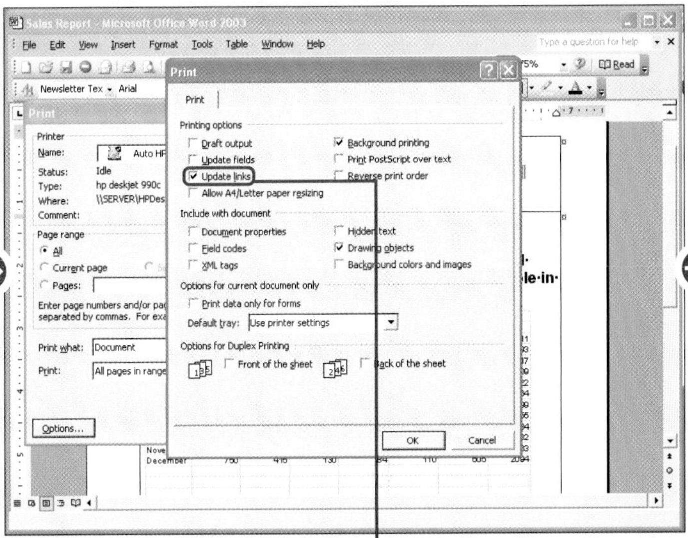

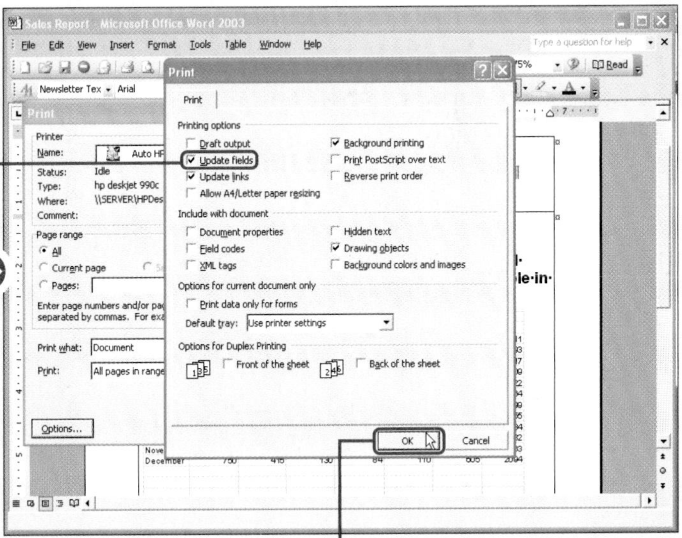

- A different Print dialog box appears.

4. Click Update links (☐ changes to ☑).

5. If you have inserted any fields in your document, click Update fields (☐ changes to ☑).

6. Click OK.

- Word updates all the links and prints the document.

Print GRAPHIC PLACEHOLDERS on draft versions

You can stop graphics from printing on draft versions of your document by using print placeholders. This option works well when you are printing a draft copy of a document to review only the text. By preventing the graphics from printing, you speed the printing time and eliminate the excess ink required to print the graphics.

When you select the placeholder option, you can quickly scroll though your document without waiting for a graphic image to load. Word draws a square box to represent the location of the graphic.

When you print a document with placeholders, the location of the placeholder is left blank. Word maintains the positioning of the text around the graphic, so the page breaks all remain the same.

To insert graphic placeholders, you need to turn on the Picture Placeholder option as well as select the Drawings option to hide the pictures in the document.

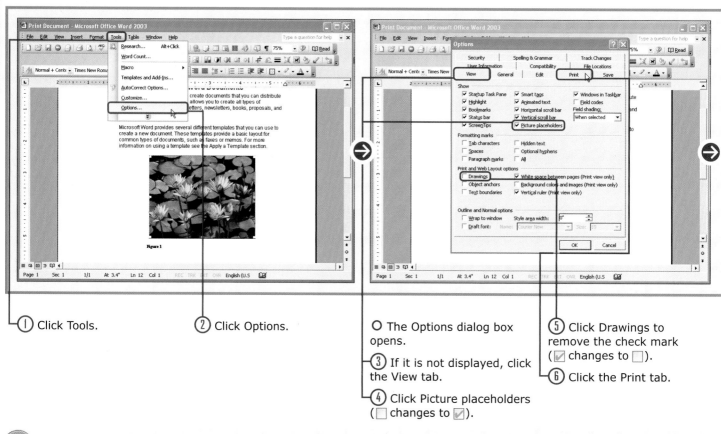

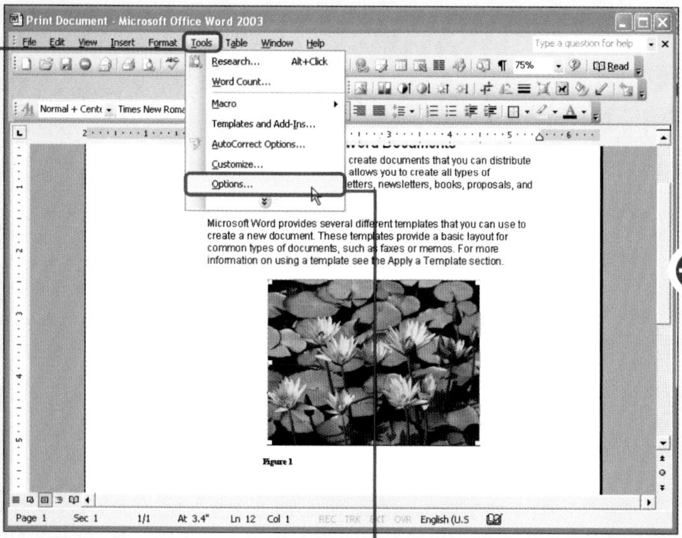

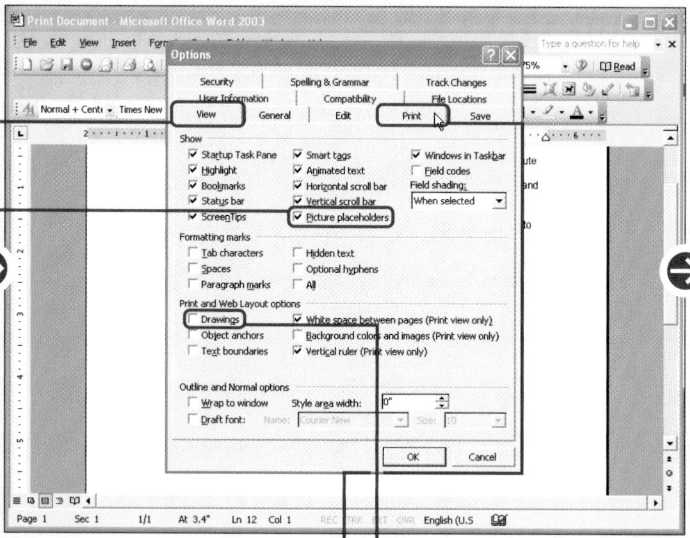

① Click Tools.

② Click Options.

- The Options dialog box opens.

③ If it is not displayed, click the View tab.

④ Click Picture placeholders (☐ changes to ☑).

⑤ Click Drawings to remove the check mark (☑ changes to ☐).

⑥ Click the Print tab.

DIFFICULTY LEVEL

Did You Know?

The Print tab in the Options dialog box is the same as the dialog box that opens when you click Options in the Print dialog box. Therefore, you can switch between the draft and final print options from either dialog box. If you remove the check mark from the Draft Output option, Word prints the document in final mode, which means that all graphics print, even if they are not displayed in the document.

Apply It!

When you print in draft mode, Word does not print all the text formatting in the document. How the draft copy compares to the final depends on the draft settings of your printer. Not all printers support draft printing.

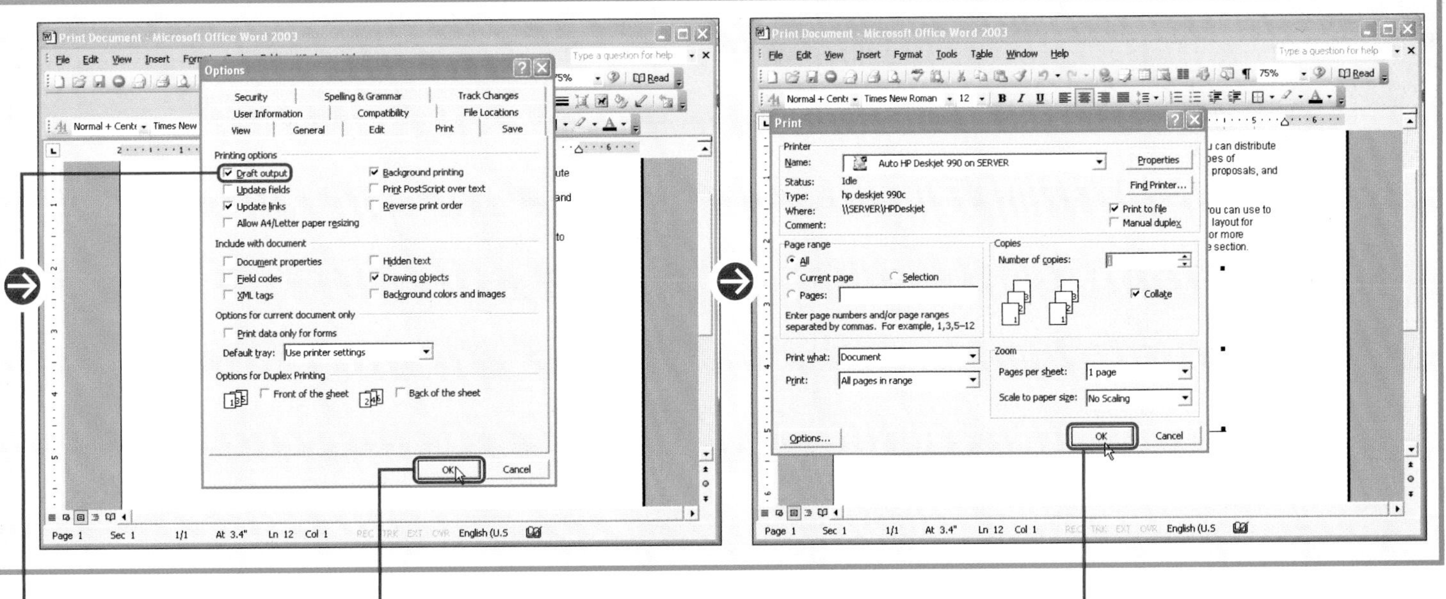

⑦ Click Draft output.

⑧ Click OK.

⑨ Click File.

⑩ Click Print.

○ The Print dialog box opens.

⑪ Select the print options that you want.

⑫ Click OK.

○ Word prints the document, leaving spaces for the embedded graphics.

Using Automation and Proofing Tools

Word provides several different tools to improve the process of creating accurate documents. Using these different automation and proofing tools also speeds up the document-creating process because they automatically insert commonly used words and phrases or correct mistyped text.

If you want to have others review a document before printing it, you can use the Send To option to e-mail the document out to the reviewers. When you use this option, Word connects you to an e-mail program to create the message. When you receive the reviews, you can compare the edits from the reviewers with the original document.

If you have text that you type frequently, especially long phrases, you can use the AutoText and AutoCorrect options to simplify the process. When you type a specific key sequence, the AutoCorrect option inserts the corresponding text.

Although Word provides an extensive dictionary, it does not contain much specialized vocabulary, such as medical terminology. You can create custom dictionaries that contain these types of custom terms. If there are words you do not want accepted, you can create an exception list to have them ignored during spell checking.

Word also provides tools for translating single words or entire documents into another language. This feature is very handy when you need to produce some international correspondence.

This chapter provides some tips about automating the creation of documents and then proofing the end result.

TOP 100

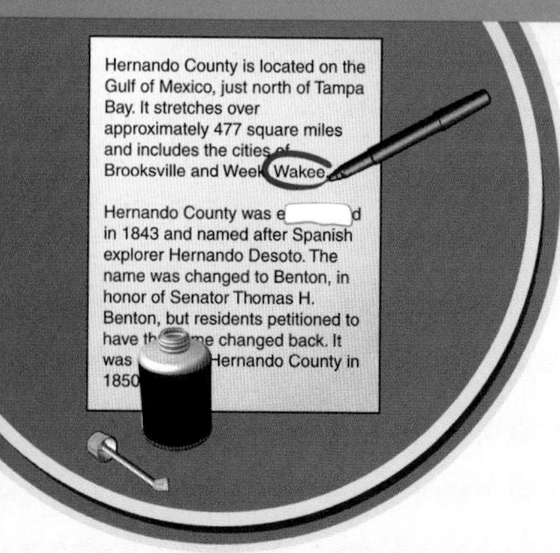

Send others a DOCUMENT FOR REVIEW

You can send documents out to other people for review. For example, you may have a document that you want other people to review before having it published. You can send the document out for review from Word and then wait for them to respond.

To use the Review feature, you must have Microsoft Outlook set up to send and receive e-mail messages. You can also use the option with Microsoft Outlook Express and Microsoft Exchange. When you select the option to mail the document out for review, Word opens up an e-mail message by linking to Outlook.

When the reviewer opens the message to review it, Word automatically opens the review tools. This ensures that any changes made by the reviewer are marked. That way, when you receive the reviewed file, you can merge the changes from each reviewer.

Each time you view a document that is out for review, the Reviewing toolbar appears for the document. When you receive the reviews, you can cancel the review process by clicking the End Review button.

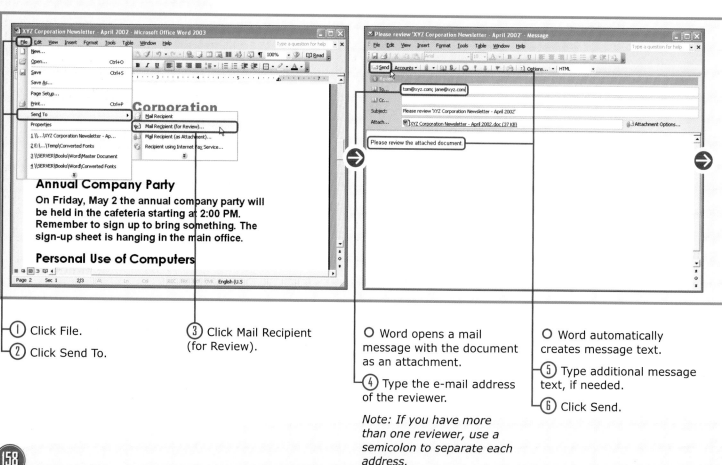

① Click File.

② Click Send To.

③ Click Mail Recipient (for Review).

○ Word opens a mail message with the document as an attachment.

④ Type the e-mail address of the reviewer.

Note: If you have more than one reviewer, use a semicolon to separate each address.

○ Word automatically creates message text.

⑤ Type additional message text, if needed.

⑥ Click Send.

DIFFICULTY LEVEL

Caution!

You should try not to send master documents out for review. A master document includes links to subdocuments. If you send that master document out for review, Word does not send the linked files. Therefore, the reviewer will only get the master document with links that do not work. If you want to have a master document reviewed, you need to send each subdocument out for review. See Chapter 6 for more information on working with master documents.

Did You Know?

When you receive the reviewed messages, you can use the Reviewing toolbar options to accept or reject the changes made by the reviewers. Click the Accept Change button ( ) to accept a change or the Reject Change button ( ) for changes you do not want to make.

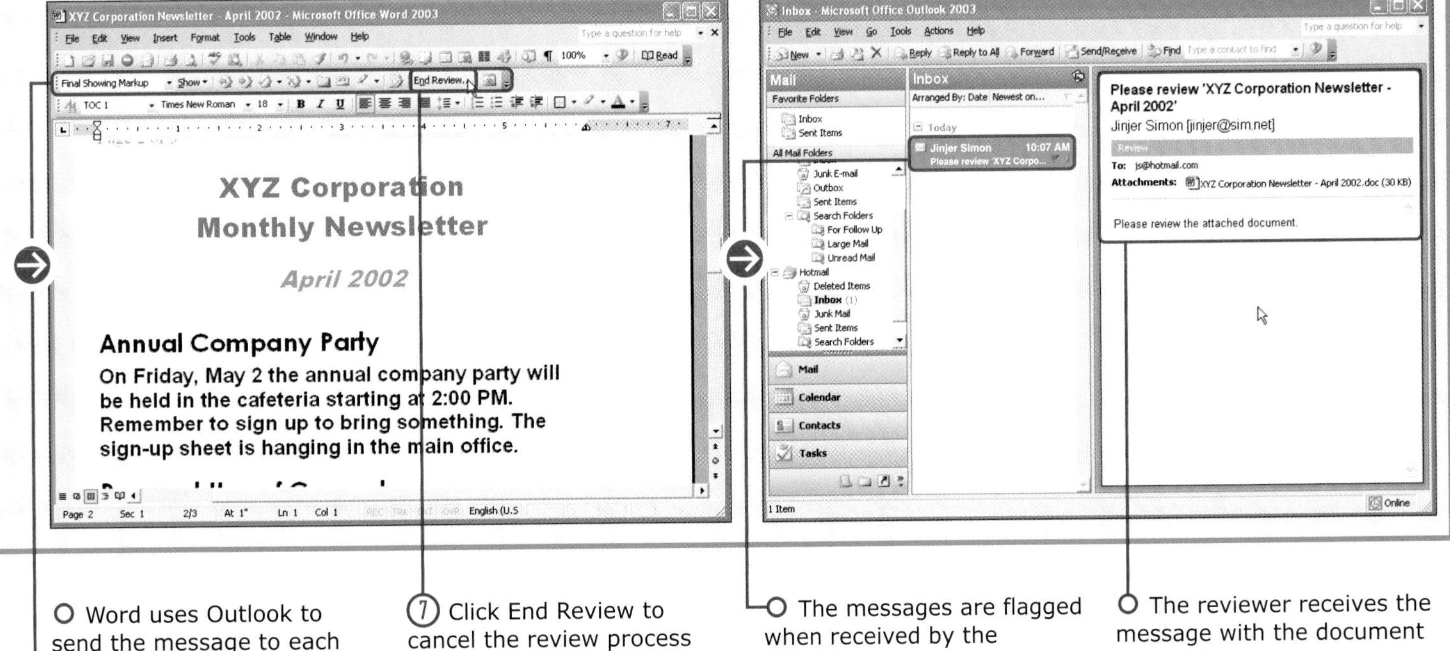

- Word uses Outlook to send the message to each reviewer.
- The Reviewing toolbar appears when you look at a document that is out for review.

7. Click End Review to cancel the review process and close the toolbar.

- The messages are flagged when received by the reviewer.
- The reviewer receives the message with the document as an attachment.

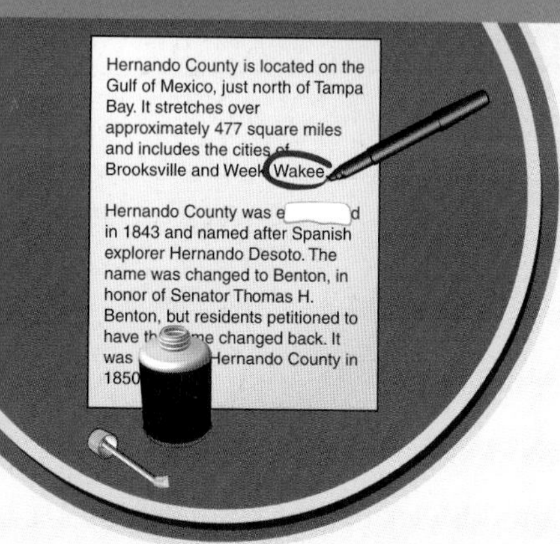

Use AutoText to INSERT COMMON PHRASES

You can use the AutoText option to store common phrases and graphic images that you use frequently. You can quickly access an AutoText entry within your documents by typing the unique AutoText name.

Before you save an AutoText entry, you need to apply any formatting that you want to the text. After you save the AutoText entry, you cannot modify the text formatting. The only way to change the formatting of an AutoText entry is to save the entry again.

When you save an AutoText entry, try to use a unique name that you can easily remember. You should avoid using text that you type frequently because each time that you type it, Word displays a pop-up message to see if you want to insert the AutoText entry. Word automatically suggests a name for the AutoText entry by using the first few characters of text.

If you decide to create an AutoText entry for a graphic, the graphic will not appear in the Preview window. This is because the Preview window displays only text.

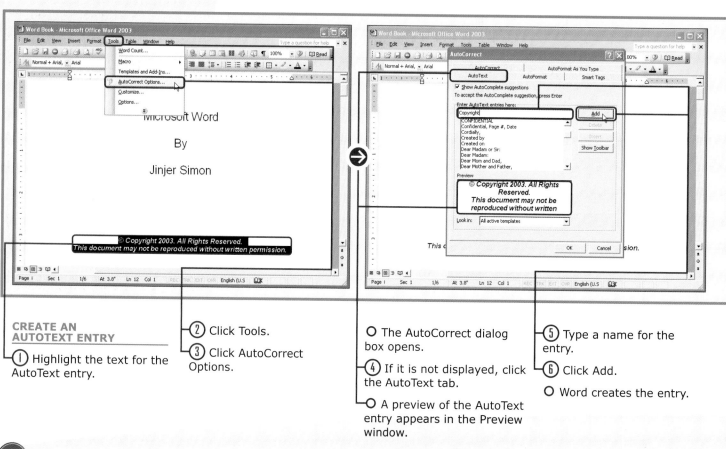

CREATE AN AUTOTEXT ENTRY

1. Highlight the text for the AutoText entry.
2. Click Tools.
3. Click AutoCorrect Options.

- The AutoCorrect dialog box opens.

4. If it is not displayed, click the AutoText tab.

- A preview of the AutoText entry appears in the Preview window.

5. Type a name for the entry.
6. Click Add.

- Word creates the entry.

DIFFICULTY LEVEL

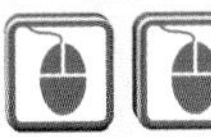

Did You Know?

You can create AutoText entries on the AutoText tab by typing the text that you want. Word uses the default text formatting of the document in which you insert the AutoText entry. Word also uses the text of the AutoText entry as the entry name.

Apply It!

You can remove unwanted AutoText entries on the AutoText tab. To do so, highlight the entry in the list box and click Delete.

Apply It!

AutoText entries work well for text that contains special characters, such as foreign words. You can create the text once with the special characters and then create the AutoText entries. Each time that you select the AutoText entry, Word will insert the special characters.

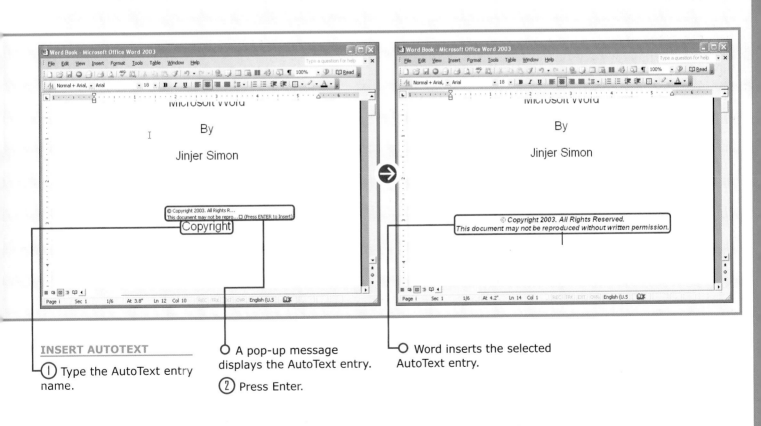

INSERT AUTOTEXT

1. Type the AutoText entry name.

- A pop-up message displays the AutoText entry.

2. Press Enter.

- Word inserts the selected AutoText entry.

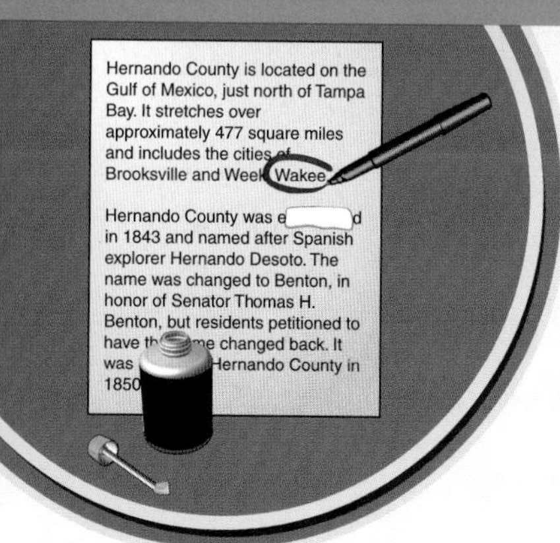

MERGE TWO VERSIONS of a document

You can merge together two versions of a document so that you have one document that shows all the changes. This option works well when you have a document that has been modified by another user. When merging two documents together, Word compares the documents and marks all the differences between them. This simplifies the process of applying changes. After you have a merged document, you can use the Reviewing toolbar options to accept and reject the changes.

When you merge two documents, you actually have three options. Your first option is to merge the first document into the second document by selecting Merge. The differences in the first document are shown as tracked changes in the new document. Second, you can merge the second document into the first document by selecting Merge into the Current Document. Finally, you can select Merge into New Document to combine both documents in a third document with the differences shown as tracked changes.

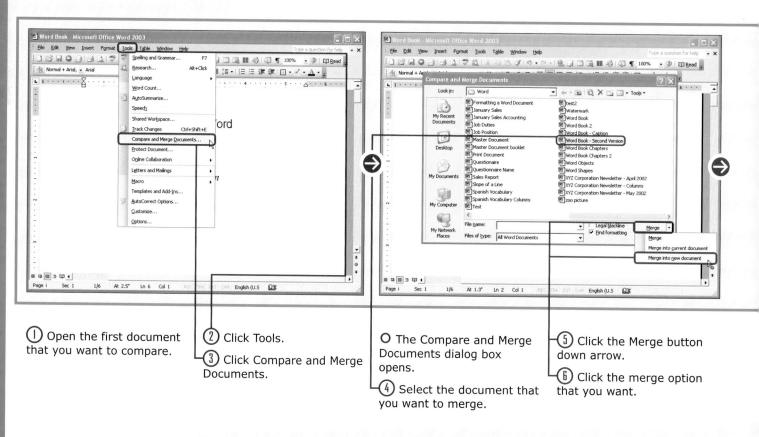

1. Open the first document that you want to compare.
2. Click Tools.
3. Click Compare and Merge Documents.

- The Compare and Merge Documents dialog box opens.

4. Select the document that you want to merge.
5. Click the Merge button down arrow.
6. Click the merge option that you want.

DIFFICULTY LEVEL

Put It Together!

You can merge the changes from several reviewers into your original document. See task #71 for information on having a document reviewed. To merge the changes, open the original document and then merge in the first document. Keep the original document open and continue merging in each reviewed document.

Did You Know?

You can also have Word compare two documents and display only the text that both documents have in common. Any additional text from the two documents is deleted. To perform this type of comparison, click Legal Blackline in the Compare and Merge Documents dialog box. When you do so, the Merge button changes to Compare. Click Compare to have Word create a new document that contains only the common text in both documents.

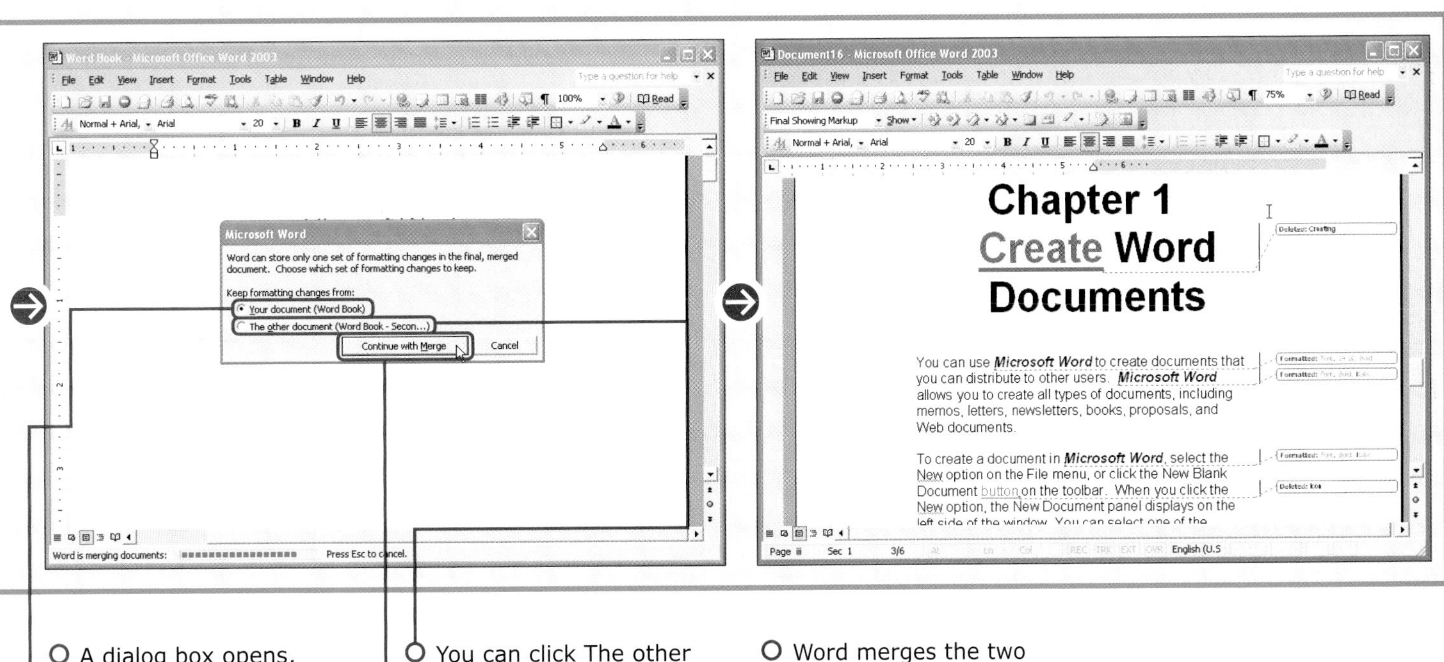

- A dialog box opens, requesting the formatting changes that you want.

7. Click Your document to use the formatting from the original document (○ changes to ◉).

- You can click The other document to use the formatting in the second document.

8. Click Continue with Merge.

- Word merges the two documents and displays the results.

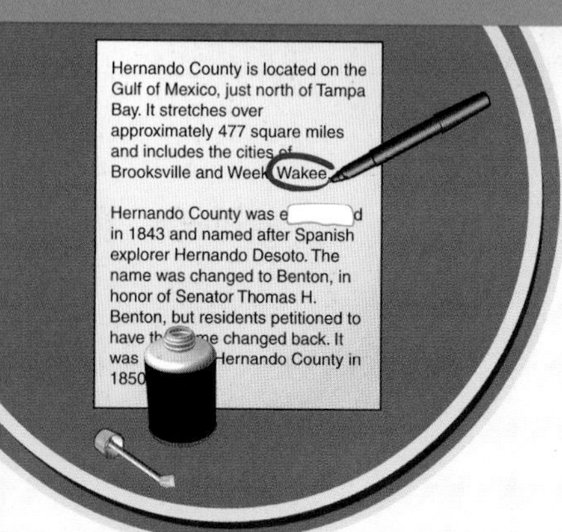

Automatically insert REPETITIVE TEXT with the AutoCorrect option

You can use the AutoCorrect option in Word to automatically insert text into your document. For example, you may have a phrase that you frequently use. If you create an AutoCorrect entry, Word will automatically insert the appropriate text when you type the corresponding text. This simplifies your work process because you simply type the text that corresponds to the AutoCorrect entry that you want, and Word automatically makes the change. Word provides several AutoCorrect entries; for example, if you type (r), Word automatically inserts the registered trademark symbol in your document.

Because Word automatically inserts AutoCorrect entries, you want to avoid using a combination that you may use as regular text. For example, if you create an AutoCorrect entry for *the,* every time you type *teh* it will be changed to the AutoCorrect entry.

You can create either a formatted or unformatted AutoCorrect entry. If you create a formatted entry, Word saves the formatting of the selected text with the AutoCorrect entry. If you create an unformatted entry, only the text is remembered.

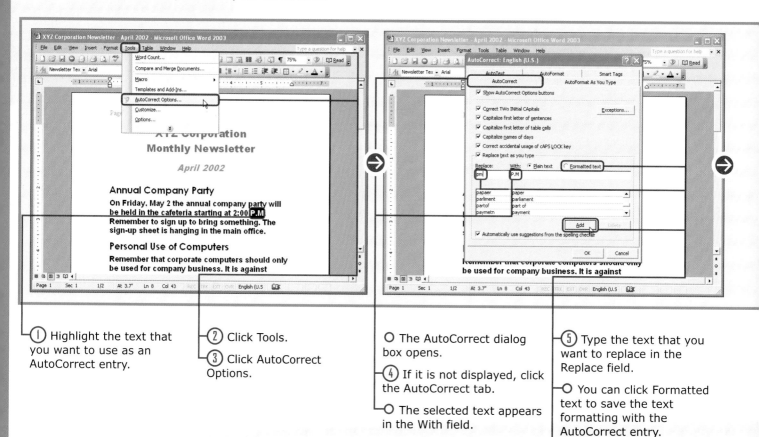

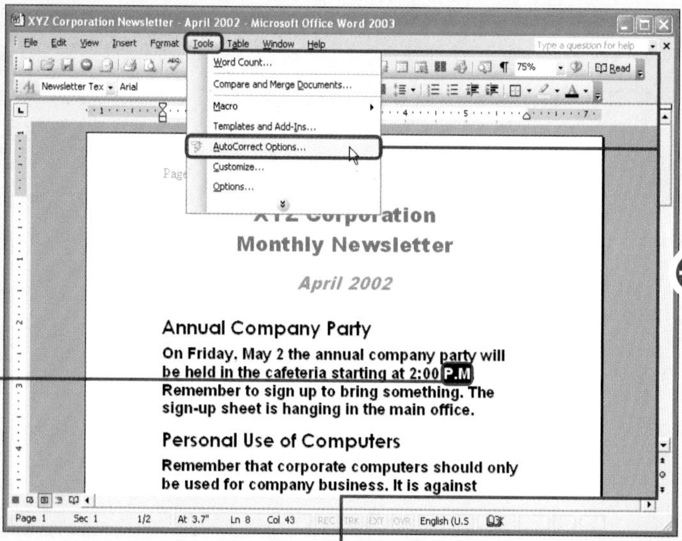

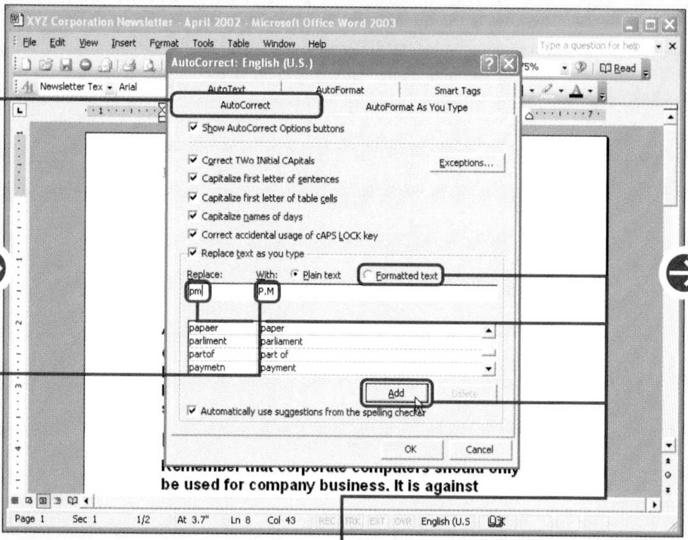

① Highlight the text that you want to use as an AutoCorrect entry.

② Click Tools.

③ Click AutoCorrect Options.

○ The AutoCorrect dialog box opens.

④ If it is not displayed, click the AutoCorrect tab.

○ The selected text appears in the With field.

⑤ Type the text that you want to replace in the Replace field.

○ You can click Formatted text to save the text formatting with the AutoCorrect entry.

⑥ Click Add.

DIFFICULTY LEVEL

Did You Know?

If you do not want an AutoCorrect entry that Word has applied, as soon as Word makes the change, press Backspace to undo the AutoCorrect.

Did You Know?

Word also provides other AutoCorrect options for correcting typing errors. For example, you can ensure that the first letter of each sentence is capitalized by clicking the Capitalize First Letter of Sentences option. You can select the correction options that you want on the AutoCorrect tab.

If you need to turn off the AutoCorrect option, you can do so by deselecting the Replace Text As You Type option. When this option is not selected, none of the AutoCorrect entries will be inserted.

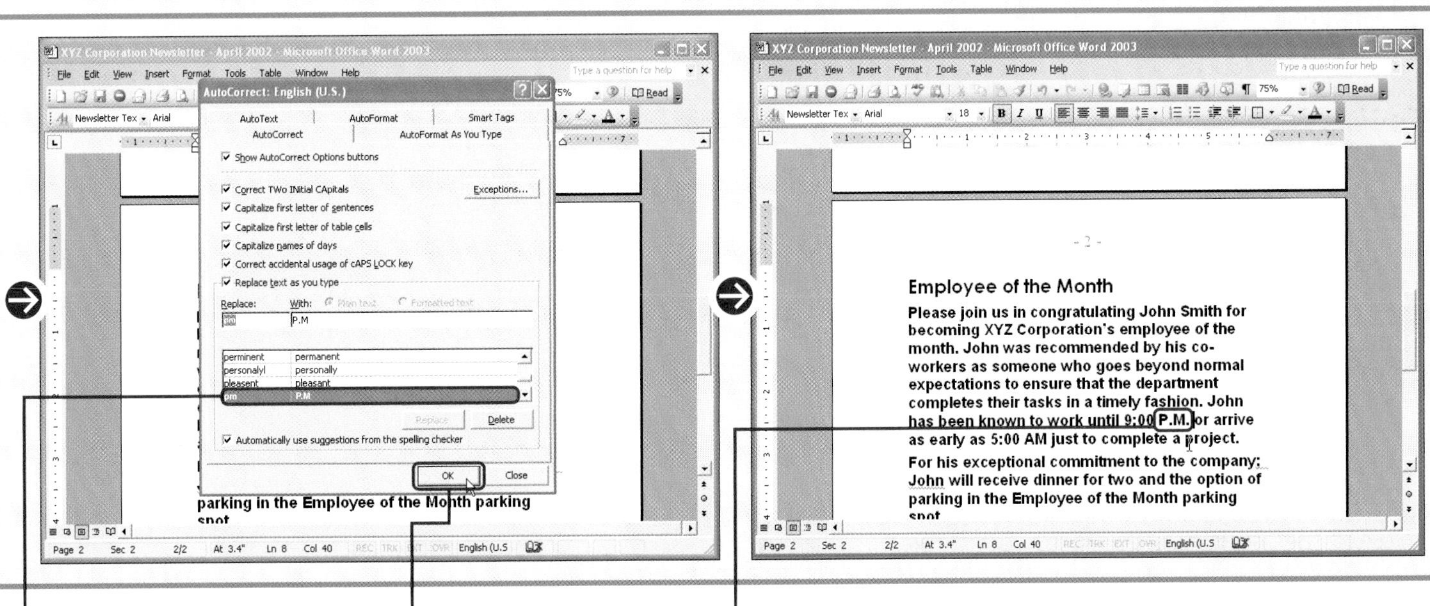

- Word adds the entry to the list box.

⑦ Repeat steps **5** and **6** to specify different text to replace with the entry.

⑧ Click OK.

- Word automatically applies the AutoCorrect entry when you type the corresponding text.

Create a CUSTOM DICTIONARY

You can create a custom dictionary that contains custom words that are not in the default Word dictionary. For example, you may have specific industry terminology that Word does not recognize. By creating a custom dictionary, you ensure that those words are spelled correctly each time you type them.

A custom dictionary is simply a list of words that you want to allow in your document. If Word finds any of the words in your custom dictionary, they are not flagged as misspellings. You can add any word to a custom dictionary as long as it is less than 64 characters and does not contain any spaces.

You create and modify custom dictionaries using the options in the Custom Dictionaries dialog box. Microsoft stores all custom dictionaries you create in the Proof folder, but you can also create and store dictionaries in other locations if you want to share them with other users.

Word uses the custom dictionaries that are selected whenever you perform a spell check. Make sure that the check mark remains next to each custom dictionary you want to use.

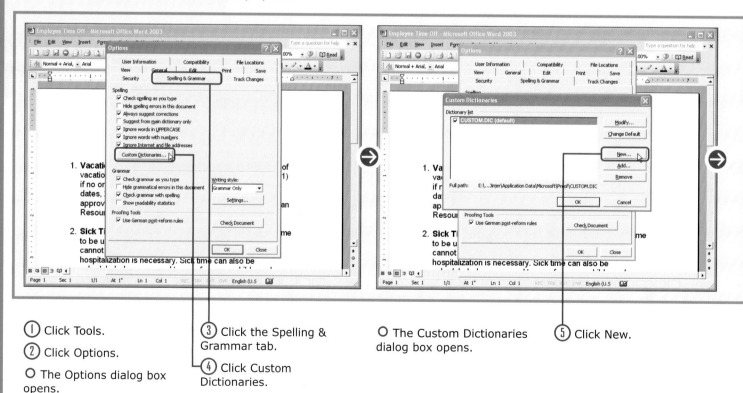

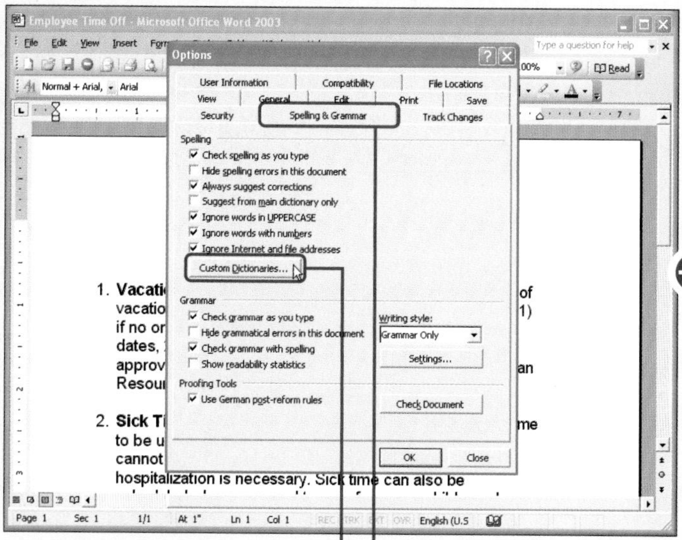

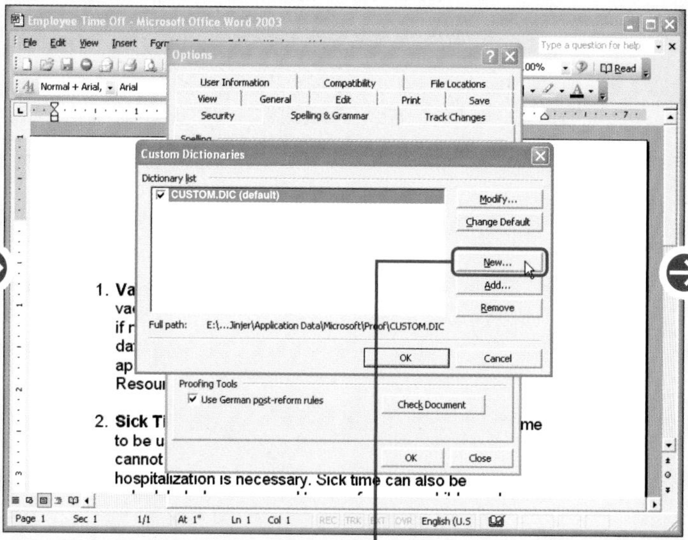

① Click Tools.

② Click Options.

○ The Options dialog box opens.

③ Click the Spelling & Grammar tab.

④ Click Custom Dictionaries.

○ The Custom Dictionaries dialog box opens.

⑤ Click New.

DIFFICULTY LEVEL

Did You Know?

You can add a custom dictionary created by another user, such as a medical dictionary. To load an existing dictionary, click Add in the Custom Dictionaries dialog box. In the Add Custom Dictionary dialog box, locate the dictionary you want to add.

Did You Know?

If you create dictionaries for different languages, the Custom Dictionaries dialog box sorts the dictionaries by language. You specify the language for a dictionary in the dialog box that opens when you click Modify. As a default, Word uses the dictionary for all languages.

Did You Know?

You can eliminate the use of all custom dictionaries by selecting Suggest from Main Dictionary Only on the Spelling & Grammar tab of the Options dialog box.

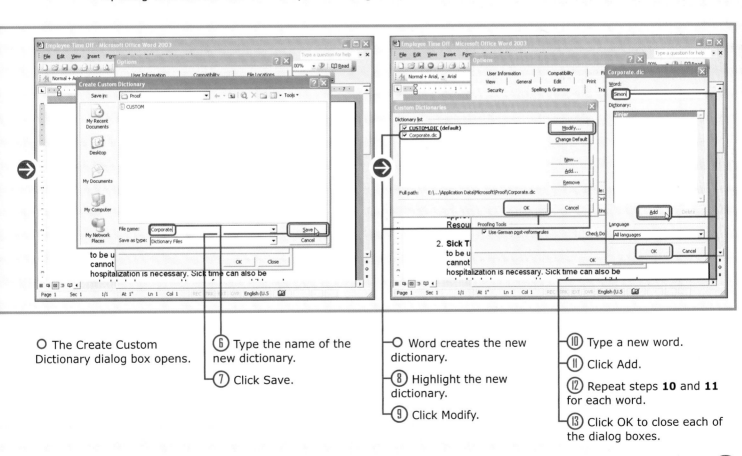

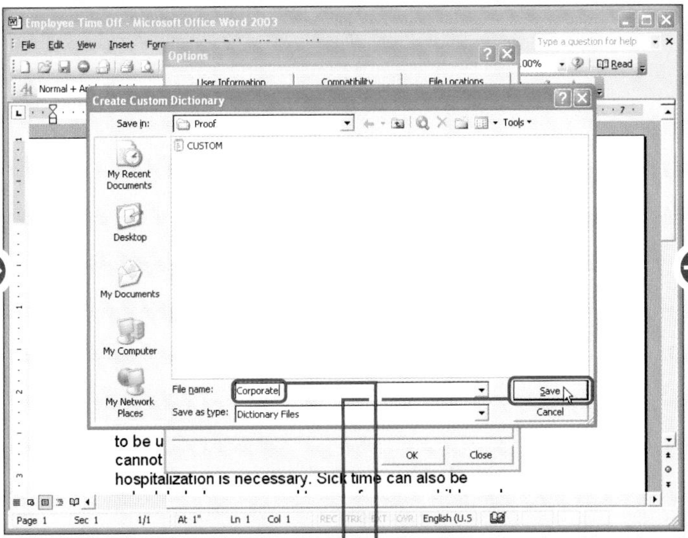

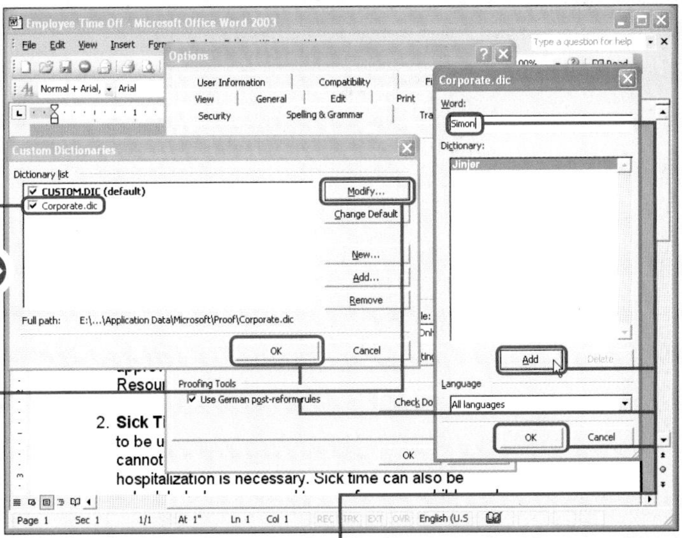

- The Create Custom Dictionary dialog box opens.

6. Type the name of the new dictionary.
7. Click Save.

- Word creates the new dictionary.

8. Highlight the new dictionary.
9. Click Modify.
10. Type a new word.
11. Click Add.
12. Repeat steps **10** and **11** for each word.
13. Click OK to close each of the dialog boxes.

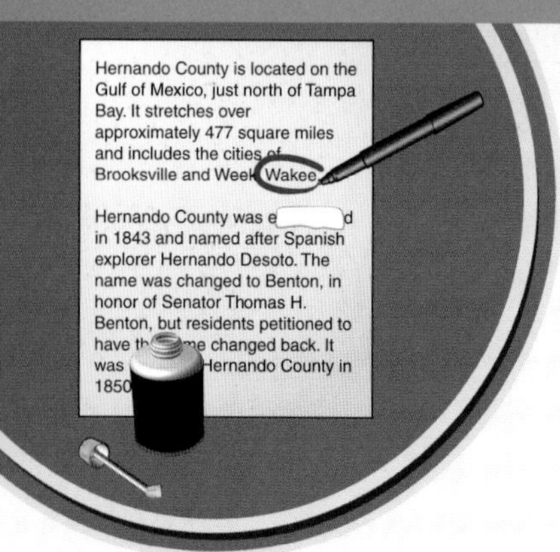

SPECIFY THE SPELLING

that you want for a word

You can eliminate spellings of Words that you do not want to appear in your documents. For example, the main Word dictionary allows you to use both *center* and *centre.* You can indicate the words that you want to be considered incorrect spellings by creating an exclusions list.

To create an exclusions list, you need to create a plain text document containing the words that you want to exclude. You need to press the Enter key after each word so that only one word exists on each line of the document.

You need to save the exclusion file with an .exc file extension and save it in the same folder as your other custom dictionaries. You can find the custom dictionaries in the following folder, where username represents your login username for Windows:

C:/Documents and Settings/username/Application Data/Microsoft/Proof

You need to name the exclusions file to match the main dictionary name. For example, the English dictionary is Mssp3en.lex, so you need to name the exclusions file Mssp3en.exc.

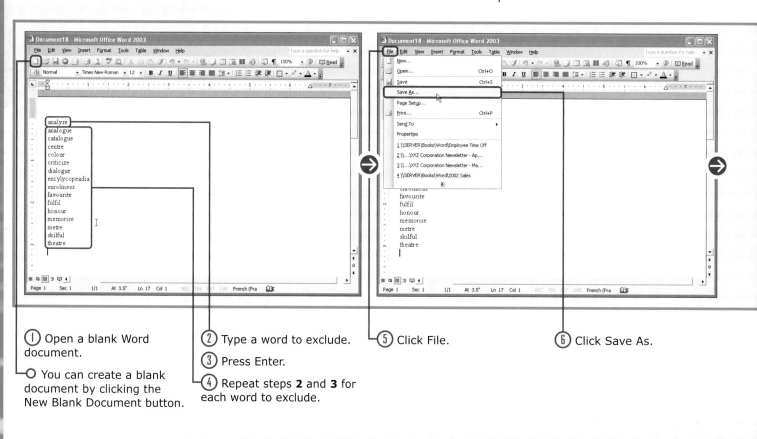

① Open a blank Word document.

- You can create a blank document by clicking the New Blank Document button.

② Type a word to exclude.

③ Press Enter.

④ Repeat steps **2** and **3** for each word to exclude.

⑤ Click File.

⑥ Click Save As.

DIFFICULTY LEVEL

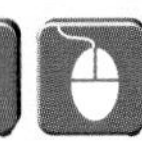

Did You Know?

The exclusion dictionary is not active until you close and reopen Word.

Did You Know?

The exclusion dictionary is available only to users logged on with the same username. If you have other login options on your machine, you need to save the dictionary in the corresponding folder for each username.

Apply It!

If you use a dictionary for another language, such as Spanish, you need to determine the dictionary name. Microsoft stores all Microsoft Office dictionaries in the C:\Program Files\Common Files\Microsoft Shared\Proof folder. All dictionary names begin with MSSP3, followed by two letters that identify the language. For example, the Spanish dictionary is named Mssp3es.lex.

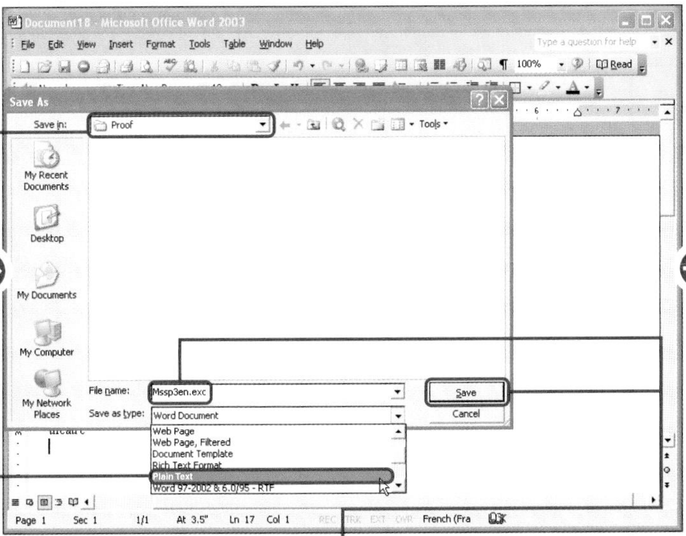

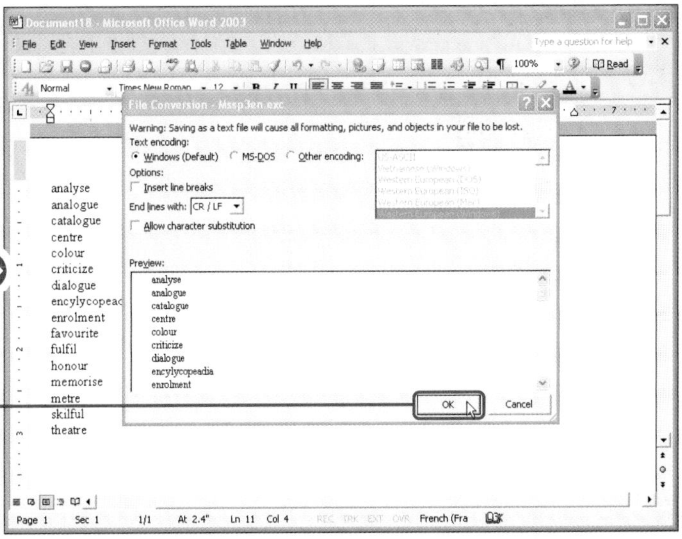

- The Save As dialog box opens.

7 Locate the Proof folder.

8 Click the down arrow and select Plain Text.

9 Type **Mssp3en.exc**, replacing `Mssp3en` with the name of the main dictionary.

10 Click Save.

- The File Conversion dialog box opens.

11 Click OK.

- Word creates the exclusion list.

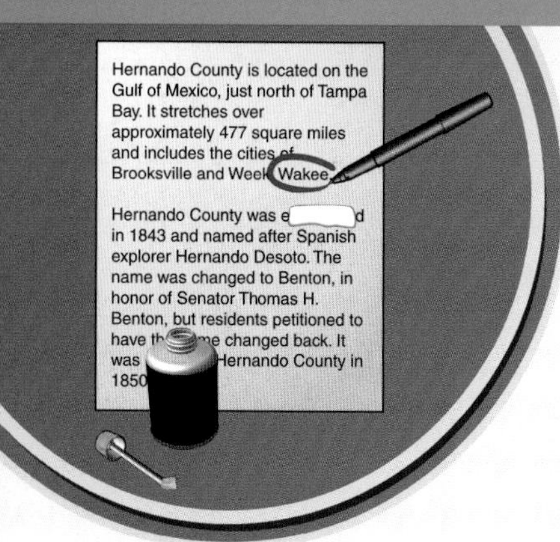

TRANSLATE A DOCUMENT

into another language

You can translate text in your document into another language by using the Translate option. For example, if you need to send a document to a customer in Mexico, you may want to translate the document from English to Spanish.

Microsoft Office provides dictionaries from other languages that you can use to look up and translate specific words in your document. If you want to translate the entire document, Word uses a machine translation option over the Web. Therefore, you need to make sure that you are connected to the Internet in order to select the Translate Whole Document button. When you select this option, Word sends your document to the machine and a translated version of the document appears in your Web browser.

If you want to use that translation, you can copy the text and paste it into a Word document. Keep in mind, however, that the translation was done using a computer and may not be totally accurate. Depending on the importance of your document, you may want to pay for a professional translation.

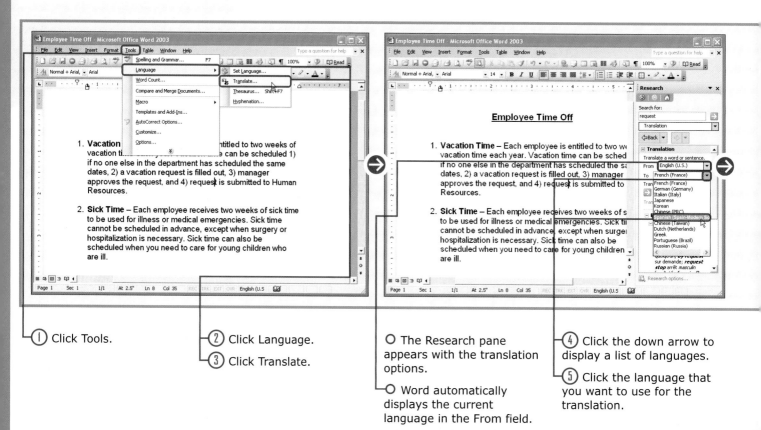

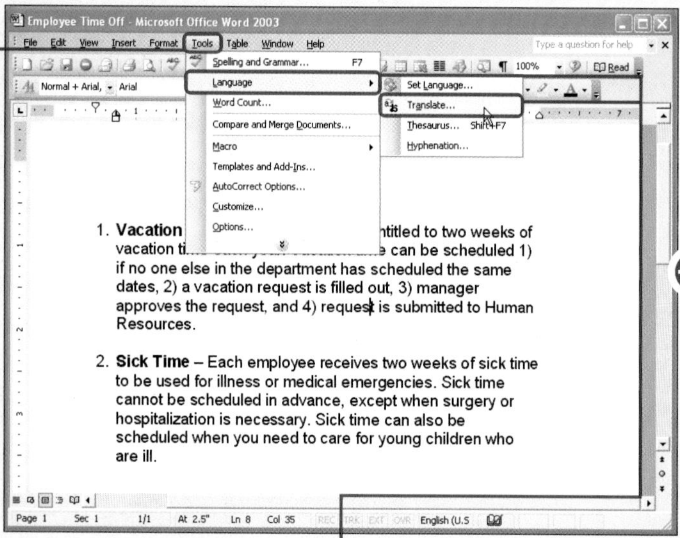

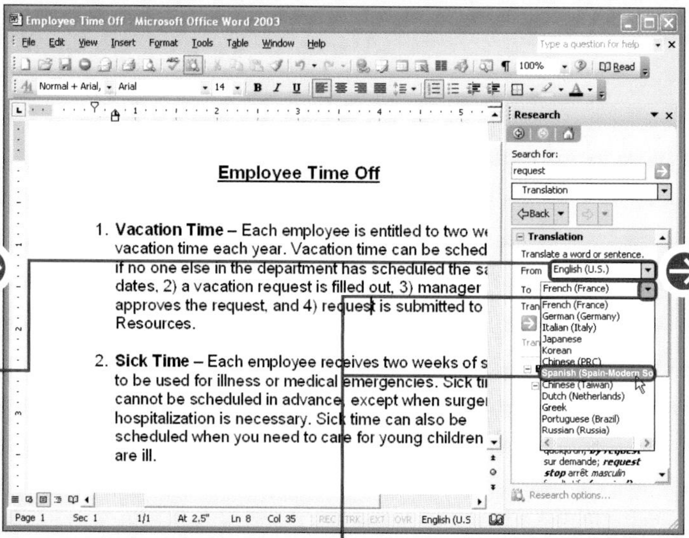

1. Click Tools.
2. Click Language.
3. Click Translate.

- The Research pane appears with the translation options.
- Word automatically displays the current language in the From field.

4. Click the down arrow to display a list of languages.
5. Click the language that you want to use for the translation.

DIFFICULTY LEVEL

Did You Know?

You can request a human translation of your document from Word. When you translate a phrase, Word displays the option of getting a quote for having a human translate the text.

Did You Know?

You can translate a phrase or single word in your document. To do so, highlight the text that you want to translate, press Alt, and click the text. The selected text appears in the Search For text box on the Research pane, and Word translates the text.

Apply It!

You can look up words that are not in your document by typing the words that you want to translate in the Search For box and clicking the arrow next to it.

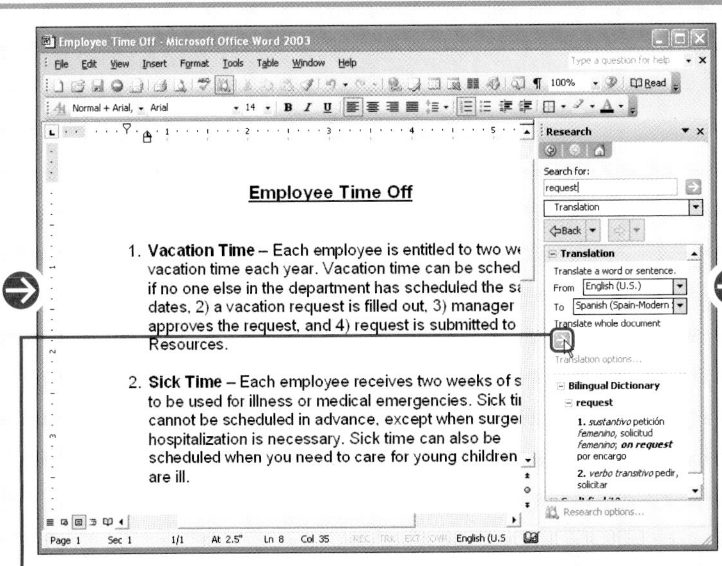

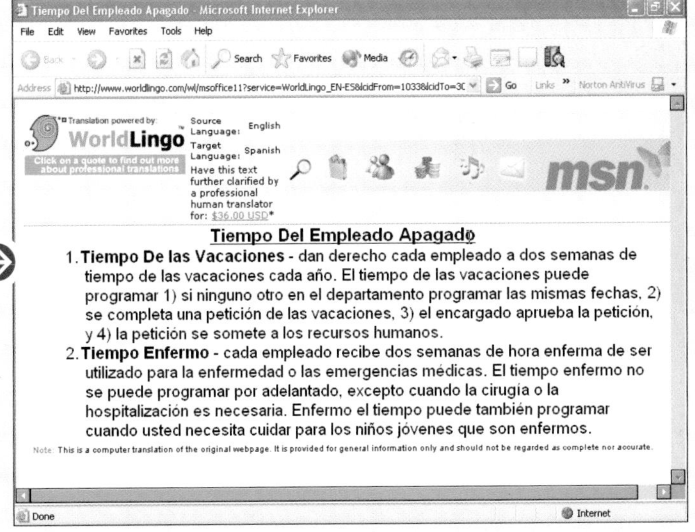

6 Click the Translate whole document button.

- Word sends the document to the translation machine over the Web, and the results appear in your browser.

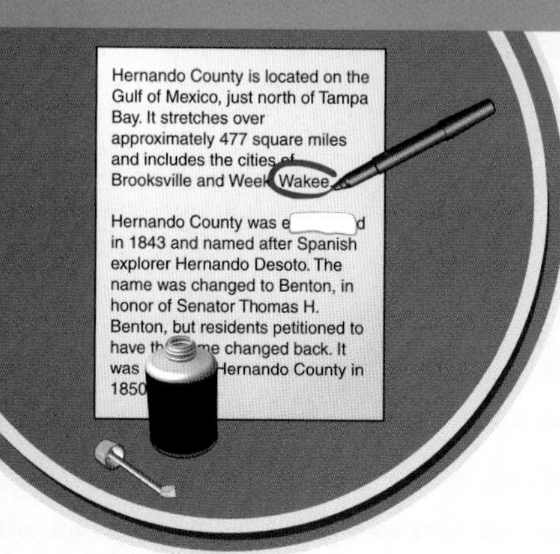

LIMIT THE CHANGES

that can be made to a document

You can protect a document to ensure that only limited changes are made to it. This is an important feature when you have a document that contains critical information that you do not want altered by other readers. This is also useful when you create a form and want the reader to modify only certain parts of the form.

You set document protection on the Protect Document pane. You can limit any formatting or editing changes in the document. You can choose from four different editing restrictions: No Changes, Comments, Tracked Changes, and Filling in Forms. If you do not want any changes made, select No Changes. If you select the No Changes or Comments options, you can select portions of the document that can be modified by certain users. Highlight the portions of the document that can be modified and click the check boxes next to the appropriate users. The Everyone check box allows everyone that reads the document to modify the marked sections.

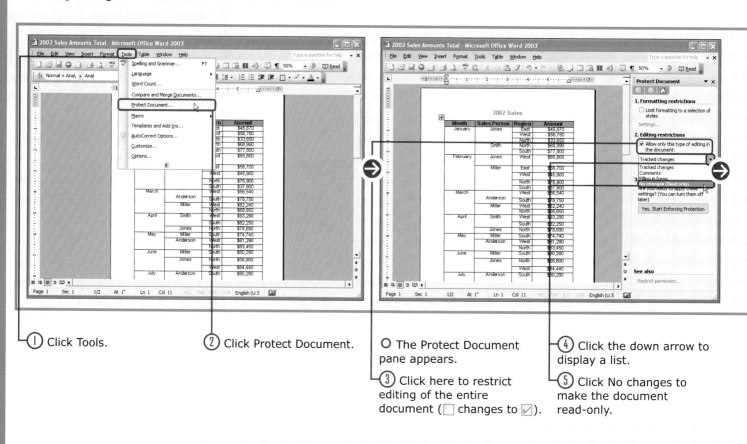

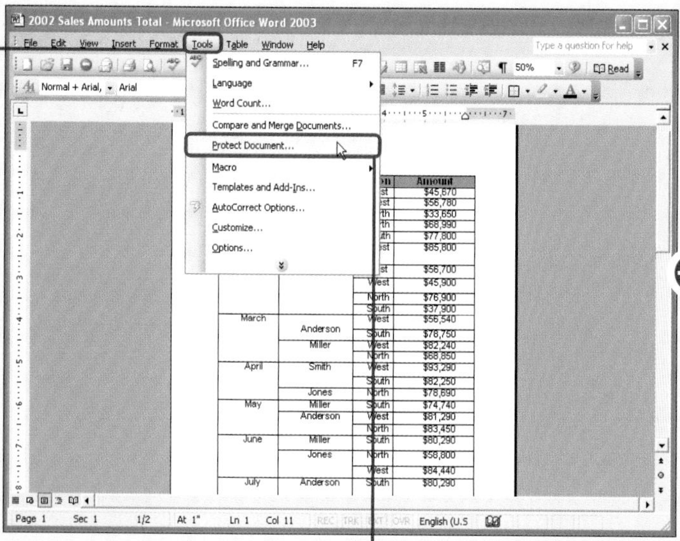

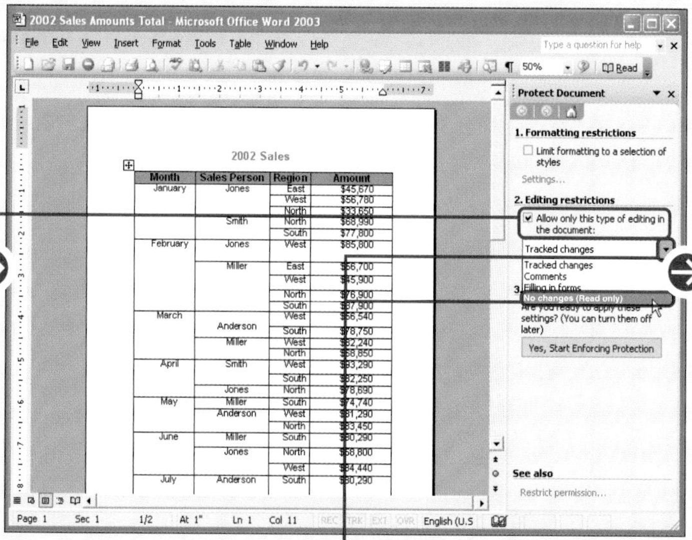

1. Click Tools.
2. Click Protect Document.

- The Protect Document pane appears.

3. Click here to restrict editing of the entire document (☐ changes to ☑).
4. Click the down arrow to display a list.
5. Click No changes to make the document read-only.

#78

DIFFICULTY LEVEL

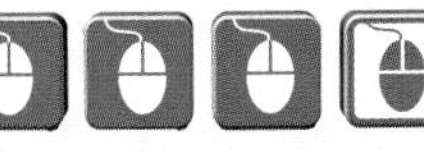

Did You Know?

If you want to restrict the formatting of the document, you need to specify the specific styles that you want to allow to be modified. As a default, if you select the Limit Formatting option, Word selects all styles. To specify the styles to protect, click Settings and select only the styles than can be applied to the document.

Apply It!

When you view a document that is protected, the Protect Dialog pane displays the protection information. You can view the areas that are unprotected by clicking the Highlight the Regions I Can Edit option on the pane. Any portions of the document that are unprotected are indicated with yellow square brackets.

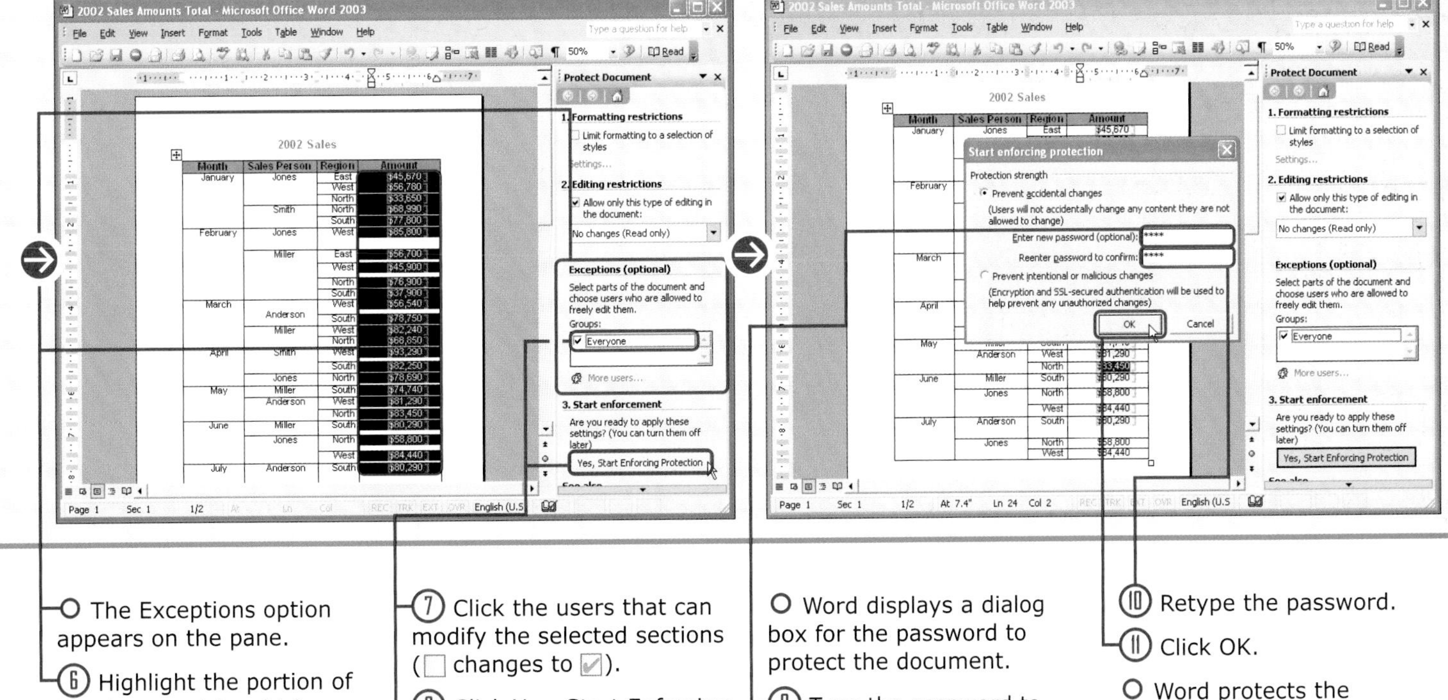

- The Exceptions option appears on the pane.
- 6 Highlight the portion of the document to which you want to allow modifications.
- 7 Click the users that can modify the selected sections (☐ changes to ☑).
- 8 Click Yes, Start Enforcing Protection.
- Word displays a dialog box for the password to protect the document.
- 9 Type the password to unprotect the document.
- 10 Retype the password.
- 11 Click OK.
- Word protects the document from changes.

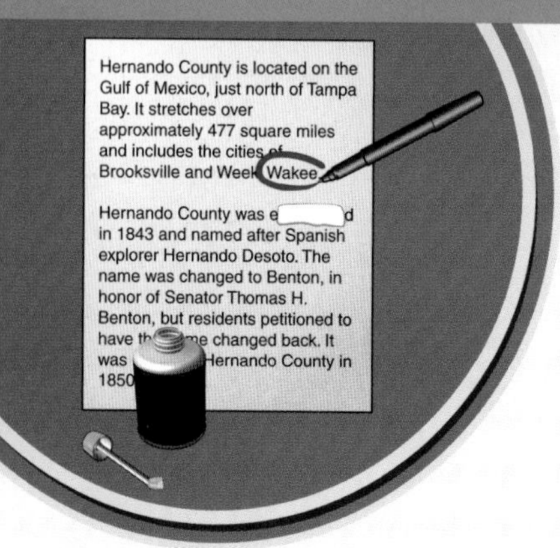

AUTOMATICALLY SUMMARIZE

a long document

You can have Word automatically summarize a long document for you. For example, you may want to be able to quickly identify the key points of a document that someone sent you without reading the entire document.

Word analyzes the selected document and finds the key points by finding words that occur frequently within the document. Word assigns a scoring system to the sentences based on the frequency of the identified key words. The sentences that use the most keywords get a higher score.

When you select the AutoSummarize option, you specify the percentage of the document you want to see in the summary. Word uses that percentage to display the sentences with scores within that percentage.

You can select from four different summary methods. You can have Word highlight the key points directly within the document or create a separate summary. If you create a summary, you can place it at the top of the document or in a separate document, or you can hide all but the summary portion of the document.

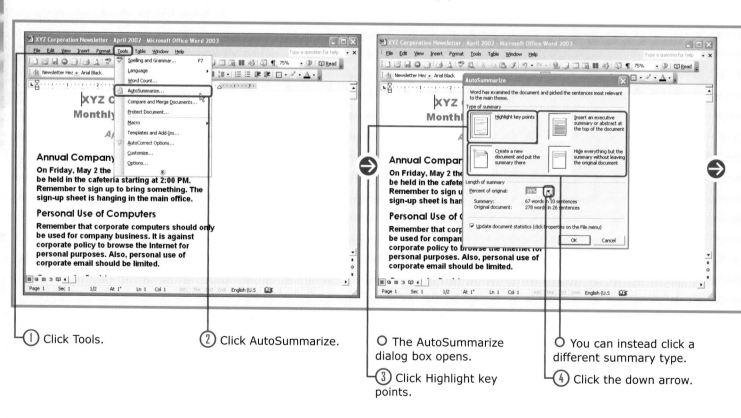

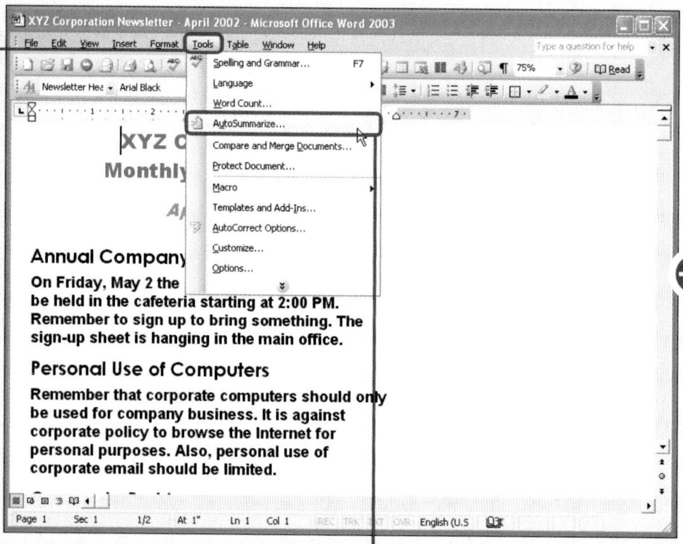

① Click Tools.

② Click AutoSummarize.

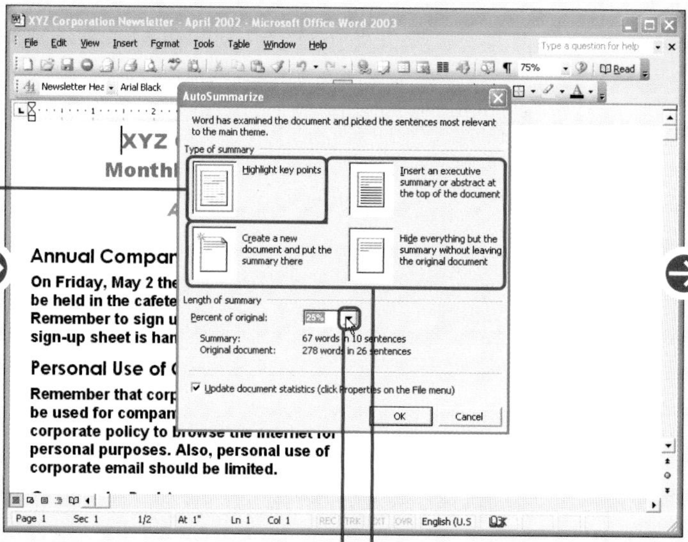

○ The AutoSummarize dialog box opens.

③ Click Highlight key points.

○ You can instead click a different summary type.

④ Click the down arrow.

DIFFICULTY LEVEL

Did You Know?

You can add summary information to the document properties. To create the summary information, click Update Document Statistics in the AutoSummarize dialog box. Word automatically updates the Keywords and Comments fields on the Summary tab.

Did You Know?

You can cancel a summary in progress by pressing the Esc key.

Caution!

Be careful about using the highlight feature to summarize text in a document. Word highlights the summarized text in yellow. You cannot change the summary color, so if you have other text highlighted in yellow, it may create confusion. If you use the highlight feature with a document that contains text highlighting, make sure that none of the document is highlighted in yellow before selecting the AutoSummarize option.

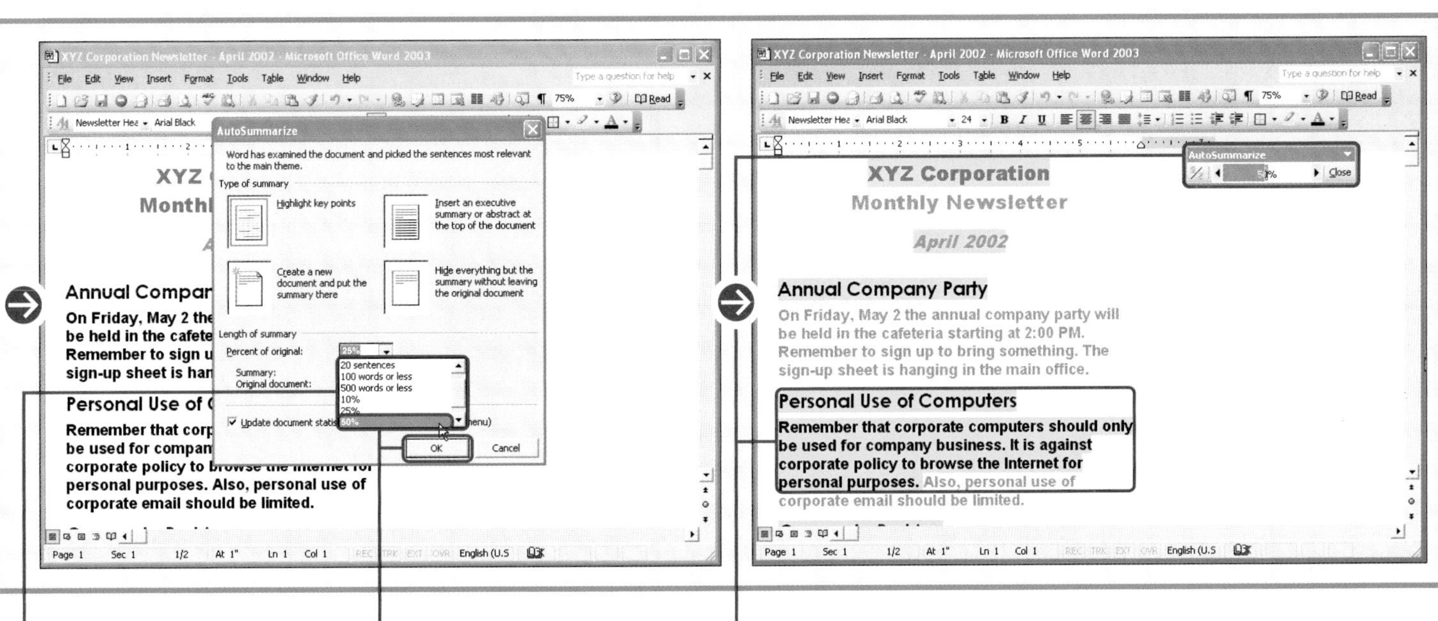

- A menu of options appears.

5. Click the portion of the document that you want.
6. Click OK.

- Word highlights the most relevant portion of the selected document.
- The AutoSummarize toolbar appears.
- Click the left arrow and right arrow to change the summary percentage.

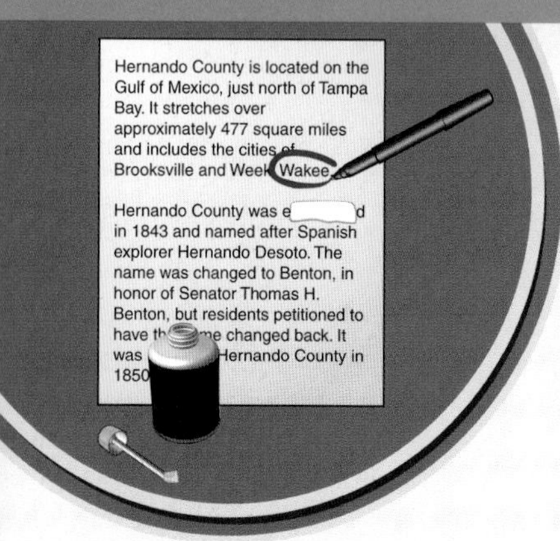

Turn off SMART TAGS

You can eliminate the display of smart tags in your document by turning them off. You may want to turn off the smart tags to make the document more readable, especially if you are reading the document online.

Smart tags are text values that Word recognizes as a particular type of data within your document. For example, Word recognizes all contacts from your Outlook e-mail recipient list and marks them as smart tags. Smart tags are marked with a dotted purple line under the corresponding text. When you drag your cursor over a smart tag, the Smart Tag button appears. You can click the button to get a menu that displays the options available for the specific smart tag.

You can turn off individual smart tags, or you can turn off all smart tags within a document. When you turn off the smart tags, Word no longer recognizes those smart tags. Although you cannot undo the action, you can have Word recheck the document to apply smart tags.

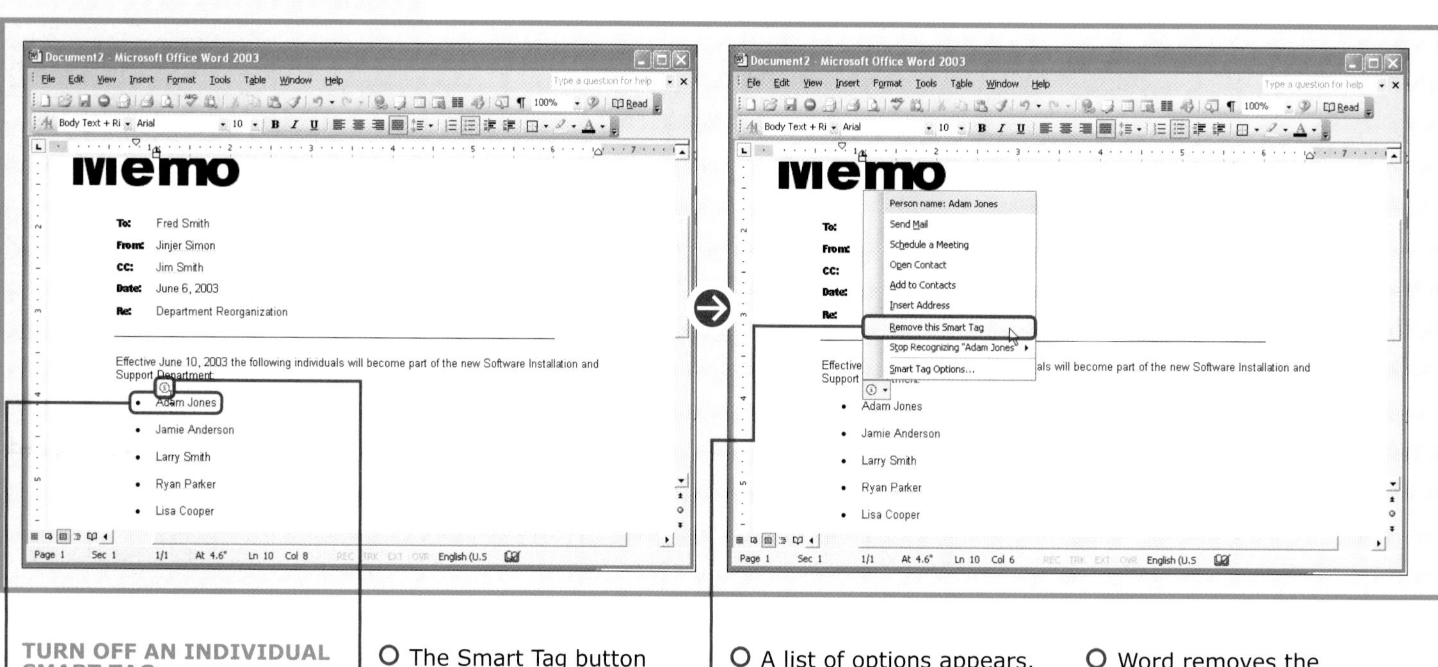

TURN OFF AN INDIVIDUAL SMART TAG

① Drag the cursor (↖) over the smart tag.

○ The Smart Tag button appears.

② Click the Smart Tag button.

○ A list of options appears.

③ Click Remove this Smart Tag.

○ Word removes the selected smart tag, so the purple underline no longer appears.

DIFFICULTY LEVEL

Put It Together!

After turning off all the smart tags, if you want to display them again, click Recheck Document on the Smart Tags tab. Word goes through the current document and finds all the smart tags.

Apply It!

You can add smart tags from other sources. Microsoft provides several different types of smart tags that you can download. To get additional smart tags, click More Smart Tags on the Smart Tags tab to display a Web site in your browser. Follow the instructions there to download smart tags.

Did You Know?

Word selects only the smart tags matching the recognizers selected on the Smart Tags tab. You eliminate the future selection of a type of smart tag by deselecting the corresponding recognizer.

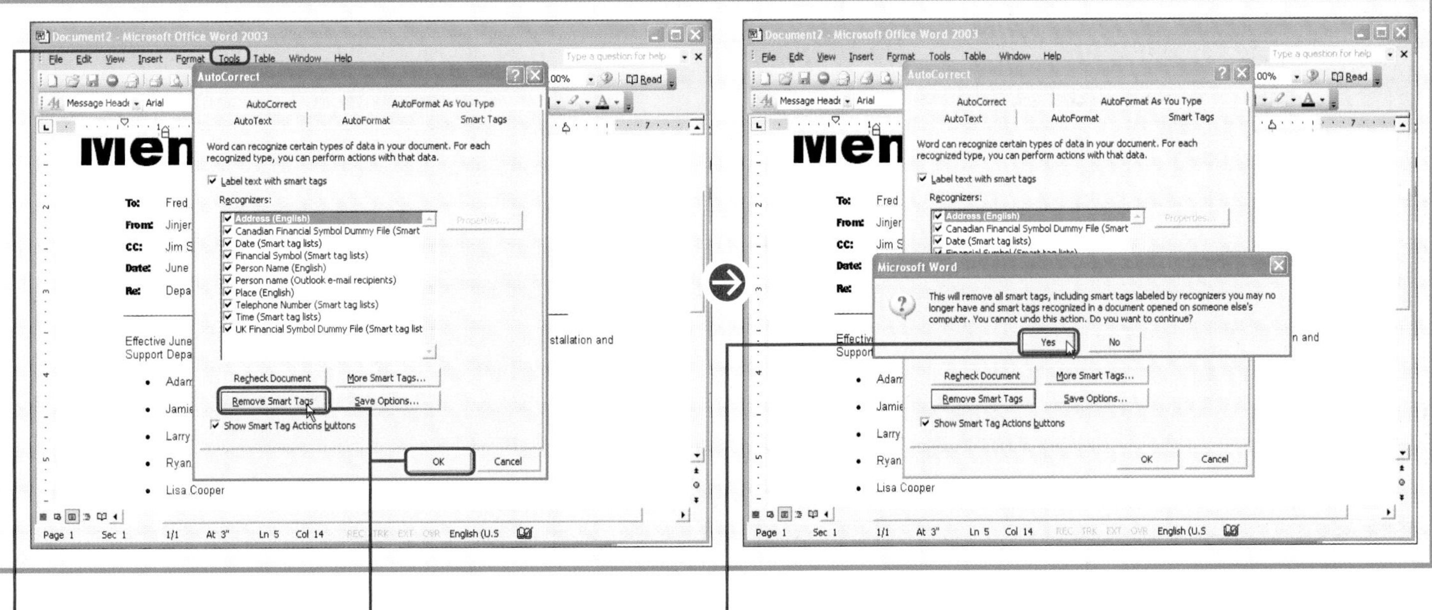

TURN OFF ALL SMART TAGS

1. Click Tools.
2. Click AutoCorrect.

- The AutoCorrect dialog box appears.

3. On the Smart Tags tab, click Remove Smart Tags.
4. Click OK.

- Word displays a dialog box to ensure that you want to continue.

5. Click Yes.

- Word removes all smart tags from the document.

CHAPTER 9

Create Web Pages

Although Word is not the ideal Web page creation software, you can use it to design and save Hypertext Markup Language (HTML) pages that you can use on your Web site. Keep in mind, however, that for more complex Web development, you should use a Web development package such as Microsoft FrontPage.

With Word, however, you can create some fairly sophisticated Web pages. For example, you can design a Web form to gather information from a user. You can even have the information sent back to you through e-mail.

You can include the most common form fields on your Web page, including text boxes and radio buttons. You can customize the properties for each of the form fields.

You can also design frame pages in Word. This enables you to design a page that contains multiple windows, called *frames,* each one containing a separate Web page. Frames are a popular Web site feature because they enable you to maintain a consistent feel as the user views multiple pages.

Word enables you to use different formats of Web pages. If you want to e-mail a Web page to another user, you can create an encapsulated file that contains all text and graphics. This compares to the traditional Web page where all graphics are stored in separate files, requiring you to send all graphic files when you e-mail a Web page.

This chapter examines several features related to working with Web pages in Word. It looks at how to take different types of documents and display them on the Internet.

TOP 100

Create a WEB PAGE DOCUMENT

You can use Word to create a page to display on a Web site. For example, you may want to provide specific information about your company or products. You can create the desired page within Word and then save the document as an HTML file that can be placed on a Web site.

When you create a Web page, Word creates an HTML file, automatically generating the HTML code for you. HTML is the standard language used to create Web pages. The nice thing about using Word is that you do not need to worry about reading or modifying the HTML code; Word does all of that for you. You simply lay your document out as you want it to appear on the Web page.

Keep in mind that it is not necessary to start with a Web document; you can also save an existing Word document as a Web document. If you initially create a Web document, you can add only the Word elements that can be viewed on a Web page. For example, you do not add page numbering to a Web document.

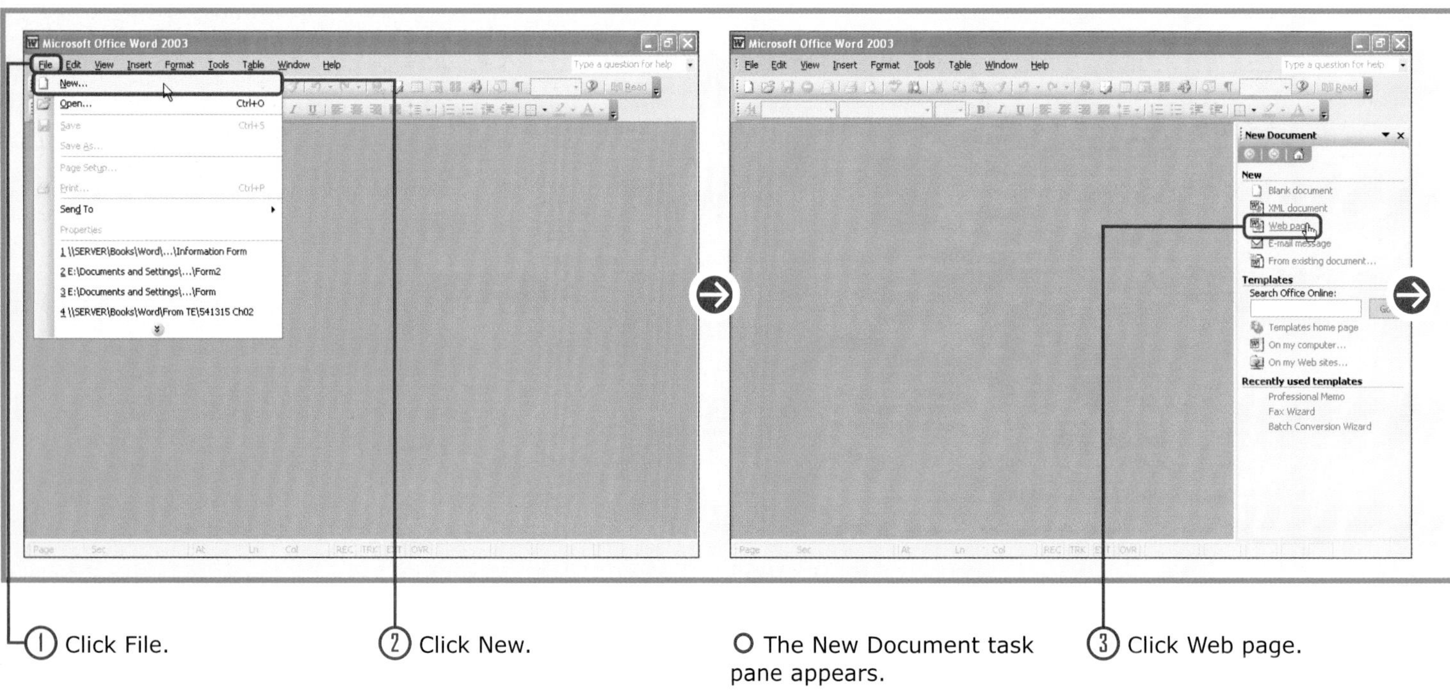

1. Click File.
2. Click New.

- The New Document task pane appears.

3. Click Web page.

Did You Know?

You can create Web pages for specific Web browsers to eliminate features that a browser does not support. To specify a browser type, click Tools ➪ Options and click the General tab. Click Web Options and then the Browsers tab. In the People Who View This Web Page Will Be Using field, click the down arrow and select the browser type.

Did You Know?

You can save your Web document in one of the following types:

Format	Description
Single File Web Page	Saves all elements of the Web page, text and graphics, in a single file.
Web Page	Creates a standard HTML page with graphics and other objects stored in other files.
Web Page, Filtered	Reduces the file size by removing Word-specific tags.

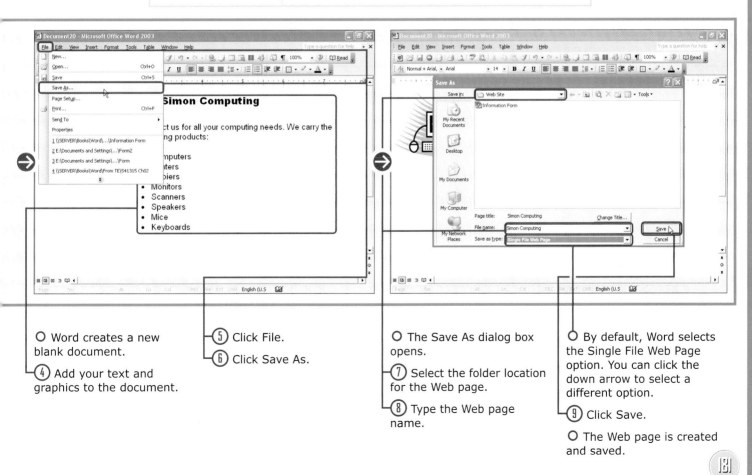

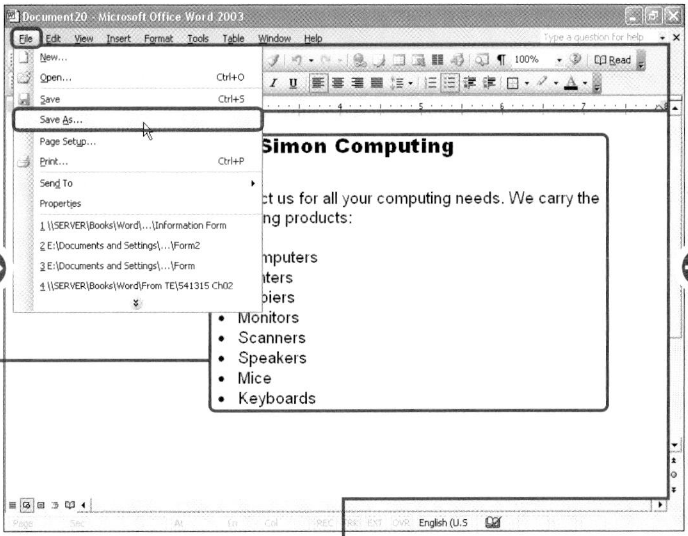

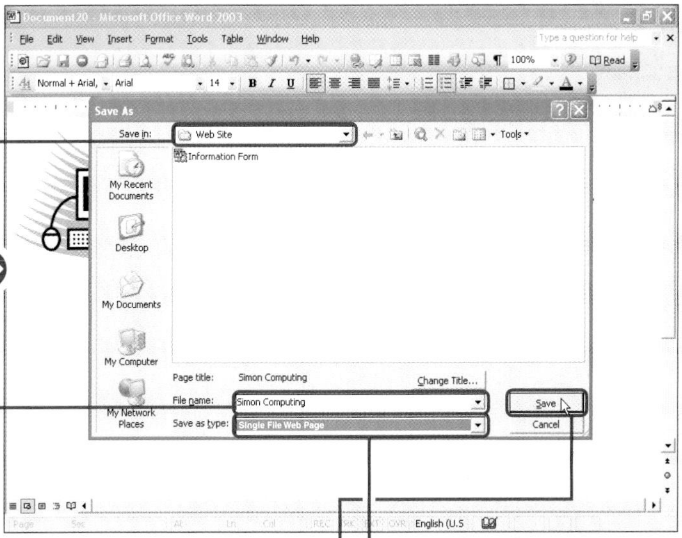

- Word creates a new blank document.

4 Add your text and graphics to the document.

5 Click File.

6 Click Save As.

- The Save As dialog box opens.

7 Select the folder location for the Web page.

8 Type the Web page name.

- By default, Word selects the Single File Web Page option. You can click the down arrow to select a different option.

9 Click Save.

- The Web page is created and saved.

The Food Critic
Honest Reviews of Current Favorites
This Month:
Geano's Pizza

Design a WEB FORM

You can use Microsoft Word to create a form to display on a Web page. For example, you may want to create a form to gather information about a perspective client.

To create a form, you need to use the form fields on the Web Tools toolbar. This toolbar enables you to create form fields such as text boxes, check boxes, drop-down lists, and buttons.

To add a field to your Web page, you need to be in Design mode. When you are in this mode, you add a field at the cursor location by clicking on it. You can type text around the fields to tell the user the purpose of the field.

When you add the first field to the page, Word automatically creates a form around the field. When you are in Design mode, the top and bottom of the form are indicated. You want to keep the fields that you add between the top and bottom lines.

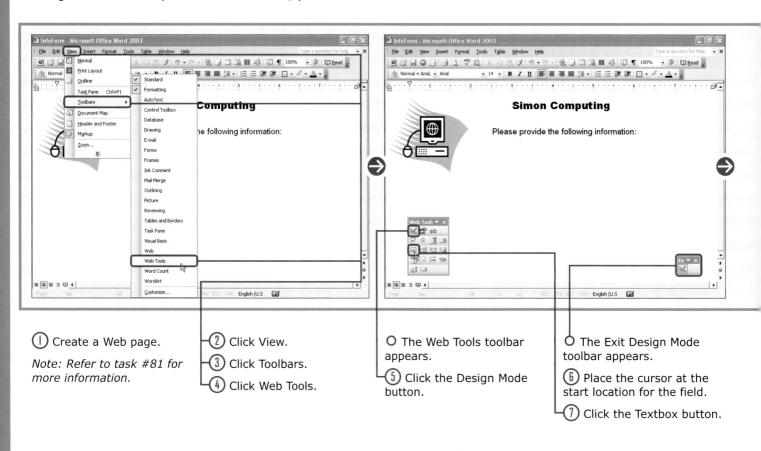

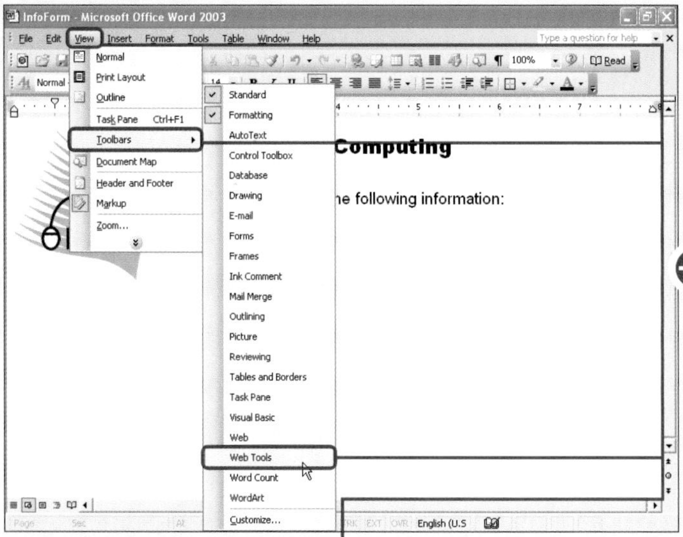

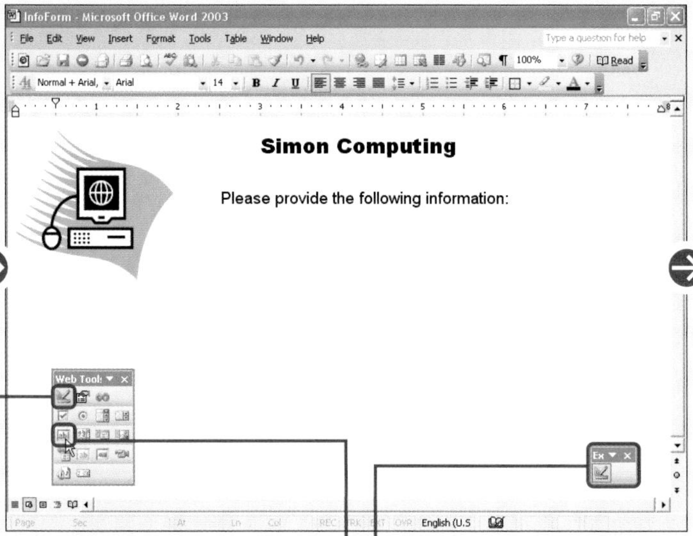

1. Create a Web page.

Note: Refer to task #81 for more information.

2. Click View.
3. Click Toolbars.
4. Click Web Tools.

- The Web Tools toolbar appears.

5. Click the Design Mode button.

- The Exit Design Mode toolbar appears.

6. Place the cursor at the start location for the field.
7. Click the Textbox button.

Did You Know?

You can change the size of the field that you insert on a Web page. To resize a field, click the field to select it and drag the side or bottom of the field until it is the size that you want.

Put It Together!

To make your form useful, you need to capture the results entered on the form by the user. One method is to have the results e-mailed to you. See task #83 for more information.

Did You Know?

You can have Word display your form in a browser window so that you can preview it. To preview a form, click File ➪ Web Page Preview.

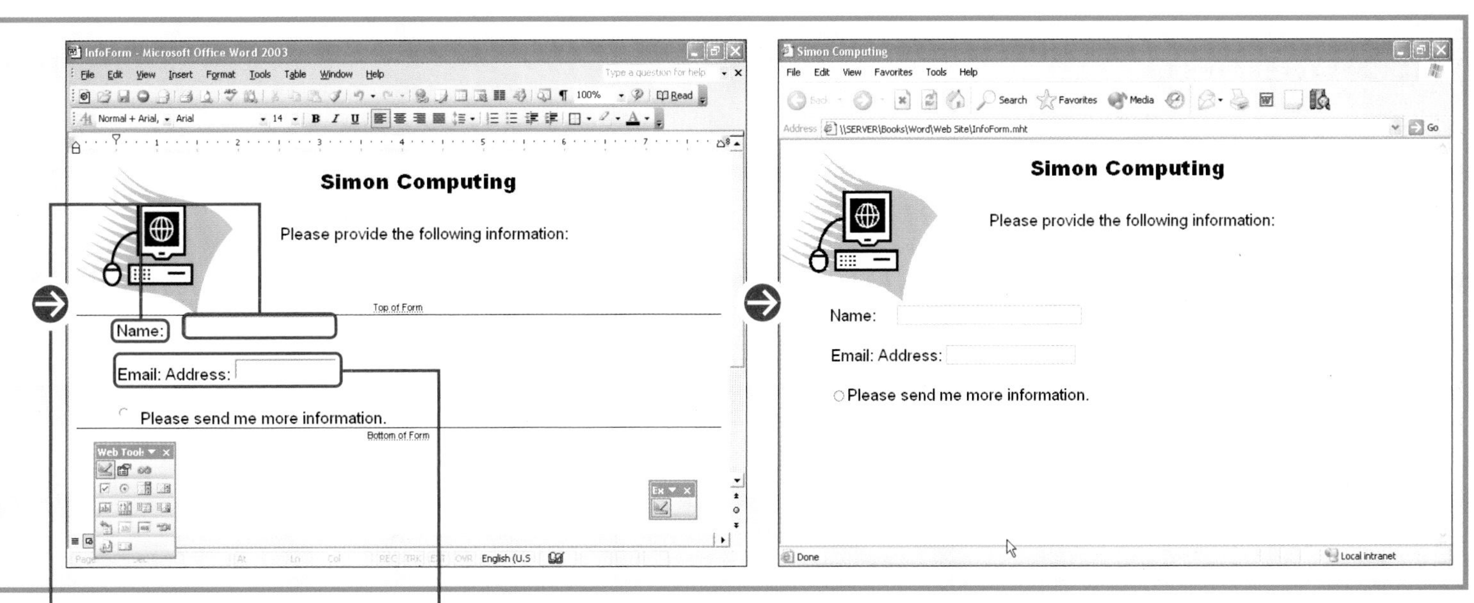

- Word creates the specified field.
- 8 Add descriptive text for the field.
- 9 Repeat steps **6** to **8** to add additional fields to the form, using different types of fields in step **7** when necessary.
- When you save, Word creates a Web form that is visible from a Web browser.

The Food Critic
Honest Reviews of Current Favorites
This Month:
Geano's Pizza

Have FORM RESULTS e-mailed back to you

You can have the results of a Web form that you create in Word e-mailed back to you when the user fills it in. This method is useful for capturing the information specified by the user.

When you have the form e-mailed to you, the browser uses the default e-mail program on the user's computer. Keep in mind that this type of page is not secured, so you should avoid requesting personal information from the user.

In order to have information sent via e-mail, you need to add a Submit button to your form. You need to set the properties of the Submit button to indicate what should occur when the button is clicked. You can also change the text that appears on the button.

When the user clicks the Submit button, an e-mail message is sent containing a file attachment. The file attachment contains the responses to the form.

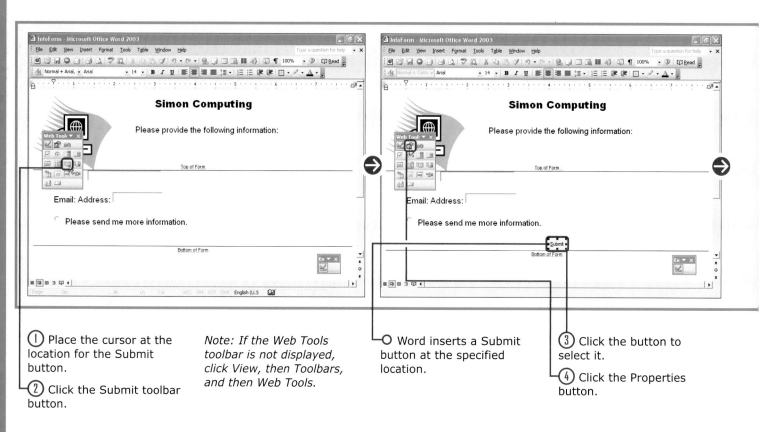

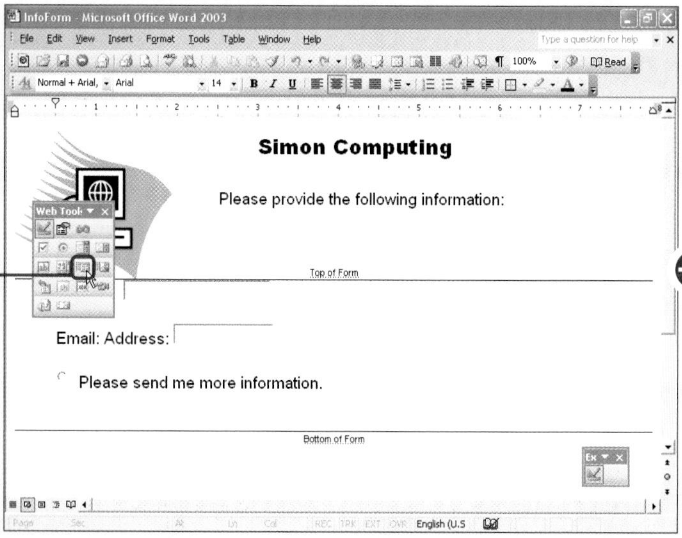

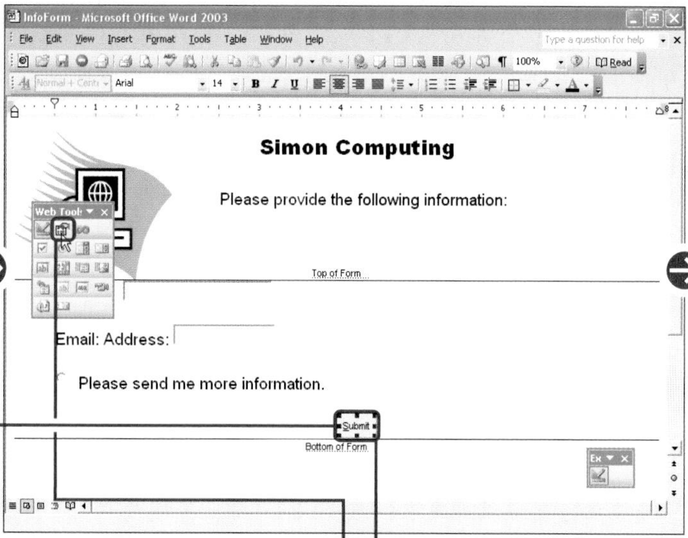

① Place the cursor at the location for the Submit button.

② Click the Submit toolbar button.

Note: If the Web Tools toolbar is not displayed, click View, then Toolbars, and then Web Tools.

○ Word inserts a Submit button at the specified location.

③ Click the button to select it.

④ Click the Properties button.

Did You Know?

When you receive a response from the Web page, you will get a file named POSTDATA.ATT as an attachment. You can view the file in any text editor, such as Notepad.

Apply It!

When you read the text file, you will see that the information from the Web page is in one continuous line. The file is laid out so that the field name is displayed with an equals sign and then the response. If there was a space in the response, an underscore character is displayed. An ampersand sign (&) separates each field.

Did You Know?

You can use the Properties window to customize each field on the form. For example, you should set a field name so that you receive field names with the response.

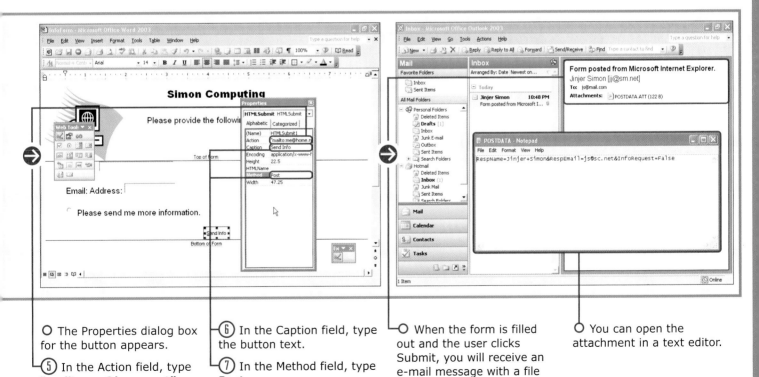

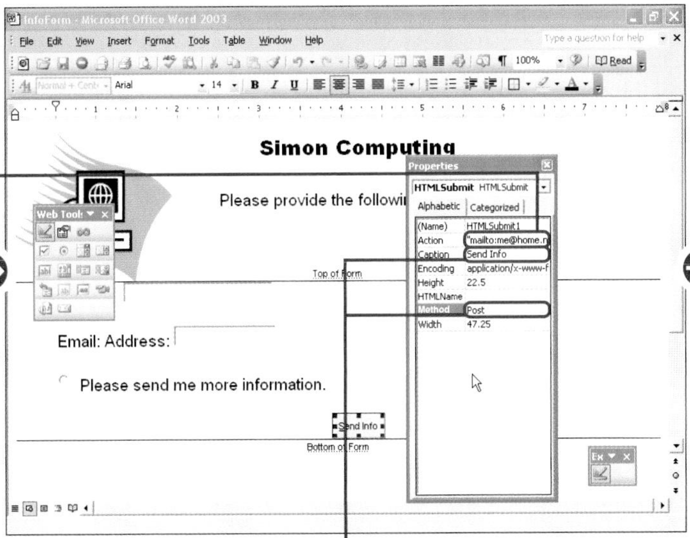

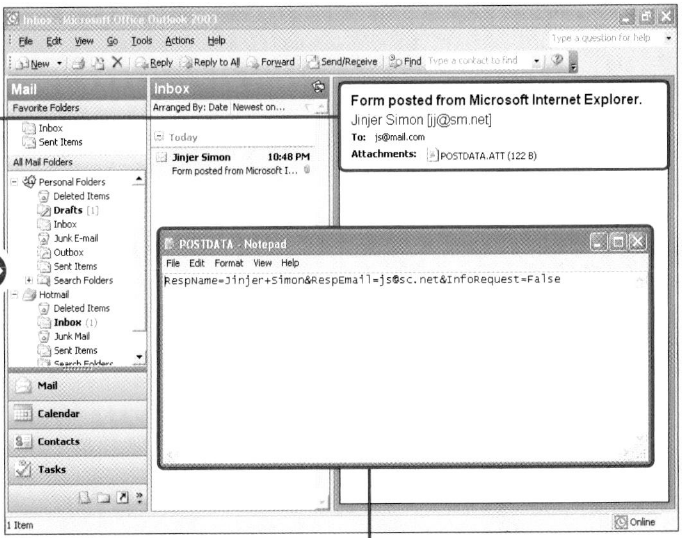

- The Properties dialog box for the button appears.

5. In the Action field, type **"mailto:me@home.net"**, replacing me@home.net with the e-mail address to receive the responses.

6. In the Caption field, type the button text.

7. In the Method field, type **Post**.

8. Save the form.

- When the form is filled out and the user clicks Submit, you will receive an e-mail message with a file containing the responses.

- You can open the attachment in a text editor.

The Food Critic
Honest Reviews of Current Favorites
This Month:
Geano's Pizza

Create a Web page ad with SCROLLING TEXT

You can insert text that scrolls in a box on your Web page. This feature works well for advertising information or text you want to emphasize.

You specify how you want the scrolling text to appear in the Scrolling Text dialog box. Word provides three different effects, or *behaviors,* for the text: Scroll, Slide, and Alternate. Slide slides the text from the specified direction and stops. Alternate slides the text from one side to the other. With both Slide and Alternate, you can specify how many times you want the text to scroll across the page. You can also adjust the speed of the text movement. You can see the results of the settings in the Preview window.

Word inserts the scrolling text as a field on the page. In Design mode, you need to resize the scrolling text to the desired height and width. The field needs to be sized large enough to read the text. The width specifies the window in which the text will scroll. Keep in mind that the text will not scroll while working in Design mode.

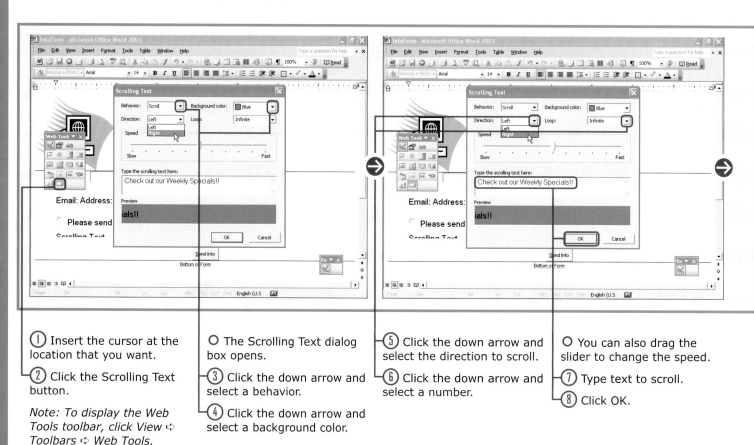

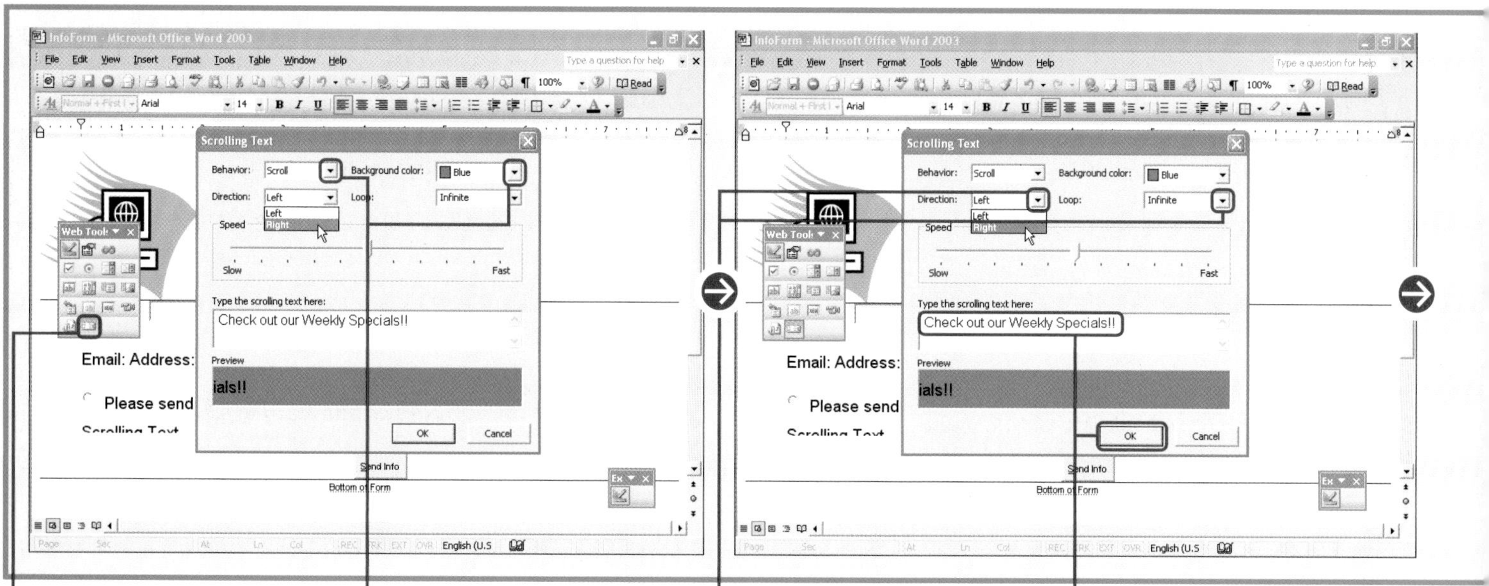

1. Insert the cursor at the location that you want.
2. Click the Scrolling Text button.

Note: To display the Web Tools toolbar, click View ⇨ Toolbars ⇨ Web Tools.

- The Scrolling Text dialog box opens.

3. Click the down arrow and select a behavior.
4. Click the down arrow and select a background color.
5. Click the down arrow and select the direction to scroll.
6. Click the down arrow and select a number.

- You can also drag the slider to change the speed.

7. Type text to scroll.
8. Click OK.

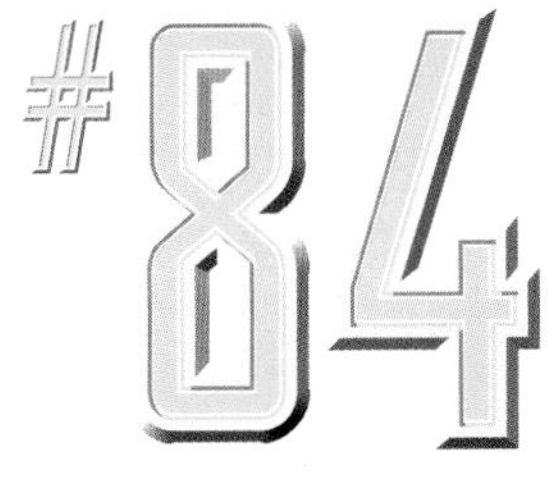

Did You Know?

Word uses the font attributes at the cursor location to create the scrolling text. For example, if you are using 12-point Arial text for your other text, that is the font and size that will be used for the scrolling text. If you want different font attributes, make the font selections before clicking the Scrolling Text button.

Did You Know?

Some Web browsers do not support scrolling text. If this is the case, the text will display as a static text within the field.

Apply It!

When you resize the scrolling text field, Word centers the text vertically within the field. Make sure that the field is wide enough to view all the text.

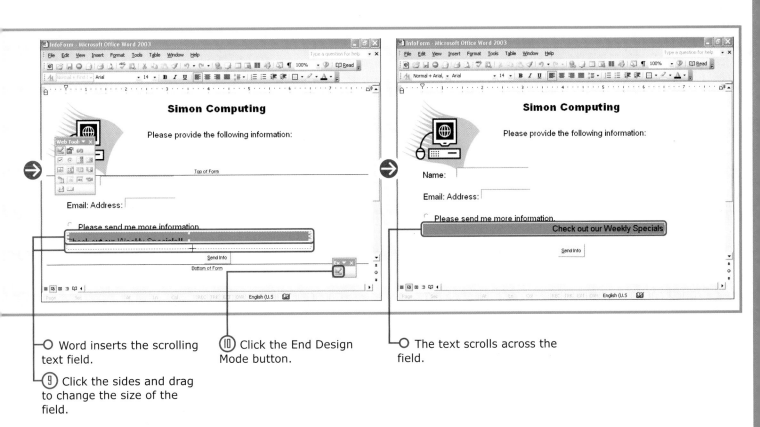

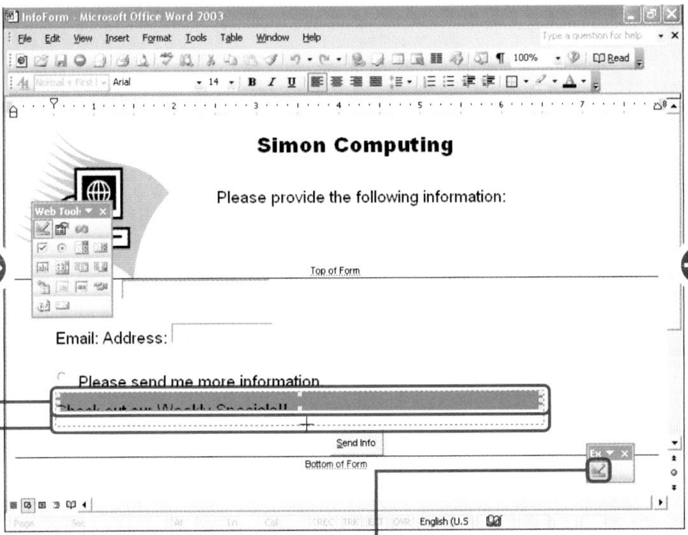

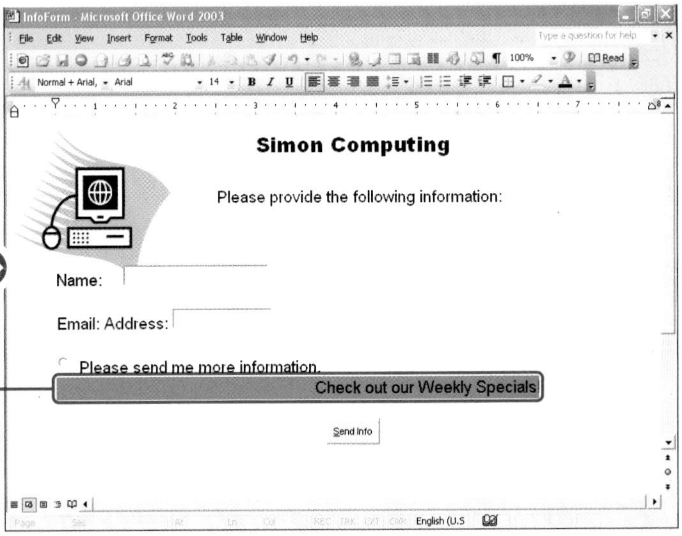

- Word inserts the scrolling text field.

9. Click the sides and drag to change the size of the field.

10. Click the End Design Mode button.

- The text scrolls across the field.

The Food Critic
Honest Reviews of Current Favorites
This Month:
Geano's Pizza

CREATE A HYPERLINK

in a document

You can create hyperlinks in your documents. A *hyperlink* is text that opens another file when it is clicked. On a Web page, a hyperlink typically opens another Web page or opens a mail message to a specified e-mail address. Although you can put hyperlinks in all your Word documents, they typically work best in Web pages that will be viewed online.

If you have automatic formatting of hyperlinks turned on, Word automatically formats any text that resembles a link as a hyperlink by changing the text color to blue and underlining it. Although this is an easy method to create a hyperlink, it does not enable you to customize the text that displays for the hyperlink. For example, although you are linking to www.wiley.com, you may want the link to say John Wiley & Sons, Inc.

You customize the hyperlink in the Insert Hyperlink dialog box. You specify the text to display and the appropriate hyperlink. You can select from hyperlinks of pages that you have visited or a file on your site, or you can even type a different hyperlink.

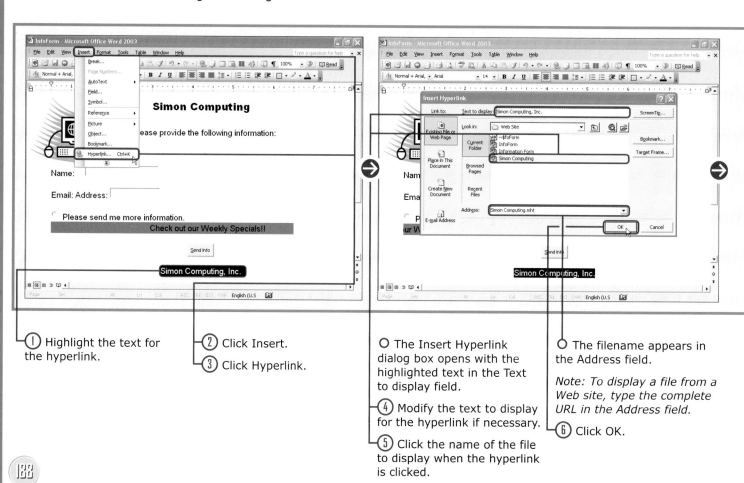

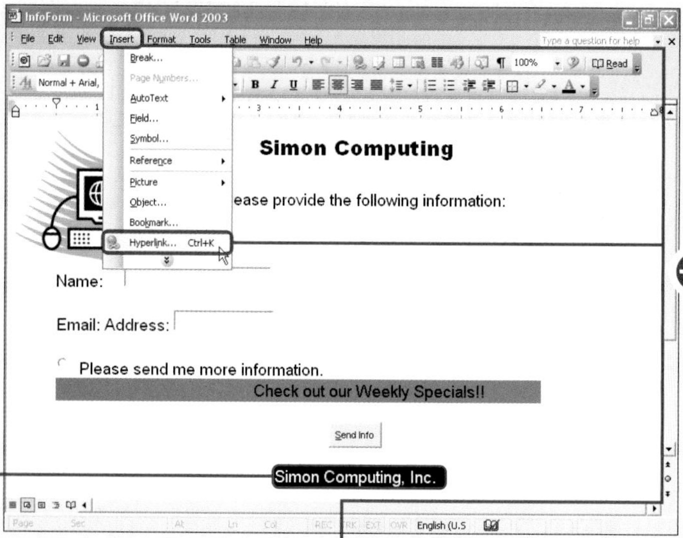

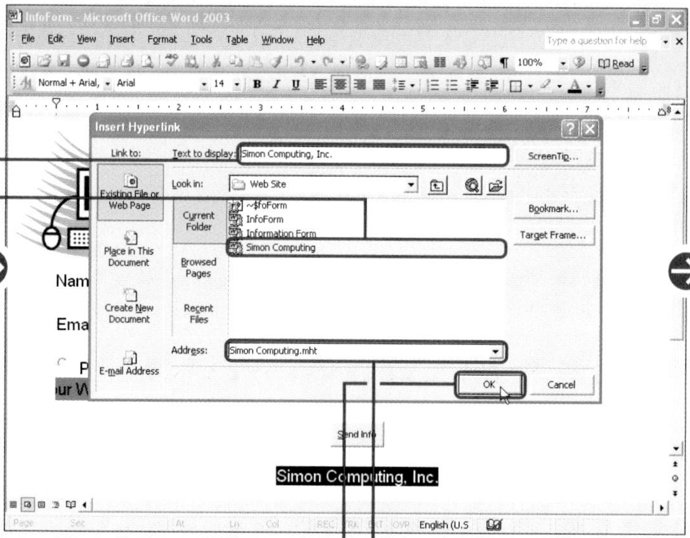

1. Highlight the text for the hyperlink.
2. Click Insert.
3. Click Hyperlink.

- The Insert Hyperlink dialog box opens with the highlighted text in the Text to display field.

4. Modify the text to display for the hyperlink if necessary.
5. Click the name of the file to display when the hyperlink is clicked.

- The filename appears in the Address field.

Note: To display a file from a Web site, type the complete URL in the Address field.

6. Click OK.

DIFFICULTY LEVEL

Apply It!

If you place a hyperlink on a Web page containing frames, you can specify which frame should display the link. To do so, click Target Frame in the Insert Hyperlink dialog box. See task #87 for more information on working with frames.

Apply It!

To create a hyperlink for a graphic, select the graphic before displaying the Insert Hyperlink dialog box. The Text to Display field will be read-only and contain the text <<Selection in Document>>.

Did You Know?

You can create a screen tip that appears when the user drags the cursor across the hyperlink. Click ScreenTip in the Insert Hyperlink dialog box and type up to 256 characters for the screen tip.

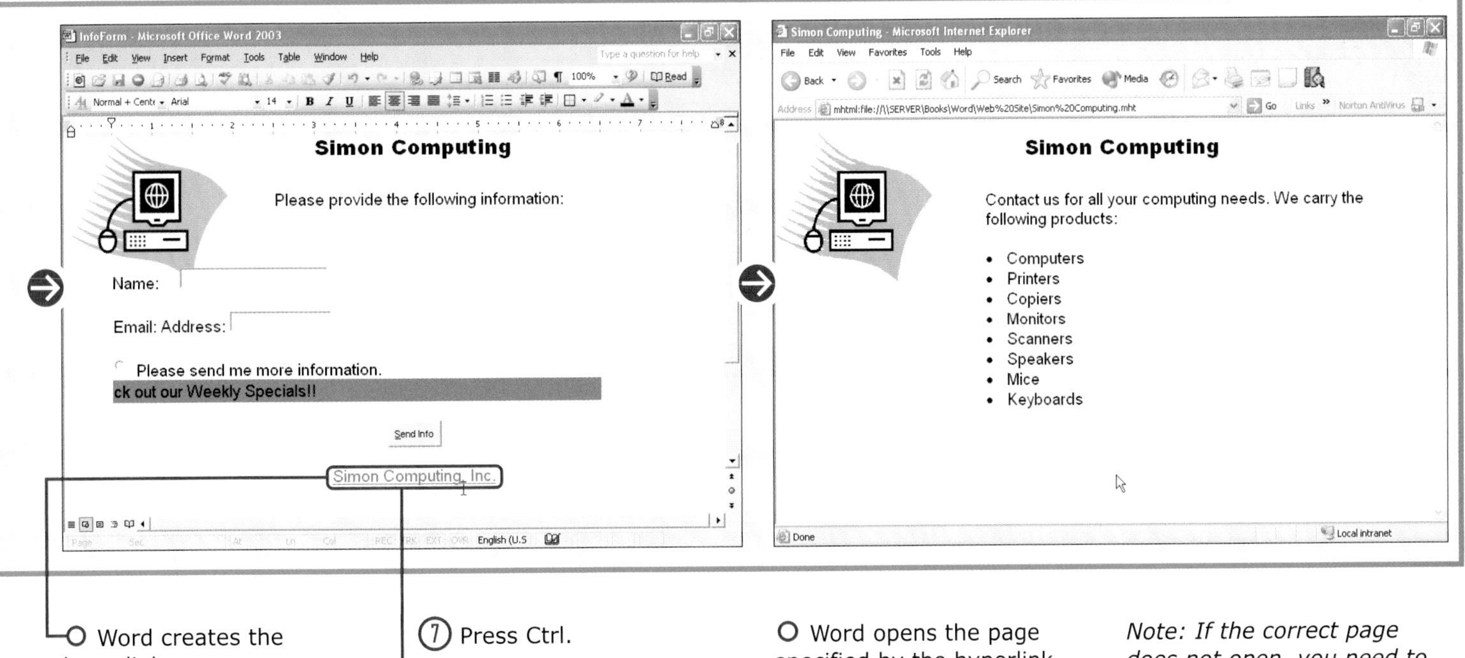

- Word creates the hyperlink.

7. Press Ctrl.
8. Click the hyperlink.

- Word opens the page specified by the hyperlink in your Web browser.

Note: If the correct page does not open, you need to verify the link specified in the Address field in the Insert Hyperlink dialog box.

SPECIFY ALTERNATIVE TEXT

for images on a Web page

You can specify alternative text for all graphics and movies that appear on your Web page. Some Web browsers do not display graphics and movies. Some users also may choose to turn off the display of graphics to improve the download time with a slow connection. By creating alternative text, you still have the opportunity to provide the user with information that may be lost if the user does not view the graphics or movie.

When a graphic is not displayed, the browser typically shows a box with a small icon indicating the location of the graphic that was not loaded. If you specify alternative text, that text appears in the box next to the icon.

You can specify as much text as you want. Keep in mind, though, that most browsers will probably truncate the text that does not fit within the box drawn for the missing graphic.

Another thing to keep in mind is that many search engines use the alternative text to identify Web pages.

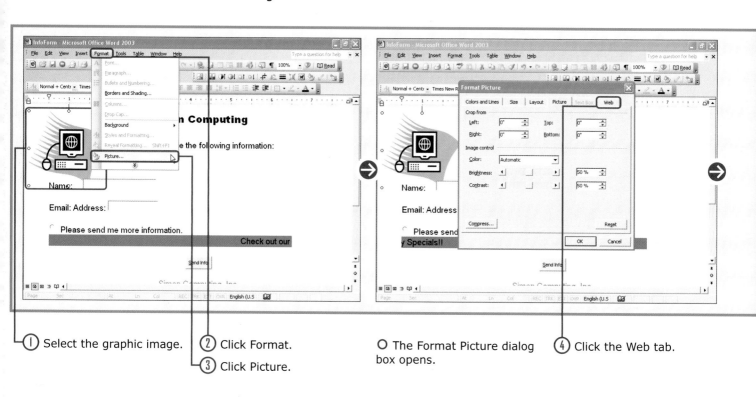

1. Select the graphic image.
2. Click Format.
3. Click Picture.

- The Format Picture dialog box opens.

4. Click the Web tab.

Did You Know?

You can eliminate the display of graphics in Internet Explorer by clicking Tools ➪ Internet Options. In the Internet Options dialog box, click the Advanced tab. Under the Multimedia section, remove the check mark from the Show Pictures option. Remove the check mark from Play Videos in Web Pages to not play any movies. Keep in mind that these changes affect all Web pages you view in the browser.

Did You Know?

If you have a movie on your Web page, you can specify an alternative text for the movie when you insert it in your document using the Movie button on the Web Tools toolbar. You can also specify an alternative graphic image. That way, if the browser does not support movies, the graphic image will be displayed.

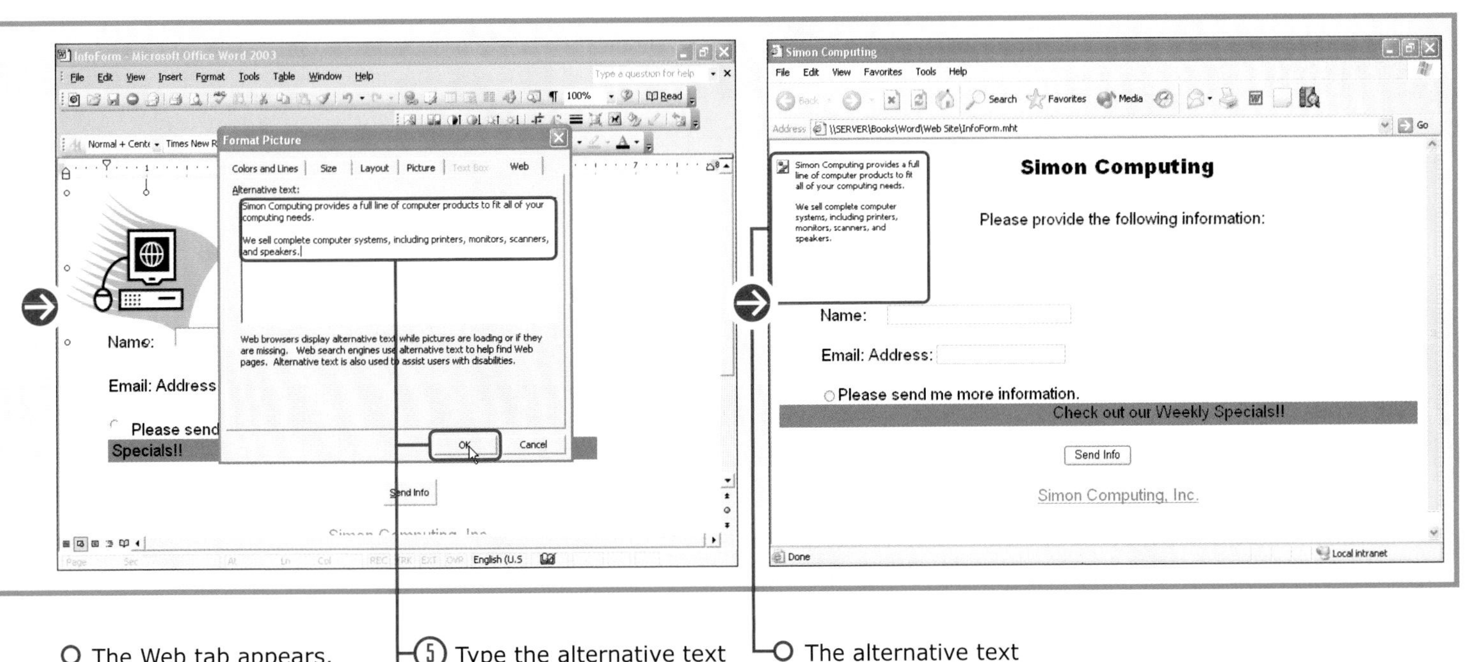

- The Web tab appears.

5 Type the alternative text for the graphic.

6 Click OK.

- The alternative text appears when the graphics are not loaded.

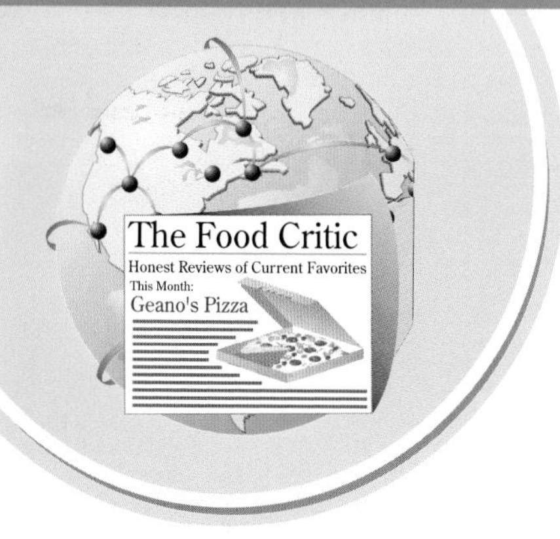
The Food Critic
Honest Reviews of Current Favorites
This Month:
Geano's Pizza

Design a FRAMES PAGE

You can use Word to create a Web page that contains frames. Frames enable you to display multiple pages of information on one Web page. Each separate frame can function independently, and you can scroll information in that frame only. Frames are often used to create a consistent layout for pages on a Web site. For example, you may choose to have a specific header on all pages that do not scroll. You can do this by placing the header text and images in a frame.

In the main frames page, you lay out the frames. You can insert a frame above, below, to the right, or to the left of the current cursor location using the buttons on the Frames toolbar. Before you start clicking the buttons, you need to determine your frame layout. For example, if you want a frame to go across the top of the page, you need to insert that frame first. Then move the cursor into the bottom frame and create the vertical frames.

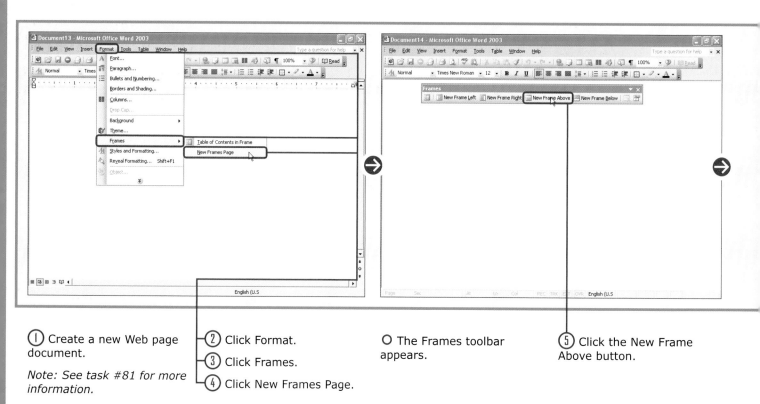

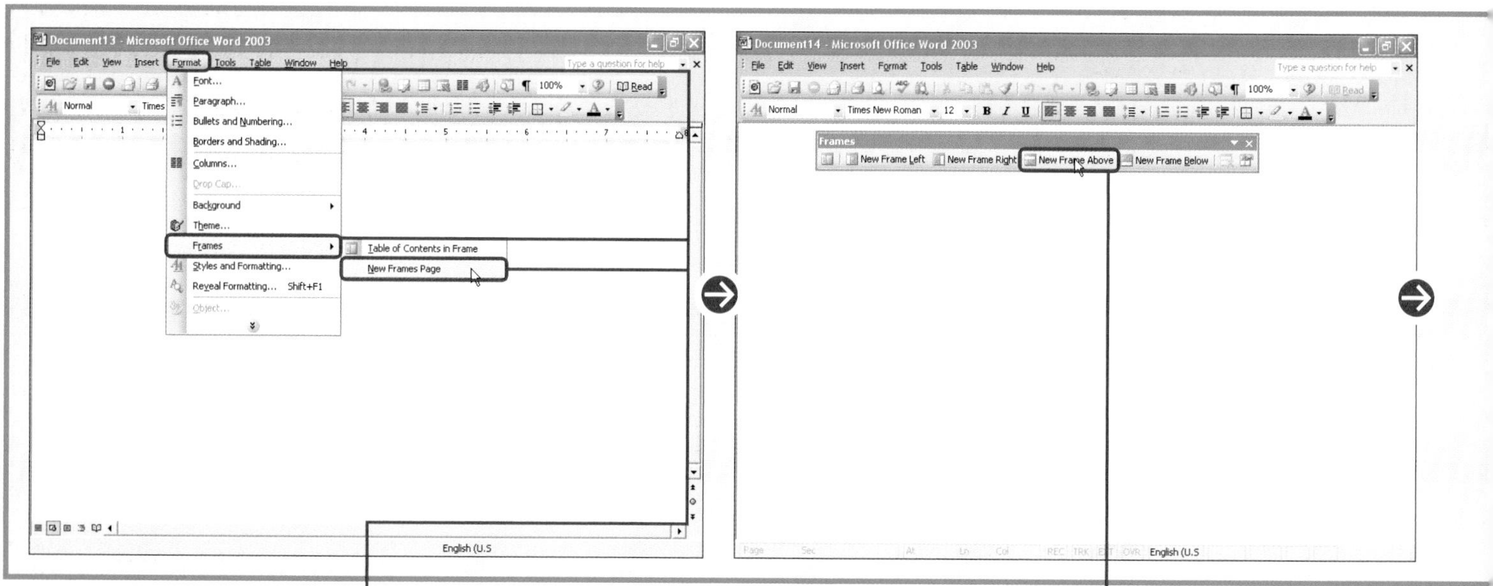

① Create a new Web page document.

Note: See task #81 for more information.

② Click Format.

③ Click Frames.

④ Click New Frames Page.

○ The Frames toolbar appears.

⑤ Click the New Frame Above button.

#87

DIFFICULTY LEVEL

Did You Know?

If you decide that you want to remove a frame from the page, you need to click inside the frame and then click the Delete Frame ( ) button. You cannot use the Undo command to remove a frame from a page.

Did You Know?

The frames on the page contain only a link to another Web page; they do not contain any actual content. You specify the links for each frame individually. See task #88 for more information on specifying frame links.

Apply It!

You can set the exact size for a frame in the Frame Properties dialog box. See task #88 for more information on setting the properties for each frame.

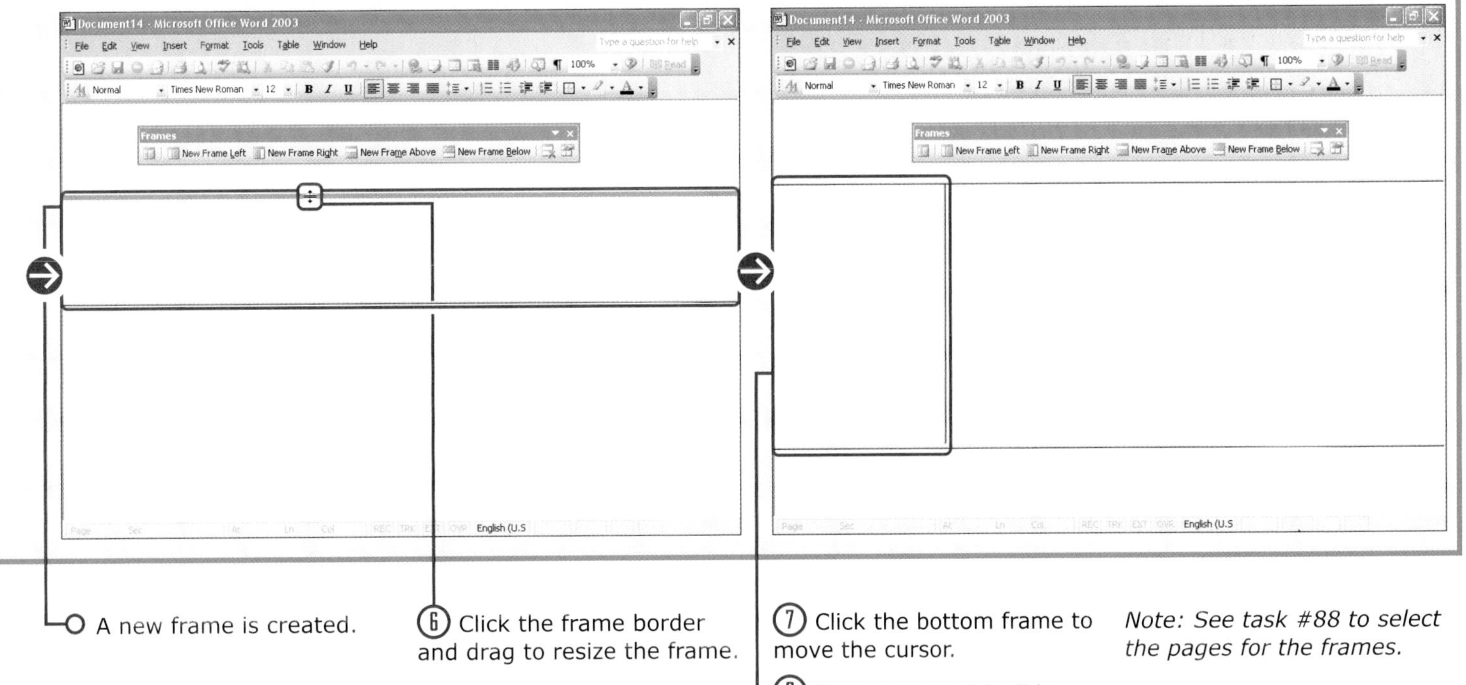

- A new frame is created.

6. Click the frame border and drag to resize the frame.

7. Click the bottom frame to move the cursor.

8. Repeat steps **5** to **7** to create each frame, clicking other frame buttons in step **5**.

Note: See task #88 to select the pages for the frames.

The Food Critic
Honest Reviews of Current Favorites
This Month:
Geano's Pizza

Set FRAME PROPERTIES

You set the properties of a frame to specify the initial page that should appear in that frame. You need to do this for each frame on your page so that the Web browser knows which pages to display when the frame page opens.

To assign initial Web pages to the frame, you must create the Web pages or have links to pages on other Web sites. A frame can open any valid Web page. If you specify a Web page from another Web site, you need to type the entire URL. For example, to open the Web site for Wiley Publishing, Inc., you would type the URL www.wiley.com.

Before specifying the frame links, you should make sure the frame page is saved in the appropriate folder. This allows Word to create links to pages on the server relative to the frame page.

Word automatically selects the Link to File option in the Frame Properties dialog box. This means that a dynamic link is created to the page. Any changes that occur in the original page will be displayed when you open the frames page.

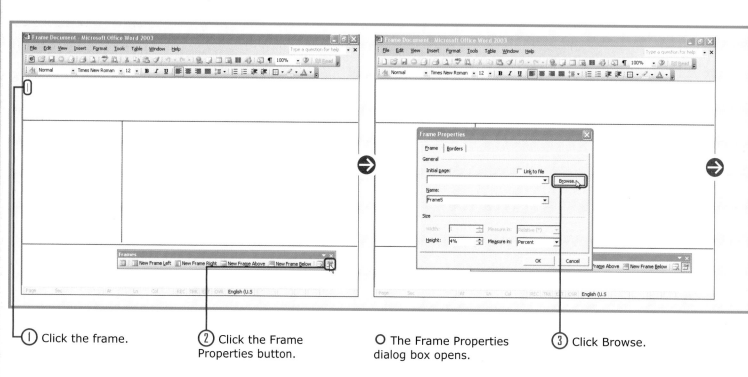

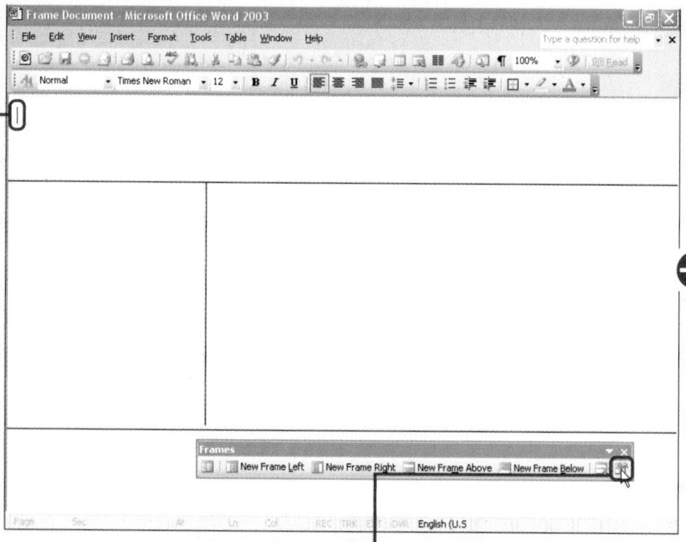

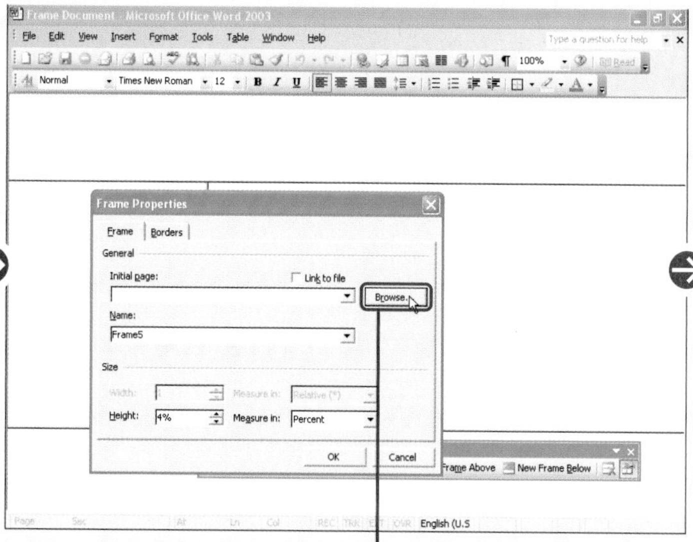

1. Click the frame.
2. Click the Frame Properties button.

- The Frame Properties dialog box opens.

3. Click Browse.

Did You Know?

You can remove the scroll bars from a frame that you do not want to scroll, such as a header frame. Click the frame and then click the Frame Properties button. In the Frame Properties dialog box, click the Borders tab. Make sure the Frame Is Resizable in Browser option is not selected. Click the Show Scrollbars in Browser down arrow and select Never.

Apply It!

You remove the borders from the frames on a page in the Frame Properties dialog box. On the Borders tab, click the No Borders option.

Apply It!

You customize the borders for all frames on a page on the Borders tab of the Frame Properties dialog box. You can change the border width and color.

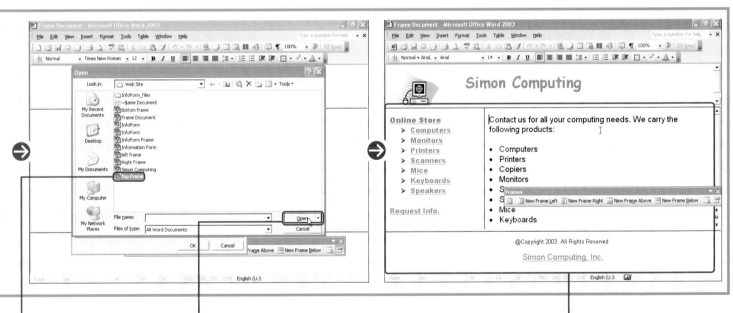

- The Open dialog box appears.

4. Click the page that you want for the frame.

- Alternatively, you can type an entire URL if the page is from another Web site.

5. Click Open.

- Word displays the specified page in the frame.

6. Repeat steps **1** to **5** for any other frames on the page.

The Food Critic
Honest Reviews of Current Favorites
This Month:
Geano's Pizza

Create a TABLE OF CONTENTS for a Web page

You can save a large document as a Web page so that it has links similar to a table of contents. This option works well when you want to convert a lengthy document so that others can access it over the Internet. When you provide links to the sections of the document, users can quickly move to the portion that they want.

When you create a table of contents for a Web page, you are actually creating a frame page that contains two frames. The left frame contains a list of links to the headings, and the right frame contains the actual document. To do this, you must have heading styles applied to the document using the same method used to create a standard table of contents. See task #56 for more information about creating a table of contents.

After you have the heading levels applied to your document, you can save the document as a Web page. When you save, Word actually creates two files, the new frame page document and a separate document for the table of contents.

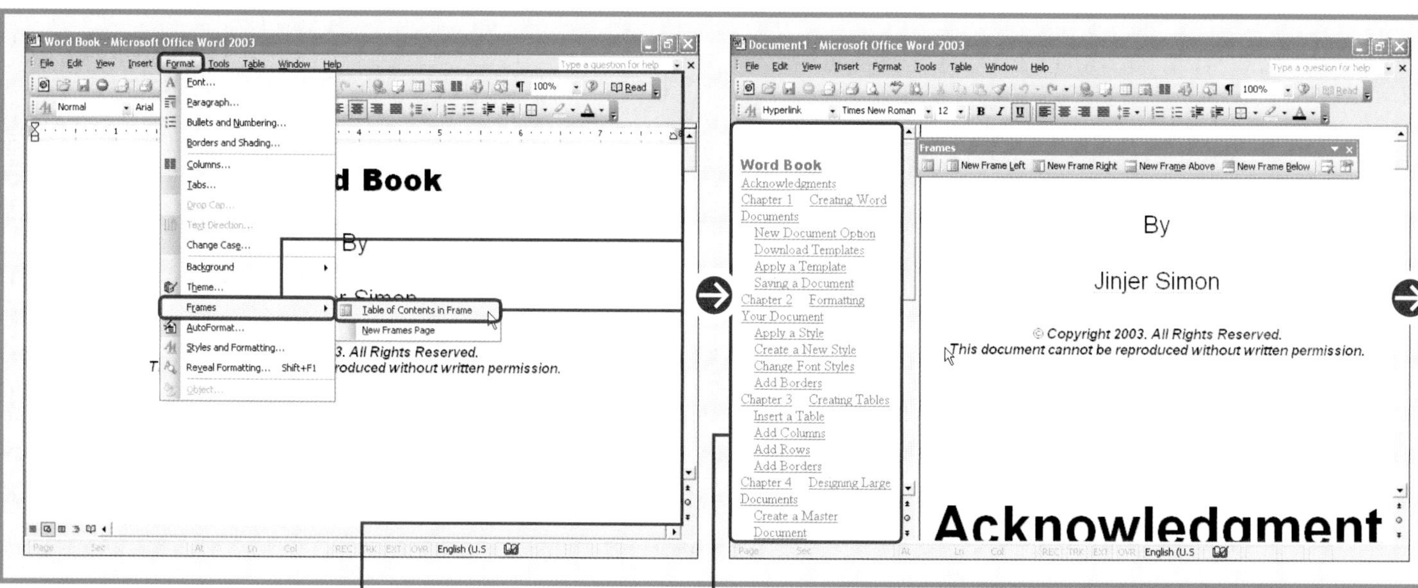

1. Save your document as a Web page.

Note: See task #81 for more information on saving files.

2. Click Format.
3. Click Frames.
4. Click Table of Contents in Frame.

- Word creates a frames page with a table of contents on the left side.

5. Make any desired edits to the table of contents.

Caution!

Make sure you save the frame page in the Web Page format. This creates a file with an .htm file extension. If you use the Single File Web Page format, Word assigns a file extension of .mht. Although browsers can display that file type, the table of contents links do not work properly.

Did You Know?

When you save the frames page, Word also creates a folder that contains files needed to generate the table of contents. If you move the frames page, you also need to move the corresponding folder. To avoid any errors from missing files, if you need to move the frames page to another location, open it again in Word and save it to the appropriate spot. Word places all the required files in the specified location.

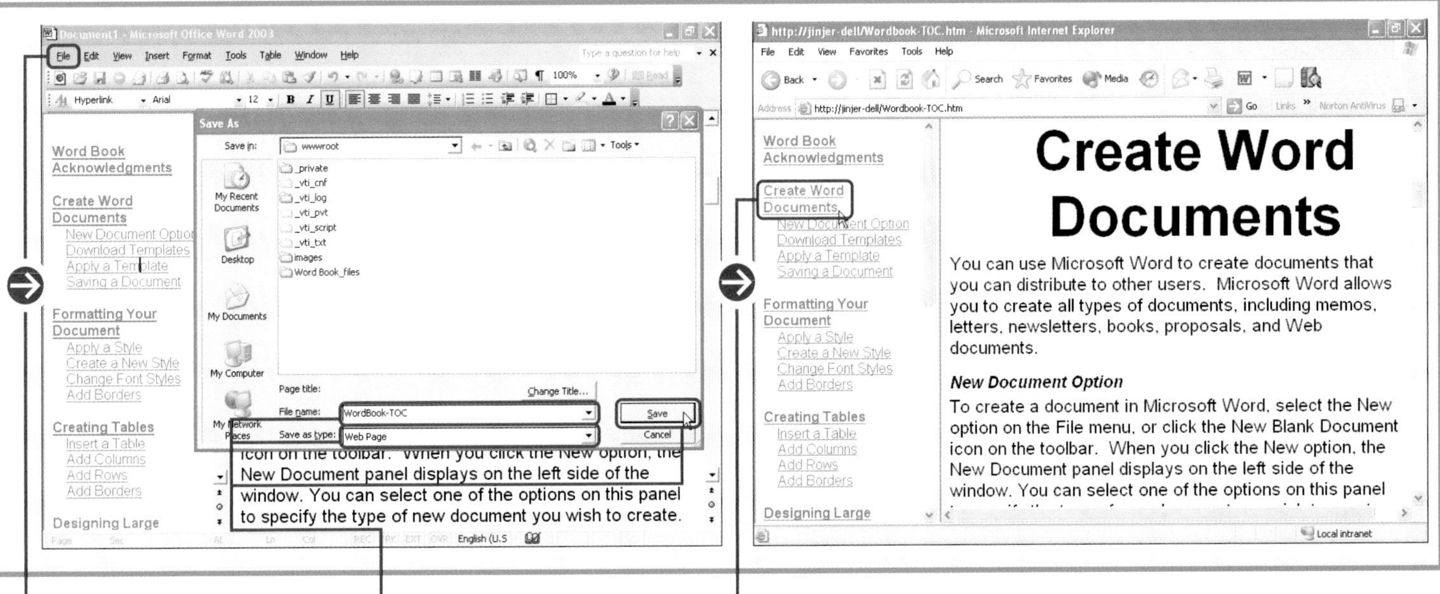

6. Click File.
7. Click Save As.

- The Save As dialog box opens.

8. Type the name for the frames page.
9. Click the down arrow and select Web Page.
10. Click Save.

- When you click a link on the Web page, it jumps to the corresponding location on the page.

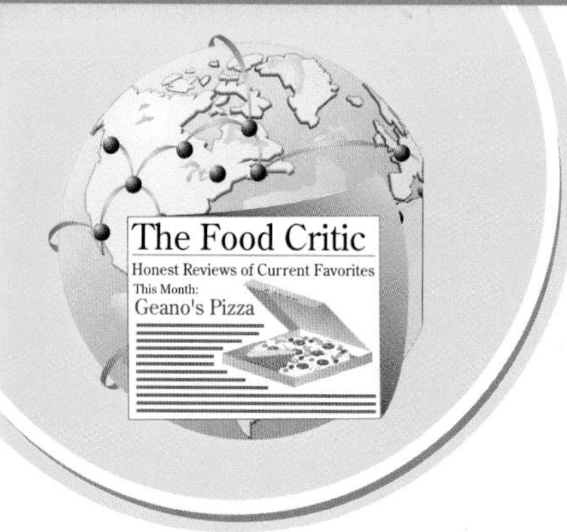
The Food Critic
Honest Reviews of Current Favorites
This Month:
Geano's Pizza

ELIMINATE EXCESS WORD TAGS

from an HTML file

You can streamline the amount of time required to load a Web page created in Word by eliminating any unneeded coding. When Word saves a Web page, it creates extra coding that is specific to Microsoft Word. This coding ensures that the page displays the same way each time you open it in Word. However, the excess coding makes the file size larger; therefore, it takes longer for someone to download the page over the Internet.

You can have Word eliminate the excess coding when you save it. When you do so, only the codes necessary to open the page in a Web browser remain in the file. If you look at the file size of the Web page before and after filtering the codes, you will see that the file is drastically smaller.

Unfortunately, the file will no longer have the same appearance when you open it again in Word. To make the process easier, you should wait to save the Web page in a filtered format until you have completed all editing. That way, you maintain all the features in Word.

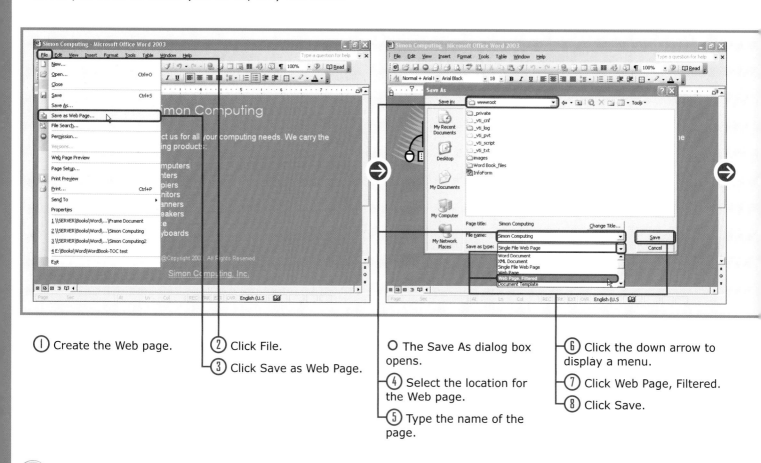

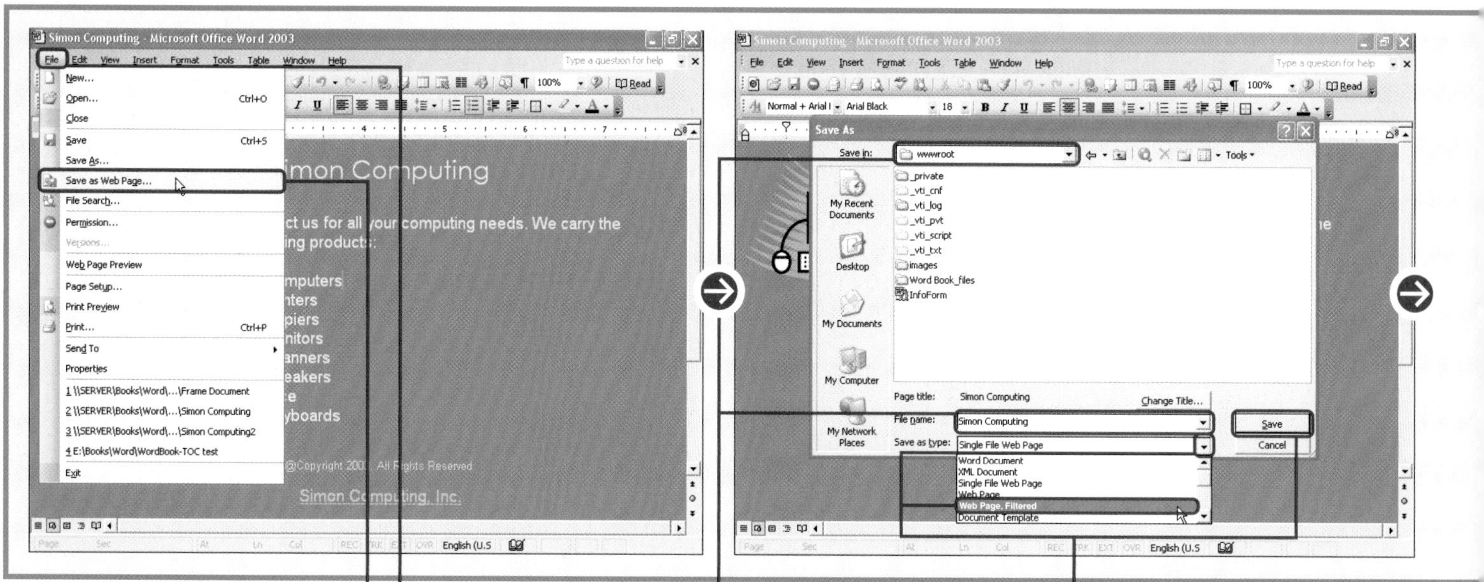

1. Create the Web page.
2. Click File.
3. Click Save as Web Page.

- The Save As dialog box opens.

4. Select the location for the Web page.
5. Type the name of the page.
6. Click the down arrow to display a menu.
7. Click Web Page, Filtered.
8. Click Save.

Apply It!

Before editing a Web page in a Web publishing package such as Microsoft FrontPage, you should save the file as a filtered Web page first. This eliminates the excess Word tags and makes the file easier to work with.

Apply It!

You should save the filtered file with a different name than your original Web page document so you can maintain the original file for future edits.

Did You Know?

When you save a filtered Web page, Word saves all graphics in the file in a separate folder. For example, if the filtered file is SComp.htm, the graphic images are saved in a folder called Scomp_files. If you move the filtered file, make sure to move the corresponding graphics folder.

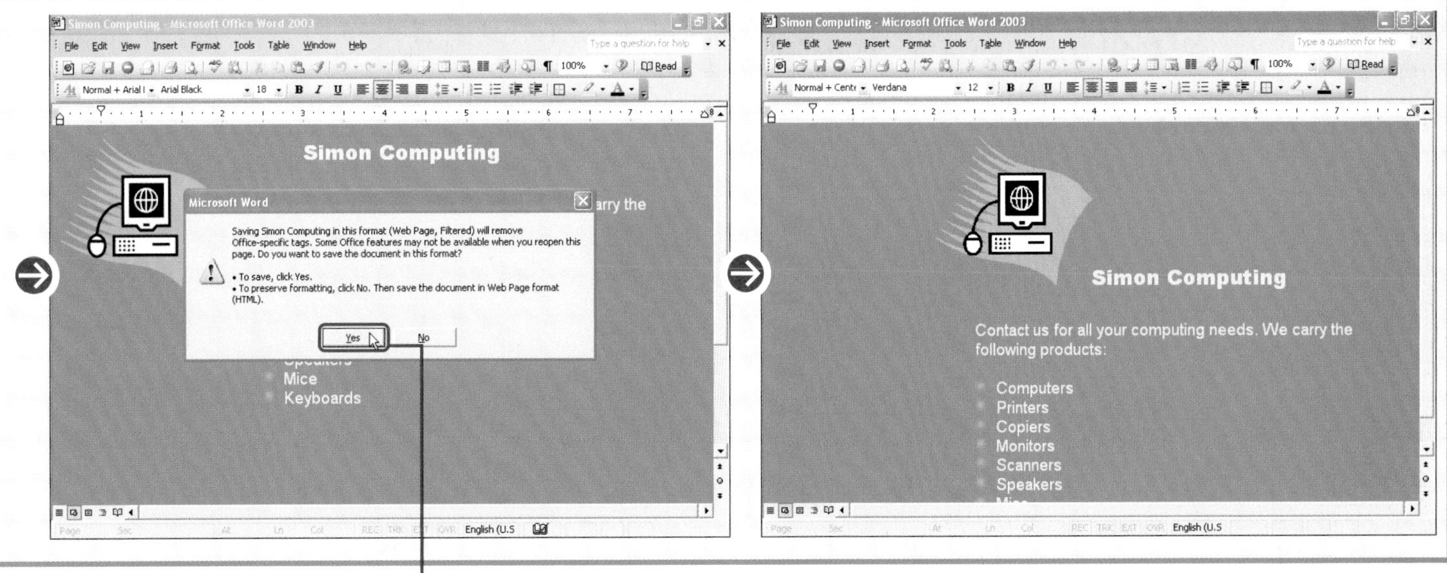

○ Word displays a dialog box to make sure that you want to save the file in the specified format.

9 Click Yes.

○ Word creates the filtered file.

Note: If you open the Web page file again in Word, it will appear different because it no longer contains the Word codes.

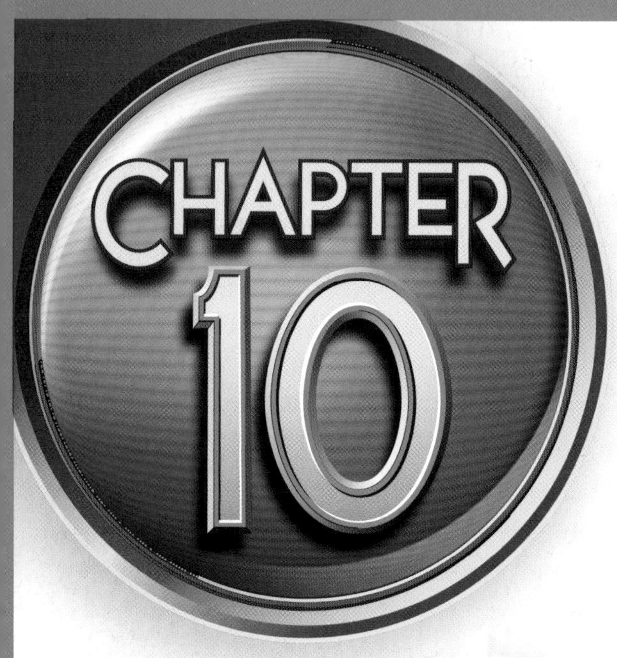

Using Mail Merge

Word provides mail merge features that you can use to create documents that you want to send to multiple recipients. For example, you may want to create a letter that you send out to multiple people. Although the text of the letter may be the same, you need to address each letter to match the recipient. You can use mail merge to easily accomplish this feature.

With the mail merge features, you create your document and use a specific data list to add the recipient information. The recipient information is merged into the documenst, creating multiple documents that you can print or e-mail as needed.

The mail merge feature is designed to help you create letters, e-mail messages, envelopes, labels, and directories. You can create the documents using the Mail Merge Wizard or create them manually. With either process, you have to create your data list or specify a data source containing the data list that you want to use.

After you load your data list, you can merge the entire list or just select individual recipients. You can also merge recipient information from your Microsoft Outlook contact list.

Although the merge process typically happens quite quickly, you can have Word request specific information for each record during the process. For example, you may want to change the text of a letter based on the recipient. You can accomplish this by using the fields available for mail merge.

TOP 100

Create a DATA LIST

You can create a data list in Word that you can use with multiple documents. This enables you to create a list of recipients without the need of another database program, such as Microsoft Access. In other words, if you have a list of people to whom you routinely send documents, you can create the list once and reuse it for each document.

Although Word enables you to use other data sources, such as SQL databases, Excel worksheets, and Access databases, you can create your own source list using the options available on the Mail Merge task pane. To create your own list, you select the Type a New List option under Select Recipients. When you use this option, you are actually creating an Access database that you can modify directly within Microsoft Access.

You can create a data source from any of the document types. Because all mail merge documents deal with name and address information, you can create one data source and reuse it for other types of documents.

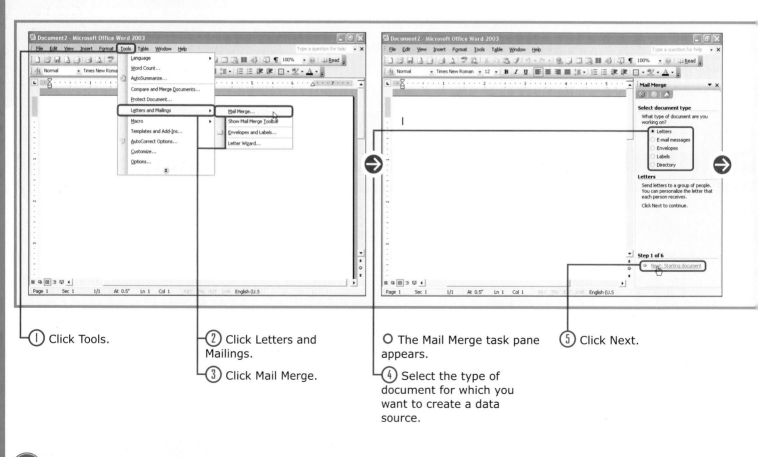

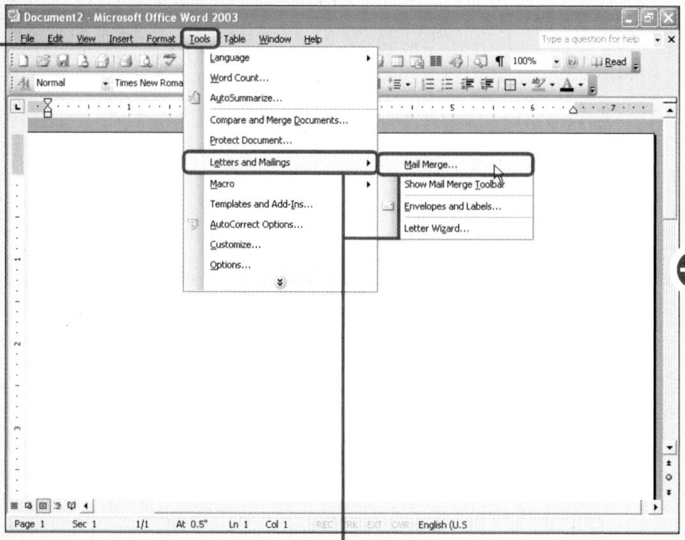

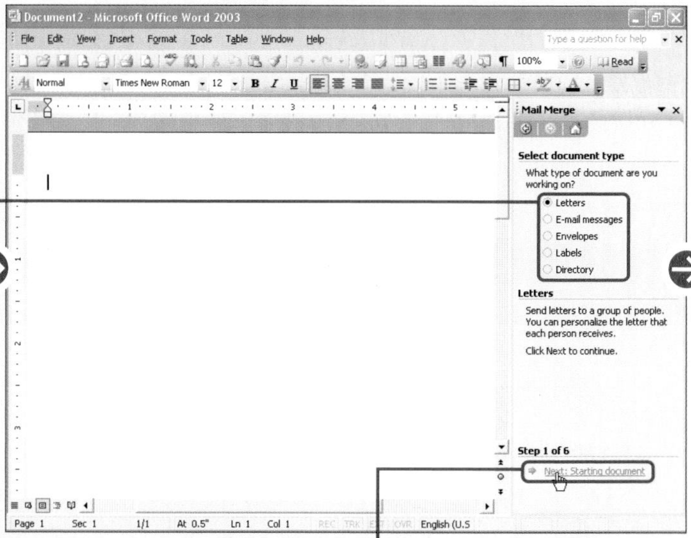

1. Click Tools.
2. Click Letters and Mailings.
3. Click Mail Merge.

- The Mail Merge task pane appears.

4. Select the type of document for which you want to create a data source.
5. Click Next.

DIFFICULTY LEVEL

Did You Know?

When creating a new mail merge document, you have three options: using the current document, using a template, or copying another existing Word document. If you decide to use a template, Word opens the Select Template dialog box with some default templates listed on the Mail Merge tab. Microsoft provides additional templates that you can download from its Web site by clicking the Templates on Office Online button.

Put It Together!

You can use the contacts that you have set up in Microsoft Outlook as your recipient list during the mail merge. See task #97 for more information on working with Outlook contacts.

CONTINUED

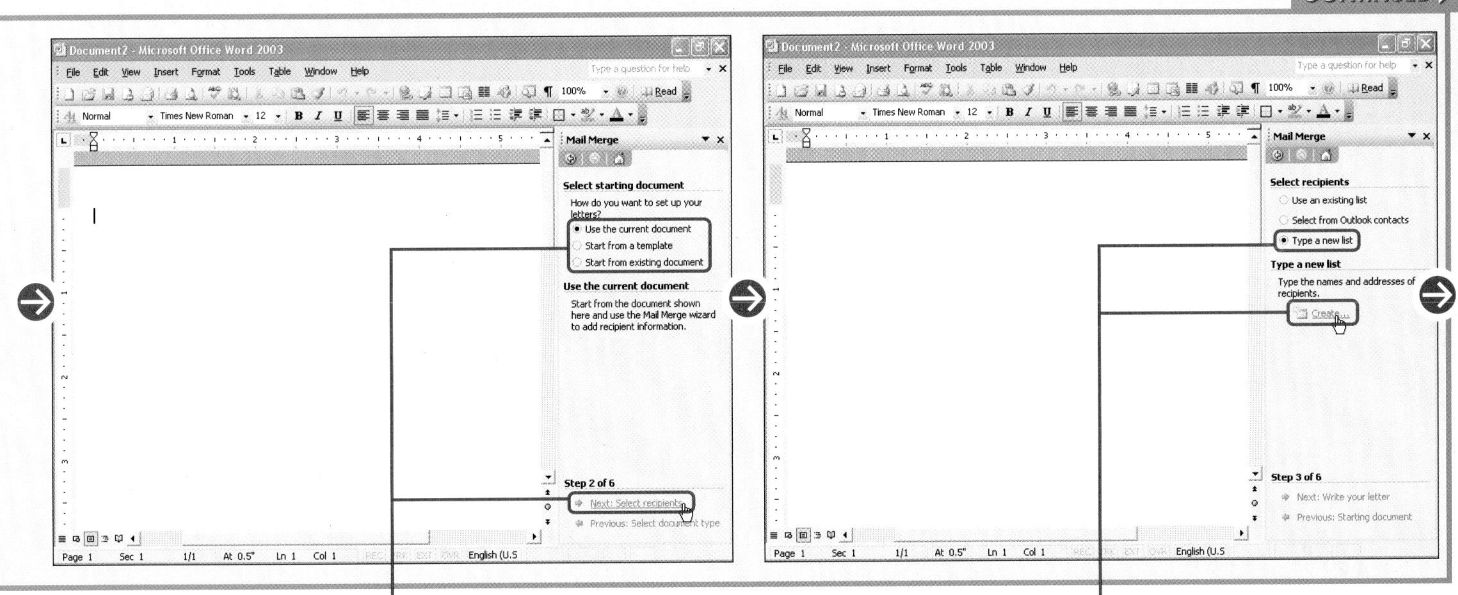

- The next step of the Mail Merge Wizard appears on the task pane.

6. Select the starting document for your mail merge document.
7. Click Next.

- The next step of the Mail Merge Wizard appears on the task pane.

8. Click Type a new list.
9. Click Create.

Create a DATA LIST

You use the New Address List dialog box to create each entry for your data list. You can type values for any of the data fields listed in the dialog box. For example, you may only want to specify first and last names for your list entries.

Although you can save the list that you create in any location, Word saves it by default in the My Data Sources folder. Word uses this folder because it is the default folder that is checked each time that you want to load a new list. If you select another location, you need to remember the location so that you can find the list for a future mail merge.

After you have specified your list entries, Word displays the data list in the Mail Merge Recipients dialog box. If your list looks correct, you close the dialog box to assign the list to the current mail merge document. You can also select specific recipients from the list. For more information on selecting recipients, see task #94.

CONTINUED

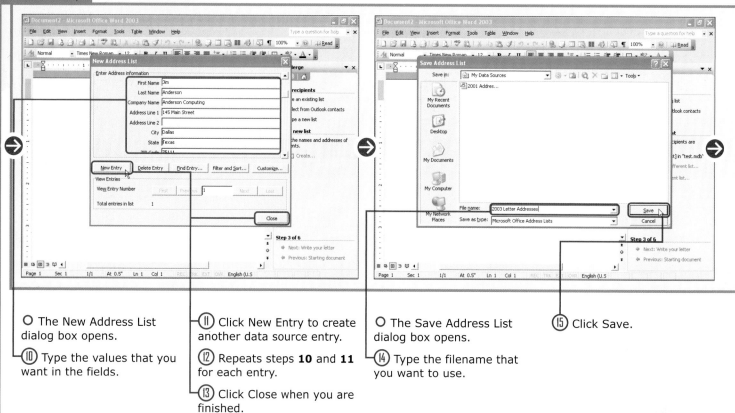

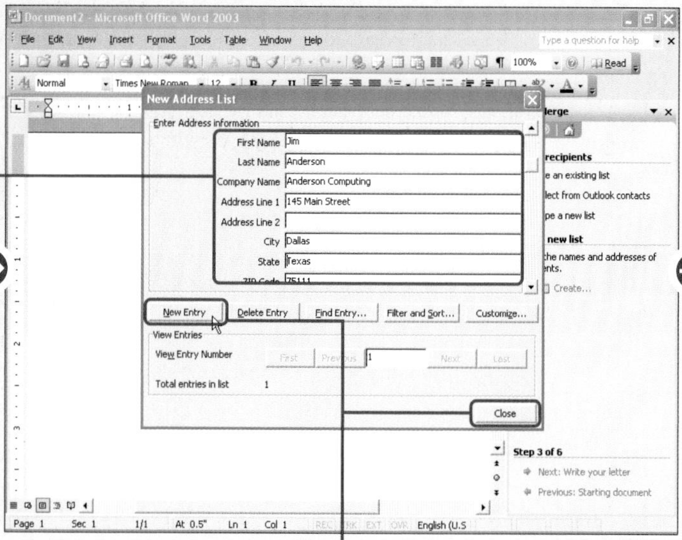

- The New Address List dialog box opens.

10) Type the values that you want in the fields.

11) Click New Entry to create another data source entry.

12) Repeats steps **10** and **11** for each entry.

13) Click Close when you are finished.

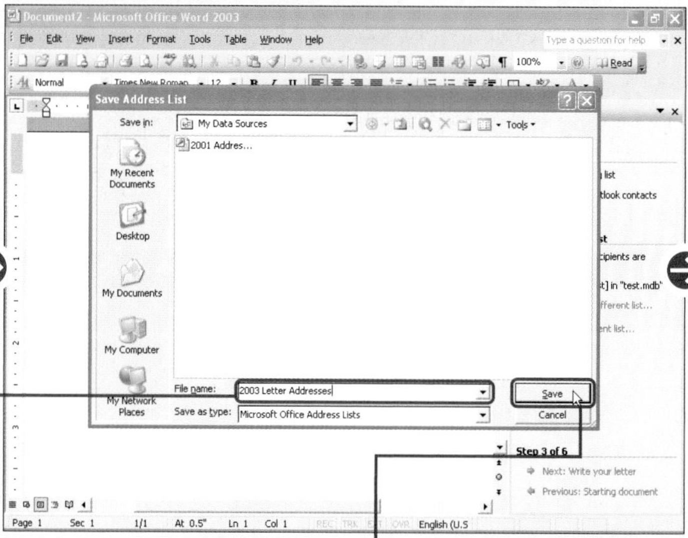

- The Save Address List dialog box opens.

14) Type the filename that you want to use.

15) Click Save.

Did You Know?

You can remove fields that you do not need from the New Address List dialog box by clicking the Customize button. In the Customize Address List dialog box, highlight the fields that you do not want to use and click Delete.

Did You Know?

If you need additional or different fields in the New Address List dialog box, you can add them by clicking the Customize button. In the Customize Address List dialog box, click Add to display the Add Field dialog box. Type the field name that you want.

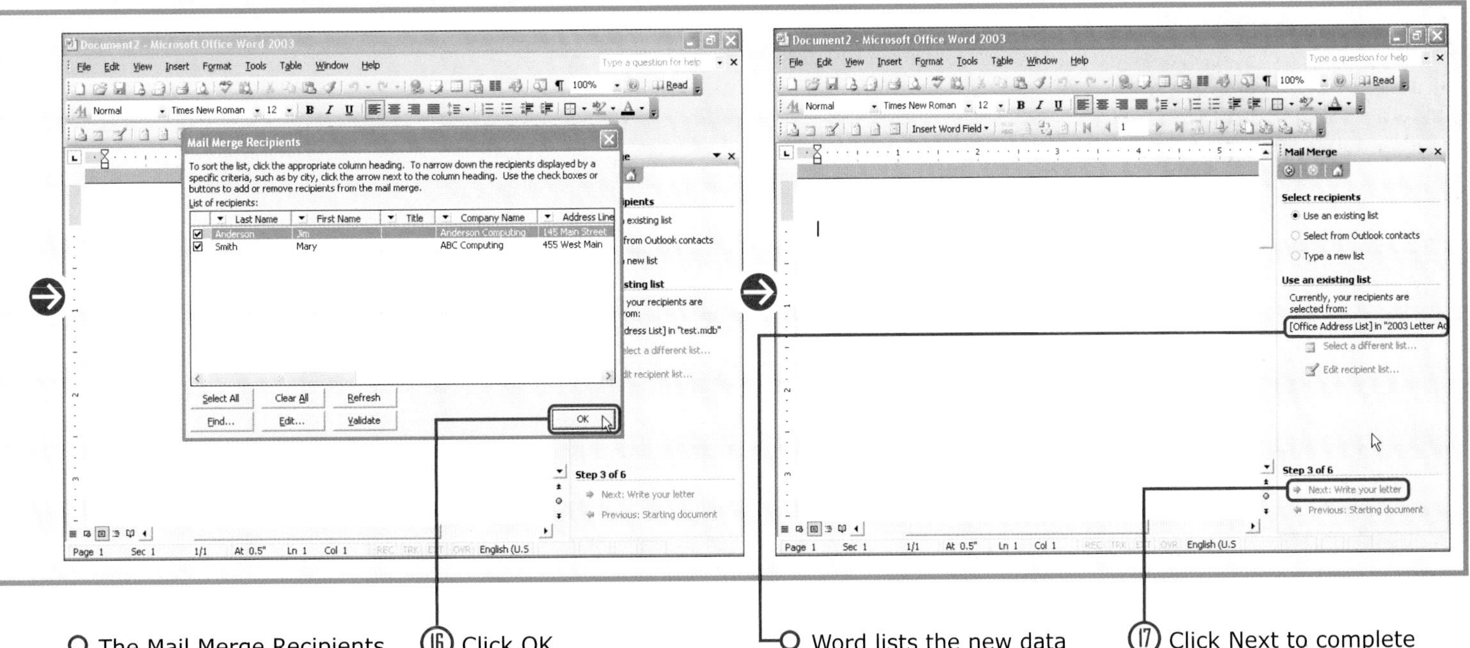

- The Mail Merge Recipients dialog box opens with all the recipients listed.

16. Click OK.

Note: See task #94 for more information on selecting recipients from a data source.

- Word lists the new data source as the selected data source for your mail merge document.

17. Click Next to complete the mail merge process by creating the document and selecting the recipients.

Use Word to ADDRESS AN ENVELOPE

You can create envelopes in Word so that you can print address information. You can create a single envelope or use the mail merge options to print envelopes for multiple recipients.

When you create an envelope in Word, you need to specify the size of the envelope on which you want to print. Word provides several default envelope sizes, or you specify a custom envelope size. For example, if you are using standard 4⅛-inch by 9½-inch envelopes, you would select size 10.

You need to verify the best envelope printing process for your printer. For example, you need to indicate whether to feed the envelope into the printer face up or face down.

When you place an address block on the envelope using the attached address list, you can specify how the address is laid out. For example, you specify the appearance of the recipient's name or whether to display the company name.

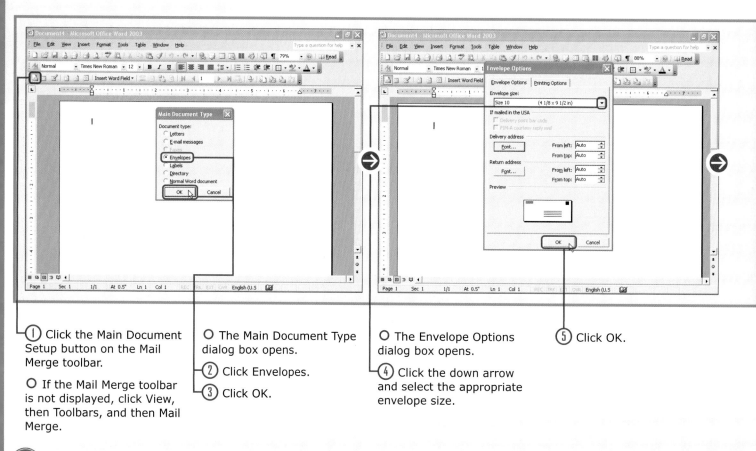

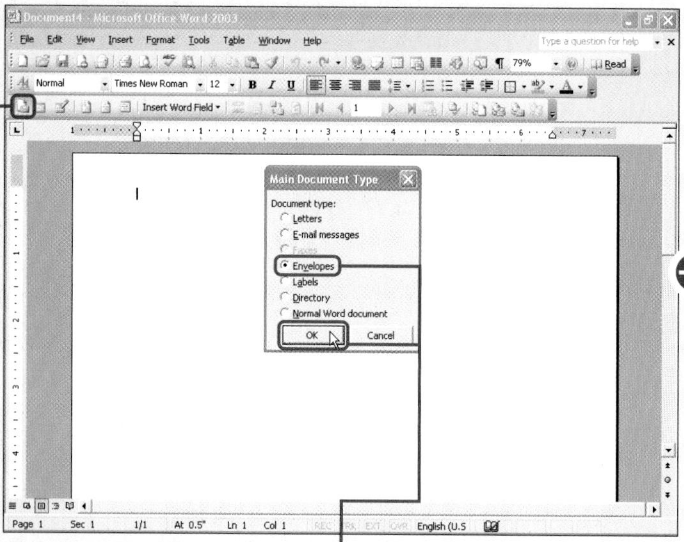

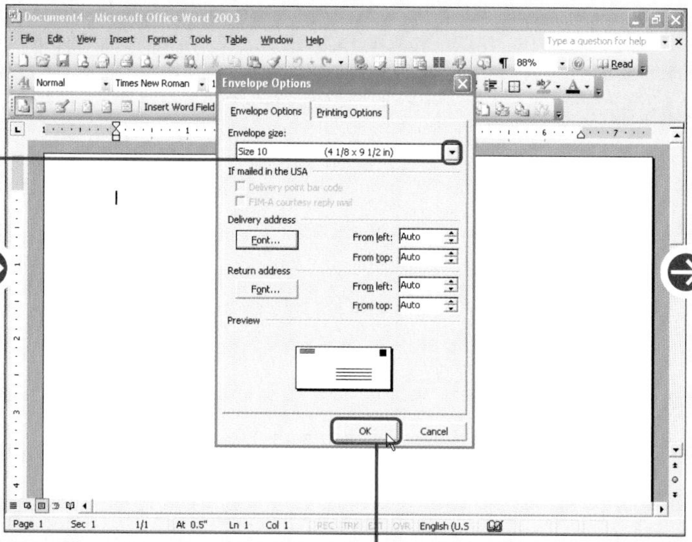

1 Click the Main Document Setup button on the Mail Merge toolbar.

- If the Mail Merge toolbar is not displayed, click View, then Toolbars, and then Mail Merge.

- The Main Document Type dialog box opens.

2 Click Envelopes.

3 Click OK.

- The Envelope Options dialog box opens.

4 Click the down arrow and select the appropriate envelope size.

5 Click OK.

Did You Know?

If you cannot find the appropriate size for the envelope in the Envelope Size drop-down list in the Envelope Options dialog box, you can create a custom envelope size. To do so, click the Custom Size option on the Envelope Size drop-down list to display the Envelope Size dialog box. Type the appropriate width and height for the custom envelope.

Customize It!

You can change the placement of the delivery and return addresses on the envelopes by using the From Left and From Top fields in the Envelope Options dialog box.

Did You Know?

You can see what the envelopes will look like with the appropriate addresses by clicking the View Merged Data button on the Mail Merge toolbar.

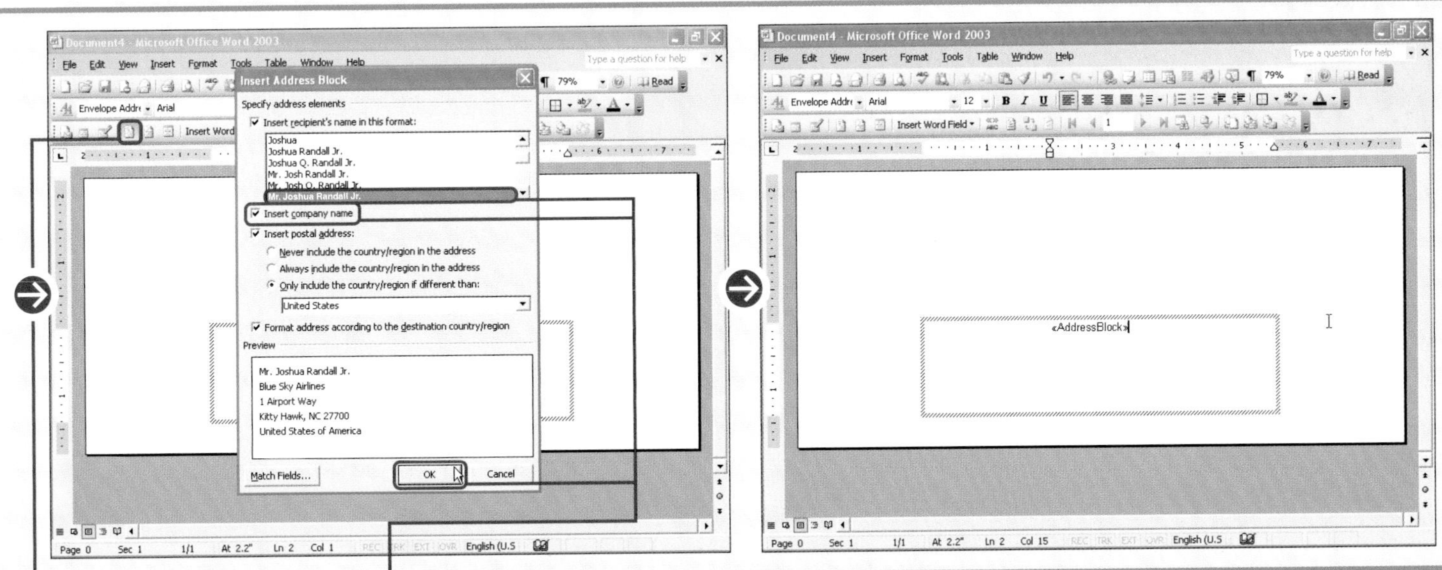

- Word creates the envelope layout.
- ⑥ Click the Insert Address Block button.
- The Insert Address Block dialog box opens.
- ⑦ Click the name format that you want for the envelope.
- If you do not want to print the company name, deselect Insert Company Name (☑ changes to ☐).
- ⑧ Click OK.
- Word displays the AddressBlock field.

LOAD AN ADDRESS LIST from a data source

DIFFICULTY LEVEL

When working with a mail merge document, you need to select the data source that contains the address list you want to use in your document. For example, you may have a list of addresses you created for another mail merge document. You need to make sure that a data source is selected before you print your merged document.

After you attach a data source to a document, the data source remains attached until you specify a new data source.

Did You Know?

You can use other data sources, such as SQL Server databases. If you need to connect to a new database, click the New Source button on the Select Data Source dialog box and select the type of data source that matches your database. Follow the steps of the Data Connection Wizard to set up the appropriate data source.

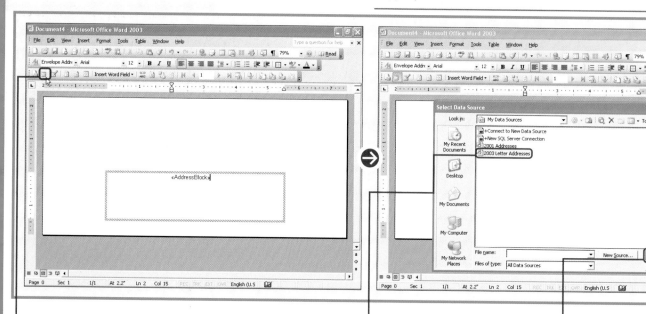

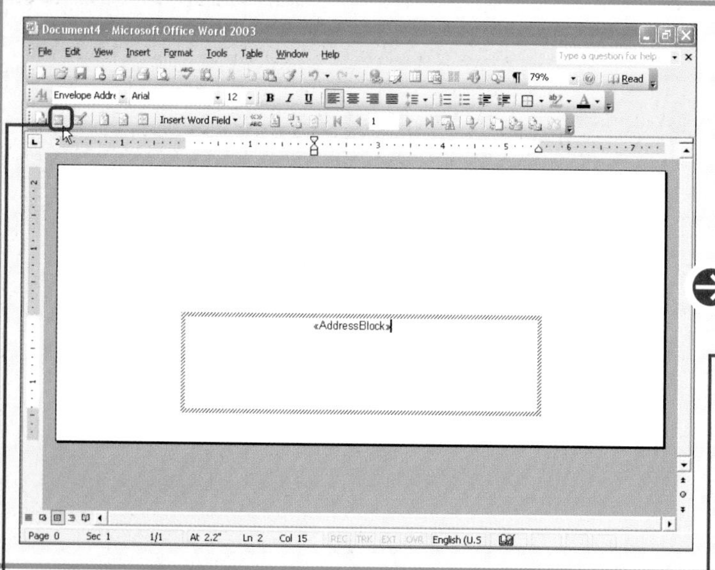

1. Click the Open Data Source button on the Mail Merge toolbar.

- If the Mail Merge toolbar is not displayed, click View ➪ Toolbars ➪ Mail Merge.

- The Select Data Source dialog box opens.

2. Click the data source that you want.

3. Click Open.

- Word uses the selected data source with the mail merge document.

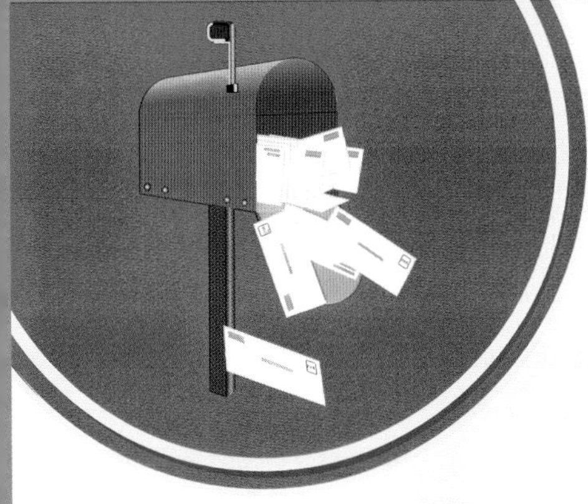

SELECT RECIPIENTS from a list of names

DIFFICULTY LEVEL

You can select the specific individuals that you want to receive a copy of your mail merge document from any data list. For example, you may want to use a list of names you created containing all company names but only want to send the letters to the individuals in the programming department.

To identify the recipients that you want, you use the check box next to each recipient in the list. When you deselect a recipient, the recipient remains in the list but is not included in the current document mail merge process.

Did You Know?

You can use the Mail Merge Recipients dialog box to add names to your list. To do so, click to select a blank row and click the Edit button. In the dialog box, specify a value for each field and click Close. Word adds the new item to the list.

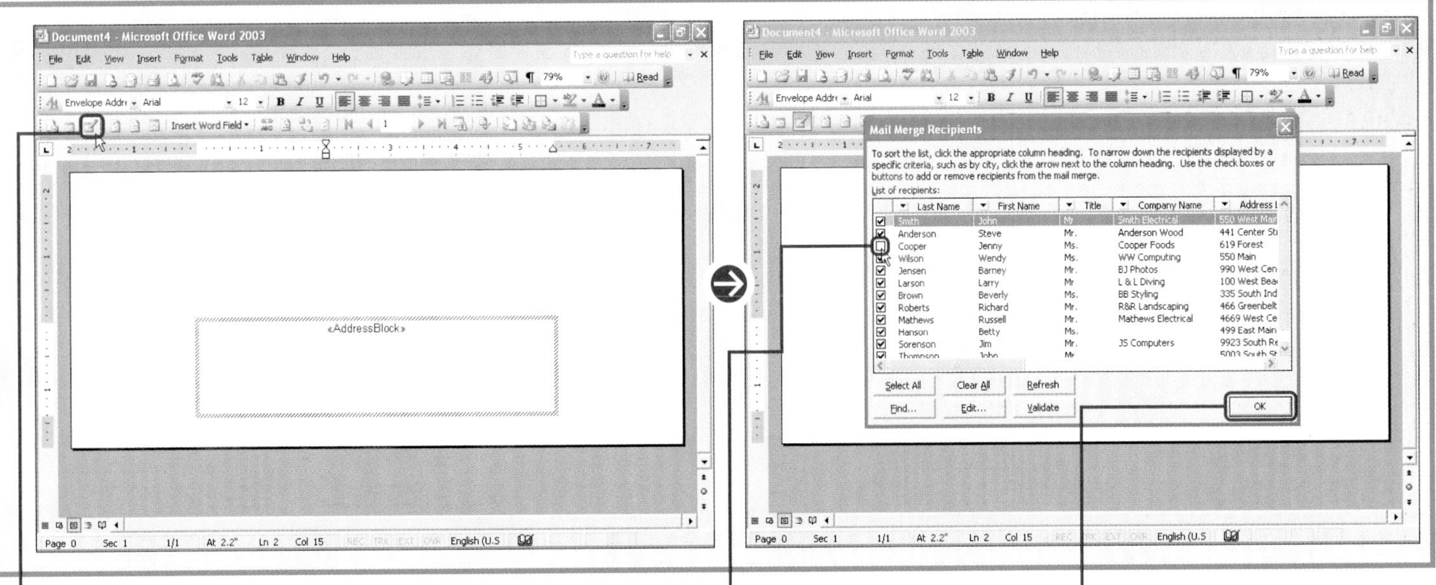

① Click the Mail Merge Recipients button on the Mail Merge toolbar.

○ If the Mail Merge toolbar is not displayed, click View ➪ Toolbars ➪ Mail Merge.

○ The Mail Merge Recipients dialog box opens.

② Click to remove the check mark next to the recipient that you do not want to receive your document (☑ changes to ☐).

③ Repeat step **2** for all the recipients that you want to exclude.

④ Click OK.

REQUEST INFORMATION during the merge

You can request information during the mail merge process by using one of the request fields in your document. For example, you may need to place different text on a document for each individual. You can have Word request the information as the names are merged creating each document.

The Fill-in field works well for requesting information during a mail merge. With this field, you can specify a default value for the field. The easiest method for inserting the Fill-in field in your document is to use the Insert Word Field drop-down button on the Mail Merge toolbar. You can also add the Fill-in field using the Field dialog box. See Chapter 5 for more information on working with fields in Word documents.

You can also customize the prompt that appears for the Fill-in field to identify each recipient. To do so, you need to reveal fields and then add the appropriate recipient fields to the Fill-in field code. Each prompt for the Fill-in field then contains the specified value from the recipient.

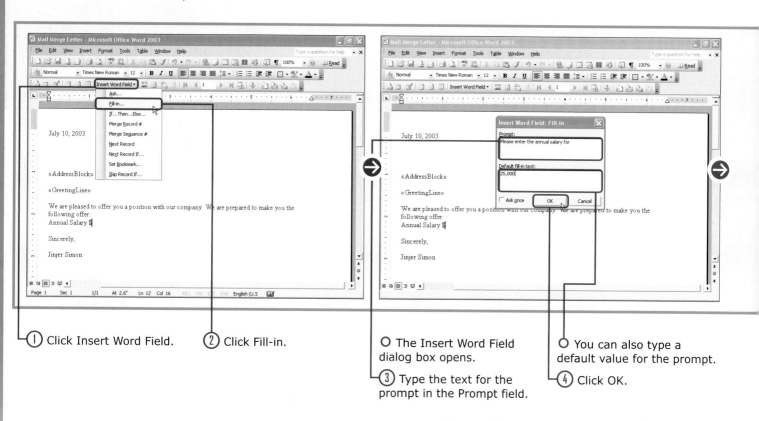

1. Click Insert Word Field.
2. Click Fill-in.

- The Insert Word Field dialog box opens.

3. Type the text for the prompt in the Prompt field.

- You can also type a default value for the prompt.

4. Click OK.

Did You Know?

You can also use the Ask field to request information during the merge process. The Ask field creates a bookmark in the document that is updated with the specified response.

Did You Know?

If you click Ask Once in the Insert Word Field dialog box, the prompt displays only at the beginning of the mail merge process. If you have a value in a document that you want to update once for the entire merge, select this check box.

Did You Know?

You can use Shift+F9 to toggle between displaying the field codes and the default text for the selected fields within your document.

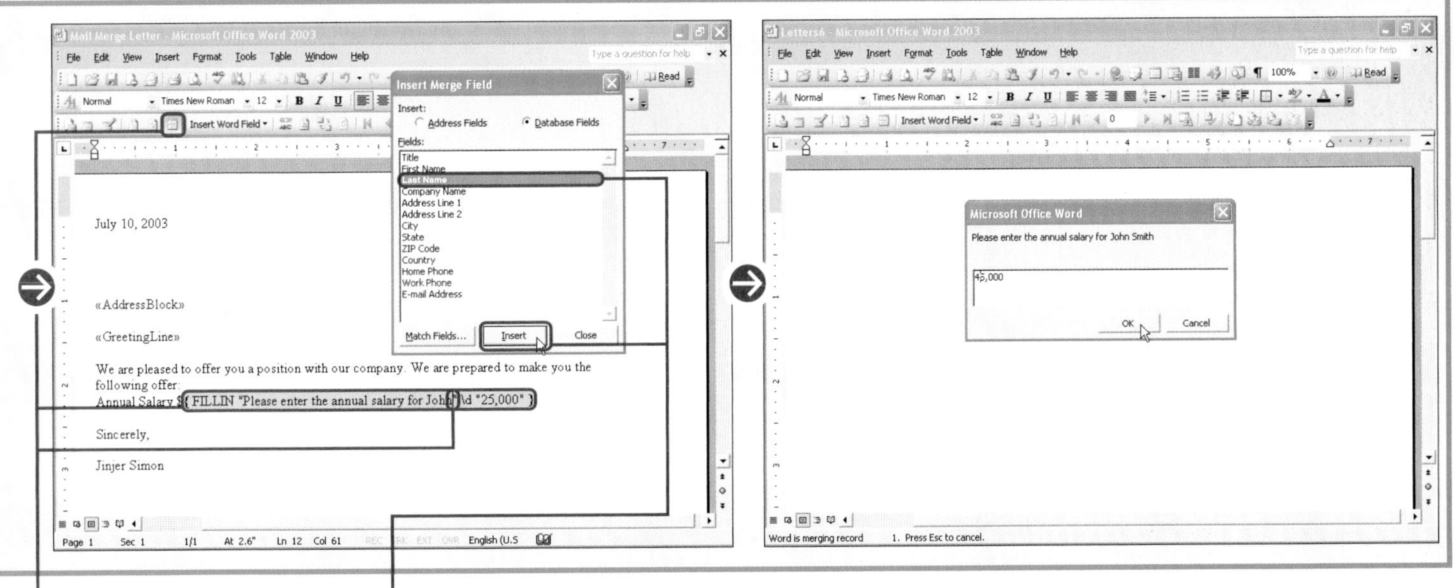

5. Select the field and press Ctrl+F9 to reveal the field codes.
6. Click at the location that you want in the field.
7. Click the Insert Merge Field button.

- The Insert Merge Field dialog box opens.

8. Select the field that you want.
9. Click Insert.

- When you merge the document, the prompt displays for each recipient.

CONDITIONALLY MERGE

information from a file

You can conditionally merge information from a file based on specific information about the recipient. For example, you may want to change the greeting line on your letter depending on whether the recipient is male or female.

You create a conditional merge statement using the If . . . Then . . . Else field. When you select this field in your mail merge document, you are able to perform an action based on the value of a field for a recipient. For example, you can create a conditional statement that looks at the Title field to determine whether the recipient is male or female based on whether it contains the value Mr. or Ms.

When you use the If . . . Then . . . Else field, you can select the type of comparison that you want to perform. For example, if you want to have specific text appear every time the value matches specific text, you select the Equal To comparison. Keep in mind that when you use Equal To and Not Equal To, Word looks for an exact string match.

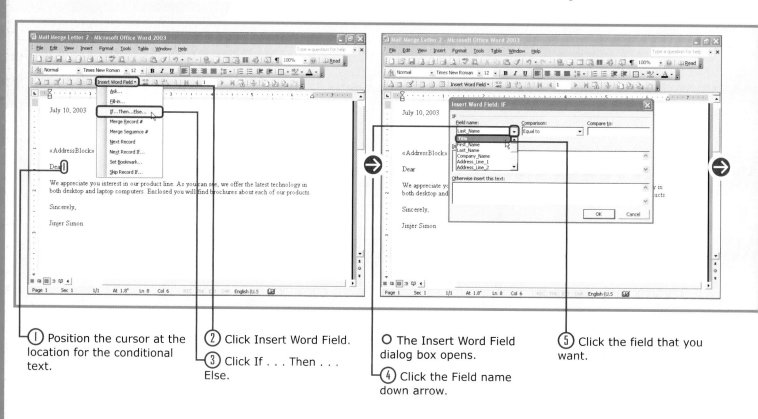

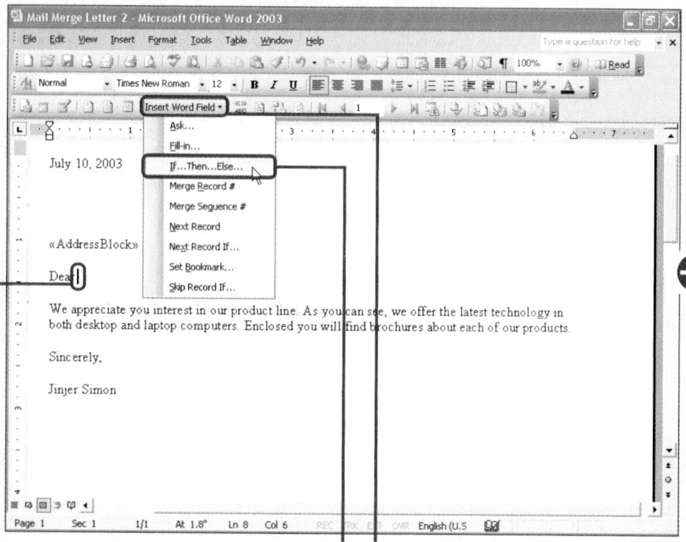

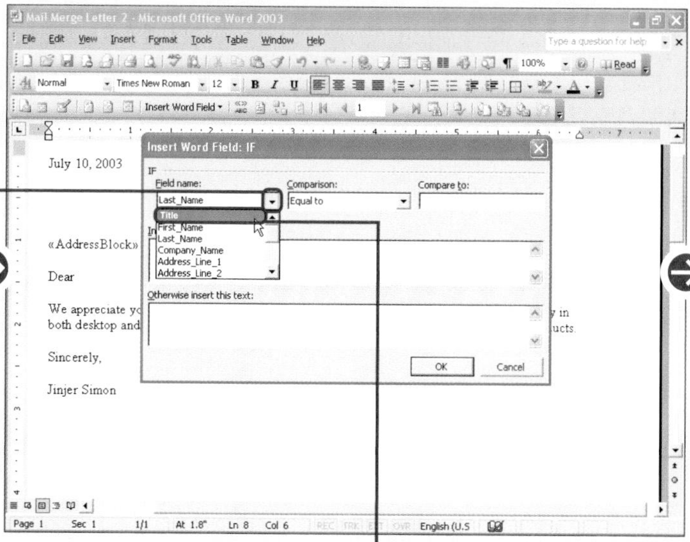

1 Position the cursor at the location for the conditional text.

2 Click Insert Word Field.

3 Click If . . . Then . . . Else.

- The Insert Word Field dialog box opens.

4 Click the Field name down arrow.

5 Click the field that you want.

Did You Know?

The If . . . Then . . . Else field provides eight different comparisons that you can apply, as outlined in the following table.

Operator	When the Condition Is True
Equal To	The field exactly matches the value.
Not Equal To	The field does not match the value.
Less Than	The field is less than the value.
Greater Than	The field is greater than the value.
Less Than or Equal	The field is less than or equal to the value.
Greater Than or Equal	The field is greater than or equal to the value.
Is Blank	The field is blank.
Is Not Blank	The field contains any value.

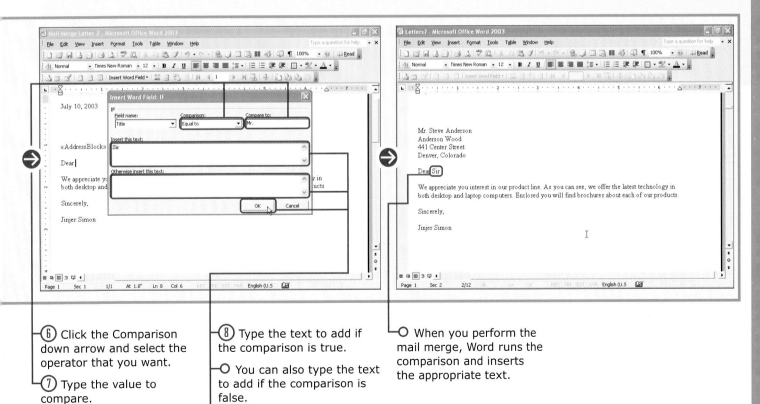

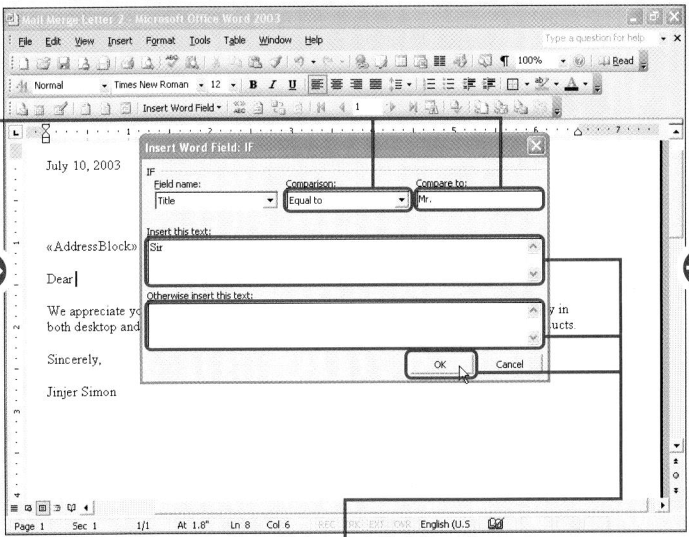

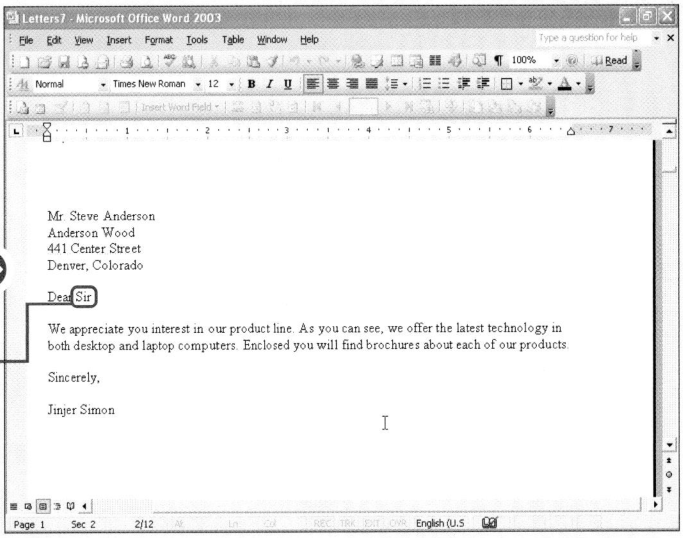

6. Click the Comparison down arrow and select the operator that you want.
7. Type the value to compare.
8. Type the text to add if the comparison is true.
   - You can also type the text to add if the comparison is false.
9. Click OK.

- When you perform the mail merge, Word runs the comparison and inserts the appropriate text.

Use an OUTLOOK ADDRESS on an envelope

You can use the address information available in your Microsoft Outlook contact list to address an envelope in Word. For example, you may want to mail a letter to one of your customers whose address information is in your Outlook contact list.

To add an address from Microsoft Outlook, you use the Envelopes and Labels dialog box. You can use your Outlook contact list to add both the delivery and return addresses by clicking the appropriate buttons.

When you use the Envelopes and Labels dialog box, you have the option of creating the envelope and immediately printing it or attaching it to the current document to print later. With either option, you need to make sure that the envelope settings are correct for your printer. Word displays an icon in the bottom-right corner of the dialog box indicating how the envelope will be fed into the printer. You can click the icon to change the printer settings.

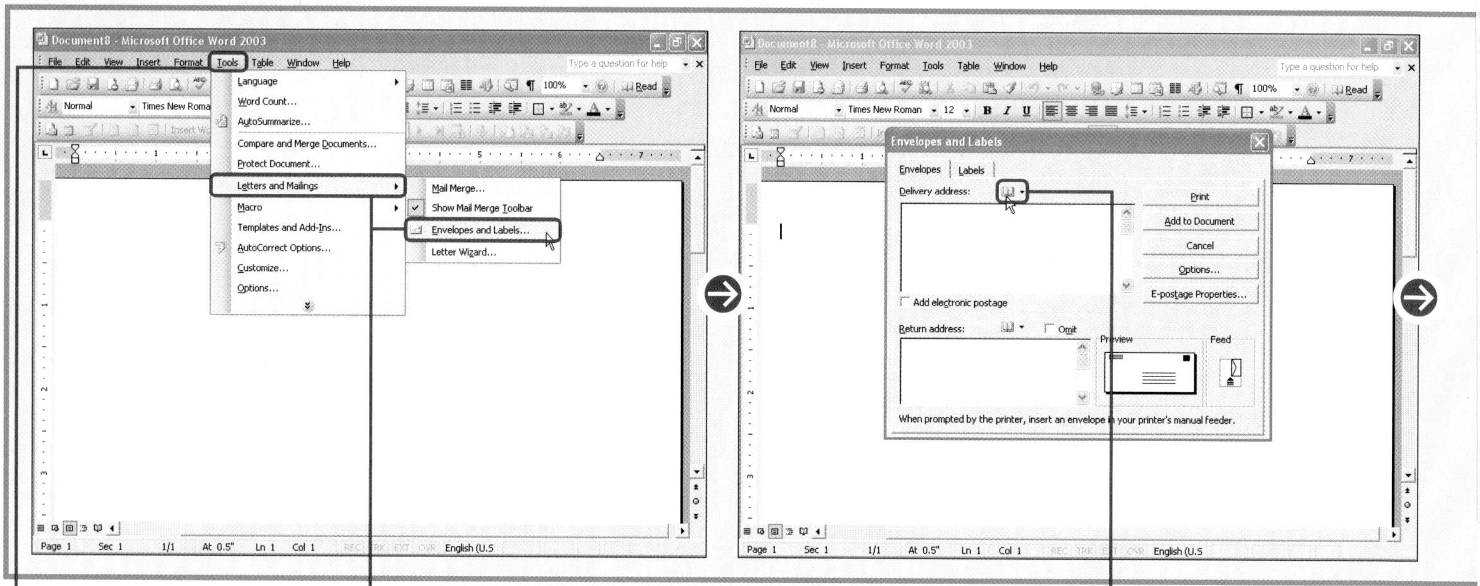

1 Click Tools.

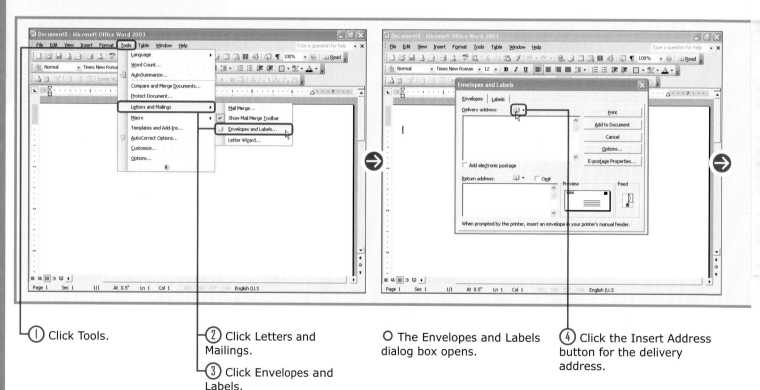

2 Click Letters and Mailings.

3 Click Envelopes and Labels.

- The Envelopes and Labels dialog box opens.

4 Click the Insert Address button for the delivery address.

Did You Know?

You can change the font settings for both the delivery and return addresses on an envelope. To do so, click the Options button in the Envelopes and Labels dialog box. In the Envelope Options dialog box, click the Font button for the address that you want to change. On the Font tab of the Envelope Address dialog box, select the font options that you want.

Did You Know?

You can print electronic postage directly onto your envelope from Word. To do so, you need to install electronic postage software. An electronic postage software add-in is available on the Microsoft Office Web site (www.microsoft.com/office/).

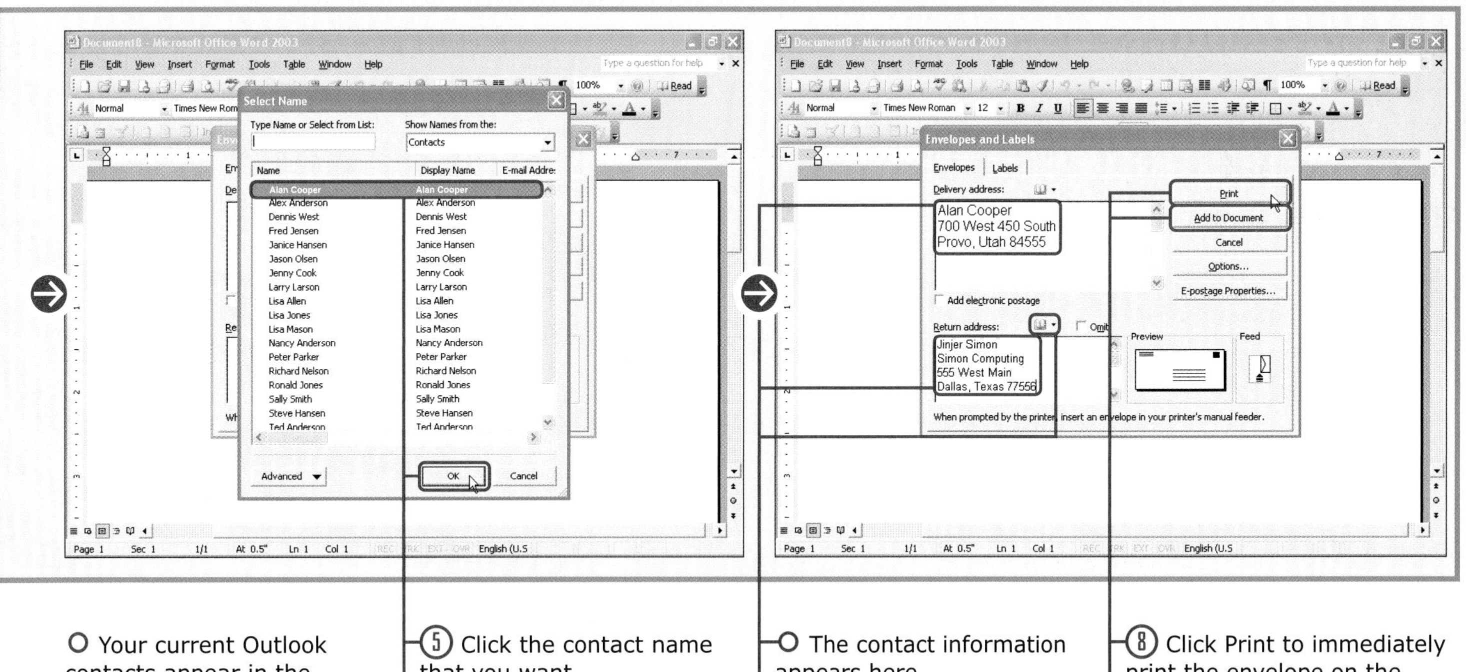

- Your current Outlook contacts appear in the Select Name dialog box.

5 Click the contact name that you want.

6 Click OK.

- The contact information appears here.

7 Type the return address information.

- Alternatively, you can click the Insert Address button and select from your contacts list.

8 Click Print to immediately print the envelope on the default printer.

- You can click Add to Document to save the envelope with the current document.

Create CUSTOM-SIZED LABELS

You can create and print custom-sized labels in Word. Although Word has default label sizes for the common label sizes, you may not find a size that matches the labels that you want to print. If that is the case, you can customize a label size.

When you specify the custom label sizing, you need to specify the exact sizing for not only the labels but also the margins around the edge of the page. You also need to indicate how many labels are on the page by selecting the number of labels across and the number of labels down the page. Make sure that the correct page size is selected.

Word displays a preview of the custom label size in the Preview window of the New Custom label dialog box. As you make modifications to the settings, the Preview window is updated.

Word remembers the custom label size that you create so that you can select that label size the next time you print labels.

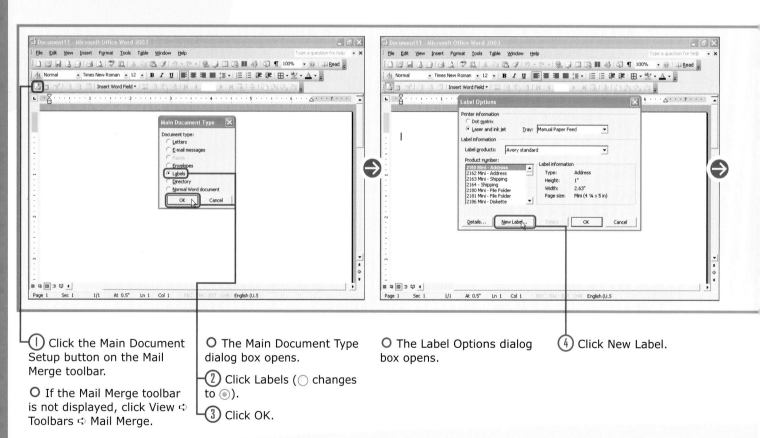

① Click the Main Document Setup button on the Mail Merge toolbar.

○ If the Mail Merge toolbar is not displayed, click View ➪ Toolbars ➪ Mail Merge.

○ The Main Document Type dialog box opens.

② Click Labels (○ changes to ◉).

③ Click OK.

○ The Label Options dialog box opens.

④ Click New Label.

DIFFICULTY LEVEL

Did You Know?

You can modify any predefined label size to create your custom labels. Locate the predefined label by selecting the name of the manufacturer in the Label Products field and then selecting the product number in the Product Number field. After you have selected the label, click New Label to modify that label size.

Did You Know?

You can resize the labels directly in the Word document by clicking on the separators and dragging them to the desired sizes.

Did You Know?

If you want to add the same type of information to all labels in your document, select the fields you want for the first label and then click the Propagate Labels button to have the same information copied to the remaining labels.

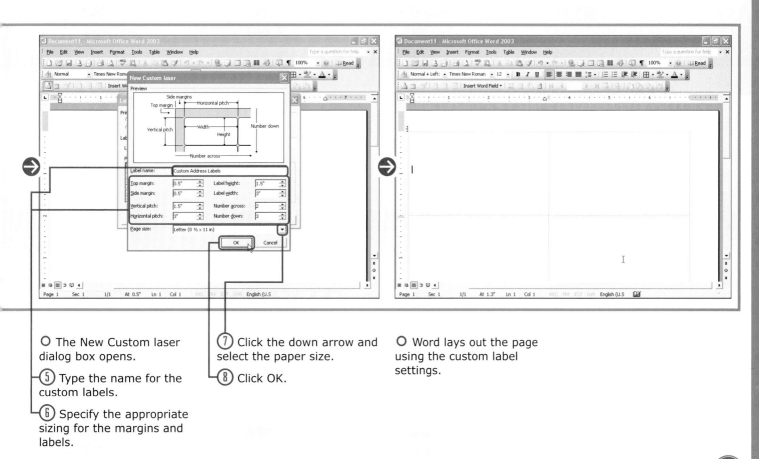

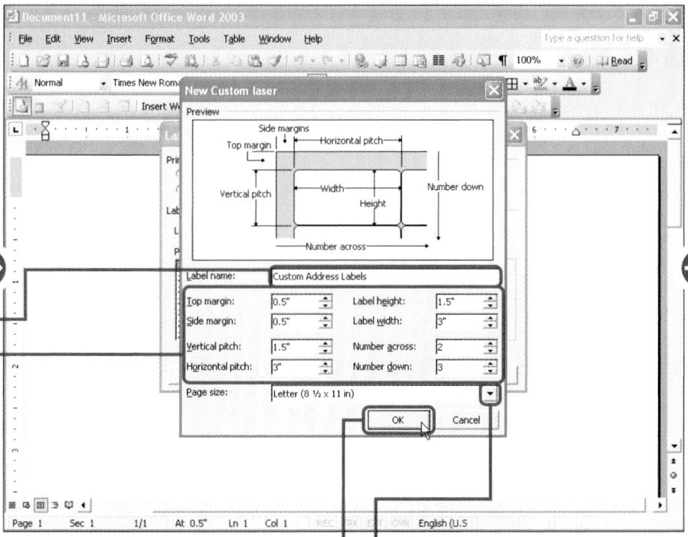

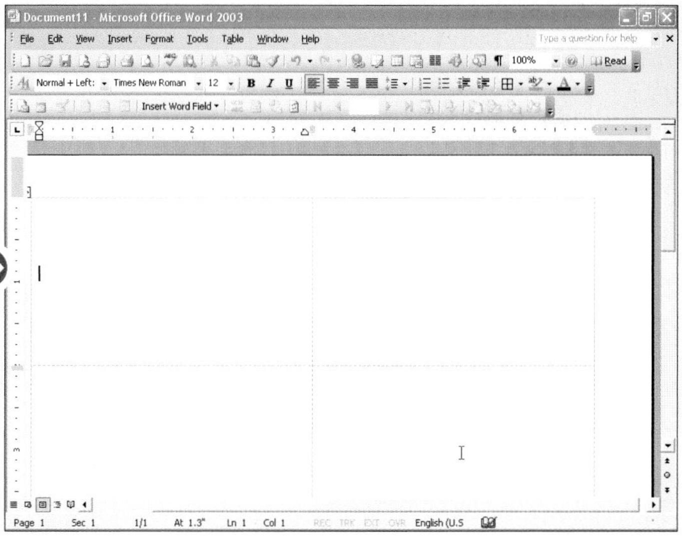

- The New Custom laser dialog box opens.

5 Type the name for the custom labels.

6 Specify the appropriate sizing for the margins and labels.

7 Click the down arrow and select the paper size.

8 Click OK.

- Word lays out the page using the custom label settings.

Set the formatting of MERGED NUMERIC VALUES

You can specify the formatting for Word to apply to numeric values when they are merged into your document. For example, you may want to specify the layout of phone numbers so that all phone numbers display the area code in parentheses.

To format a numeric value that will be merged into your document, you use the numeric formatting switch \#, followed by the formatting you want to use. For example, to format a number to always display with two decimal places, you specify the numeric switch with the number format, as follows: \# "0.00"

You need to specify the formatting for the number as part of the field code. To do so, use the Reveal Codes command and then add the numeric formatting at the end of the MERGEFIELD. For example, if you are merging a field called Amount, the field code would have the format {MERGEFIELD "Amount" \# "0.00"}.

Each 0 (zero) represents one digit in the numeric layout. If the number does not include two decimal places, a zero is added for each missing decimal value.

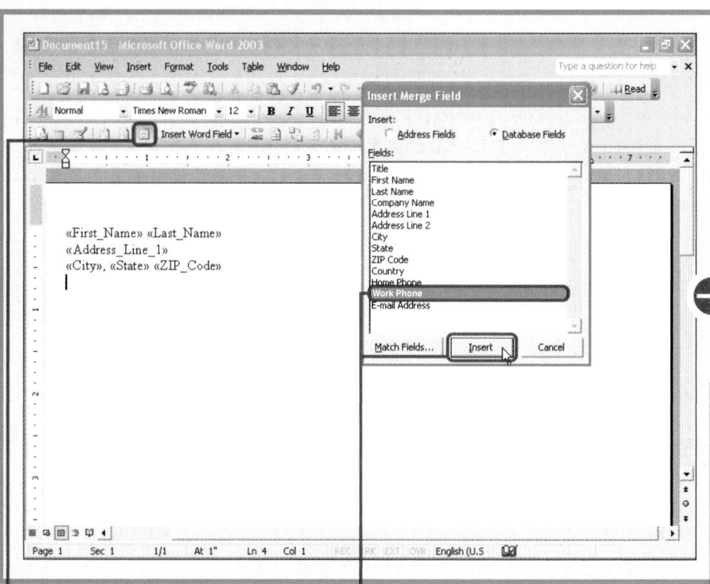

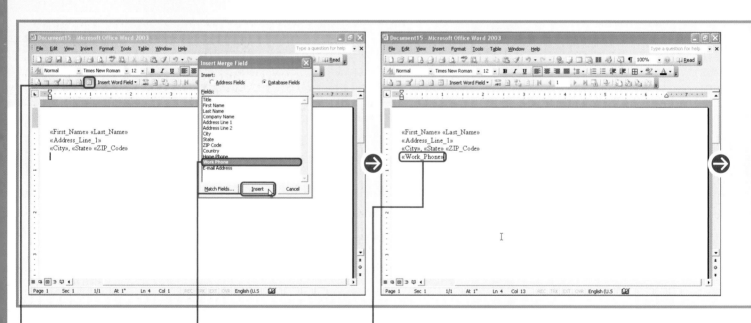

① Click the Insert Merge Field button on the Mail Merge toolbar.

○ If the Mail Merge toolbar is not displayed, click View ⇨ Toolbars ⇨ Mail Merge.

○ The Insert Merge Field dialog box opens.

② Click the phone number field that you want.

③ Click Insert.

④ Click Close to close the Insert Merge Field dialog box.

○ Word adds the selected fields to the document.

⑤ Press Alt+F9 to display the field codes for the fields in the document.

DIFFICULTY LEVEL

Did You Know?

You can combine text characters and numeric formatting characters. For example, to separate the digits in a phone number, you can use a '–' character. You need to place single quotes around text characters within the formatting string. If you omit the quotes, Word treats the – as a minus sign.

Did You Know?

If you want to change the font characteristics for a merge field, you can apply any of the font settings that you want to the field code. When Word merges the field values, the specified formatting is applied to the merged text.

Did You Know?

You can display a field in all uppercase or all lowercase characters by using the appropriate switches. Type *Upper for all uppercase or *Lower for all lowercase characters.

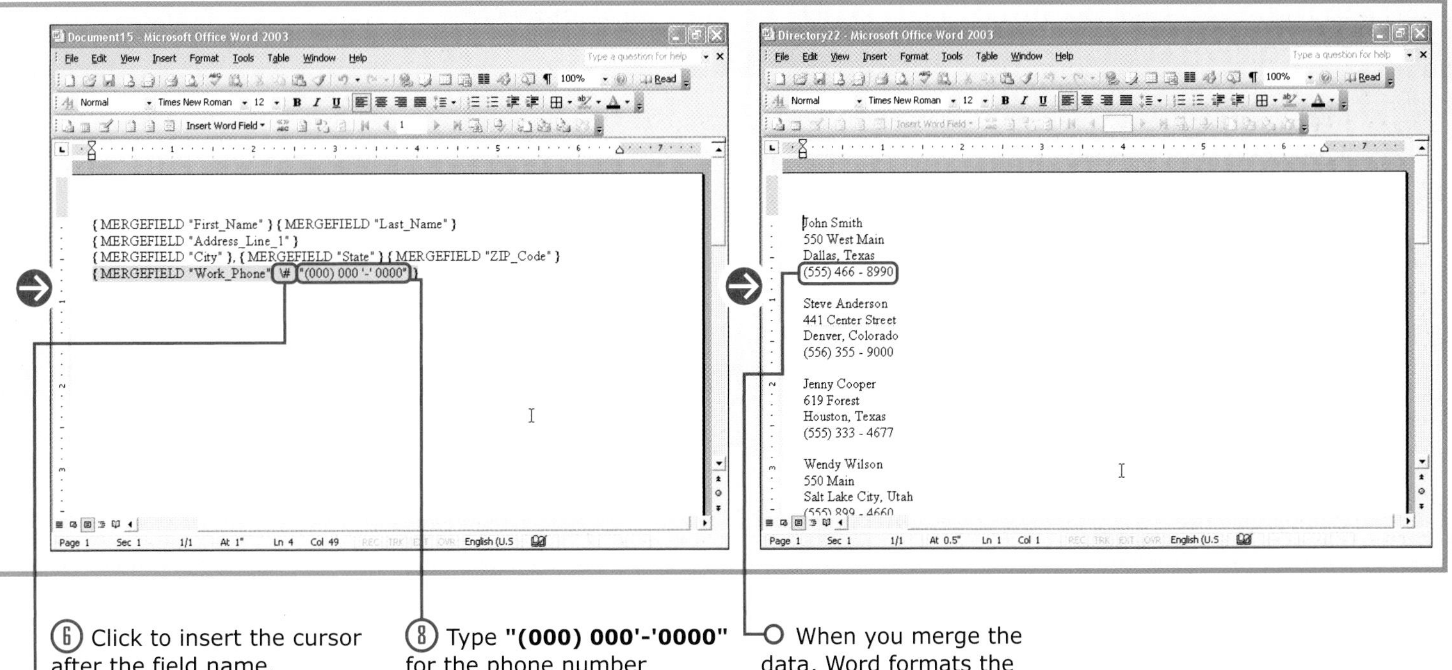

6 Click to insert the cursor after the field name.

7 Type **\#** to indicate a numeric formatting switch.

8 Type **"(000) 000'-'0000"** for the phone number formatting.

- When you merge the data, Word formats the phone number using the specified numeric formatting.

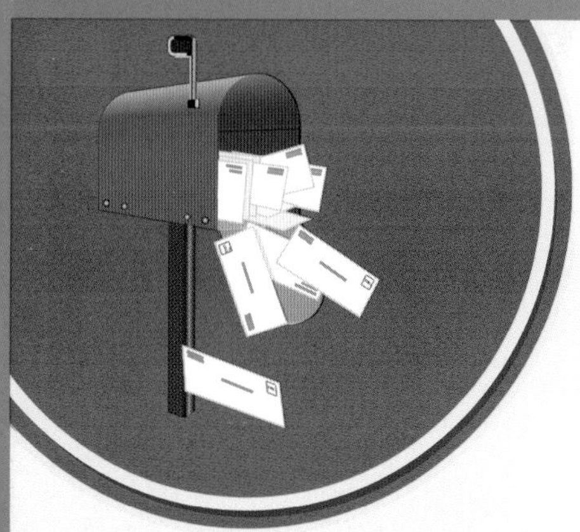

PRINT A RANGE
of merged documents

You can print a specific range of merged documents instead of printing the entire set. For example, you may need to reprint a group of letters that were misplaced. You can specify that range of documents instead of printing the entire set of letters.

You specify the range of documents to print in the Merge to Printer dialog box. You need to specify page numbers for the range of documents that you want. Keep in mind that the documents print in the same order as the recipient names are listed in the data list.

You can also print the entire assortment of documents by clicking the All button.

You need to make sure that you use the Merge to Printer button instead of selecting the File ➪ Print option. If you do not select the Merge to Printer option, Word does not merge the field values, and the printed document contains the field codes only. When you click the Merge to Printer button, Word displays the Print dialog box so that you can make the appropriate printer selections.

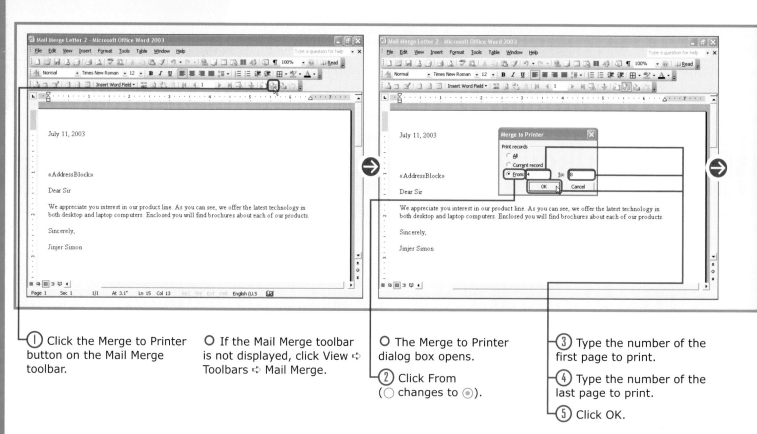

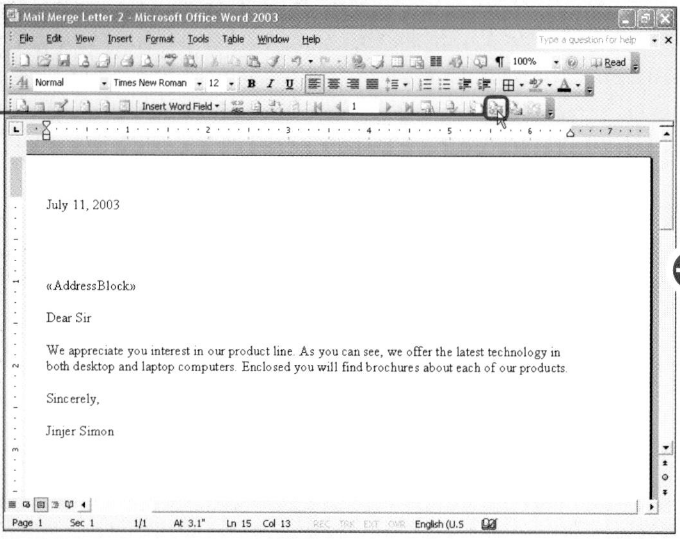

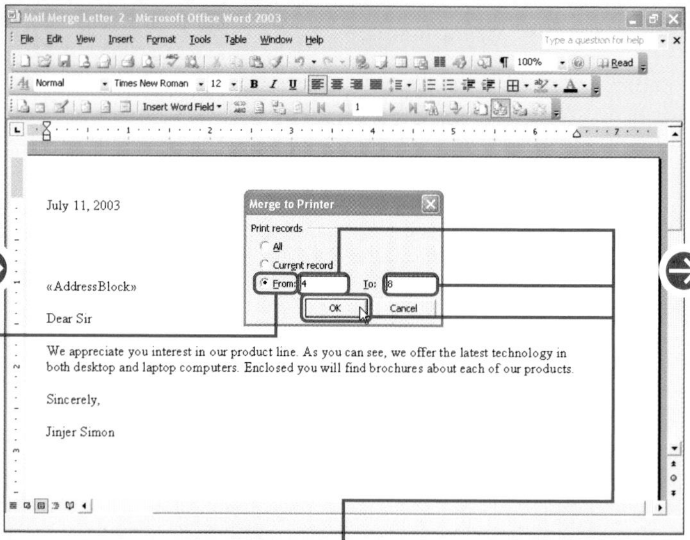

1 Click the Merge to Printer button on the Mail Merge toolbar.

○ If the Mail Merge toolbar is not displayed, click View ➪ Toolbars ➪ Mail Merge.

○ The Merge to Printer dialog box opens.

2 Click From (○ changes to ◉).

3 Type the number of the first page to print.

4 Type the number of the last page to print.

5 Click OK.

Did You Know?

Word merges the recipients' values in a document based on the order that the recipients' names are listed in the data list. For example, if you have the list sorted alphabetically by last name, a recipient with a last name of Anderson prints before Cooper. You can determine the order the recipient documents will print in the Mail Merge Recipients dialog box. To sort the list by a specific value, click the appropriate column heading; for example, to sort by last name, click the Last Name heading.

Did You Know?

You can view the documents in the order they will print by clicking the View Merged Data button. Use the Next Record and Previous Record buttons on the Mail Merge toolbar to scroll through the documents.

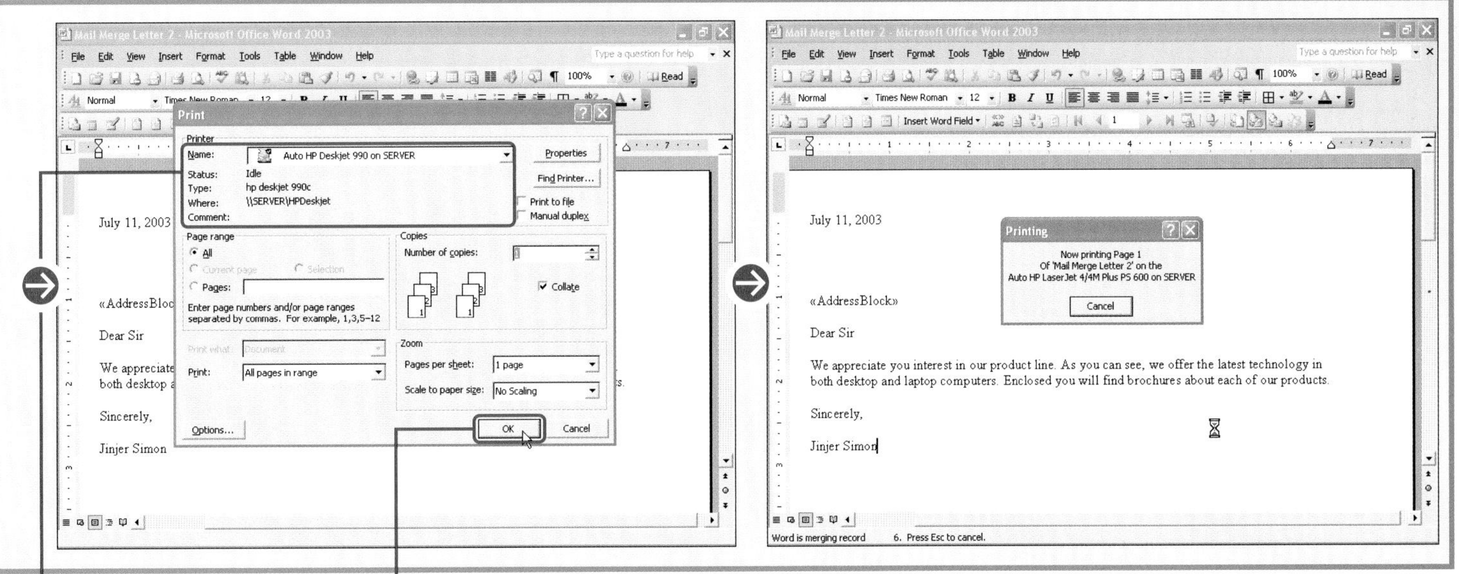

- The Print dialog box opens.

6 Verify the printer selection.

Note: Refer to Chapter 7 for more information on printing.

7 Click OK.

- Word prints the selected pages by merging the appropriate field values.

INDEX

A

B

C

D

E

F

G

INDEX

R

S

T

U–V

W–Z